Pascal's Pensées

Pascal's Pensées

TRANSLATED WITH AN
INTRODUCTION BY
MARTIN TURNELL

Harper & Brothers
PUBLISHERS NEW YORK

Printed in Great Britain

239
P27

GENERAL LIST OF CONTENTS

21405

INTRODUCTION

Great writers divide the critics. While there is general agreement about Pascal's status as a writer, he is a difficult author because his work invites wildly differing personal interpretations. The difficulty has been aggravated by almost insoluble textual problems. His Apology for religion is not only unfinished; we do not know, we shall never know for certain, in what order he would have assembled his material, what he would have included and what he would have omitted. The work of interpretation therefore begins as soon as an editor sits down to prepare his text. The problems of the first editors are described by Mme Périer in her life of her brother, but it is not unfair to say that the rot started with the earliest or Port-Royal edition in which the boldness of Pascal's thought was toned down in the interests of peace and quietness. In the eighteenth century Condorcet produced a selection from the *Pensées* arranged in a way that turned it into a sort of 'Agnostic's Apology'. The Romantics invented 'the anguished Pascal', who has been succeeded in our own time by Claudel's 'sick man' and Mr Aldous Huxley's 'life-hater'. It is only during the past twenty-five years that, thanks to the researches of MM. Lafuma, Mesnard and Tourneur, opinion is moving in another direction: a Christian humanist is emerging, a little shakily it is true, from the confusion of the texts.

Pascal was the child of a troubled age. Christians had been profoundly disturbed in their faith by the religious wars of the sixteenth century and by the advances in the physical sciences. Unbelief was widespread, open, militant. For the Reformation had not simply cut Christendom in two: it had brought into the open doubts, denials and divisions which had existed largely behind the scenes until the split came. France was not divided merely into Catholic and Protestant or Christian and unbeliever: the divisions had been carried inside the Catholic community itself.

It is well known that whenever upheavals take place or new and explosive ideas begin to circulate, there is a twofold reaction, that society divides into two camps which can be broadly described as 'conservative' and 'progressive'. Conservatives see nothing but danger and disaster in the changes and cling tenaciously to tradition, try to shut out the new ideas, in religion become rigorists. Progressives either jettison old beliefs and embrace the new, or they try to come to terms with the new ideas. Although we are inclined to think of the Reformation as a revolution which brought medieval Christendom to a violent end, in intention it was fundamentalist and claimed to be a return to primitive Christianity, to the simplicity of the Gospels shorn of the accretions and abuses of fifteen hundred years of Rome. The split between conservative and progressive was repeated inside the Church in France by the feud between Jansenist and Jesuit. Jansenism sprang from the desire of a small group of people to withdraw from the new world and devote their lives not merely to the service of God, but to serving him in a form which was purged of certain elements of which they disapproved as much as the Protestants. The Jesuits were founded as the shock troops of the Papacy of the Counter-Reformation. Their aim was certainly to combat heresy, but not by going back to the past: it was to sift and test what was new, to see to what extent it could be harmonised with Truth.

A French priest has written a book called 'the heresy of Port-Royal'.[1] Jansenism will always be associated with Port-Royal which was its headquarters and its stronghold. The abbey of Port-Royal-des-Champs was a thirteenth-century Cistercian foundation standing in the misty valley of the Chevreuse some fourteen miles south-west of Paris. A second house, known as Port-Royal-de-Paris, was opened in 1626.[2] At the close of the

[1] L. Cristiani: *L'Hérésie de Port-Royal*, Paris, 1955.
[2] Port-Royal-des-Champs was razed to the ground by Louis XIV's soldiery in 1709 in a final attempt to stamp out Jansenism: Port-Royal-de-Paris is today a maternity hospital.

sixteenth century religious life at the abbey had grown slack and the rule was relaxed there as in so many other French religious houses. In 1597 Jacqueline Arnauld, one of the twenty children of Antoine Arnauld, a famous but impoverished barrister and a notorious enemy of the Jesuits whom he had accused in 1594 of complicity in the assassination of King Henri III, had entered the abbey as Mère Angélique at the tender age of seven. It was the beginning of the domination of the French religious scene by the Arnauld family. Four years after her entry, at the age of eleven, Jacqueline found herself Abbess of Port-Royal. Six years later she was much impressed by some Lenten sermons preached by an itinerant Capuchin friar and resolved to set her house in order. On 25 September 1609, which came to be known as the 'Journée du Guichet', she refused entry to the monastery to her parents who had neglected her as a child and whom she had never liked. She thus revealed the stubborn, headstrong self-will which was characteristic of the family. Jacqueline was a niece of Arnauld d'Andilly, a considerable reprobate who was converted in his later years, and a sister of Antoine Arnauld the younger, who became known as 'Le Grand Arnauld' and played one of the leading roles in the Jansenist-Jesuit controversy. In 1640 there were no less than fifteen members of the Arnauld family living either at Port-Royal-des-Champs or at Port-Royal-de-Paris. In addition to the community there were the 'solitaries', the pious laymen like Antoine Le Maître who had given up their careers and withdrawn from the world in order to practise the austerities which they thought becoming to genuine religion.

The year 1640 was the year of decision. It saw the publication of a long posthumous Latin treatise called the *Augustinus* in which Cornelius Jansen, sometime Bishop of Ypres, gave an interpretation of St. Augustine's teaching on Grace. While a correct assessment of its implications will always remain a matter of controversy, its author was undoubtedly the founder of what became known as Jansenism. Although Jansenism had a doctrinal basis and was coloured by Protestant theories of the Fall, Predestination and Grace, it was much more an attitude of mind than a matter of precise beliefs. The feeling that the Fall had led to the complete ruin of human nature, that salvation was a sort of lottery, produced a singularly joyless religion which was to leave an indelible mark on Pascal's *Pensées*. While therefore the quarrel between Jansenist and Jesuit may appear to turn on intricate questions of theology, it was primarily a conflict between opposing outlooks. In the framework of the age Jansenism represented an intensely puritanical reaction against the undoubted laxity of faith and practice. The Jansenists were hostile to the Jesuits because they thought, not without reason, that the Society with its elegant opportunism and its cultured *mondain* outlook stood for compromise with the spirit of the age, that it was ready to settle for a minimal instead of an integral Catholicism, and was attempting to convert the unbeliever by toning down 'hard sayings' of the Gospels and rounding off the jagged edges of the Catholic faith: an attitude which was reflected in the title of a contemporary devotional work called *La Dévotion aisée*.

The controversy which followed the publication of the *Augustinus* was serious and involved the Holy See. In 1653 Innocent X began by condemning as heretical five propositions extracted from the book. The Jansenists, led by Arnauld, proceeded to draw a distinction between the questions of 'right' and 'fact'. While admitting that the condemned propositions were heretical, they maintained that 'in fact' they were not to be found in the *Augustinus*. In 1656 Alexander VII put the matter beyond doubt by condemning the book lock, stock and barrel.

Arnauld had come into conflict not merely with the Jesuits, who were in the forefront of the campaign against the *Augustinus*, but with the doctors of the Sorbonne who decided to sit in judgement on his activities. They went to extravagant lengths to secure the verdict that they wanted by packing the jury with theologians who were known to be hostile to his views, and succeeded by a comparatively narrow majority. Arnauld was condemned on 14 January 1656. He was a theologian and a voluminous writer both of the heavier kind of theological treatise such as his *Livre de la fréquente communion* (described by one of his enemies as a 'Treatise on Infrequent Communion'), and of pamphlets. His aim, when he found himself condemned by the Sorbonne, was to widen the conflict, to carry it beyond the clerical world and the world of the specialists and obtain a hearing from the Catholic community at large. He appears to have realised that whatever his talents as an expositor of theological arguments, he was not the man to present the issues persuasively to the wider public. He had recently met Pascal. At one of the meetings he is said to have appealed to him with the words: 'You're young. Can't you do something?' That was how Pascal became one of the central figures in the bitterest theological controversy of the century.

Blaise Pascal was born on 19 June 1623. He was the second of the three surviving children of Étienne Pascal and Antoinette Begon. His elder sister, Gilberte, was born in 1620 and in 1641 became the wife of her cousin Florin Périer. The younger sister, Jacqueline, to whom Pascal was fanatically devoted, was born two years after her brother in 1625.

Although Mme Périer's life of her brother is not always accurate on points of detail and was clearly written for the purpose of edification, it is a remarkable portrait of the man: deeply religious, obstinate, hot-tempered, irascible—'highly inflammable with a low flash-point', remarks a recent biographer —and altogether a decidedly grim figure.[1] 'A sick man' said Claudel who was clearly referring to his mind as well as his body. Mme Périer gives a vivid account of his physical ailments, but there is a passage at the beginning of the memoir by his niece, Marguerite Périer, which deserves verbatim quotation. The first of Pascal's illnesses, or perhaps we should say the first signs of his illness, occurred when he was only one year old.

'At this time', wrote Marguerite Périer, 'the child fell into a state of apathy which resembled the state known in Paris as "falling into a decline", but his condition was

[1] Ernest Mortimer: *Blaise Pascal*, London, 1959, p. 136.

accompanied by two unusual factors: the first was that he could not bear the sight of water which threw him into a violent state of agitation; the other, which is far more unusual, was that he could not bear to see his father and mother close to one another: he liked being petted by them singly, but the moment they both came to him he began to cry and fling himself about with an exaggerated violence. This lasted for more than a year, and during it his illness grew worse until it reached the point where he was believed to be at death's door'.[1]

M. Jean Mesnard has thrown doubt on the value of Marguerite Périer's testimony, but though it is mixed up with a bizarre story of witchcraft her account, with its almost clinical precision, bears the stamp of veracity. Pascal's symptoms are less surprising to us than they were to the seventeenth century. Liquids, as we know from Gilberte Périer's life, were to be a constant worry to him. While this was no doubt due to some extent to his internal troubles, we may suspect that his chronic sickness and his allergy to liquids were in some degree nervous in origin. His violent reaction to contact between his parents is less difficult to explain: the intemperance that he displayed even at this age was to remain with him all his life.

Pascal's childhood and youth were very much those of an infant prodigy. He concentrated on mathematics and while still in his early teens argued on equal terms with some of the foremost mathematicians of the day. The family settled in Paris some five years after the death of the mother. In 1638 Étienne Pascal incurred the displeasure of Richelieu by protesting against certain fiscal measures and was obliged to seek refuge in his native Auvergne in order to escape incarceration in the Bastille. The following year Jacqueline, who herself was something of a prodigy, was presented to Richelieu and obtained her father's pardon. He was made the King's commissioner for taxes at Rouen where he was associated with the ruthless repression of an uprising provoked by the imposition of new taxes.

[1] *Oeuvres complètes*, Ed. J. Chevalier (Bibliothèque de la Pléiade), Paris, 1954, p. 35.

Pascal's first published work, a mathematical treatise called *Essai pour les coniques*, appeared in 1640 when he was only seventeen. Two years later he began work on the famous calculating machine which was originally designed to help his father in his work as commissioner of taxes, and which continued to occupy him for the next ten years as he continually sought to improve it.

In 1646 Étienne Pascal fell and dislocated a thigh. He was tended by two reformed swashbucklers who were followers of the Abbé Saint-Cyran, the friend of Jansen and spiritual director of the nuns of Port-Royal from 1636 until his imprisonment by Richelieu in this same year. Blaise was the first of the family to be impressed by their teaching. It produced in him that deepening of the spiritual life which is known as his first conversion. The rest of the family followed his example. One year later there occurred the incident of the attack on the former Capuchin for his heretical views which is related at length by Mme Périer. This was the year that Pascal and Jacqueline left Rouen and went to live in Paris. He met Descartes, had a discussion on mathematics with him, but it is clear from contemporary accounts that the two men did not take to one another. In the meantime, Pascal who had become preoccupied with the problem of the vacuum, which had attracted attention owing to the experiments of the Italian mathematician, Torricelli, carried out experiments of his own with the assistance of his father and continued his mathematical work.

During the period of the Fronde the family removed once more to Clermont and only returned to Paris in 1650 when the troubles were over. Étienne Pascal died in 1651. In spite of strong opposition from her brother and sister, Jacqueline Pascal entered Port-Royal as a nun the year following her father's death. This marked the beginning of what is known as Pascal's 'worldly period'. He spent some six months at Clermont at the end of 1652 and the beginning of 1653. On his return to Paris he renewed his opposition to Jacqueline's vocation. It appeared that he intended to impose some sort of sanction by withholding the money for her dowry. The Abbess of Port-Royal offered to take her without a dowry; Pascal relented and made a generous settlement. Jacqueline took her vows.

Pascal then travelled to Poitou with its governor, the Duc de Roannez, and two of his *libertin* friends, Damien Mitton and the Chevalier de Méré. This might be described as the last episode of 'the worldly period'. Although Mme Périer was to call it, somewhat primly, 'the worst spent period of his life', we may feel some reservations about her judgement. Mitton and Méré were both highly accomplished men of the world: the first an incorrigible gambler; the second an equally incorrigible womaniser; both free-thinkers. Mitton wrote little, but his published works included a treatise on the immortality of the soul, which in private he referred to frivolously as a treatise on the mortality of the soul. Méré was a much more voluminous writer and is credited with perfecting the definition of the *honnête homme*. It should be emphasised that though free-thinkers they were no idle scoffers; they were exceptionally cultivated and sympathetic men; and Méré was described by someone as a man of no faith but abundant charity. They were undoubtedly Pascal's main link with the world of fashionable unbelief, but as it was of this world that he was thinking when he wrote his Apology no one can suppose that a first-hand knowledge of it was a disadvantage for his purpose. There are references in the Apology to 'Miton', who appears as the tardy and dilatory 'seeker', though in his last years he became devout.[1]

On his return to Paris Pascal paid frequent visits to Jacqueline at Port-Royal. It is to her that we owe most of the information that we have about his state of mind at this period. In a letter written on 8 December she said that for more than a year her brother had experienced 'a great contempt for the world and a great distaste for the people who compose it'. On 25 January 1655 she remarked, in another letter, that towards the end of the previous September he had seen her and expressed his aversion for the world, but without feeling in the least drawn

---

[1] The references are editorial inferences. The name is difficult to decipher in the manuscript and looks like 'Marton', but it may well have been Mitton whom Pascal intended.

to God. The same feeling is expressed in the *Écrit sur la conversion du pécheur*, which was probably written by Pascal, where the first stage on the convert's journey is described as disgust with the world without any attraction towards God. Clearly, in many conversions there is what might be called the neutral moment: the moment of lassitude and discouragement which spiritually and psychologically is the prelude to a new life.

It seems evident that Jacqueline was 'working' on her brother in the autumn of 1654. The results were sudden and startling. The turning point came on the night of 23 November when Pascal had that religious experience which like so many aspects of his life and work has attracted the attention of people of every shade of belief. This is not the place to speculate on the precise nature of his experience. That he did have an overwhelming experience is not in doubt. It is generally referred to as his 'second conversion'. It was a religious conversion in the sense that it produced that transformation of the whole man which is recognised alike by the theologian and the psychologist as the essential factor in religious conversion. Mme Périer was exaggerating, or was misinformed, when she alleged that after his experience he ceased to take any interest in the secular sciences with the exception of a mathematical work produced at a time when he was seriously ill and in great pain. What is certain is that from this time onwards religion became the centre of his life, and that his one desire was to achieve Christian perfection. It was to remind himself of this and of what he regarded as the most important event of his life that he wrote a description of his experience on the piece of parchment known as the *Mémorial*, which he kept sewn in the lining of his coat for the rest of his days.

At the beginning of 1655 Pascal went for a fortnight's retreat to Port-Royal-des-Champs. There he had the famous conversation with M. de Saci which he afterwards recorded in the *Entretien avec M. de Saci*. From Port-Royal-des-Champs he moved to Port-Royal-de-Paris where he spent some days before returning to his own home in the Faubourg Saint-Michel. In the spring he was in Poitou again, staying with the Duc de

Roannez whom he proceeded to convert. Nor had his own conversion led him to throw over his 'worldly' friends. He was still
in contact with Méré and Mitton.

It has been said that Pascal was not a Jansenist and he himself maintained that he did not belong to Port-Royal. Jansenism
was so contagious and so pervasive that traces of it can still be
detected in certain circles—particularly among writers and
intellectuals—in France. It undoubtedly left its mark on all
Pascal's religious writings. He may not have belonged in any
formal sense to Port-Royal, but he was clearly not merely a
sympathiser: he was one of its most effective allies. He was in
continual contact with the community in the months following
his conversion and it was when he went to make another short
retreat at Port-Royal-des-Champs that he met Arnauld: a
meeting which, as we have already seen, was to have such
momentous consequences.

M. Jean Mesnard has described the *Provincial Letters* as
'collective', 'anonymous' and 'clandestine'[1]. They were 'collective' in the sense that they were produced by a team: the theological material was provided by Arnauld and Nicole; the style
in the widest sense by Pascal. They were published under the
pseudonym of Louis de Montalte, which proved a transparent
disguise, and 'clandestine' in the sense that Pascal spent very
little time at his own home, for fear of arrest, during the period
of their publication. The first letter appeared on 23 January
1656; the eighteenth and last on 1 June 1657. On 6 September
of the same year they were placed on the Index. They had
begun as pamphlets written for Arnauld's defence, but during
the eighteen months over which their publication was spread
they broadened into a more general controversy over Jansenist
theology and finally developed into a frontal attack on the
Jesuits' methods of casuistry, if not into a frontal attack on the
Society itself.

The *Provincial Letters* are a masterpiece of French prose: it is
hardly too much to say that from every other point of view their
effect was wholly bad. Their effect on religious life was bad

[1] *Pascal: his Life and Works*, Eng. tr., London, 1952, p. 75.

because they fostered that internal strife which is always a scandal to the unbeliever, and which undoubtedly weakened the Church in France and contributed to her collapse at the time of the French Revolution. Their effect on the writer was bad because as they grew more polemical they provided a release for feelings to which Pascal was only too prone and of which no Christian can really approve.

Little more than a month after the condemnation of the *Provincial Letters* Alexander VII issued the definitive Bull condemning the *Augustinus* as a whole. The Bull was officially 'received' by Louis XIV in January 1657. The Assembly of Clergy, who had already produced one formula, proceeded to draw up a fresh one which removed the distinction between the questions of 'right' and 'fact', intending to call on every priest and religious to sign it. Before a papal bull could become law in France it had to be 'registered' by Parliament. At this point Parliament, feeling perhaps that there was a danger of Rome interfering with the jealously guarded privileges of the Gallican Church, refused to impose signature of the formula on the clergy. When the matter came up again four years later on 1 February 1661, it took a different attitude. For by this time Louis had decided that Port-Royal and the Jansenists were a pocket of resistance to the royal despotism which he was no longer prepared to tolerate: Church and State found themselves on the same side and Parliament registered the four-year-old Bull which made the decree of the Assembly of Clergy binding on the faithful. The State closed the 'little schools' of Port-Royal: the Assembly set to work to obtain the signatures.

There was a split in the Jansenist camp. Arnauld thought that with certain reservations the new formula could be accepted. He would sign on the question of 'right' and preserve a ' respectful silence ' on the question of 'fact'. This produced painful conflict on the part of the nuns of Port-Royal and though they signed on 22 June and 28 November it seems to have shaken their faith. This was particularly true of Jacqueline whose death on 4 October of that year is said to have been hastened by the conflict.

Pascal behaved with an intransigence which contrasts with the more moderate attitude of Arnauld and caused something like a breach between them. As a layman he did not have to sign, but there can be little doubt that his advice was responsible for a great deal of the heartburning caused by the decision to sign or not to sign. His writings, or rather the writings attributed to him, on this issue suggest that he had an imperfect understanding of what was involved and failed to see where his intransigence was leading him. He appears to have thought that though the five propositions could be interpreted in a heretical sense, there was another sense, which he attributed to Jansen, in which they were perfectly orthodox. As a seventeenth-century Catholic, he was not required to believe in papal infallibility, but it is difficult to reconcile what amounted to an accusation of a theological blunder on the part of the Pope and the bishops with his emphasis on Church unity and his declarations of his own attachment to the Apostolic and Roman Church.

The end of the story is obscure. In October or November 1661 Pascal withdrew from all public controversy. He was a sick man by this time in spite of the fact that in the following year he launched what must rank as the first omnibus service in the world in Paris, and it was natural that he should go into retirement and shun any form of controversy. The events preceding his death are described in Mme Périer's Life. In the years following his death the Archbishop of Paris obtained a statement from Father Beurrier who heard his confession and gave him the Last Sacraments while in the present century Beurrier's memoirs have been published. Although the priest was insistent on Pascal's complete submission to the Church, his testimony is not of great historical value nor is it particularly easy to see how the problem could have been resolved in different circumstances. Pascal had always considered himself a loyal son of the Church and believed firmly in the orthodoxy of his own views. Nevertheless, he had been involved in a controversy in which his position had been that of accusing the Pope and the bishops of a serious theological error and counselling the faithful not to conform to a decree of the Assembly of Clergy. Although he had withdrawn from public controversy he had retracted nothing because, in a sense, there was nothing for him to retract. In spite of the characteristically lively defence of the Abbé Bremond, we can hardly avoid the conclusion that he went to his grave in the firm belief that Rome had been wrong and Blaise Pascal right.

The years 1656 to 1658, when he enjoyed comparatively good health, were fertile ones in Pascal's career. He wrote the *Provincial Letters*, the letters to Mlle de Roannez, the *Écrits sur la Grâce*, collected and wrote down most of the material for the *Pensées*. He also continued his mathematical work, held an international competition for a solution of the problem of the 'curve' (known in France as *la Roulette*), which caused a considerable amount of bad feeling, and engaged in a controversy with Father Noël in which he showed himself sadly lacking in the normal courtesies and in which, as in the religious controversies, he displayed his customary intemperance.

He had become seriously ill in 1659 which not only brought to a virtual end his writing, but appears to have interrupted his classification of the material for the Apology.[1] The result was that when they came to examine his papers after his death, his family received what M. Lafuma describes as 'a disagreeable surprise'. 'We found the papers all pinned together in different bundles, but without any order or arrangement,' said Pascal's nephew, Étienne Périer, who wrote the Preface to the Port-Royal Edition of 1670. Although the work appeared to the family to have been written on scraps of paper and pinned together 'without any order or arrangement', they did one very sensible thing. They had the papers copied in the precise order in which they found them. Their action in doing so prevented the extremely difficult problem of the order of the *Pensées* from becoming totally insoluble. There are only two guides to the way in which Pascal intended to arrange his material. One

[1] But the reference in the *Pensées* to the death of Cromwell and the restoration of the English monarchy shows that there were at least additions as late as 1660.

is the lecture that he delivered at Port-Royal which probably took place in May 1658 before his health finally began to fail. Filleau de la Chaise, a friend of the family, claimed to have been present at the lecture. In 1668 he wrote his *Discours sur les Pensées de M. Pascal*, which purported to give an account of it and was intended to serve as the Preface to the Port-Royal edition. In the event, Étienne Périer decided to write the Preface himself and simply reproduced that part of Filleau's discourse dealing with the plan of the Apology. Scholars have since expressed doubts whether Filleau was really present at the lecture, and have pointed out that he seems in any case to have relied on the copy of the manuscripts rather than on recollections of a lecture heard some ten years before he wrote his treatise. The copy is of the utmost importance because of what happened to Pascal's own manuscript. When the copy had been made, the family unpinned the fragments, pasted them on to large sheets of paper and had the sheets bound into albums. Owing to various mishaps, the original order of the sheets became confused with the result that the copy is the only reliable guide to the order in which Pascal left his papers.

It has been shown that the family were mistaken in believing that Pascal jotted down his thoughts on any scrap of paper that he happened to have by him and then strung them together at random, or in the order in which they were written. He wrote them down on large sheets of paper, cut them into strips and then pinned the separate thoughts together in the bundles in which they were found. The papers appear to divide into two main groups: those which had been classified and pinned together, and those which had in fact been left 'without any order or arrangement' and were awaiting classification. This has led to the inference that the bundles, or *liasses*, represent a first attempt by Pascal himself to arrange his material in the order he had in mind and was only interrupted when he became too ill even to undertake an almost mechanical exercise of this nature.

Editors of the Apology have adopted two different methods of classification. They have either decided that it was impossible

even to guess what order Pascal would have followed and have
arranged the material in an order which seemed reasonable and
coherent to them, or more recently they have relied on the copy
and the discourse in an endeavour to produce something which
could be described as an 'objective' edition approximating to
Pascal's intended order. This does not mean that they have
simply reproduced the copy as it stands. The unclassified
material contains work which evidently belongs to one or other
of the classified bundles, and they have fitted it into what appeared to them to be the likeliest places. In addition to material
evidently destined for the Apology, there is another group of
writings consisting of miscellaneous material on which earlier
editors have drawn and which includes *Le Mystère de Jésus* and
the *Mémorial*. This is relegated by M. Lafuma to a separate
section which he calls 'Personal Notes'. His method, as we shall
see, has the great advantage of clarifying the plan of the
Apology and removing material which obscured its essentially
dialectical movement.

It has to be remembered that though some parts of the
Apology are much more polished and more highly finished
than others, which really are no more than jottings, the manuscript left by Pascal was basically a first draft. Parts of it are not
merely corrected or rewritten: they exist in two or more separate
versions. This means that even the best of recent editions contain repetitions, alternative versions of the same idea, and a
good deal of very roughly drafted material. There are, however,
great compensations. In spite of repetition and duplication the
text of M. Lafuma, which I have used here, does possess an
order and a shapeliness for which we shall look in vain in any
of the other editions. No one will pretend that it is the definitive
edition, but it seems to me to be by far the best at present
available and for this reason I have preferred it to M. Chevalier's text in the 'Bibliothèque de la Pléiade' which has many
admirers, among them the late Albert Béguin who was the
author of a vivid and discerning *Pascal par lui-même* in the well-
known series, 'Écrivains de Toujours'.

In M. Lafuma's edition we find a short foreword, some introductory matter and twenty-seven headed chapters or sections that are believed to correspond to Pascal's own Table of Contents which existed at the time of his death and was subsequently lost. The foreword is a general address to the reader and deals with the problem of arranging one's material in the best order which faces every author. The introductions contain some account of the audience, the fashionable unbelievers, whom he wished to convert, and from the passion and eloquence with which parts of them were written, particularly those pointing out the need to understand religion before either dismissing it or attacking it, we may suppose that they were intended to produce a preliminary softening up of the unbeliever.

What is most arresting about M. Lafuma's edition is the way in which it restores the essentially dialectical movement and pattern of the Apology. The antithesis between the 'greatness' and 'wretchedness' of man has long been a commonplace of Pascal criticism. It is based on the doctrines of the Fall and Redemption, but in this edition it is seen to be the first of a series of antitheses: Religion and the religions; the Church and the churches; Philosophy and the philosophies; unity and multiplicity; the infinite and nothingness; the infinitely great and the infinitely small; head and heart; faith and reason. It is the continual interplay between them, the way in which themes interweave, the switch from one to its opposite, which give the Apology its dramatic quality and make the reading of it a cumulative experience that transcends the particular effect of the separate chapters.

This becomes apparent as soon as we look at the contents of the chapters. The first chapter, 'Order', provides the reader with a sketch of the ground which Pascal intends to cover and the method he proposes to adopt. The next four chapters describe the plight of man without religion. In chapter 2, 'Vanity', we see him without any sense of direction leading a life of futility and frivolity, vainly trying to find a way of escape from the gnawing sense of uneasiness among the vanities of the world. Chapter 3, 'Wretchedness', examines the fundamental cause underlying the surface frivolity described in the previous chapter. In Chapter 4, 'Ennui and Essential Qualities of Man', Pascal analyses what might be called the symptoms of human wretchedness.

> 'Nothing', he says, 'is so intolerable to man as a state of complete repose . . . In such a state he becomes aware of his nothingness . . . There at once wells up from the depths of his soul weariness, gloom, misery, exasperation, frustration, despair.'

He is, indeed, such a poor creature that he can only be propped up by a high degree of social organisation. But in the fifth chapter, 'Cause and Effect', the positive forces—custom, law, justice—are seen to be no more than illusions which are effective up to a point simply because of their appearance of authority, which rests either on nothing or on tyranny.

In the sixth chapter, Pascal suddenly turns on us and proceeds to explain that in spite of the poor figure that he cuts, man possesses 'greatness', that he is great precisely because he is aware of his essential 'wretchedness'. In Chapter 7, 'Contradictions', he gathers up his twin themes and reveals man as a strange mixture of contradictions:

> 'What sort of a monster then is man? What a novelty, what a portent, what a chaos, what a mass of contradictions! Judge of all things, a ridiculous earthworm who is the repository of truth, sink of uncertainty; the glory and scum of the world.'

'Who', he asks, 'shall unravel such a tangle?' That in fact is the task he has set himself. Chapter 8, 'Diversions', illustrates the way in which Pascal counterpoints his themes. It is a reference back to the chapter on vanity and describes man's attempt to escape from himself and his problems by plunging into the world of amusements, by living in such a whirl that he has no time to sit and brood, which is to run the risk of allowing himself to be submerged in the suffocating ennui which rises from the depths of his being and reduces him to impotence and despair. Chapter 9 is a survey of the inadequacy of the different philosophical systems which have offered themselves for man's guidance and simply cancel out, leaving him in a greater state of perplexity than when he started. Chapter 10 focuses our attention on the Sovereign Good, but recalls the conclusions of the philosophers when they tried to discover what it was: 'For the philosophers, two hundred and eighty sovereign goods', he remarks caustically. Chapter 11, with its heading, 'At Port-Royal', may, as some authorities believe, have been used for his address at the monastery. It dwells on some of the central themes of the Apology, but it also places man's dilemma—his fundamental dilemma—fairly and squarely before the reader:

'It is in vain, O men, that you seek within yourselves the cure of your miseries.'

In these first eleven chapters Pascal has drawn a picture of man's plight. His aim has been to disturb the reader, to make him dissatisfied with his lot, but also to hold out hope of a better one if he will make the effort, will take the apologist's advice and embark on 'the search'. All through these chapters we have seen the main themes being repeated, combining or clashing, and gradually forming a pattern: the hopelessness of man without God; the duty to seek, to consider the arguments for the existence of God and the truth of the Catholic religion seriously instead of simply glancing through a chapter or two of the Bible, having a chat with an ecclesiastic, and then pretending that one has sought God 'without success'.

Now that he has induced in the reader, as he hopes, a little good will, Pascal settles down to the proofs of religion in earnest. That is why the twelfth chapter is called 'Beginning'. He imagines man as a prisoner in the condemned cell and asks whether he would simply sit down to a game of cards if there were only an hour to go before his execution instead of trying everything possible to have his conviction quashed. Next he sees him oscillating between infinity and the void. Characteristically, he suddenly turns on him and produces the 'wager'. In the state in which he finds himself he is bound to take a chance and wager either that God exists or that he does not. In Chapter

13, 'Submission and Use of Reason', he deals with the usefulness of reason as a starting point for the 'search' and its limitations. In Chapter 14 he describes the merits of his own method.
'We only know God through Jesus Christ,' he says. 'Without
the Mediator all communication with God is removed.' 'The
metaphysical proofs of the existence of God are so remote from
men's methods of reasoning that they produce little impact; and
even if they did help, the effect would only last for a few
moments while they were watching the demonstration, but an
hour later they would be afraid that they had made a mistake.'
We pass in the next chapter from the knowledge of man to that
of God. In Chapter 16 he disposes of the falsity and inadequacy
of other religions—a reference back to his treatment of the
philosophers with their two hundred and eighty sovereign goods
—as a prelude to establishing that there is only one true religion. The next chapter deals with the attractions of religion
and is intended, as Pascal says in the most explicit terms, to
make the unbeliever wish that it were true as a preliminary
to the final demonstration.

Pascal was a mathematician and a pragmatist. He had little
use for metaphysics. In his attacks on fashionable unbelief he
used the pragmatical proofs that appealed to his own mind, the
visible tangible proofs: history and miracles. He insists on the
uniqueness of the Jewish religion and shows that it leads
naturally to Christianity which is its fulfilment. In the chapters
dealing with Judaism and Christianity there is the same back-
wards-and-forwards movement that we have seen in earlier
chapters. When he has established a necessary connection
between Judaism and Christianity, he turns back to Judaism to
show in greater detail how particular prophecies were fulfilled
by the coming of the Messiah, how certain incidents in the Old
Testament are 'symbols' which prefigure what happened in the
New Testament. Chapter 25 consists of no more than four lines,
but it is evident that Pascal would have filled it in with a series
of special or particular symbols, and the key is contained once
again in his insistence on duality: 'double law, double tables of
the law, double temple, double captivity'. Chapter 26, 'Chris-

tian Morality', dwells again on contradictions and dualism. The last chapter closes the debate with a final appeal to the unbeliever: 'What a vast difference there is between knowing God and loving him.'

It has been argued by believers and unbelievers alike that much of Pascal's apologetic is out of date, that he was mistaken in his belief that Moses was the author of the Pentateuch—a matter on which he sets great store—and that some of his history is uncertain. It must be remembered that the Apology was written at a particular moment in history for a particular section of society, that it was essentially a 'tract for the times'. Pascal marks the change from one form of apologetics to another: the change from metaphysics to psychology, from the ontological proofs of the existence of God to the study of the mental processes of the believer.

In spite of the pragmatist's insistence on history and miracles, it is the analysis of human nature in the earlier rather than the historical arguments in the later chapters which is the most original and impressive part of the *Pensées*. Pascal is relentless in carrying out his declared intention of giving the unbeliever no rest. He makes a clean sweep of the props and palliatives, the subterfuges and illusions, which enable the common run of men to muddle through life from the cradle to the grave without open disaster, and probes into the deepest recesses of man's being in the attempt to discover something permanent and unchanging—an essential nature—beneath the mass of inherited or acquired habits. He does not analyse human faculties in isolation or in the abstract. He treats man, to borrow a distinction of Fortunat Strowski's, not as a 'will', but as a 'nature', as a complex being functioning at different levels or, as Pascal himself puts it, according to different 'orders'. Man was created by God who must be the centre of his life and the goal of all his actions. Sin inflicted an incurable wound on man's primary nature, caused him to fall from his high estate, estranged him from God and led to the corruption of all his faculties. But though it plunged him into 'wretchedness', he retains something of his former 'greatness'. It is this inborn sense of his 'greatness' which is responsible for his feeling of incompleteness and bewilderment in the world. His aim must therefore be to make what is great in him prevail over his 'passions', to put aside 'distractions' which deflect him from his goal, and seek to unite himself to God. And this can only be done through the mediation of Jesus Christ.

In the end, the reader finds himself driven into a dialectical corner and forced to choose between two conflicting conceptions of the nature and destiny of man. He can only disbelieve by doing violence to his nature and his faculties. Without God there is no means of unravelling the 'tangle': man remains a 'chaos' suspended over an 'abyss'.[1]

Sceptics have dealt harshly with the 'wager' and with the 'heart' as an instrument for revealing the existence of God, but it is here that Pascal most clearly appears as a 'modern' and as one of the founders of the line of apologists which runs through Maine de Biran and Newman (who disapproved of him) to Kierkegaard and Bergson. The 'wager' anticipates Kierkegaard's 'Either-or'.[2] The 'heart' is no more capable than any other organ of providing us with irrefragable proofs of the existence of God, but it is used by Pascal to designate a valid form of insight which has clear affinities with Maine de Biran's *sens intime*, Newman's 'illative sense', and Bergson's intuition.

One of the great verities which emerges from Pascal's Apology is that the truth of religion can never be proved absolutely like a mathematical proposition. There are simply different arguments which lead people to make the act of faith. When all these arguments, all the different pieces of evidence are put together, they do in fact add up to an overwhelming case, but they only do so provided that the person who is considering them is a man of good will and recognises the duty of seeking God with an unprejudiced mind. Clearly some argu-

[1] 'Pascal has thrown a shirt of Nessus over our shoulders which devours, burns, consumes us, and which we must tear off' (H. Lefèbvre in *Blaise Pascal: l'homme et l'oeuvre* (Cahiers de Royaumont: Philosophie No. 1, Paris, 1956, p. 203).
[2] See Romano Guardini: *Christliches Bewusstsein*, 3rd Ed., Munich, 1956, pp. 199 *et seq.*

ments appeal more forcibly at some periods than at others, to some people than to others. What Pascal does is to produce the array which seems to him to be the most effective in the age in which he is living and for the man whom he has in mind.

This brings us to what we may call Pascal the artist. He was a great mathematician whose place in the history of mathematics is secure. He was not a philosopher; he was still less a theologian; but he was an immensely intelligent man who was able to use these disciplines for his purpose. In the last analysis, however, what makes him unique is not his intelligence or his personality as such, but his sensibility. It was because he was a great artist who was endowed with a unique sensibility that his work has had vast repercussions among people of the most divergent views, has been a solace to the honest doubter and a scandal to the aggressive unbeliever. For Pascal seldom leaves people indifferent. He either provokes the profoundest admiration or an equally violent antipathy such as we find in Valéry's famous onslaught, and sometimes a combination of the two that we find in the hostile critic who recently declared that he reads him with a 'sacred horror'.[1]

MARTIN TURNELL

[1] H. Lefèbvre: *Art. cit.*: *loc cit.*

The Life of Monsieur Pascal

WRITTEN BY MADAME PÉRIER,
HIS SISTER, WIFE OF MONSIEUR PÉRIER,
COUNSELLOR AT THE
COUR DES AIDES
AT CLAIRMONT

My brother was born at Clairmont on 19 June 1623. My father's name was Étienne Pascal, and he was a judge of the Cour des Aides; my mother's name was Antoinette Begon. As soon as my brother was old enough to talk, it became clear that he possessed a mind of exceptional ability from his concise little answers to questions that were put to him, but still more from the questions that he himself asked about the meaning of things. This early promise was never belied because, as he grew older, his intellectual powers increased and were very far beyond those of his age.

My mother died in 1626 when my brother was only three years old. When my father found himself alone, he devoted himself assiduously to the care of his family. As he had no other son except my brother, his position as only son and his other qualities so endeared him to my father that he could never bring himself to entrust the child's education to anybody else. He made up his mind to educate him himself which he did, for my brother never went to school and never had any masters except my father.

My father retired in 1632, and took us with him when he moved to Paris where he decided to make his home. My father's retirement greatly assisted his plans for the education of my brother who was only eight at the time, because it is unlikely that he would have been able to give him the same attention in the provinces, where the exercise of his profession and the large number of people who came to see him would have kept him too busy to occupy himself with my brother. But in Paris his time was his own; he applied himself wholly to him with the complete success that was to be expected from the care of a father who was as intelligent and devoted as it is possible for a father to be.

The principle which governed the child's education was to ensure that he was more advanced than the work he was doing; it was for this reason that my father would not teach him Latin until he was twelve so that it would come more easily to him. In the meantime, he did not let him waste his time, but discussed everything with him that he found him capable of grasping. He explained the general theory of language to him; he showed him that language had been reduced to grammar by the application of various rules, that the rules had certain exceptions which he was careful to point out, and that in this way people had discovered the means of transmitting all languages from one country to another. This general conception clarified his mind and enabled him to understand the reasons for the rules of grammar, with the result that when he came to learn them he understood why he was doing it and applied his mind to precisely those things which required the greatest concentration.

After teaching him these subjects, my father taught him others. He often talked to him about the extraordinary effects of nature such as gunpowder and other things which, when we think about them, are a source of wonder to us. My brother enjoyed these talks, but he wanted to know the reason for everything; and since the reasons are not always known, when my father did not tell him or only gave him the conventional ones, which are really a sign of defeat, he was not satisfied. He always possessed an admirable clarity of mind which invariably enabled him to detect what was false, and it is fair to say that at all times and in everything truth was the sole object of his mind, because nothing ever satisfied him except his own personal knowledge. Thus, when he was still a child, he was only able to accept things which seemed to him to be obviously true, so that when people were unable to give him sound reasons, he sought them for himself, and once he had taken something up he refused to abandon it until he had found a convincing reason for it.

It so happened that on one occasion someone at table tapped a porcelain plate with a knife and he noticed that it gave off a loud sound, but that the sound was muffled the moment you put your hand on the plate. He at once wanted to know the reason and this experiment with sound led him to make many others. He made so many observations that, at the age of eleven, he wrote a treatise on sound which was considered to be very cogently argued.

His genius for mathematics began to show itself when he was still under twelve owing to an incident which was so extra-ordinary that it deserves to be described in detail. My father was an excellent mathematician and knew all the ablest mathematicians of the day who used to come to his home. But as he intended to teach my brother languages and as he knew that mathematics was a subject which people found peculiarly fascinating and which was inclined to absorb their minds completely, he did not want my brother to know anything about it for fear that he would neglect Latin and the other languages that he was anxious for him to learn. For this reason he did not allow him to read mathematical works. He refrained from talking about mathematics to his friends in his presence: but all these precautions did not prevent the child's curiosity from being aroused, and he often begged my father to teach him mathematics. But my father said that he would only do so as a reward. He promised him that as soon as he knew Latin and Greek he could go on to mathematics.

When he noticed his reluctance, my brother asked him one day what mathematics was and what it dealt with. My father replied that, in general terms, it was a method of producing accurate figures and showing the connection between them. At the same time he forbade him to discuss it any further or even to think about the subject. But my brother could not accept these restrictions and as soon as he was given the opening, that mathematics provided the means of producing figures which were bound to be accurate, he began to reflect and during his spare time, when he was in the room where he used to play, he picked up some coal and began to draw figures on the floor, looking, for example, for a way of producing a circle which was perfectly round, a triangle whose sides and angles were equal, and other things of the same kind.

He discovered the solutions by himself without the slightest difficulty; then he went on to investigate the relations of the figures to one another. But my father had taken such care to keep all these things from him, that he did not even know their names, and was compelled to invent them for himself. He called a circle a 'round', a line a 'bar'; and did the same with other figures. After he had invented these terms, he produced some axioms and then some perfect demonstrations, and as we go from one thing to another in these matters, he went on and pushed his researches so far that he came to the thirty-second proposition of the first book of Euclid. When he had reached this point my father happened to walk into the room without my brother's hearing him. He found the child so deeply immersed in what he was doing that it was a considerable time before he noticed his presence. It is impossible to say who was the more surprised, the son at seeing his father while he was doing work that was forbidden, or the father at finding the son in the midst of all these operations. But the father's surprise was much greater when, on asking his son what he was doing, he received the answer that he was seeking something which turned out to be the thirty-second proposition of the book of Euclid.

When my father asked where the idea had come from, he replied that he had discovered something; and when my father repeated his question, he spoke to him about several other demonstrations that he had done; and finally, by going backwards and using the terms 'rounds' and 'bars', he came to his definitions and axioms.

My father was so appalled at the greatness and power of his intellect that he left him without a word, and went to see Monsieur Le Pailleur who was a close friend and also a very learned man. On his arrival he stood stock-still like a man in a trance. When Monsieur Le Pailleur noticed it and also noticed that he was weeping, he was thunderstruck and begged him not to hide the cause of his distress from him. My father said to him: 'I am not weeping out of grief, but for joy. You know what care

I took to prevent my son from knowing anything about geometry, for fear of distracting him from other subjects. Now look what has happened.' And he told him what the child had discovered, which really meant that he had discovered mathematics.

Monsieur Le Pailleur was no less surprised than my father, but he told him that he did not feel that it was right to go on keeping such a mind in captivity and withholding the knowledge of mathematics from him; that he should let him have the books without trying to hold him back any longer.

My father agreed and gave my brother the *Elements of Euclid* to read in his spare time. He read and understood it by himself without needing any explanation. And while he was studying the book, he worked out the propositions and made such rapid progress that he became a regular attendant at the weekly lectures to which all the ablest people in Paris came in order to bring their own works and examine those of other people.

My brother was very well able to hold his own both in the discussion of the works of others and the production of original work himself, because he was among those who most often brought something new. The meeting frequently dealt with problems which had been sent from Germany and other foreign countries; people asked his opinion on everything and did so with greater respect than they showed anybody else; because he was gifted with such vivid insight that he often discovered mistakes which had escaped other people. Yet he only studied mathematics in his spare time because at this period he was learning Latin according to the rules which my father had drawn up specially for him. But as he discovered in mathematics the truth which he had always sought with such ardour, he was so pleased that he applied the whole of his mind to it, and short though the time was that he was able to spend on it, he made such progress that at the age of sixteen he wrote a *Traité des coniques* which was considered so brilliant that people said that nothing of such outstanding merit had been produced since the time of Archimedes.

All those competent to judge thought that it should be published at once saying that, though it would always remain an admirable piece of work, nevertheless if it were published at the time when the author was still only sixteen, this fact would greatly enhance its merit. But as my brother never cared about fame, he did not pay any attention to the suggestion with the result that the work was never published.

During the whole of this period he continued to learn Latin and Greek. In addition, my father used to talk to him at meal times about logic, physics, and the other branches of Philosophy; this was all the instruction that he had in them because he never went to school and never had other teachers for this subject any more than he did for the rest.

It is easy to imagine the delight that my father took in my brother's progress in all branches of knowledge; but he did not realise that such great and continual concentration of mind at this tender age might have a serious effect on his health, and indeed signs began to appear as soon as he reached the age of eighteen. But as the discomforts that he experienced at this time were not very serious, they did not prevent him from pursuing all his normal occupations so that it was at this period, when he was nineteen, that he invented the Arithmetical machine with which you can not only carry out all sorts of calculations without pen or slips, but you can also do so without knowing a single one of the rules of Arithmetic and with absolutely unimpeachable accuracy. It was regarded as something decidedly novel to have reduced to a mechanical operation a form of knowledge which belongs completely to the mind, and to have discovered the means of carrying out all the calculations with complete certainty and without the need of working out anything. His invention tired him very much, not because of the thought or the calculations which went into it and which he managed without any trouble, but because of the effort needed to explain everything to the workpeople. The result was that it took him two years to bring it to its present state of perfection.

But his fatigue and the precarious state of health from which he had suffered for several years led to disabilities from which he was never to be free again, and he sometimes said that from the age of eighteen he had never known a day without pain. His sufferings were not always equally violent and as soon as he experienced some alleviation, his mind at once applied itself to fresh discoveries.

It was during one of these periods, when he was twenty-three, that after seeing Torricelli's experiment, he proceeded to devise and carry out another experiment which is known as the *experiment on the Vacuum* and which proves conclusively that all the properties previously attributed to the vacuum are caused by the heaviness of the atmosphere. This was his last work in the field of secular learning, and though he was later to invent the *Roulette*, it does not conflict with what I have said; because he discovered it without systematic thought and without any of the intellectual concentration which I shall describe in its proper place. Immediately afterwards, when he was still under twenty-four, Providence placed him in a position which forced him to read some works on religion; and by means of these holy readings God opened his eyes so effectively that he understood perfectly that the Christian Religion demands that we shall live only for God and have no other object but him. And this truth appeared so obvious to him, and of such importance, that it put an end to all his scientific researches. The outcome was that at this time he abandoned all other branches of knowledge in order to devote himself exclusively to the one thing that Jesus Christ describes as necessary.

Up to that time he had been preserved by a special protection of Providence from all the youthful vices and what is still stranger with a mind of this calibre and character, he had never indulged in free thought in Religion because he had always confined his researches to natural phenomena. He told me on several occasions that, in addition to all his other obligations towards him, his father, who had the greatest respect himself for religion, had imbued him with the same respect when he was still a child and had laid down, as a precept, that everything that is the object of faith cannot be the object of reason.

These precepts, which were often repeated to him by a father for whom he had the highest regard and in whom he saw great learning combined with very clear and powerful reasoning, made such a deep impression on his mind that whatever perorations he happened to hear on the lips of free-thinkers, he was not in the least influenced by them, and though very young he considered them as people who sub-scribed to the mistaken principle that human reason is above everything and who did not understand the nature of faith.

For this man, who was endowed with such a vast, profound and inquiring mind, who was so determined in his search for the cause and reason of everything, was at the same time as sub-missive as a child in all matters pertaining to Religion. And his simplicity governed the whole of his life; with the result that from the time when he made the decision not to work at any subject save Religion, he never occupied himself with difficult problems of Theology, but applied the whole power of his intellect to the study and practice of the perfection prescribed by Christian Morality, to which he devoted all the talents which God had bestowed on him, and did nothing else for the rest of his life except meditate day and night on the law of God. But though he had not made a special study of Scholasticism, he was not unaware of the Church's condemnation of the various heresies which had been evolved by the ingenuity and waywardness of the human mind. It was against this kind of speculation that he felt most strongly, and it was at this time that God gave him an opportunity of displaying his zeal for religion.

He was living at the time at Rouen, where my father was employed in the service of the King and where in those days there was a man who taught a new Philosophy which attracted the curious. My brother went to see him with two young men who had pressed him to accompany them; but they were very surprised, during the talk they had with the man, to find that when expounding the principles of his philosophy, he drew con-clusions on points of faith which were contrary to the teaching of the Church. He proved by his arguments that the body of

Jesus Christ was not formed of the blood of the Virgin and several other things of a similar nature. They tried to refute him, but he remained firm in his view. With the result that after reflecting on the danger of leaving the instruction of the young in the hands of a man whose opinions were erroneous, they resolved first of all to warn him and then, if he refused to heed the warning, to denounce him. That is what happened because he listened to the warning with contempt; so they thought that it was their duty to denounce him to Monsignor du Bellay who for the time being was carrying out episcopal duties in the diocese of Rouen by the commission of the Archbishop. Monsignor du Bellay sent for the man, but when he had questioned him he was taken in by an equivocal confession which he wrote out and signed with his own hand, besides which he did not attach much importance to a warning by three young men on such a serious topic. Nevertheless, as soon as the young men saw the profession of faith they realised its inadequacy; this led them to pay a visit to the Archbishop of Rouen, at Gaillon, and he looked into the matter, decided that it was so important that he wrote out a patent for his council and gave a firm instruction to Monsignor du Bellay to call on the man to recant on all the points on which he had been accused, and not to accept anything from him except by the intermediary of those who had denounced him. The order was executed and the man appeared before the council of the Archbishop and withdrew all his opinions; we can assume that he was sincere because he never showed any ill-will towards those who had brought the matter up, which suggests that he himself had been deceived by the false conclusions which he drew from his false premises. It is therefore perfectly true that the young men had no intention of harming him and no object except to make him realise his errors and prevent him from misleading young people who in such complex questions would not have been capable of distinguishing between true and false. Thus the affair ended quietly. And as my brother continued more and more to seek ways of pleasing God, his love of perfection became so ardent that at the age of twenty-four it permeated the whole house. My father, who was in no way ashamed to take lessons from his son, began to lead a more regular life through the practice of the virtues until the time of his death, which was thoroughly Christian.

My sister, who possessed extraordinary intellectual gifts and, while still a child, acquired a reputation which few girls achieve at a more advanced age, was also so moved by my brother's homilies that she decided to give up all the comforts which she had enjoyed until then and devote herself entirely to God. As she had plenty of intelligence, the moment that God touched her heart, she like my brother understood everything that he said about the holiness of the Christian Religion; and as she could not abide the state of imperfection in which she believed herself to be living in the world, she became a nun at a very strict house, the Abbey of Port-Royal-des-Champs, and died there at the age of thirty-six after embarking on the most difficult tasks and wearing herself out in a short time through merits that other people only acquire after many years.

My brother was now twenty-four; his disabilities had been increasing all the time and had reached a stage when he was unable to swallow any liquid unless it was hot, and even then only drop by drop. But as he also suffered from an almost intolerable headache, a burning feeling in his belly and many other infirmities, the doctors ordered him to purge himself every other day for a period of three months. He was therefore obliged to take all the medicines as best he could, that is to say, warmed up and drop by drop. It was a veritable torment, and those who were with him were filled with horror at the very sight of it; but my brother never complained. He regarded everything as a gain for himself. For, as he knew no other science but virtue and as he knew that virtue is perfected by suffering, he joyfully accepted all his suffering as a penance, remarking on the advantages of Christianity in all things. He often said that at other times his infirmities had interfered with his studies which had distressed him, but that a Christian finds his reward in everything, and more especially in suffering, because through suffering he comes to know Christ crucified, which must be the whole knowledge of a Christian and the one glory of his life.

The continuation of his treatment, and the new remedies prescribed for him, brought him some relief, but not perfect health. The result was that the doctors thought that, in order to cure him completely, it would be necessary for him to give up every form of intellectual exertion which had any adverse effects on him, and to seize every opportunity he could to rest his mind by engaging in activities which he found attractive and enjoyable, by which they meant normal social intercourse; for there was no other kind of relaxation which was suited to my brother. But how could a man in his position make up his mind to it? In fact, to begin with, he experienced great difficulty. But everyone pressed him so hard that he ended by yielding to the specious argument that it would restore his health: people convinced him that it is a gift that God wishes us to turn to good account.

He therefore went into society: on a number of occasions he found himself at Court where experienced people noticed that at first he adopted its airs and manners with as much enjoyment as if he had been there all his life. It is true that when he spoke about the world of fashion, he was so skilful in analysing its outlook that it was easy to see that he was perfectly capable of responding to it, and, in so far as he thought it reasonable, doing everything necessary to adapt himself to it.

It was the worst spent period of his life; for though by the mercy of God he was preserved from vice, in the last resort the atmosphere of the world is very different from that of the Gospels. God, who demanded a greater degree of perfection from him than from other people, was not disposed to leave him there for long, and used my sister as an instrument to withdraw him from it, as he had earlier used my brother to extricate my sister from her commitments in the world.

Since her entry into religion, she had grown daily in fervour and all her sentiments were permeated by an undiluted holiness. That is why she could not endure the fact that the person to whom, after God, she was most indebted for the graces which she enjoyed, did not share the same graces; and as my brother saw her often she spoke to him as often of them, until at last she did so with such determination that she convinced him, as he had been the first to convince her, that he must renounce the world and all its works. For the most innocent of them are nothing more than a round of unending futilities, completely unworthy of the Christian holiness to which we are all called and of which Jesus Christ has provided us with the model.

The reasons of health which had previously been responsible for his attitude appeared so pathetic to him that he himself was ashamed of them. The light of true wisdom made him see clearly that salvation must be preferred to everything else, and that it is false reasoning which makes us worry about the momentary well-being of our body when the eternal well-being of our soul is at stake.

He was thirty when he decided to withdrawn from the new commitments which he had undertaken in the world; he set to work to change his environment, and in order to break more completely with his existing habits he went to live in the country. When he returned from a prolonged stay there he showed so unmistakably that he wished to renounce the world that the world ended by renouncing him.

In the last resort he always acted according to principles in everything: his mind and heart were so made that he could not behave otherwise. Thus the principles which he adopted during his retreat from the world were the solid precepts of true piety; one was to give up all forms of pleasure, the other to go without everything except the barest necessities.

In order to put the first of these principles into practice, he began at once, as he always did afterwards, to dispense with servants in so far as it was possible: he made his own bed; he had his meals in the kitchen; he brought back his own dishes and, in short, only used his staff for those things which he was absolutely unable to do for himself.

It was impossible for him not to use his senses; but when he was compelled by necessity to do something which gave him pleasure, he displayed a marvellous skill in disengaging his mind so that it did not participate in it. We never heard him praise the food which was served to him at table, and when we sometimes went out of our way to choose a dainty morsel for him and asked him if he found it good, he answered simply: 'You ought to have warned me beforehand because I no longer remember and I must confess that I did not pay attention.' And when somebody remarked casually on the goodness of one of the dishes, he could not bear it and called it sensuality, though the dish may have been a very ordinary one. 'It was,' he said, 'a sign that people were eating because they liked the taste of the food, which was always wrong, or at any rate were using the language of sensuality, which was not becoming in a Christian who must never say anything which has not at least an air of sanctity.' He had never allowed anyone to make any sauce or relish, or to give him orange or verjuice grape, or anything that stimulated his appetite though by nature he was fond of all these things.

At the beginning of his withdrawal from the world he had settled the amount of food that was necessary to satisfy the needs of his stomach; and from that time onwards he never exceeded it, however good his appetite, and he always made himself eat the prescribed amount, however repugnant food might be to him. When anyone asked him why he behaved in this way, he replied that we ought to satisfy the needs of our stomach and not of our appetite.

But the mortification of the flesh was not confined to cutting down on anything that was pleasant, whether it was food or medicines for his illness: for four years on end he took beef tea without showing the slightest sign of repugnance. It was sufficient for someone to prescribe a thing for him to swallow it without a murmur, and when I expressed surprise that he took certain very revolting medicines without displaying the least sign of disgust, he laughed at me and told me that he himself could not understand why people were so nauseated when they took something of their own free will after being told that it was nasty; and that only violence or astonishment should produce such reaction. It will be apparent from what follows how careful he was to give up all kinds of intellectual pleasure in which self-esteem might play some part.

He was no less scrupulous in observing the second principle which followed from the first: to give up whatever was super-fluous . . . He had gradually reduced himself to the state of no longer having a carpet in his bedroom because he did not con-sider it necessary and was not obliged to have one out of polite-ness. For the only people whom he saw were those to whom he never ceased to recommend privations, and who in consequence were not surprised to see that he practised what he preached.[1]

We have already observed that he had cut out superfluous visits and no longer wished to see anybody.

But as we always seek out a treasure wherever it happens to be and as God does not permit a lamp which is lighted to illuminate people to be hidden under a bushel, a certain num-ber of people, including persons of intelligence, whom he had known earlier, came to see him in his retirement and to ask his advice. Others who had doubts in matters of faith and who knew that he possessed great insight into them, also came to him for help; and both parties, some of whom are still living, always left him well satisfied, and even today take every oppor-tunity of asserting that they are indebted to his explanations and advice for the good which they know and do.

Although he only took part in these conversations for purely charitable reasons and though he kept a careful watch on him-self to ensure that he lost nothing of what he was trying to ac-

[1] The editions of 1684 and 1686, which were published respectively by Abraham Wolfgang of Amsterdam and Guillaume Desprez of Paris, contain the following paragraph which is not in MS. 4546:
[That is the way in which he spent five years of his life, from thirty to thirty-five, working ceaselessly for God or his neighbour, or himself, by try-ing to achieve a greater and greater degree of perfection; and it could al-most be said that it was the whole of his life because during the four remain-ing years that God granted to him, he was constantly ailing. It was not pre-cisely a new illness which attacked him, but an aggravation of the ailments to which he had been subject since youth. But at this period they attacked him with such virulence that he succumbed to them; and during all this time he was unable to work at all on his great book on religion, or help the people who had appealed to him for advice either verbally or in writing: for his illness was so grave that he could do nothing for them in spite of his great desire to help them.]

quire in his retirement, he soon began to feel distressed and to fear that self-esteem might tempt him to take pleasure in the talks; and his rule was not to indulge in any enjoyment which might be due to self-esteem. On the other hand, he did not feel that he could refuse people the help of which they stood in need. He was therefore faced by something resembling a conflict. But the spirit of mortification, which is the very spirit of charity and reconciles all things, came to his help by giving him the idea of having an iron belt studded with spikes and placing it next to his naked flesh every time that he heard that these Gentlemen had come to call on him. He did so, and as soon as he was aware of any sense of vanity, or felt that he was enjoying the conversation, he dug his elbow into himself to intensify the pain of the spikes and remind himself of his duty. This practice appeared to him to be so useful that he also used it as a remedy against the lack of concentration from which he suffered so much during the last years of his life. As he was reduced to a state in which he could neither read nor write, he was obliged to remain unoccupied and to go for walks without being able to think coherently about anything. He was afraid, with good reason, that lack of any form of work, which is the root of all evil, might make him lose the thread of his thoughts. And in order to keep himself always on the alert he had, so to speak, incorporated this voluntary enemy which, by pricking his body, continually spurred his mind to cling to its fervour, and provided him with the means of certain victory. But he kept these things such a close secret that we knew nothing about them and only heard of them after his death from a person of great virtue of whom he was fond and whom he had been obliged to tell for reasons which concerned that person.

The whole of the time that was not given up to the charitable work which we have just described, was devoted to prayer and to reading Holy Scripture. It was, so to speak, the core of his existence from which he derived all his joy and the repose brought by his withdrawal from the world. It is true that he possessed a special gift for tasting the fruits of these two precious and holy occupations. It could even be said that for him there was no difference between the two because he meditated on Holy Scripture while he prayed. He often used to say that Holy Scripture was not a knowledge of the mind but of the heart, that it is only intelligible to those whose heart is upright, that anyone else discovered only obscurities in it, that the veil which lies over Scripture for the Jews is also there for bad Christians, and that charity was not only the object of Scripture, but also the means of entering into the spirit of it. He went further and said again that we are only in a fit state to understand Holy Scripture when we hate ourselves and love the life of mortification of Jesus Christ. It was in this frame of mind that he himself read Holy Scripture and he applied himself to it with such determination that he almost knew it by heart, with the result that one could not misquote it to him and he declared positively: 'Either it is not in Scripture or it is,' pointing out the exact place and usually everything which served to give one a perfect understanding of all the truths of faith and morality.

He possessed such an admirable turn of mind that it enhanced everything he said and though he learnt a number of things from books, when he had absorbed them in his own way they appeared quite different because he always expressed himself in a way that fixed them in people's minds.

He was a man of extraordinary natural gifts; but he had worked out for himself very special rules of expression which enhanced his gifts still more. It was not a question of what are known as fine thoughts, which merely possess a sham brilliance and mean nothing: he never used big words and seldom employed metaphorical expressions, or said anything obscure or crude or overbearing, or omitted anything important, or included anything irrelevant. But he thought of eloquence as a method of expressing things in a way that is easy of understanding and is a pleasure to the listener. He believed that the art lay in appealing to inclinations situated in a region midway between the mind and heart of the listener, and the thoughts and expressions which we employ, but that the relations between the two are only properly adjusted by the turn that we give our thought. That is why he had made a profound study of the mind

46

and heart of man: he understood their inclinations perfectly. When a thought came to him, he put himself in the place of those whom he wished to understand it, and by examining it to see whether everything was in the correct perspective, he perceived what form he should give it, and he was not satisfied until he saw clearly that one was absolutely made for the other, that is to say, that he had thought for the mind of the person whom he was about to see; that, when thought and expression were perfectly matched, it was impossible for the mind not to grasp it with pleasure. He did not make small things great, or great things small. It was not enough for a thing to appear beautiful; it was necessary that the expression should fit the subject, that there should be nothing superfluous about it, but also nothing lacking. In short, he was such a master of his own style that he said everything that he wanted to say, and what he said always produced the effect that he intended. And his simple, vigorous, precise, agreeable, and natural manner of writing was at once so well suited to him and so personal that as soon as the *Provincial Letters* were published, everyone knew that he had written them in spite of the care that he had taken to hide the fact even from those who were closest to him.

It was at this time that it pleased God to cure my daughter of a lacrymal fistula from which she had suffered for three and a half years. The fistula was so bad that the ablest surgeons in Paris regarded it as incurable; and at last God took it upon himself to cure it by the touch of a Holy Thorn at Port-Royal; the miracle was vouched for by several surgeons and doctors, and confirmed by the solemn verdict of the Church.

My daughter was my brother's goddaughter; but he was more deeply moved by the miracle because God was glorified in it and because it happened at a time when the faith of the majority of people was at a low ebb. His joy was so great that he was entirely absorbed by it, and as he never turned his mind to anything without a great deal of reflection, this particular miracle provided him with the opportunity for a number of very important reflexions on miracles in general in both the Old and New Testaments. If there are miracles, it follows that there must be something above what we call nature. The argument is eminently sensible: we only need to be convinced of the certainty and authenticity of miracles. Now there are rules for judging them which are also a matter of good sense, and the rules turn out to be right for the miracles of the Old Testament. The Old Testament miracles are therefore true: there is therefore something above nature.

But there are still other signs that the principle behind miracles is God; and in the case of the miracles of the New Testament in particular, that he who worked them was the Messiah for whom men were waiting. Thus the miracles of the Old and New Testaments prove that there is a God, while those of the New prove specially that Jesus was the true Messiah.

He unravelled it all with admirable insight, and when we heard him talk and he dwelt on all the circumstances of the Old and New Testaments in which miracles were described, they at once became clear to us. It was impossible to deny the truth of these miracles, or the arguments which he drew from them to prove the existence of God and the Messiah without coming into conflict with ordinary everyday principles which enable us to accept all sorts of things that are regarded as being beyond doubt. Some of his reflexions on the subject have been preserved; but they amount to very little and I should feel obliged to expand what I have said, in order to provide a clearer picture of his opinions, if one of his friends had not given us a treatise on the works of Moses in which everything is admirably explained in a manner which would not be unworthy of my brother. I must refer you then to his book and I merely add, what it is important to observe at this point, that my brother's various reflexions on miracles gave him a fresh insight into religion. As all truths follow from one another, it was sufficient for him to apply himself to one of them for the rest to come crowding in on him and they were analysed in such a manner that he was carried away by what he told us; and it was on one of these occasions that he felt so strongly against atheists that, perceiving by means of the insight which God had given him, how he could convince them and reduce them to final confusion, he began work on his book on religion. The parts which have been preserved fill us with the deepest regret that he was unable to edit them himself, because what we already have coupled with the material that he might have added would undoubtedly have produced a finished work of compelling power. He was certainly capable of doing it, but God who had given him all the intelligence necessary for such a great undertaking did not give him the health required to bring it to perfection.

He claimed to show that the Christian Religion possessed as many marks of certainty as those things which in life are accepted as being absolutely beyond doubt. He did not make use of the metaphysical proofs: it was not that he did not think them worthy of respect when properly used. But he said that they were very far removed from men's ordinary mode of thinking, that not everyone was capable of grasping them; that to those who were, they were only convincing for the moment and that an hour later they would not know what to think of them, but would be afraid that they had been mistaken. He also said that proofs of this kind could only lead to a speculative knowledge of God, and that to know God in this way meant that we did not know him. Nor did he use the ordinary arguments based on nature; he respected them, however, because they were consecrated by Holy Scripture and in conformity with reason, but he believed that they were not sufficiently in tune with the mind and temper of those whom he wanted to convince. He had learnt from experience that, far from winning them over by these methods, nothing was more likely to repel them and dash their hopes of discovering truth, than to try to convince them simply by this kind of argument against which they had so often set their face; that the hardness of their hearts had made them deaf to the voice of nature; in short, that they were in a state of blindness from which they could only emerge with the help of Jesus Christ, without whom all contact with God is taken from us, because it is written that no one shall know the Father except through the Son and him to whom it pleases the Son to reveal him.

The Godhead of Christians does not consist in a God who is merely the author of mathematical truths and the natural order: that is the pagan idea. It does not consist in a God who in his providence watches over the lives and possessions of men in order to guarantee them a prosperous and a carefree life: that is the Jewish view. But the God of Abraham and of Jacob, the God of Christians, is a God of love and consolation: he is a God who fills the soul and heart of those who possess him. He is a God who makes them feel within themselves their wretchedness and his infinite mercy, who unites himself to them in the depths of their soul, who fills them with humility, with faith, with trust and love, who makes them capable of an end which is something other than themselves.

The Christian God is a God who makes the soul feel that he is its sole good, that its place lies in him, that it will only find joy in loving him and who, at the same time, makes it hate the obstacle which holds it back and prevents it from loving him with all its strength. The self-love and sensual pleasure which hold it back are intolerable to it; God makes it aware that this residue of self-love is there and that he alone can cure it.

That is what is meant by knowing God as a Christian. But in order to know him in this way, man must also be conscious of his wretchedness, his unworthiness, and his need of a mediator for approaching God and uniting himself to him. We must not separate these forms of knowledge because once they are separated they are not merely useless, but harmful. A knowledge of God without a corresponding knowledge of our wretchedness makes for pride; a knowledge of our wretchedness without Jesus Christ drives us to despair. But a knowledge of Jesus Christ frees us from pride and despair, because in him we find God who is our only comforter in our wretchedness and our only means of curing it.

We can reach a knowledge of God without a knowledge of our wretchedness, or a knowledge of our wretchedness without a knowledge of God, or even a knowledge of God and our wretchedness without discovering the means of escaping from the miseries which overwhelm us. But we cannot know Jesus

Christ without at the same time knowing both God and our wretchedness, because he is not simply God, but a God who redeems us in our wretchedness.

Thus all those who seek God without Jesus Christ do not find any light which satisfies them or which truly helps them, because they either do not reach the point of knowing that there is a God, or if they do it is useless because they create for themselves a means of contact with this God without a mediator, with the result that they fall into Atheism or Deism, which are two things that are almost equally abhorrent to the Christian.

We must therefore strive uniquely to come to a knowledge of Jesus Christ, because it is through him alone that we can claim to know God in a manner which is of practical value to us. He is the true God of mankind, of the wretched and the sinners: he is the centre of all and the object of all and anyone who does not know him knows nothing of the order and nature of the world, or of himself, for not only do we know God only through Jesus Christ, but we only know ourselves through Jesus Christ.

Without Jesus Christ man is condemned to a life of vice and wretchedness; with Jesus Christ man is delivered from vice and wretchedness. He is our whole happiness, our virtue, our life, our light, our hope; outside him there is only vice, misery, darkness and despair; and we see only darkness and confusion in God's nature and our own. These are his actual words, and I felt that I should reproduce them here because they reveal admirably the spirit of his work, and show that the manner in which he intended to set about it was undoubtedly the one most likely to make an impression on men's hearts.

One of the main rules of style that he laid down was not only not to say anything that was not understood, or only understood with difficulty, but also to say things which interested his hearers, because he could feel assured that from then onwards self-esteem itself would never fail to make us think them over, and moreover that since the attitude which we could adopt towards things was of two kinds (for they either cause us pain or comfort us), he believed that we must never cause pain without offering consolation, and that to organise everything well was the secret of style.

This was how he handled the proofs of the existence of God and the truth of the Christian religion; he did not wish to say anything which was beyond the comprehension of those for whom it was intended or in which man did not feel called upon to take part, either by an inner feeling that all the things to which his attention was drawn were good or bad, or by perceiving clearly that he could not adopt a sounder or more reasonable attitude than to believe that there is a God in whom we may rejoice and a mediator who having come that we might deserve grace, brings us greater happiness in this life by the virtues that he awakens in us than we could expect from anything that the world offers, and gives us the assurance that we shall be perfectly happy in heaven if we deserve happiness by following the path that he has revealed and the example that he himself has given us.

Although he felt certain that everything that he had to say about religion was perfectly clear and convincing, he did not think that it would appear so to those who had fallen into a state of apathy and who, because they did not discover in themselves the light necessary to convince them, neglected to seek it elsewhere, above all in the Church where it is striking in its abundance. For he regarded two truths as certain: that God has given, particularly in the Church, positive signs by which he can be recognised by those who seek him sincerely, and that he has nevertheless concealed them in such a way that he will only be found by those who seek him with all their heart.

That is why, when he had discussions with atheists, he never began by argument or by stating the principles that he wished to establish, but wanted to know beforehand whether they were seeking truth with all their heart, and he handled them according to their answer, in order to help them to find the light that they did not possess if they sought it sincerely, or to induce them to seek it and to regard the search as the most serious business of their lives before giving them any instruction, if they wanted his instruction to be of value to them. His infirmities prevented him from devoting himself further to his task. He was thirty-four when he began work on it; he spent a whole year in preparation for it, in the manner permitted by his other occupations, which was to collect the different thoughts that had come to him, but at the end of the year, that is to say, his thirty-fifth year, which was the fifth year of his withdrawal from the world, he suffered such a serious relapse in health that he was able to do nothing more during the four years of life which remained to him, if one can use the word 'life' of the pitiful state of prostration in which he spent them.

It is impossible to think of this undertaking without feeling a very deep sense of distress at seeing what is perhaps the finest and most valuable work of the century in which we are living left unfinished. I dare not go so far as to say that we were unworthy if it. Whatever the reason, it was God's will to show by this fragment what my brother was capable of achieving through the greatness of his intellect and the gifts that God had bestowed on him; and if the work were to be completed by another person, I am convinced that such a great benefit could only be attained by renewed prayer.

The recurrence of my brother's ailments began by a toothache which completely prevented him from sleeping. But how could a mind like his remain awake without thinking of anything? That is why, during the periods of insomnia which were frequent and exhausting, there came to him one night some ideas on the cycloid. The first was followed by a second, the second by a third; and last of all by a swarm of ideas which came tumbling out one after the other. They enabled him, in spite of himself, to perceive a solution of the problem of the cycloid which came as a surprise to him. But as he had long ago given up the study of mathematics, it did not even occur to him to put anything down in writing. Nevertheless, when he had talked it over with someone whom he regarded with great deference both on account of his respect for his ability and out of gratitude for the affection that he received from him, the person suggested that the discovery should be used for a purpose whose only aim was to glorify God, and he persuaded my brother to write down all his views and have them printed.

It is incredible with what speed the whole thing was done, because he did nothing but write as fast as his hand could go and it was finished in a very few days. He did not keep a copy, but sent the pages to the printer as each one was finished. Another of his writings was sent to the printers in the same way, so that he was providing them simultaneously with copy for two different works.[1] It was no undue burden for his mind, but his body could not stand up to it; it was this final strain which ended by ruining his health completely and reducing him to the distressing state in which, as we have said, he was unable to swallow things.

But if his ailments prevented him from helping other people, they were not without value for himself, because he endured his sufferings with such patience that there are grounds for believing, and for consoling ourselves with the thought, that God chose these means to make him as he wished him to be when he appeared before him. In fact, he thought of nothing else but that and always bore in mind the two precepts that he had laid down for himself—the renunciation of all pleasure and all superfluity—and he observed them with still greater fervour as though bowed down by the weight of charity, and the feeling that he was nearing the centre where he would enjoy eternal rest.

But there is no better way of discovering the special disposition in which he supported all his new ailments during these four years than by reciting the admirable *prayer* which we learnt from him and which he composed at that time *to ask God to teach us the proper use of illness.* For we cannot doubt that all these things were in his heart because they were in his mind and he only wrote them down because he practised them. We can even give an assurance that we ourselves witnessed it and that if anyone has written better about the right use of illness, no one

[1] Either the *Cinquième écrit des curés de Paris* (11th June 1658), or the *Sixième écrit des curés de Paris* (24th July 1658).

has ever practised it with greater edification for all those who saw him.

A few years earlier he had written a letter on the death of my father from which we can see that he understood that a Christian must regard this life as a sacrifice, and that the different misfortunes which befall us should only be taken into account in so far as they interrupt or further this sacrifice. That is why the moribund state to which he was reduced during the last years of his life was a means of accomplishing the sacrifice which was completed by his death. He looked on his state of prostration with joy, and we saw every day that he blessed God for it out of the fulness of his gratitude. When he spoke to us of death, which he believed was closer than in fact it turned out to be, he always spoke at the same time of Jesus Christ, saying that without Jesus Christ death is horrible, but that in him it is lovable, holy and the joy of the believer, and that in truth if we were innocent a horror of death would be reasonable because it is contrary to the order of nature for the innocent to be punished; that in these circumstances it would be right to hate it if it could separate a holy soul from a holy body; but that, as things were, it was right to love it because it separated a holy soul from an impure body; that it would have been right to hate it if it destroyed the peace between soul and body, but not at a time when it calms the irreconcilable conflict between them, when it takes away from the body the unhappy freedom of sin, when it places the soul under the blessed necessity of only being able to praise God and to be eternally united with him. That we must not, however, condemn the love of life that nature has given us because we have received it from God himself; that it must be used for the same life for which God gave it, which is an innocent and a blessed life, and not for some object opposed to it. That Jesus Christ had loved his life because it was innocent, that he had feared death because in him it came to a body which was acceptable to God. But that since things are not the same in our life, which is a life of sin, we should teach ourselves to hate a life which was the opposite to that of Jesus Christ, to love and not to fear a death which, in thus putting an end to a life of sin and misery, sets us free to go with Jesus Christ to meet God face to face, to worship, bless and love him eternally and unreservedly.

It was in accordance with these same principles that he displayed such a love of penance because he said that we must punish a sinful body, and punish it unstintingly by continual penance for without penance it rebelled against the spirit and against all thought of salvation. But since we do not possess the courage to punish ourselves, we ought to feel very grateful to God when he is good enough to do it for us; that is why he never ceased to bless the sufferings that God had sent him, why he regarded them as a fire which gradually purged him of his sins by daily sacrifice and prepared him in this way while he waited until it should please God to send death to him as a consummation of the perfect sacrifice.

He always had such a great love of poverty that it was continually in his mind; so that, as soon as he thought of embarking on anything or anyone asked his advice, his first idea was to see whether there was any opportunity of practising poverty. But his love of that particular virtue became so much stronger at the end of his life that I could give him no greater pleasure than to discuss it with him and listen to what he was always ready to tell us about it.

He never refused alms to anyone though he was not a rich man and the cost of his illnesses exceeded his income. He never gave alms except out of the monies which he required for his own needs. But when this was pointed out to him, particularly when he made a number of substantial gifts, he was upset and said to us: 'I have noticed that, however poor people are, they always leave something when they die.' There were occasions when he went so far that he was reduced to entering into legal obligations in order to live and to make inroads into his capital because he had given all he had to the poor, and did not wish to ask for anything from his friends for he had made it a rule never to allow other people to feel that their needs made them importunate to him, and always to be afraid of appearing importunate to others on account of his own.

As soon as the case of the carriages was settled, he told me that he wished to ask for an advance of a thousand *livres* on his own account, so that he could send the money to the poor of Blois and its neighbourhood who at that time were reduced to a state of great need. When I pointed out that the result of the case was still uncertain and that he ought to wait another year, he replied that he did not see any great inconvenience in that because if those for whom he was negotiating lost, he would give them money out of his own pocket, and that he was against waiting another year because their needs were too pressing. Nevertheless, as things cannot be settled overnight, the poor of Blois were helped from another source and my brother's only contribution was his good will, which demonstrates the truth of what he had said to us on many occasions, that he only desired money so that he could help the poor, because the moment he thought that he was going to have any he began to give it away in advance and even before he was certain that he would actually receive it.

We must not be surprised if a man who knew Jesus Christ so well was so devoted to the poor, and if the disciple even gave away what he needed for himself because he had implanted in his heart the example of his master who had given himself. But the rule which he had imposed on himself, to give up every form of superfluity, was for him the foundation stone of his love of the poor. For one of the points on which he examined himself most closely, in the light of this rule, was the excess represented by the desire to excel in everything, which in particular cases impels us, in the use we make of the things of this world, always to demand the best, the finest, the most convenient. That is why he could not tolerate the wish to have the best workmen, but told us that we must always choose those who were the poorest and the most deserving, and give up the idea of an excellence which is never essential; he was also a severe critic of those who paid too much attention to their own convenience, such as having everything at their elbow, a room in which nothing was lacking, and other things of the same kind in which people indulge without the slightest scruple; because taking as his guide the spirit of poverty, which should be in all Christians, he believed that everything which was opposed to it, even if authorised by what was regarded as proper behaviour in the world, was always a sign of excess since we had renounced such things in baptism. He sometimes declared: 'If I were as poor in heart as in spirit, I should be very happy; because I have a wonderful conviction that the spirit of poverty and the practice of this virtue is a great means of gaining one's salvation.'

All these observations made us withdraw into ourselves, and sometimes they also made us seek the general rules which cover every contingency, and we suggested it to him. But he did not think that it was a good idea; he told us that we were not concerned with the general, but with the particular: and that he thought that the way of helping the poor which was most pleasing to God was to help the poor poorly, that is to say, according to the means at one's disposal, without embarking on those grandiose schemes which turn into an ostentatious search for the kind of excellence that he always criticised both in theory and practice. It was not that he considered the foundation of general hospitals a bad thing, but he said that these great undertakings were reserved for certain people whom God had chosen for them and whom he led to them almost imperceptibly; but that it was not a vocation which was common to everybody, such as the private individual's daily succour of the poor.

He would have liked me to devote myself to performing ordinary services for them, and to do it as a punishment which I had inflicted on myself for my life. He exhorted me with great eloquence to bring my children up to do it. And when I told him that I thought it would lead me to neglect my family, he replied that it was only lack of good will on my part and that, as there are various degrees in the exercise of virtue, we can very easily find time for it without interfering with household duties, that charity itself imbues us with the spirit and that we have only to follow it. He said that there was no need of any special sign to decide whether or not one was called to it, that it was the vocation of all Christians; that because it was according to

this that Jesus Christ would judge the world, it was sufficient
that the need was common for us to devote ourselves to satisfying it by every means in our power, and when we see from the
Gospels that the mere neglect of this duty was the cause of eternal damnation, this thought alone should be sufficient to lead
us to strip ourselves of everything and to give ourselves a hundred times over, if we had faith. Again, he often said that contact with the poor was extremely useful because through constantly seeing the burden of their misery and observing that
they often lacked the prime necessities, we should have to be
very hard-hearted not to give up useless conveniences and
superfluous frills of our own free will. That is part of the teaching he gave us which was designed to encourage us to love the
poor who occupied such a large place in his own heart.

He was no less insistent on the importance of purity, and he
had such respect for this virtue that he was continually on his
guard to prevent the least offence against it by himself or other
people. It is difficult to imagine how strict he was in the matter.
I even felt rather embarrassed, to begin with, because he had
some comment to make on almost everything you heard said in
company, even when it appeared to be completely innocent. If,
for example, I happened to mention that I had seen a beautiful
woman, he came down on me, and told me that I ought never
to speak like that in front of servants and young people because
I could not tell what sort of ideas it might give them. I hardly
like to mention that he would not even tolerate the embraces
that I received from my children. He asserted that it could only
do them harm, and that there were a thousand other ways of
showing my affection for them. It was more difficult for me to
accept his view, but I later realised that he was just as right
about this as about everything else, and I learnt from experience
that I was right to do as he told me.

This all took place in the home; but about three months
before his death, God gave him an opportunity of displaying his
zeal for purity outside the home. One day, as he was on his way
back from Saint-Sulpice where he had been to hear Holy Mass,
a girl of about fifteen came up and asked him for alms. He at

once thought of the danger to which she was exposed and after learning that she lived in the country, that her father was dead, that on that very day her mother had been taken to the Hôtel-Dieu, so that the poor girl was on her own and did not know what would become of her, he thought that God must have sent her to him, and he at once took her to the seminary where he placed her in charge of a good priest to whom he gave money and asked him to find her a post where she would be safe. And to spare him trouble, he said that the next day he would send him a woman who would buy clothes for the girl and everything else that was necessary to enable her to find work. In fact, he sent a woman who co-operated so well with the good priest that, shortly afterwards, they found a suitable position for her. The ecclesiastic did not know my brother's name, and at first it did not occur to him to ask it because he was occupied with the girl. But when she was placed, he thought about my brother's action which he considered such a fine one that he wished to know the name of the person who was responsible for it. He asked the woman, but she replied that she had been forbidden to tell anybody. 'Please get his permission,' he said; 'I promise that I will never mention it during his lifetime. But if it were God's will that he died before me, it would be a great consolation to me to be able to tell people what he has done, for I find it so fine and deserving to be known that I could not bear it to be forgotten.' But he obtained nothing and realised that the person, who wished to remain anonymous, was no less modest than charitable, and that if he was zealous in preserving the purity of other people, he was no less zealous in preserving his own humility.

My brother had a great affection for his friends and for those whom he thought were on the side of God; and if we can say that no one has ever been more worthy of affection, no one has known better how to love or practised it better than he. But his affection was not simply the effect of his temperament because, though his heart was always ready to melt for the needs of his friends, he was never moved except in accordance with the precepts of Christianity which reason and faith placed before his eyes: that is why his affection never developed into an attachment and why it was always free from flattery.

He could not be fonder of anyone than he was of my sister, and he was right. He saw her often; he talked to her about everything without the least reserve; everything that she said and did met with his approval because, temperamentally, they were so alike that they agreed about everything; and certainly their hearts were but a single heart and they found in one another a source of comfort which can only be understood by those who have enjoyed something of the same happiness and who know what it means to love and be loved with complete trust and without fearing that anything could come between them, and where everything is a source of mutual satisfaction.

Yet on learning of my sister's death, which took place ten months before his own, he said nothing except: 'May God grant us the grace to die such a Christian death as hers.' And later, he only spoke to us of the graces which God had bestowed on my sister during her life and of the circumstances and the time of her death; then raising his heart to heaven, where he believed her to be among the blessed, he said to us with some emotion: 'Blessed are they who die and die thus in the Lord.' And when he saw that I was grieved (for it is true that I was deeply distressed by her loss) he was upset; he told me that it was not good and that we ought not to feel like that over the death of the righteous, but that on the contrary we ought to praise God for rewarding her so soon for the small services that she had performed for him.

This was his way of showing that he was fond of people without becoming attached to them; and we had a further proof of it at the time of my father's death for whom he certainly had all the feelings that a grateful son should have for a very devoted father. We saw from the letter that he wrote about his death that, if his heart was touched, reason soon gained the upper hand and that, when he considered the event in the light of faith, his soul was moved not to mourn for the father whom he has lost so far as this life was concerned, but to look on him in Jesus Christ in whom he had won him for heaven.

He distinguished two kinds of affection: one emotional, the other rational. He admitted that the former had some small value in the eyes of the world. He maintained, however, that merit played little part in it and that decent people should only attach importance to a reasonable affection which according to him lay in associating ourselves with everything that happens to our friends in all the ways approved by reason at the expense of our pocket, our convenience, our freedom and even of our life if it is someone who deserves it; and he will always deserve it if it is a question of helping him for God who must be the unique object of the love of all Christians.

'A man must be hard-hearted,' he said, 'if he is aware of the anxieties of his fellows and resists the pressing obligation to associate himself with them, but he shows a tender heart when he enters into them naturally by way of the sentiments that reason bids us have for others in such circumstances; who rejoices when it is right to rejoice; who is sad when it is right to be sad.' But he added that tenderness can only be perfect when reason is illuminated by faith and prompts us to act in accordance with the precepts of charity. That is why he saw no great difference between tenderness and charity, any more than between charity and friendship. He merely thought that as friendship assumes a closer relationship and this relationship a more particular application, we are less likely to refuse to help our friends when they are in need because their needs are better known to us and we are more easily convinced that they are genuine.

That is how he understood tenderness and those are the sentiments that it inspired in him without leading to attachments or dalliance, for since charity can have no end but God, it could only attach itself to him, and could not dally with things that amuse because it knows that there is no time to lose and that God, who sees and judges everything, will call us to account for everything that happens in our life which is not a further step along the path that alone is permissible, which is the way of perfection.

But he was not only without attachment to others, he did not wish other people to become attached to him. I am not speaking here of criminal and dangerous attachments, because it is obvious and everyone understands it; I am speaking of the most innocent friendships whose delight contributes to the ordinary pleasures of human society. It was one of the things in which he watched himself most carefully in order to avoid falling into it and to put a stop to it as soon as he perceived the slightest sign of it; and since I was very far from this degree of perfection and thought that I could not take too great care of a brother like him, who was responsible for the happiness of the family, I did not neglect any of those attentions which were necessary to assist him and to show my affection for him in every way that I could. In the end I came to realise that I was attached to him and that I regarded it as a merit to show him all the consideration that I felt was his due; but he did not look on it in the same light and because, as it seemed to me, he did not give sufficient outward signs of responding to my feelings for him, I was not satisfied and went to my sister from time to time to open my heart to her, and nearly got to the point of complaining about him. My sister did her best to put things right by reminding me of the occasions on which I had needed my brother and on which he had taken such trouble and done it with such affection, that I ought to be in no doubt that he was very fond of me. But the mystery of his reserved behaviour towards me only became clear to me on the day of his death; when a person who was distinguished for his greatness of mind and his piety, to whom he had had so much to say about the practice of virtue, told me that he had always laid it down as a fundamental rule of piety not to permit anyone to become attached to him, and that it was a fault about which we did not examine ourselves with sufficient care, which had serious consequences, and which was all the more dangerous because it often appears to us to be free from danger.

After his death we had still another proof that the principle was deeply embedded in his heart; for in order to ensure that it was always present to his mind, he had written it down in his own hand on a separate scrap of paper which we found on him and which we often remembered seeing him read. This is what was on it: 'It is wrong for people to attach themselves to me though they do so with pleasure and of their own free will. I should be deceiving those in whom I inspire the wish; because I am no one's final end and I do not possess what is necessary to satisfy them. Am I not near to death? Thus the object of their attachment will die. Therefore, as I should be to blame if I made them believe something that is false in spite of the fact that I convinced them by gentle methods and it would give me pleasure: so I am doing wrong if I make people fond of me and attract them to me; because they ought to spend their lives and devote their attention to attaching themselves to God and seeking him.'

It was in this way that he gave himself instructions and carried them out so well. It was in this way that I made a mistake in judging the manner in which he behaved towards me because I attributed to a want of affection something which in him was a perfection of his charity.

But if he did not wish creatures, who exist today, who perhaps will no longer exist tomorrow and who moreover are so incapable of making themselves happy, to grow attached to one another in this way, we see that it was in order that they might attach themselves to God alone, and in fact that is the meaning of order; we cannot judge it otherwise if we give our attention to it seriously and wish to follow the true light. That is why we must not feel surprised if he who was so enlightened and whose heart was so well ordered had adopted such just rules and was so exemplary in observing them.

This did not apply only to the first principle which is the foundation of Christian morality; he displayed such great zeal for the order of God in all other matters which follow from it, that he could not bear to see it infringed in the slightest degree: that is what made him so zealous in the service of the King that he stood up to everybody at the time of the troubles in Paris. He dismissed as pretexts all the reasons that were given in justification of the rebellion. He said that if a state were established like the Republic of Venice, it was a great wrong to put in a king and suppress the freedom that God had given to the people; but that in a State where the royal power is established, we cannot violate the allegiance that we owe the king without being guilty of a kind of sacrilege, because the power with which God has invested him, being not only a symbol but a participation in the power of God, we could not oppose it without openly opposing the order of God. And what is more, that civil war which is one of the results of rebellion, being the greatest wrong that we can commit against our neighbour, it is impossible to exaggerate the greatness of the fault; that the first Christians taught us not rebellion, but patience when princes did not fulfil their duties properly. He usually said that he felt just as much repugnance for this sin as for murder or highway robbery; in short, that there was nothing which was more contrary to his own nature and less of a temptation to him, which led him to forgo substantial benefits for himself by refusing to play any part in the disorders.

Those were his views on the service of the King: he was therefore irreconcilable towards all those who opposed them. And we can see that it was not a question of temperament or attachment to his own comfort from the fact that he displayed an admirable gentleness towards those who offended him personally; with the result that he never treated them differently from anyone else, and forgot so completely anything which only affected him personally that it was difficult to make him remember it: it could only be done by recalling the exact circumstances. And as people sometimes expressed surprise, he said: 'Do not be surprised; it is not through virtue but forgetfulness; I do not remember it.' And yet he possessed such an excellent memory that he never forgot anything that he wished to remember. But the truth is that offences which only concerned him personally did not make any impression on a great soul like his, who could no longer be moved by things except in so far as they related to the eminent order of charity because everything else seemed to be outside him and no concern of his.

It is a fact that I have never met a soul who was more naturally superior to all the corrupt impulses of human nature; and it was not only towards personal affronts that he appeared indifferent; he behaved in the same way over matters which offend everybody else and become the source of their greatest passion. He certainly possessed a great soul but without ambition, not desiring to be great or powerful, or honoured in the world and regarding such things as leading to wretchedness rather than to happiness. He desired wealth only in order to share it with others and found his delight in reason, order, justice, in everything, in fact, which provided the soul with sustenance, rather than in material things.

He was not without faults, but he gave us complete freedom to draw his attention to them and was extremely submissive to the views of his friends when he considered that they were right; and even when they were not, he always listened to them gently. The extreme vivacity of his mind made him so impatient that he was difficult to satisfy; but as soon as one drew his attention to it or he himself noticed that he had made someone angry by his impatience, he at once made amends for his fault by behaviour which was so becoming that it never deprived him of anyone's friendship.

The self-esteem of others was never offended by his own, and it could even be said that he did not have any because he never talked about himself or about things in relation to himself; and we know that he preferred a well-bred man to avoid talking about himself and even the use of the words *I* or *me*. What he was used to saying on the subject is that 'Christian piety annihilates the human self and human civility hides and suppresses it.' He regarded it as a rule, and it is precisely what he practised.

Nor was he disagreeable to anyone about their failings, but once he had committed himself to speaking about things he spoke frankly without hiding anything; and as he did not know what it was to humour people by flattering them, he was equally incapable of not speaking the truth when he felt obliged to do so. Those who did not know him were surprised at first when they heard him engaged in one of these conversations because it always seemed as though he preserved the upper hand with a sort of domination; but it was the vivacity of his mind which gave this impression, and you could not be with him for long without realising that even in this there was something lovable, or without coming in the end to feel as pleased with his manner of speaking as with what he said.

For the rest, he had a horror of every kind of untruth, and the least form of deceit was intolerable to him: with the result that his mind was naturally penetrating and just, and his heart upright and without guile, the key to his character and conduct, to his sincerity and loyalty.

We found a note by him in which he had no doubt described himself, so that by always keeping his eyes fixed on the path which God had chosen for him, he could never stray from it. This is what the note says: 'I love poverty because Jesus Christ loved it. I love wealth because it offers us the means of helping the poor. I keep faith with everybody. I do not return ill to those who do me ill; but I desire for them a state like my own in which one suffers neither good nor ill at the hands of the majority of people. I try always to be sincere, true and loyal to all men, and I feel a tenderness in my heart for those to whom God has united me most closely; and though I am strong in the sight of men, in all my actions I have my eyes on God who will judge them and to whom I should devote them. Those are my views, and every day I bless my Redeemer who implanted them in me and who out of a man riddled with weaknesses, with misery, with sensual desires, with ambition and pride, has made a man free from all these vices by the power of his greatness to which all glory is due because my natural state is one of misery and error.'

We could no doubt add a great deal to this portrait if we wished to complete and perfect it; but I will leave to others more competent than myself the task of putting the finishing touches, which only belong to the masters, and merely add that the man who was so great in everything displayed the simplicity of a child in matters of religion. Those who saw him as he usually was were surprised. His behaviour was free from any suspicion of cant or hypocrisy, but as he was able to penetrate into the realm of the loftiest virtues, so he was able to stoop to practice of the humblest of the virtues which are the basis of true piety. All things were great in his heart when they served to glorify God. He practised them like a child. His chief amusement, particularly in the last years of his life when he was unable to go on working, was to go and visit churches where relics or other pious objects were on view, and he had provided himself for the purpose with a *Spiritual Almanach* from which he found out the places where all these devotions were practised: but he did it with such piety and simplicity that those who saw him were surprised and among them a very virtuous and enlightened person who explained them in these fine words: That the grace of God makes itself known in great minds by little things and in commonplace minds by big things.

He had a marked love for the whole of the office (that is to say, the prayers of the breviary) and disciplined himself to recite as much of it as he could; but above all the little hours which are composed from Psalm CXVIII in which he discovered so many admirable things that he always experienced a fresh joy when he said it; and when he discussed the beauty of the Psalm with his friends he was carried away and communicated the same enthusiasm to all those to whom he happened to be talking. When he was sent his spiritual guide for the month, as is done in a number of parishes, he studied it assiduously, and never omitted for a single day to read the homily. It was the same with everything that related to piety and could edify him.

The parish priest of Saint-Étienne, who visited him during his illness, was also an admirer of this simplicity, and was constantly saying: 'He's a child; he's as humble and as submissive as a child.' And, on the eve of his death, an ecclesiastic who was a man of great learning and virtue, who had come to see him and stayed an hour with him, was so edified that as he was leaving, he said to me: 'Come, you should feel comforted by the thought that if God is calling him to himself, you have every reason to be thankful for the graces that he has bestowed on him. He is dying with the simplicity of a child. It's unheard of for a man with a mind like his; I wish with all my heart that I were in his place; I can think of nothing more splendid.'

His last illness began with a peculiar nausea which overtook him two months before his death. He had living with him an old fellow with the whole of his family and his household who did not in the event perform any services for him; but he kept them as though they were something that had been entrusted to him by the providence of God of which he took the greatest care. One of the old man's children became ill with smallpox so that there were two sick people at my brother's home—himself and the child. It was essential for me to be with my brother and as there was a danger of my breathing the infected atmosphere of the smallpox and giving it to my children, there was some talk of the child's being made to leave the house, but in his charity my brother took a very different decision: he made up his mind to leave his own home and come to mine. He was already very ill, but he said that it was less dangerous for him to be moved than the child, so it had to be he and not the child. And in fact he had himself moved to our house.

This charitable action had been preceded by forgiveness of an offence which touched him in a very tender spot by someone who was under a great obligation to him. My brother behaved in his usual way not only without showing the slightest resentment, but with a gentleness and the kind of consideration which is necessary to win a person over. And it was no doubt owing to God's special providence that during his last days, when he was so near to appearing before God, that he had the opportunity of performing two acts of mercy which are the signs of predestination in the Gospels, so that when he came to die he had direct proof in these two charitable actions that God would forgive his own sins and give him the place in his Kingdom which he had prepared for him because he gave him the grace to forgive the faults of others with such simplicity, and to help them in their need. But we shall see that God had prepared him for the death of one truly predestined by other actions which are no less comforting.

Three days after his arrival at our house he was seized with a violent colic which made it absolutely impossible for him to sleep; but as he possessed great strength of mind and great courage, he did not hesitate to get up every day and take his medicines and would not allow anyone to perform the least service for him.

The doctors who visited him declared that his illness was serious; but as he had no temperature they did not think that there was any immediate danger. But on the fourth day of the colic and before he was made to keep to his bed, my brother, who did not wish to take any chances, sent for the parish priest of Saint-Étienne and made his confession; but at this early stage he did not receive Communion. Nevertheless, as M. le Curé came to see him from time to time with his customary vigilance, my brother did not lose a single one of these opportunities of making his confession over again; but he did not say a word about it to us for fear of alarming us. There were days when he was slightly less ill; he took advantage of them to make his will in which the poor were not overlooked, and he had to restrain himself from giving them more. He told me that if M. Périer had been in Paris and if he had agreed, he would have left the whole of his estate to the poor.

At the last, he had no room in his heart and mind for anything except the poor, and he sometimes said to me: 'How is it that I have never yet done anything for the poor although I have always been so devoted to them?' And when I answered: 'It is because you were never sufficiently well off,' he said: 'Then I ought to have given them my time and trouble; that is where I failed. And if the doctors are right and God allows me to come through this illness, I am determined for the rest of my life not to have any other occupation or interest but the care of the poor.' This was his frame of mind at the time God took him.

His patience was no less great than his charity; and those who were with him were so edified that they declared that they had never seen anything like it. When they told him from time to time that they were sorry for him, he replied that personally he was in no way distressed by his condition, that he was even afraid of the idea of being cured, and when he was asked the reason, he said: 'Because I know the dangers of health and the advantages of illness.' And as we could not help being sorry for him, particularly when the pain was greatest, he said: 'Don't feel sorry for me; illness is the natural state of Christians because when we are ill, we are in the state in which we should always be, that is to say, in the midst of suffering, pain, deprived of all comforts and all the pleasures of the senses. Is not that the way in which Christians ought to spend their lives? And is it not a great piece of good fortune when we find that we are of necessity in the state which is properly ours?' And, in fact, we could see that he liked the state, which is something of which few people are capable. For there is nothing else to do but to submit humbly and quietly. That is why he asked nothing of us except to pray to God to grant him this grace. It is true that after listening to him there was nothing left that we could say to him, so much so that we felt ourselves animated by the same spirit as himself to desire suffering and to realise that it was the state in which all Christians ought to spend their lives.

He felt an ardent desire to receive Communion, but the doctors were against it because they did not consider that he was sufficiently ill to receive the viaticum, and they did not think that it was fitting that it should be brought to him at night, when he had to be fasting, unless his condition took a turn for the worse. Since the colic persisted, however, they prescribed waters which brought him a few days' relief, but on the sixth day of the waters he suffered from severe giddiness accompanied by a violent headache. Although the doctors were in no way surprised by the incident and said that it was only the vapour from the waters, he lost no time in making his confession and demanded, with the greatest urgency, that he should be given Communion and that in the name of God they should find some way of removing all the obstacles that they had put in the way of it; he was so pressing that someone who was there said that it was not a good thing and that he should abide by the views of his friends, that he had scarcely any temperature, and that he should judge for himself whether it was right to have the Blessed Sacrament brought to the house because he was better, and whether it was not more suitable to wait and receive Communion in church where he would soon be well enough to go. He replied: 'They do not feel my illness; they are mistaken; there is something extraordinary about my headache.' Nevertheless, seeing that his wish was meeting with such opposition, he dared not say any more about it. But he said to me: 'As this grace has been refused me, I should like to make up for it by some good action, and since I cannot have Communion in the Head I should like to do so in the members, and for that I thought that I might have here some poor sick person to whom the same services can be rendered as to me. For I am distressed and confused at finding myself with such assistance while a vast number of poor people, who are sicker than I, are deprived of the barest necessities. Let a nurse be engaged specially for the purpose and let there be no difference between him and me. It will lessen the pain which I feel at finding that I lack nothing, and which I can no longer bear without the consolation of knowing that there is a poor man here who is being as well cared for as I; I beg you to go and ask M. le Curé for one.'

I sent to M. le Curé at once who replied that there was not a single one who was in a fit state to be moved; but that as soon as my brother was better he would find an opportunity for him to exercise his charity by giving him an old man of whom he could take care for the rest of his life; for M. le Curé had no doubt that he would recover.

When he saw that he could not have a poor man with him at the house, he asked me to have him moved to the hospital for incurables because he felt a great desire to die among the poor. I told him that the doctors did not consider it appropriate to move him in his present state. He was obviously upset by my reply, and proceeded to make me promise that, if there was any improvement in his condition, I would carry out his wish.

But I did not have to suffer this pain because his suffering increased so much that, when it reached its climax, he asked me to arrange a consultation; but at the same time, being overcome by scruples, he said: 'I fear that I am going too far in asking this.' But I lost no time in doing it. The doctors ordered him to drink a little milk and kept on assuring him that there was no danger, that it was only the effect of his migraine and the vapours from the waters. Nevertheless, no matter what they said, he did not believe them. He begged me to send for a priest to spend the night with him, and I myself thought him so ill that, without saying a word to anyone, I gave orders for the candles to be prepared and everything that was necessary for him to have Communion the following morning.

These preparations were not without their use, but they were needed sooner than we expected. For about midnight he was seized with such a violent convulsion that when it had passed, we thought that he was dead. And on top of everything else, we had the extreme unhappiness of imagining that he had died without receiving Communion after asking for it so often and so insistently.

But God, who wished to reward such an ardent and such a righteous desire, put an end to his convulsions as though by a miracle, and restored his mental faculties completely as though he were in perfect health; with the result that when M. le Curé came into his room with Our Lord, saying: 'Look, I am bringing you Him whom you have so greatly desired,' his words woke him. M. le Curé went towards him to give him Communion; he made an effort and half raised himself on his own in order to receive it with greater respect; and when M. le Curé interrogated him, in accordance with his usual practice on the principal mysteries of the faith, he replied devoutly: 'Yes, Monsieur, I believe them all with my whole heart.' And afterwards he received the Holy Viaticum and Extreme Unction with such devotion that tears came into his eyes. He replied to everything and, at the end, thanked M. le Curé, and when he blessed him with the

73

Blessed Sacrament he said: 'May God never abandon me!' which were, so to speak, his last words. For the moment that he had made his thanksgiving, the convulsions returned and did not leave him a moment's respite; they continued until his death which took place twenty-four hours later: that is to say, on the nineteenth of August 1662 at one o'clock in the morning, at the age of thirty-nine years and two months.

Pascal's Pensées

WITH THE PREFACE TO THE
PORT-ROYAL EDITION

PREFACE TO THE PORT-ROYAL EDITION

(1670)

Describing the manner in which the Pensées were written and col-
lected; what delayed their publication; what M. Pascal's aim
was in his book; and how he spent the last years of his life.

When he was still very young M. Pascal gave up mathematics,
physics and the other branches of secular learning, in which he
had made such great progress that there have certainly been
very few people who have advanced further than he in the particular subjects which he studied, and about the age of thirty
began to apply his mind to higher and more serious matters and
to devote himself exclusively, in so far as his health permitted, to
the study of Scripture, the Fathers and Christian morality.

But though he was no less distinguished in these subjects
than he had been in the others, as he has shown in works which
are regarded as being as nearly definitive as such works can be,
we can nevertheless say that, had God allowed him to spend
more time on the work which he intended to write on religion
and to which he intended to devote the rest of his life, the book
would greatly have surpassed all the others that he wrote;
because in fact the views which he held on the subject were far
above those which he had on all others.

I do not think that anyone can fail to be convinced of this
simply by reading the small selection, however imperfect it may
appear, that we are giving here, and by knowing how he worked
and the manner in which the selection was made. This is how it
all happened.

M. Pascal planned his book some years before his death, but
we need feel no surprise that he waited for so long without

putting anything in writing because he had always been accustomed to giving a great deal of thought to things and arranging them in their proper order in his mind before writing them down. This was done to enable him to consider carefully what should come first and what last, and to ensure that they were presented in the order that would create the effect which he desired. He had an excellent memory—a memory which might even be described as prodigious—and often asserted that he never forgot anything that he had really taken in. When, therefore, he had spent some time on a subject, he had no fear that thoughts which he had once had would ever escape him; and that is why he often postponed writing them down, either because he lacked time or because his health, which was almost always sickly and precarious, was not sufficiently robust for concentrated work.

That is why his death deprived us of the greater part of the work that he had already done on the subject. For he put into writing practically none of the main arguments on which he intended to rely, the foundations on which he claimed to base his work, and the order that he wished to preserve in it, which was certainly very considerable. It was all so deeply engraved in his mind and memory that, having omitted to put it on paper when he might perhaps have been able to do so, he found that when he wished to he was in no condition to work at all.

There was, however, an occasion ten or twelve years ago on which he was obliged not to write down what he had in his mind on the subject, but to say something about it orally. He therefore did it in person at the instigation of several important people among his friends. He explained the plan of his entire work to them in a few words; he told them about the subject and content; he gave them an abridged account of its arguments and principles, and explained the order and sequence of the topics with which he intended to deal. His audience, who were very well qualified to form an opinion on matters of this nature, said that they had never heard anything finer, more forceful, more touching, or more convincing, that they were delighted by it; and that what they saw of his plan and its scope in an address lasting some two or three hours, gave them a good idea of the way in which it would turn out if it were ever written down and brought to completion by a man whose powers and ability were known to them; who was accustomed to working hard on his books, who was never satisfied with his first thoughts, however excellent they might appear to other people, and who had often rewritten a piece of work as many as eight or ten times which anyone except himself would have considered admirable in its original draft.

After he had shown which arguments made the greatest impact on people's minds and were the most likely to convince them, he undertook to prove that there were as many signs and as much evidence of the certainty of the Christian religion as of those things which the world regards as being absolutely beyond doubt.

When unfolding his plan, he began first of all by a portrait of man in which he overlooked none of the things which would give him an understanding of everything, inside and outside him, down to the most mysterious impulses of his heart. He then went on to imagine a man who had always lived in a state of complete ignorance and indifference towards everything, including himself. He eventually comes across this portrait and asks himself what he is. He is surprised to discover in it an infinite number of things which had never occurred to him; and he could not observe without surprise and admiration everything that M. Pascal made him feel about his greatness and baseness, his good qualities and his weaknesses, the small amount of light that remained to him, and the darkness enveloping him on almost every side; and lastly, all the astonishing contradictions to be found in his own nature. After that, he can no longer remain in a state of indifference if he has a spark of reason left; and however insensitive he may have been up to then, as soon as he has discovered what he is, he is bound to wish to know where he comes from and what will become of him.

Once he had made him feel that he ought to try to clear up his doubts on a matter of such importance to him, M. Pascal proceeded to deal with the philosophers; and it was at this point, when he had explained everything that the greatest philosophers of all the different schools had had to say on the subject of man, that he drew his hearers' attention to so many failings, so many weaknesses, so many contradictions and so many falsities in everything that the philosophers had said about him, that it is not difficult for man to realise that this is not the path which he ought to follow.

Next, he took him through the whole universe and all the ages in order to point out the infinite number of religions to be found there; but he showed him, at the same time and by such powerful and convincing arguments, that all these religions were such a conglomeration of vanity, folly, errors, aberrations and extravagances that he would find nothing in them which was capable of satisfying him.

Lastly, he invited him to glance at the Jewish people, and he pointed to circumstances which were so extraordinary that he had no difficulty in attracting his attention. After showing him what is so unusual about the Jewish people, he took special care to emphasise a unique book by which the people governed themselves and which contained between its covers their history, their law, and their religion. The reader has scarcely opened the book before he learns from it that the world is the work of a God, and that he is the same God who created man in his own image and endowed him with all the advantages of body and mind which fit his condition. Although there is nothing so far to convince him that it is true, it at once appears attractive to him, and reason alone enables him to realise that the supposition that a God is the creator of men and of all that exists in the universe is more plausible than all the things that these same men have imagined by the unaided power of their own minds. What holds his attention at this stage is to see from the picture that he is given of man, that he is far from possessing all the advantages that he should have had when he emerged from the hands of his creator. But he does not remain in doubt for very long because as soon as he goes on reading this same book, he finds that after being created by God in a state of innocence and with every sort of perfection, man's first action was to rebel against his creator, and to use all the gifts with which he had been endowed to offend him.

M. Pascal then made him realise that, as man's crime was from every point of view the most heinous of all crimes, it had been punished not merely in the first man who had at once fallen from his first state into a state of misery, weakness, error and blindness; but that it had also been punished in all his descendants to whom the first man transmitted his corruption, and will continue to transmit it for the rest of time.

M. Pascal went on to take the reader through different parts of the Bible in which he had discovered this particular truth. He pointed out that henceforth the Bible only speaks of the weakness and disorder of man's condition; that it often says that all flesh is corrupt, that men have abandoned themselves to their senses, and that they have a tendency towards evil from the time of their birth. He also made him see that the first fall was the source not only of what is most incomprehensible in human nature, but also of an infinite number of effects which were outside it and whose cause is unknown. Finally, he showed him that man was so well portrayed all through the Bible that he does not appear any different at the end than he was on the first page.

It was not enough to show the reader the full wretchedness of man's state; M. Pascal proceeded to show that in the same book he would find something to comfort him. And in fact he pointed out that it is said that man's remedy was in the hands of God; that it was to him that we must turn in order to acquire the strength that we lacked; that he would allow himself to be swayed and that he would even send men a saviour who would atone for them and cure their weakness.

After making a large number of very special observations on the book of the Jewish people, he pointed out that it was the only one to have spoken fittingly of the Sovereign Being and to have provided the conception of a true religion. He showed that its most striking characteristics were those which the book taught; and he drew particular attention to the fact that the essence of this religion lay in the love of God whom the people worshipped; that it was this that gave their religion its special character and clearly distinguished it from all other religions whose falseness was evident from the absence of this one essential sign.

Although M. Pascal, who had carried those whom he wished to convince by imperceptible degrees so far with him, had not yet said anything which could convince him of the truths which he had revealed to him, he had nevertheless placed him in a state of mind in which he could accept them with joy provided that it was possible to make him see that he ought to accept them, and even to desire with all his heart that they were solid and well founded because he discovered in them so much that would contribute to his peace of mind and the removal of his doubts. This should also be the state of mind of every reasonable man if he had once embarked upon the sequence of events which M. Pascal had just described to him. There are grounds for believing that, after that, the reader would be ready to accept all the proofs which M. Pascal would later produce in support of the important truths of which he had spoken, and which are the foundation of the Christian religion, which is what he set out to demonstrate.

Let us say a few words about the proofs. After M. Pascal had shown in general terms that the truths with which he was dealing were contained in a book whose truth no man of good sense could doubt, he dwelt mainly on the book of Moses where the truths are particularly in evidence, and he made one reader see by many arguments which were beyond question that it was alike impossible that Moses should have written down things which were false, or that the people to whom he left them should have allowed themselves to be taken in even if Moses were capable of dishonesty.

He also spoke of the great miracles which are related in the book; and since they are of immense importance for the religion which it teaches, he proved that it was not possible for them not to be true, not merely on account of the authority of the book in which they are recounted, but still more by all the circumstances which surrounded them and which place them beyond doubt.

He further explained the sense in which the whole of the Mosaic law was symbolic; that everything that had happened to the Jews had only been a prefiguration of what happened when the Messiah came and that, once the veil which hid the symbols had been lifted, it was easy to see its fulfilment and perfect consummation in favour of those who accepted Jesus Christ.

M. Pascal next embarked upon the task of proving the truth of religion from the prophecies, and he devoted far more time to this subject than to the others. As he had done a lot of work on it and held views which were peculiarly his own, he explained them in a manner which was very easy to grasp; he showed their meaning and the way in which they were linked with a marvellous ease: and he stated them in all their clarity and all their force.

Lastly, after going through the books of the Old Testament and making a number of further observations which were intended to serve as foundations and proofs, he went on to speak of the New Testament again and to draw his proofs from the truth of the Gospel itself.

He began by Jesus Christ; and though he had already proved his claims conclusively from the prophecies and from all the symbols of the law which received their perfect fulfilment in him, he brought many more proofs still which were based on his very person, his miracles, his teaching and the circumstances of his life.

He next dwelt on the Apostles; and to prove the truth of the law which they loudly proclaimed everywhere, after showing that it was impossible to accuse them of falseness except by supposing either that they were rogues or had been deceived themselves, he showed clearly that both these suppositions were unthinkable.

In short, he overlooked nothing which would help to prove the truth of the Gospel story, making some penetrating observations on the Gospels themselves, on the style of the evangelists and on their personalities; on the apostles in particular and on their writings; on the prodigious number of miracles; on the martyrs; on the saints; in fact, on all the ways by which the Christian religion has been completely established. And although he did not have time, in a single address, to deal at length with such a vast subject as he intended to do in his book, he nevertheless said enough to convince us that it could not all be the work of men, and that only God could have been responsible for an event with so many different effects which all contribute equally to proving beyond doubt the truth of the religion that he himself came to establish among men.

Such in substance were the main topics which he discussed in the course of his address and which he only placed before his audience as a summary of the great work that he was planning, and it is thanks to one of those who were present that we have since learnt the small amount that I have just described.

Something of M. Pascal's grand design can be seen from the fragments which are now being offered to the public, but only a very small part of it; and the ideas themselves which will be found there are so imperfect, so undeveloped and so far from being digested, that they can only give a crude idea of the way in which he meant to deal with them.

For the rest, the reader must not be surprised if, in the small selection that we are giving, we have not preserved his order and his arrangement of the material. As we had practically nothing which followed in logical order, it would have been pointless to keep to this order; and we have arranged the material in more or less the order that we regarded as the most fitting and most suitable for what was actually in our possession. We would even go so far as to express the hope that there will be few readers who once they have a thorough grasp of M. Pascal's plan, will not be able to fill in the gaps for themselves, and who when they consider carefully the various subjects mentioned in the fragments, will not be able to decide without difficulty where they should be placed in accordance with the ideas of the man who wrote them.

If only we possessed the address written out in full and in the way in which it was delivered, we should have some grounds

for consoling ourselves for the loss of the work, and it could even
be said that, though very imperfect, we had at any rate a small
sample of it. But God did not permit him to leave us either of
them; because shortly after he had fallen sick of a wasting,
weakening disease, which continued for the last four years of
his life and which, though there was little to be seen outwardly
and though it did not compel him to remain in bed or in his
room, very soon interfered seriously with his faculties and made
him almost incapable of concentrating on anything: with the
result that the greatest concern and the principal occupation of
those who were with him was to persuade him not to write or
even to speak of matters which required any degree of concentration or mental application, and only to talk to him about
unimportant things which would not tire him.

Yet it was during those four years of sickness and languor
that he thought out and put on paper all we have of the book
that he was preparing, and the whole of those parts which are
now being given to the public. For though he was waiting for
the complete restoration of his health before really beginning
serious work on it, and before writing down the things that he
had already absorbed and arranged in his mind, yet when new
ideas and new views came to him, or even some turn of phrase
or expression which he thought might one day be useful for his
plan, as he was not at the time in a condition to apply himself
with the same strength as when he was in good health, he preferred to jot something down on paper to avoid forgetting it;
and he would pick up the first scrap of paper which happened
to be at hand and write down his thought in a few words, very
often only in abbreviated form; because he was only writing for
himself; and that is why he was content to do it very briefly, so
that he would not tire his mind, and only put down the
minimum that was necessary to remind him of his ideas and
opinions.

That is the way in which the major part of the fragments to
be found in the present collection were written. The reader
must therefore not be surprised if some of them appear somewhat imperfect, too condensed and insufficiently explained,

and even if in some of them he comes across terms and expressions which are not altogether suitable or very elegant. Nevertheless, it sometimes happened that when he found himself with a pen in his hand, he could not prevent himself from following his bent, developing his ideas and elaborating a little more on them, though it was never done with the power and mental concentration with which he would have been able to do it had he been in perfect health. And that is why we shall find that some of his ideas are more developed and better written, some chapters more coherent and better done, than others.

Such is the way in which the thoughts were written down. And I think that there will be few people who will not easily realise from these modest beginnings, these feeble exercises of a sick man, written for himself alone and only intended to keep in mind thoughts which he feared might be lost and which have never been revised or touched up, what the complete book would have been like if M. Pascal had recovered his health and given it its definitive form—he who knew so well how to place things in the best light and in such an excellent order, who gave so special, so noble and so elevated a turn to everything that he wished to say, who intended to do more work on this book than on all the others that he had previously written, who wanted to draw on the whole of his mental powers and all the gifts that God had bestowed on him and of which he had often said that he would need ten years to finish it.

As we knew of M. Pascal's intention to write about religion, we took very great care, after his death, to collect everything that he had written on the subject. We found the papers all pinned together in different bundles, but without any order or arrangement because, as I have already said, they were only the first drafts of his thoughts which he wrote down on the little scraps of paper as they came to mind. And it was all so unfinished and so ill-written that we had the greatest difficulty imaginable in deciphering it at all.

The first thing we did was to have them copied as they were and in the same state of confusion in which they had been found. But when we saw them in that state, and were able to read and examine them with greater ease than in the originals, they appeared at first to be so shapeless, so lacking in order, and for the most part so little explained, that for a long time we never even gave a thought to the idea of having them printed though a number of people of the highest standing often asked us to do so with the most anxious and pressing solicitation; for we thought that if we published them as they stood, they would not fulfil people's hopes or come up to their expectations of the book of which we had already heard them speak.

But in the end we were obliged to yield to the impatience and to the great desire that everybody expressed to have them printed. And we did so all the more willingly because we thought that those who would read them would be sufficiently fair-minded to distinguish between a mere outline and a finished work, and to judge the work by the sample, however imperfect it was. And so we decided to give it to the public. But as there were several ways of putting our decision into effect, we spent some time considering which of them we should adopt.

The first that came to mind, which would certainly have been the simplest, was to print them straight away in the same state in which we had found them. But we soon reached the conclusion that to do this would have resulted in the loss of almost all the beneficial results for which we were hoping: because since the most perfect, the most coherent, the clearest and most fully developed thoughts were mixed up and, as it were, submerged in so many others which were incomplete, obscure, half-digested, and since a number of them were practically unintelligible to anyone except the person who had written them, there was every reason to think that the latter would lead to the rejection of the others, and that people would only regard a book, which had been pointlessly swollen by the inclusion of so many unfinished thoughts, as a confused mass without order or coherence, which could not serve any useful purpose.

There was another way of presenting the writings to the public, which was to do some work on them in advance, to clarify obscure thoughts, to complete those which were unfinished and, by applying M. Pascal's plan to all the fragments, in a way to substitute for them the book that he had intended to write. This method would undoubtedly have been the most satisfactory, but it was also the most difficult to carry out. Nevertheless, we clung to it for quite a long time and had actually begun work on it. But in the end we decided to abandon it along with the first proposal, because we saw that it was almost impossible to enter fully into the thought and plan of an author, especially a dead author, and that we should not be publishing a book by M. Pascal, but an entirely different one.

Thus, in order to avoid the difficulties which were inherent in both these proposals for publishing his writings, we chose one that stood midway between the two, which is the one that we have adopted in the present collection. We have simply selected from among the great number of thoughts those which appeared to us to be the clearest and most complete; and we are publishing them as we found them, without adding or changing anything, except that in those places where they were without any order or connection and were simply jumbled together in a state of confusion, we arranged them in some sort of order and placed them under the same headings as those dealing with similar subjects; and we omitted all the others which were too obscure or too incomplete.

It is not that these, too, did not contain some very fine things and would not have been capable of opening up fresh perspectives for those who managed to understand them. But as we had decided not to clarify or complete them, they would have been entirely useless in the condition in which they were found. And in order to give some idea of them, I will only transcribe one of them here as an example which will enable the reader to judge all the others which have been omitted. This then is the thought in the state in which we found it among the fragments:

'A labourer who speaks of wealth, a procurator who speaks of war, of royalty, etc. But the rich man speaks well of wealth, the king speaks casually of a great gift that he has just bestowed, and God speaks well of God.'

The fragment contains a very profound thought; but there are few people who can see what it is because it is explained very imperfectly and in a very obscure manner, very briefly and in a very abbreviated form; so that if we had not often heard him utter the same thought with his own lips, it would be difficult to recognise it when it is expressed in such a muddled and confused way. This is more or less what it means.

He had made a number of very special observations on the style of Scripture and mainly on the style of the Gospels, in which he discovered beauties which had probably not been noticed by anyone before him. He admired among other things the naïveté, the simplicity or, so to speak, the coldness with which Jesus Christ appears to speak of the greatest and loftiest subject as, for example, the Kingdom of God, the glory which will belong to the saints in heaven, the torments of hell, without elaborating on them in the manner of the Fathers and everyone else who has written about them. And he used to say that the real reason is that these things, which are truly infinitely great and lofty in our eyes, are not the same in the eyes of Jesus Christ, and that there is therefore nothing unusual in the fact that he speaks of them without surprise and without admiration, just as we see, without making comparisons, that a general speaks perfectly simply and without emotion of the siege of an important town and of winning a great battle, and as a king speaks coldly of a large sum of fifteen or twenty million whereas a simple citizen or a labourer would only speak of it in exaggerated terms.

That is the thought which is contained and concealed in the few words of which the fragment is composed; and this factor together with many others of a similar nature, could undoubtedly serve, in the minds of people who are reasonable and who act in good faith, as in some manner a proof of the divinity of Jesus Christ.

I believe that this one example is sufficient not only to enable people to judge the quality of the other fragments which we have omitted, but also to illustrate the lack of concentration and, so to speak, the carelessness with which almost all of them were written down. This should convince them that, as I have said, M. Pascal had in fact only written them down for his own use, and without ever suspecting that they might one day be published in this form. And it is this which leads us to hope that people will be indulgent enough to excuse any shortcomings that they may find in them.

While there may still be some thoughts in the selection that are a little obscure, I believe that, provided people take a certain amount of trouble, they will understand them without any difficulty, and will agree that they are not among the least fine, that we were right to publish them as they are rather than to try to clarify them by long explanations which would only have made them slow and wearisome, and which would have removed one of their principal virtues, which is to say a great many things in very few words.

An example is to be found in one of the fragments in the chapter called *Proofs of Jesus Christ by the Prophecies* which is expressed in these terms:

> 'The prophecies of particular events are mixed with those relating to the Messiah, so that those foretelling the Messiah would not be without proofs and particular prophecies would not be without point.'[1]

In this fragment he gives the reason why the prophets, who were only thinking of the Messiah and who seemed under an obligation only to foretell him and what related to him, have nevertheless foretold particular incidents which appeared to be unconnected with and useless for their purpose. He said that it was in order that particular events should be accomplished from day to day in the sight of everybody, in the way in which the prophets had foretold, they should be recognised as being indisputably prophets, and that in this way people would not be able to doubt the truth and certainty of everything that they foretold about the Messiah. So that by these means the prophecies about the Messiah would in a certain sense derive their proofs and their authority from the prophecies about particular

[1] This appears to be a misreading of No. 659 *q.v. Tr.*

events and thus serve to prove and to give authority to those relating to the Messiah, which meant that they were neither useless nor fruitless. That is the meaning of the fragment when it is developed and expanded. But there is certainly no one who would not greatly prefer to discover it for himself in the obscure words in which it is expressed than to have it clarified and explained in this fashion.

In order to undeceive some people who might expect to find here mathematical proofs and demonstrations of the existence of God, the immortality of the soul and various other articles of the Christian faith, it still seems to me to be relevant to warn them that this was not M. Pascal's intention. He did not claim to prove all the truths of religion by demonstrations based on clear principles which would overcome the obstinacy of the most hardened, or by metaphysical arguments, which often bewilder rather than convince the mind, nor by commonplaces drawn from the different effects of nature; but by moral proofs which are directed more to the heart than to the mind. This means that he strove to touch the heart and induce the right mood in it rather than to convince and persuade the mind, because he knew that the passions and the vicious attachments which corrupt the heart and will are the greatest obstacles and the chief impediments in the way of faith, and that provided that these obstacles can be removed, it would not be difficult to make the mind accept the explanations and the reasons that would convince it.

The reader will see all this without difficulty when he reads the book. But M. Pascal has again explained his views on this topic in one of the fragments which was found among the rest and which has not been included in the present volume. This is what he says in the fragment in question:

'I shall not undertake here to prove by natural reasons either the existence of God, or the Trinity, or the immortality of the soul, or any of the things of that nature; not only because I do not feel myself qualified to discover anything in nature which is capable of convincing hardened atheists, but also because such knowledge, without Jesus Christ, is useless and sterile. If a man were convinced that the proportions of numbers were immaterial, eternal verities and dependent on a first truth in which they subsisted and which we call God, I should not consider that he had made much progress towards achieving salvation.'

The reader will perhaps be surprised to find in the present collection such a great variety of thoughts, several of which seem to be somewhat remote from the subject with which M. Pascal had set out to deal. But it must be understood that his plan was much wider and more extensive than might be imagined, and that he did not by any means limit himself to refuting the arguments of atheists and those who contest some of the articles of the Christian faith. His great love and the peculiar regard that he had for religion was such that he could not bear the idea that people wished to destroy it completely or even that they should harm and corrupt it in the slightest degree. With the result that he wished to declare war on all those who impugned either its truth or its holiness: that is to say, not merely on atheists, infidels and heretics, who refuse to submit the false enlightenment of their reason to faith and to recognise the truths that religion teaches; but he even wanted to declare war on Christians and Catholics who, being in the body of the true Church, nevertheless do not live according to the precepts of the Gospels, which are put forward as the model which serves as a rule for all our actions and to which they should conform.

Such was his plan and this plan was vast enough and great enough to find a place for most of the subjects which are dealt with in the selection. A few, however, may be found which have no connection with it, and which in fact were not intended for it; as, for example, most of those included in the chapter called *Miscellaneous Thoughts*, which were also discovered among M. Pascal's papers and which we considered could suitably be added to the others; because we are not offering the book simply as a work directed against atheists or about religion, but as a collection of the *Thoughts of M. Pascal on Religion and on some other Subjects.*

I think that in order to bring this preface to a close, it only remains, after speaking of his work, to say something about the author. I believe that it will not only be to the point, but that what I am about to say will be very useful in enabling people to understand how it was that M. Pascal acquired the sentiments and the regard that he had for religion, which gave him the idea of writing a book on it.

A short account has already been given in the preface to the treatises on the *Equilibrium of Fluids* and the *Heaviness of Air* of the way in which he spent his youth and the great progress that he made in a short time in every branch of human and secular learning to which he chose to apply himself, and particularly in geometry and mathematics; the strange and surprising way in which he learnt them at the age of eleven or twelve; the little works which he sometimes wrote, and which were always very much superior in power and penetration to those normally written by a person of his years; the astonishing and prodigious effort of his mind and imagination which were displayed in his calculating machine which he invented between the ages of nineteen and twenty; and finally, the splendid experiments on the vacuum which he performed in the presence of some of the leading citizens of the town of Rouen where he lived for some time when his father, President Pascal, was employed in the service of the king in the administration of justice. I shall therefore repeat nothing of that here, and shall be content to recall in a few words how he came to scorn all these things, and in what frame of mind he passed the last years of his life; in which the greatness and solidity of his virtue and his piety were no less apparent than the power, breadth and admirable penetration of his intellect had been in his earlier years.

He had been preserved in youth, by a special protection of God, from the vices to which the majority of young men succumb; and what is rather extraordinary with a mind which was as inquiring as his, he had never indulged in free thought so far as religion was concerned, but had always confined his taste for speculation to natural phenomena. And he said on a number of occasions that he added this obligation to all the others that he felt towards his father who, having himself a very great respect for religion, had imbued his son with it when he was still a child and had laid down, as a precept, that everything that is an object of faith cannot be the object of reason, and still less be subordinated to it.

These instructions, which were often repeated by a father for whom he had a great regard and in whom he saw great learning united to very clear and powerful reasoning, made such a deep impression on his mind that, whatever arguments he heard on the lips of free thinkers, he was unmoved by them; and although he was very young, he considered them as people who subscribed to the mistaken principle that human reason is above everything and did not understand the nature of faith.

But at last, after spending his youth on occupations and distractions which seem innocent enough in the eyes of the world, God touched him in such a way that he made him understand perfectly that the Christian religion demands of us that we should live only for him, and have no other object but him. And this truth appeared so obvious to him, and of such importance, that it led him to take the decision to withdraw from the world, and to renounce everything which attached him to it in order to devote himself solely to that.

His desire to withdraw and to lead a life that was more Christian and more orderly came to him when he was still very young; and it led him to abandon completely all forms of secular learning in order to apply himself only to those which could contribute to his own salvation and that of others. But the constant illnesses which attacked him interfered for some time with his plan, and prevented him from carrying it out before the age of thirty.

It was then that he really settled down to work at it and in order to do so more easily and to give up at once all his previous habits, he changed the district in which he was living, then went to live in the country where he remained for some time; and when he returned from it he showed so unmistakably that he wished to renounce the world that the world ended by renouncing him. When he was living in retirement he regulated his life in accordance with two main precepts, which were to give up all forms of pleasure and go without anything which was superfluous to his needs. He kept them constantly in mind, and he endeavoured all the time to advance and to perfect himself in the practice of them more and more.

It was the continual application of these two great precepts which enabled him to display such patience in his sickness and his ailments which throughout his life practically never left him free from pain; which made him practise such harsh and severe mortifications on himself; which drove him not merely to refuse his senses everything which might be agreeable to them, but also to submit without difficulty, without disgust and even with joy, when it was necessary, to everything which was disagreeable to them, whether by way of food or remedies for his illnesses; which made him cut down more and more every day on anything which he did not regard as being absolutely necessary whether in the way of clothing, food, furnishings and everything else; which gave him such a great and ardent love of poverty that it was always present to his mind, so that when he wished to do something, his first thought was to see whether it provided an opportunity for practising poverty; and which at the same time inspired him with such tenderness and affection for the poor that he could never refuse them alms and gave them very often and on a considerable scale, though he only did so out of what was necessary for his own requirements; which made him unable to bear people who were always thinking about their own comfort, and he criticised the curious search, the desire to excel in everything, such as to have the best workmen for everything, to have the best and the best made of everything, and scores of similar things which people do without scruple because they do not see any harm in it, but which he did not judge in the same way; and finally which led him to perform several very remarkable and very Christian actions which I shall not relate here for fear of taking too long, and because my aim is not to write a life, but simply to give those who did not know him some idea of the piety and virtue of M. Pascal; because I cannot claim to tell those who knew him and frequented him a little during the last years of his life anything fresh, and I think that they themselves will take the view that I might have said a lot of other things that I am passing over in silence.

Pensées : Contents

Pensées: Contents

*The number at the beginning of each passage is the
number of the Lafuma edition: the number in brackets
at the end is the number of the Brunschvicg edition.
Where the manuscript is not in Pascal's handwriting,
the Lafuma number is printed in italics; where this
italic number is followed by an asterisk, the manuscript
is partly in Pascal's and partly in another hand.
Except when the contrary is stated, biblical quotations
are given in the Knox translation.*

PART ONE

A. FOREWORD

1. What a difficult thing it is to put a case to another person without influencing his opinion by the way in which we do it! If we said: 'I think it's beautiful', or 'I think it's obscure', or something of that kind, we should be appealing to his imagination to subscribe to our own view; or conversely, we should drive him into adopting the opposite point of view. It is better to say nothing at all, and let him judge for himself according to the sort of person that he is at the time, to the weight that he attaches to other factors for which we are not responsible. But at all events, we shall not have tipped the scales either way; unless our silence produces its own effect, which depends on the way in which he takes it, or the interpretation that he is disposed to place on it, or the inferences that he draws from our gestures, the expression on our faces or our tone of voice, which will depend again on whether he is a physiognomist: so difficult is it to avoid distorting people's judgement, or rather, so far is opinion from being firm and stable! (105)

2. All our reasoning comes down to surrendering to feeling. But fancy is akin to feeling, and opposed to it, so that we are unable to distinguish between these two opposites. One person maintains that my feeling is fancy, another that his fancy is feeling. We really need a rule. We may think that reason will provide it, but reason can be manipulated in any way one pleases; with the result that there is no rule. (274)

3. We are surprised and delighted when we come across the natural style, because we expected to meet an author and instead find a man. This is the reverse of the attitude of people of taste who when they read a book expect to find a man, and are greatly surprised to discover an author: *Plus poetice quam humane*

locutus es.[1] People pay a fitting tribute to nature by telling her that she may discuss anything she likes, even theology.　　(29)

4. Let no one argue that I have said nothing new: the arrangement of my material is new; when we play tennis, both players use the same ball, but one of them places it better than the other.

I would sooner people said that I have used old words. And just as though the same thoughts did not add up to a different speech when they are arranged in a different order, so the same words express different thoughts when they are placed in a different order.　　(22)

5. When we want to correct another person in a helpful way and convince him that he is mistaken, we must consider the angle from which he approaches the subject. He is usually right from one point of view, and we must tell him so, but we must also explain the point of view from which he is wrong. He will be perfectly amenable because he will realise that he has not made a mistake, and that he had simply failed to look at the matter from every possible angle. Now people are not angry because they do not see everything, but they do not like to feel that they are mistaken; it may be due to the fact that man cannot in the nature of things see everything, and that he obviously cannot be mistaken from his own point of view, because his sense-perceptions are always true.　　(9)

6. We are usually more convinced by the reasons which we have discovered for ourselves than by those which are advanced by other people.　　(10)

7. . . . For we must not harbour illusions about ourselves: we are as much machines as minds; that is why the faculty which produces conviction is not the only method of demonstration. How few things there are which can be proved! Proofs only convince the mind. Habit provides us with our most effective and most widely accepted proofs; it bends the machine which carries the mind with it without our thinking about it. Who has ever been able to prove that tomorrow will come, and that we shall die? And what could be more generally believed? It is therefore

---

[1] 'You have spoken more like a poet than a man' (Petronius).

2|4 05

habit which convinces us of the fact; it is habit which makes so many people Christians; habit which makes Turks, pagans, traders, soldiers, etc. (There is the faith received in baptism which is commoner among Christians than Turks.) In short, we must rely on faith when the mind has once perceived where truth lies in order to quench our thirst and colour our minds with a faith that eludes us at every moment of the day; for we should be overdoing it if we always carried the proofs in our minds. We need a simpler faith which is habit, which without violence, without tricks, without argument makes us believe things, and predisposes all our faculties in favour of belief, so that our soul absorbs it naturally. It is not sufficient if we only believe through the strength of our convictions and when the machine in us is disposed to believe the opposite. We must therefore take care that both parts of ourselves believe: the mind by reasons which it is enough to have grasped once in our lives; and the machine by habit and by not allowing it to slip into the contrary belief. *Incline cor meum, Deus.*[1]

Reason acts slowly, with so many different views on so many principles, which must always be present to it, that it is continually dozing or wandering through failure to keep all its principles before it. Feeling does not operate in that way: it acts like a flash, and is always at the ready. We must therefore put our trust in feeling; otherwise our faith will always be precarious. (252)

8. The last thing we discover when writing a book, is what to put first. (19)

9. M. de Roannez used to say: 'The reasons come to me afterwards, but first of all the thing pleases or shocks me without my knowing why, and yet it shocks me for a reason that I shall discover later on.' I myself am convinced, not that something shocks us for reasons which we discover later, but that we only discover the reason because we have been shocked. (276)

---

[1] Incline my heart unto thy testimony, O God (Ps. cxviii, 36).

B. INTRODUCTIONS

10. To be insensitive to the extent of despising interesting things, and to become insensitive to the point that interests us most!

(197)

11. . . . Let them at least understand the nature of the religion that they are attacking before starting the attack. If religion prided itself on having a clear view of God, on possessing him openly without veils, it would be sufficient for them to say that they could discover nothing on earth which provided them with any evidence of it. But since religion says the opposite, since it maintains that men live in darkness far removed from God, that God has hidden himself from them, that this is the very name that he gives himself in the Scriptures, *Deus absconditus* [Is., xvi, 15]; in short, if religion strives equally to establish two things: that God has placed visible signs in the Church so that he will be recognised by those who seek him sincerely, and that he has nevertheless concealed the signs in such a way that he will only be seen by those who seek him with all their heart, what good does it do them when, in the indifference that they profess for the search for truth, they assert that nothing reveals truth to them, because the darkness in which they find themselves and which they use as an objection against the Church, only proves one of the things which it asserts without touching on the other and, so far from destroying it, gives support to the Church's teaching?

In order to embark on a struggle against religion, they would have to convince us that they had made every effort to find it in every possible place, even in what the Church has to offer for their instruction, but without success. If they spoke in these terms, they would indeed be attacking one of religion's claims. But I hope to show here that no reasonable person can speak in such a way, and I even venture to say that no one has

102

ever done it. We know perfectly well how people who hold these views behave. They are convinced that they have gone to great trouble to obtain information when they have simply spent an hour or two reading some of the books of the Bible, and have asked an ecclesiastic a few questions about the truths of faith. After that, they boast that they have sought without success in books and among men. But in fact I shall say to them, as I have often said, that such neglect is intolerable. It is not, in this case, a question of mild interest in some unknown person which permits them to behave in such a way; it is the question of ourselves, and of our all.

The immortality of the soul is a matter of such importance to us; it affects us so deeply that we must have lost our wits completely not to care what it is all about. All our actions and our thoughts must follow such different courses depending on whether there are eternal rewards to hope for or not, that it is impossible to take a single step with sense and judgement unless it is determined by our conception of our final end.

Thus our primary interest and our first duty must be to inform ourselves about the subject on which the whole of our conduct depends. And that is why, among people who are not convinced, I draw an important distinction between those who apply the whole of their powers to acquainting themselves with it, and those who go through life without bothering and without thinking about it.

I can feel only compassion for those who are sincerely distressed by their doubt, who regard it as the greatest of misfortunes, and who, by sparing no pains to escape from it, make the search one of their main and most serious occupations.

But I take a very different view of those who live their lives without giving a thought to the final end of life, and who solely because they do not discover within themselves the light necessary to convince them of it, neglect to seek elsewhere, and to decide after mature reflection whether belief is one of those ideas that people accept out of mere credulity, or one of those which though obscure in themselves nevertheless possess a solid and unshakable foundation.

Their neglect in a matter which vitally concerns themselves, their eternal destiny, their all, irritates me more than it moves me; it astonishes and appals me: I find something monstrous in it. I am not saying this out of pious sentiment. On the contrary, I mean that people ought to feel like this as a matter of human interest and self-respect: it calls for nothing more than that they should see what is apparent to the least enlightened of people.

We do not need to be very high-souled to realise that there is no true and solid satisfaction to be had in this world, that all our pleasures are only vanity, that our misfortunes are infinite and that death, which dogs us at every moment, must in the space of a few years inevitably bring us face to face with the dreadful necessity of being either eternally annihilated or eternally unhappy.

There is nothing more real than that, or more terrible. We may appear as brave as we please: that is what lies in store at the end of the most successful career in the world. Let people think about it and say afterwards whether it is not beyond question that the only good in this life lies in the hope of another life, that we are only happy in so far as we are approaching it and that, as there will be no more misfortunes for those who are completely sure of eternal life, so also there is no happiness for those who have no knowledge of it.

It is assuredly a great misfortune therefore to be in a state of doubt; but it is at least an indispensable duty to seek when we are in such a state; and so the man who doubts and does not seek is at once very unhappy and very unjust. That he should, in spite of everything, be calm and complacent, that he should declare himself so, and that he should regard such a state as something to boast about or as a matter for congratulation—I can find no words to describe such an extravagant creature.

Where can anyone acquire such feelings? What reason is there for rejoicing when we cannot look forward to anything but incurable unhappiness? What reason is there for vanity in finding oneself surrounded by impenetrable darkness, and how is it that such arguments can even occur to any reasonable person?

'I do not know who placed me in the world, what the world is, what I myself am; I am in a state of terrible ignorance about everything; I do not know what my body is, what my senses are, what my soul is or the very organ which thinks what I am saying, which reflects on everything and on itself, and does not know itself any more than the rest of me. I see the terrifying spaces of the universe which imprison me, and I find myself planted in a tiny corner of this vast space without my knowing why I happen to be here rather than in some other place, or why the brief space of life that is mine has been allocated to me at this point rather than another in all the eternity of time which preceded me and all the eternity of time which will come after me. I see only infinities on all sides which enclose me like an atom and like a shadow which only lasts for a second that will not return. All I know is that soon I shall die, but what I am most ignorant of all about is this very death from which there is no escape.

'Just as I do not know whence I came, so I do not know whither I am going; I only know that on leaving this world I shall fall for ever, either into the void or into the hands of an angry God, without knowing which of the two will be my lot for all eternity. Such is my state of mind, a mass of weakness and uncertainty. And the only conclusion I draw from it is that I shall spend the whole of my life without trying to find out what is going to happen to me. Perhaps I might be able to obtain some enlightenment in my doubt; but I do not want to be bothered; I do not even want to put out a hand and seek for it; and afterwards, filled with scorn for those who do take the trouble to find out (whatever certainty they obtain will be a subject for despair rather than for vanity), I shall go, without fear or foresight, to put the great event to the test, and allow myself to be softly led to death in a state of complete uncertainty about my future state in eternity.'

Who would wish to have a person who talks like that as a friend? Who would pick him out from among other people and discuss his affairs with him? Who would turn to him for comfort in adversity? In short, what use could he possibly be to anyone in life?

Truly, it is a glorious thing for religion to have such unreasonable men for its enemies; so far from being dangerous to it, their opposition is useful in establishing the truths of religion. For the Christian faith seeks little more than to establish these two truths: the corruption of nature and its redemption through Jesus Christ. Now, I maintain that if they do not serve to demonstrate the truth of redemption by the sanctity of their lives, at least they serve admirably to prove the corruption of nature by harbouring such unnatural feelings.

Nothing is of more importance to man than his state, nothing is so redoubtable to him as eternity. And so the fact that there are men who are indifferent to the loss of their life and to the peril of an eternity of unhappiness is not natural. They adopt a very different attitude towards everything else: they are afraid of the least things, foresee them, feel them; and the same man who spends so many nights and days in a rage, in an agony of despair over the loss of some office or some imaginary affront to his honour, is the same man who knows that he will lose everything by death and feels neither concern nor emotion at the prospect. It is a monstrous thing to see, in the same heart and at the same time, this concern for the most trivial of matters and this lack of concern for the greatest. It is an incomprehensible form of bewitchment and a supernatural torpor which is a proof of an all-powerful force that causes it.

There must be a strange confusion in the heart of man that he should glory at being in a state in which it seems inconceivable that anyone can exist. In the course of my experience, however, I have come across such a large number that it would be surprising if we did not know that the majority of them disguise their feelings and are not really like that. They are people who have heard it said that it is a sign of fine manners to pretend to be carried away. It is what they call casting off the yoke, and they try to imitate it. But it would not be difficult to make them see how mistaken they are in trying to create a good impression by such methods. That is not the way to do it—I mean among men of the world whose judgement of things is sound and who know that the only path to success is to appear decent, loyal, judicious and capable of helping a friend because men are by nature only fond of those who can be of use to them. Now, what advantage do we derive from hearing a man say that he has shaken off the yoke, that he does not believe that there is a God who watches over his actions, that he regards himself as sole judge of his conduct, and that he does not think of accounting for it to anyone but himself? Does he imagine that by saying this he is encouraging us to feel great confidence in him in the future and to expect comfort, advice and help from him in the difficult situations of life? Do such men imagine that they have greatly rejoiced us by telling us that they think that our soul is only a puff of wind or smoke, and still more by telling us so in an arrogant, self-satisfied tone? Is it a thing to be said cheerily? Is it not rather something to be admitted mournfully as though it were the saddest thing in the whole world?

If they thought about it seriously, they would surely see that it creates the worst possible impression, that it is so contrary to good sense, so incompatible with decency, and so far removed in every way from the genial atmosphere that they seek, that they would be more likely to cure than to corrupt those who might feel inclined to follow their example. And in fact, if you make them account for their feelings and explain their reasons for doubting the truth of religion, they will use such base and feeble arguments that they will convince you of the opposite. That is what someone said very aptly to them one day. 'If you go on holding forth like that,' he remarked, 'you'll end by converting me.' And he was quite right, for who would not be horrified at the very idea of sharing the sentiments of such contemptible individuals?

It follows that those who simply pretend to feel like that would be very ill-advised to repress their natural feelings merely in order to turn themselves into the most impudent of men. If, at the bottom of their hearts, they are annoyed at not possessing more insight, let them not hide the fact: there is nothing to be ashamed of in such an admission. The only thing that is shameful is not to feel any sense of shame. Nothing betrays more clearly an extreme weakness of intellect than not to recognise the unhappiness of a man without God; nothing betrays more clearly a bad nature than not to want eternal promises to be true; nothing is more cowardly than to brave God. Let them therefore leave their impieties to those who are sufficiently ill-bred to be really capable of them; let them at least be decent, honest men if they cannot be Christians; and lastly, let them recognise that there are only two kinds of person whom we can describe as reasonable: those who serve God with all their heart because they have found him, and those who seek him with all their heart because they have not found him.

But those who go through life without knowing or seeking him obviously feel that they are of so little value that it is not worth anyone's while to bother about them, and we must be possessed of all the charity that comes from the religion that they despise in order not to despise them to the point of abandoning them to their folly. But because religion imposes on us an obligation always to regard them, while they are still on earth, as capable of the grace which can enlighten them, to believe that in a short time they may be filled with greater faith than ourselves, while we ourselves may become the victims of the same blindness which now afflicts them, we must do for them what we should wish people to do for us if we were in their position: urge them to have pity on themselves, and at least take some steps to find out whether they are not capable of seeing the light. Let them devote to their reading a few of those hours which they spend so fruitlessly on other things: however great an aversion they feel for it, they may, perhaps, discover something, and in any case they will not lose very much; but I hope that those who embark on it with real sincerity and a genuine desire to find truth will be rewarded, and that they will be convinced by the proofs of so divine a religion which I have assembled here, and in which I have more or less followed this order. (194)

12. Before embarking on the proofs of the truth of the Christian religion, I find it necessary to draw attention to the injustice of men who live without bothering about the truth of a matter which is of such vital importance to them, and which affects them so intimately.

Of all their aberrations it is the one which most clearly convicts them of folly and blindness; the one in which it is easiest to reduce them to confusion by the first reactions of common sense and natural feeling. For it is clear beyond doubt that this life only lasts for a moment, that the state of death is eternal whatever its nature, and therefore that all our actions and thoughts must follow very different paths according to the nature of this eternity, that it is impossible to take a single step with sense and judgement unless it is done with this point in mind which should be our final goal.

Nothing is more obvious than this and therefore according to the principles of reason, the behaviour of men who follow a different course is thoroughly unreasonable.

Let us therefore judge from this point of view those who go through life without giving so much as a thought to the final end of life, who allow themselves to be led by their inclinations and their pleasures without reflexion and without uneasiness and, as though they could wipe out eternity simply by putting it out of their minds, think only of the happiness of the moment. Eternity, however, exists, and in a short time death, which will reveal it and which threatens them at every second of the day, will inevitably place them in the position of being condemned for all eternity either to annihilation or unhappiness without their knowing which of these two eternities awaits them.

It is a form of uncertainty which may have terrible consequences. They are in danger of an eternity of unhappiness; and in spite of it, as though the matter were not worth the trouble, they neglect to find out whether eternity is merely one of those ideas which the common people swallow too eagerly and too credulously, or one of those which though obscure in themselves, possess very solid but hidden foundations. Thus they do not know whether the idea is true or false, or whether the evidence for it is strong or weak. It stares them in the face; they refuse to see it, and in their ignorance they elect to do their utmost to succumb to the misfortunes which undoubtedly await them if religion is true; to wait for death in order to put it to the test, yet they are perfectly satisfied with their position; they subscribe to it openly and even boast about it. Can we think seriously of the importance of what is at stake without being appalled by such extravagant behaviour?

It is a monstrous thing to be easy in one's mind when one lives in such a state of ignorance; its extravagance and stupidity must be brought home to those who spend their lives in such a way by having it thrust under their noses, so that they will be confounded by the sight of their own folly. For this is how men argue when they choose to live in ignorance of what they are without seeking enlightenment. 'I do not know,' they say. (195)

13. That is what I see and what disturbs me. I look everywhere and everywhere I see only darkness. Nature offers me nothing that is not a source of doubt and anxiety. If I saw nothing in it which was a sign of the Divinity, I should answer in the negative; if I saw everywhere the signs of a Creator, I should live at peace in the faith. But, seeing too much for denial and too little for certainty, I am in a state which inspires pity and in which I have wished a hundred times that, if there is a God who preserves it, it should reveal him unequivocally, and that, if the signs it offers are illusory, it should obliterate them completely; that it should tell all or nothing so that I should know what attitude I ought to adopt. Instead of which, in the state in which I am, not knowing what I am and what I must do, I do not understand either my position or my duty. My whole heart is bent on knowing where true good lies in order that I may follow it; nothing would be too great a price to pay for eternity.

I envy those whom I see living so carelessly in the faith and who make such ill use of a gift which it seems to me I should put to such a different use. (229)

14. We cannot conceive either the glorious state of Adam or the nature of his sin, or the way in which it has been transmitted to us. They are things which occurred in conditions which were entirely different from our own, and which transcend our present powers of comprehension.

It is all so much useless knowledge when it comes to extricating ourselves from it; all that we need to know is that we are wretched, fallen, separated from God, but redeemed by Jesus Christ; and that is something of which we have marvellous proofs on earth. Thus the two proofs of corruption and redemption are provided by the unbelievers who live in a state of indifference towards religion, and the Jews who are its irrevocable enemies. (560)

15*. We ought to feel sorry for both; but for some it should be a pity born of love, and for the others a pity which springs from contempt.

We need to belong to the religion that they scorn in order not to scorn them.

It is not a happy state of affairs.

It shows that there is nothing that we can say to them, not because we despise them, but because they have no common sense. God must touch their hearts.

People of that sort are academics or students, and have the worst characters that I know.

You will convert me.

There is no doubt that there can be nothing good without a knowledge of God, that in so far as we are near him we are happy, and that ultimate happiness lies in knowing him with certainty; that in so far as we move away from him we are unhappy, and that final unhappiness would lie in the knowledge of the opposite.

It is therefore a misfortune to doubt, but it is an indispensable duty to seek when we are in a state of doubt, and he who doubts and does not seek is at once unhappy and unjust. That in spite of it he should be cheerful and bumptious leaves me unable to find words to describe such an extravagant creature.

Is it not sufficient that miracles happen in a particular place, and that Providence reveals itself to a particular people?

Yet it is obvious that man is so unnatural that there is a spark of joy in his heart over his state.

Is it a thing to be said joyfully? It is something to be said sorrowfully.

A fine subject for rejoicing and for bragging about with head held high like that . . . ; therefore, let us rejoice; let us live without fear or anxiety, and let us await death, since the time of its coming is uncertain, and we shall find out what becomes of us. I do not see the point.

It is the sign of a good disposition not to be complacent, and true pity lies in being tolerant of others.

Is it a sign of courage on the part of a dying man to go, in a state of weakness and agony, to meet an all-powerful and eternal God?

How delighted I should be, were I in such a state, if someone took pity on my folly and was charitable enough to rescue me from it in spite of myself.

Not to be irritated by it and not to care for it shows such weakness of mind and such ill-will.

What a joy not to have anything to look forward to except incurable unhappiness! What comfort in the despair of finding any comforter!

But the very people who seem most opposed to the glory of religion are not without their use for others. We will use them as our first argument: that it is something supernatural, for blindness of this nature is not natural; and if their folly makes them so inimical to their own interests, the horror of such a lamentable example and of a foolishness that is so deserving of pity, will serve as a warning to others.

Are they so immovable that they are insensible to everything that affects their interests? Let us put them to the test by the loss of their goods or their honours. What! It must be a form of bewitchment . . .

I am not speaking out of bigotry, but because of the way in which the heart of man is made; not out of piety or with detachment, but from a purely human principle and for reasons of interest and self-respect, because sufficiently interested to be moved by the certain knowledge that in a few years, after all

the ills of this life an inevitable death, which threatens us at
every moment of the day, must [bring us *face to face*] with the
appalling necessity of [being either eternally annihilated or
eternally unhappy].

The three conditions.

It cannot be described as an example of good sense.

It is all that a man could do who was convinced of the falseness of the news; yet he should be in a state not of joy, but of
collapse.

Nothing matters but that, and it is the one thing that they
neglect.

Our imagination magnifies the present for us to such a degree because we are continually thinking about it and diminishes
the importance of eternity so enormously owing to our failure
to think about it, that we turn eternity into nothingness and
nothingness into eternity; and it has such living roots in us that
the whole force of our reason cannot preserve us from it, and
that . . .

I would ask them whether it is not true that they themselves
are the living proof of the foundation of the faith against which
they are fighting, which is that the nature of man is in a fallen
state.   (194*ter*)

16. . . . Thus the whole universe teaches man either that he is
fallen, or that he is redeemed. Everything speaks to him of his
greatness or his misery. The abandonment of God is apparent
among the Jews.   (560 *bis*)

17. . . . They blaspheme against something which they do not
know. The Christian religion consists of two things; it is equally
important that men should know them and it is equally dangerous to be ignorant of them; and it belongs equally to God's
mercy to have given signs of both.

And yet they infer that one of these two things is not true
from the fact which ought to make them accept the other. The
wise men who said that there was only God were persecuted,
the Jews hated, the Christians even more so. They saw by their
own insight that, if there is a true religion on earth, all things
ought to tend towards it as their centre. The whole conduct of

things should have as its object the establishment of religion and its greatness; men's feelings ought to conform to the teaching of religion; in short, it ought to be so much the object and centre towards which all things gravitate, that whoever knows the principles will be able to give an explanation both of the whole nature of man in particular, and the whole direction of the world in general.

And starting from this assumption, they take it upon themselves to blaspheme against the Christian religion because they do not possess a proper knowledge of it. They assume that it consists simply in the worship of a God who is considered great and powerful and eternal; this properly speaking is deism, which is almost as far removed from the Christian religion as atheism, which is the exact opposite of it. And from this they go on to conclude that the Christian religion is not true because they fail to perceive that all things help to establish this fact: that God does not reveal himself to men as clearly as he could.

But they can come to whatever conclusions they like about deism, they will not arrive at any conclusions against the Christian religion which lies properly speaking in the mystery of the Redeemer who, uniting in himself two natures, one human and one divine, has saved men from the corruption of sin in order to reconcile them with God in his divine person.

It therefore teaches men these two truths at the same time: that there is a God whom men are capable of knowing, and that human nature is fallen and unworthy of God. It is equally important for men to grasp both these points; and it is equally dangerous for man to know God without being aware of his own wretchedness, and to be aware of his wretchedness without knowing the Redeemer who can cure him of it. One of these forms of knowledge alone will either produce in him the pride of the philosophers who have known God without being aware of their own misery, or the despair of the atheists who know their own misery without knowing the Redeemer.

And just as it is equally necessary for mankind to be aware of both these things, so it is equally a sign of God's mercy to have taught men both these things. The Christian religion does it; that is its essence.

Let us look at the order of the world from that point of view, and see whether everything does not tend to prove the two main tenets of the Christian religion: Jesus Christ is the object of everything, and the centre towards which all things gravitate. Whoever knows that, knows the reason for everything.

Those who go astray only do so through their failure to grasp one of these two things. A man may therefore be capable of knowing God and not knowing his own wretchedness, or knowing his wretchedness and not knowing God; but we cannot know Jesus Christ without at the same time having a knowledge of God and our wretchedness.

And that is why I do not intend to embark here on the proofs from nature either of the existence of God, or the Trinity or the immortality of the soul, or anything of that sort; not only because I do not think that I am sufficiently well-equipped to discover anything in nature which will convince hardened atheists, but also because without Jesus Christ such knowledge is useless and vain. If a man were convinced that numerical proportions were immaterial and eternal truths dependent on a first truth in which they subsist and which we call God, I should not consider that he had made much progress towards salvation.

The God of Christians is not a God who is merely the author of mathematical truths and the order of the elements; that is the point of view of heathens and Epicureans. He is not simply a God whose providence watches over the lives and possessions of men, so that those who worship him will enjoy a long and prosperous career; that is the Jewish idea. But the God of Abraham, the God of Isaac, the God of Jacob, the God of Christians is a God of love and consolation; he is a God who fills the soul and heart of those whom he possesses; he is a God who makes them inwardly conscious of their wretchedness and of his infinite mercy; who unites himself with them in the depths of their soul; who fills it with humility, with joy, with trust, with love; who makes them incapable of any other end but him.

All those who seek God outside Jesus Christ and who stop at nature, or who do not find any form of light which satisfies them, or who succeed in finding a means of knowing God and serving him without a mediator, end by falling into atheism or deism, which are two things that are almost equally abhorrent to the Christian religion.

Without Jesus Christ the world would not continue to exist; it would either be destroyed, or would be a sort of hell.

If the world existed in order to instruct man in the knowledge of God, his divinity would shine everywhere in a manner which was undeniable; but since it only continues to exist through and for Jesus Christ, and to bring men a knowledge both of their corruption and their redemption, everything is bursting with the proofs of those two truths.

What can be seen is not a sign either of a total absence, or of the manifest presence of the divinity, but of the presence of a God who hides himself. Everything bears this character.

Will the only being who knows nature know it solely in order to be wretched? Will the only being who knows it be the only one who is unhappy?

It is [not] necessary that he should see nothing at all; nor is it necessary that he should see enough to imagine that it belongs to him; but it is necessary that he should see enough of it to realise what he has lost; because, in order to know what he has lost, he must see and not see; and that is precisely the state of nature.

Whichever standpoint he adopts, I shall give him no rest.

(556)

18. I will not allow him to stick to either view, so that being without habitation or rest . . . (419)

19. It is a remarkable thing that no canonical author ever used nature to prove the existence of God. They all aim at making people believe in him. David, Solomon, etc., never said: 'There is no void, therefore there is a God.' They must have been shrewder than the shrewdest of their successors, who all used the argument. This is an important fact. (243)

20. Man's sensitiveness in little things, and his insensitiveness in large is the sign of a strange confusion. (198)

21. These people have no heart. We should not want to have any of them for our friends. (196)

22. *Quid fiet hominibus qui minima contemnunt, majora non credunt?*[1]

(193)

23. And what about the person who jeers at another? Who has the right to jeer? And yet this one does not mock the other, but is sorry for him. (191)

---

[1] What will become of men who scorn little things and do not believe in great ones? (Pascal.)

1. ORDER

24. The psalms sung by the whole world.

Who bears witness to Mahomet? Mahomet himself. Jesus Christ wants his own testimony to be nothing.

The quality of witnesses is such that they exist always and everywhere, and are wretched. He is alone. (596)

25. *Order by dialogue.* 'What must I do? I see everywhere nothing but obscurities. Am I to believe that I am nothing? Am I to believe that I am God?' (227)

26. 'All things change and succeed one another.' 'You are wrong, there is . . .'

'What! Did you yourself not say that the heavens and the birds prove the existence of God?' 'No.' 'And doesn't your religion say so?' 'No. For though it is true in a sense for certain souls, to whom God has given this form of enlightenment, it is nevertheless untrue for the majority of people.' (244)

27. A letter to encourage people to seek God.

And then make people seek him in the works of the philosophers, sceptics and dogmatists, who disturb the man who consults them. (184)

28. *Order.* A letter of exhortation to a friend to persuade him to seek. And he will answer: 'But what's the good of seeking? Nothing comes of it.' Reply to him: 'Do not give up hope.' And he would answer again that he would be delighted to find some form of light, but that according to religion itself, if he believed in it, it would not help him, and therefore he prefers on the whole not to seek. The answer to that is: The machine. (257)

29. *First part*: Wretchedness of man without God.

Second part: Happiness of man with God.

Or:

First part: That nature is corrupt. Nature itself is the proof.

Second part: That there is a Redeemer. Proved by Scripture.

(60)

30. *Letter which shows the usefulness of proofs. Proof by the machine.*

Faith is different from the proof of it: one is human, the
other is a gift of God. *Justus ex fide vivit*[1]: it is this kind of faith
that God himself places in our heart of which the proof is often
the instrument, *fide ex auditu*[2], but this kind of faith is in our
hearts and makes us say not *scio*, but *credo*. (248)

31. *Order*. See what is clear and unchallenged about the state of
the Jews. (602)

32. In the letter *On Injustice* we can put: the absurdity of the law
that the elder son inherits everything. 'My friend, you were
born on this side of the mountain; it is therefore just that your
elder brother should have everything.'

'Why are you putting me to death?' (291)

33. The miseries of human life are the cause of it all: since they
have seen them, men have given themselves up to amusements.

(167)

34. *Order*. After the letter 'On the need to seek God', place the
letter 'On the removal of obstacles', which is the disquisition
on the 'machine', on preparing the machine, 'seeking by means
of reason.' (246)

35. *Order*. Men despise religion; they hate it and are afraid that
it may be true. In order to cure them of this attitude, we must
begin by showing them that religion is not contrary to reason;
that it is venerable and awaken a feeling of respect for it;

Next we must show that it is gracious, make good men wish
that it were true; and then prove that it is true.

Venerable, because of its profound knowledge of human
nature.

Gracious, because it holds out the promise of true good.

(187)

36. *Order*. I should be much more afraid of making a mistake

---

[1] The just man liveth by faith (Rom. i, 17).
[2] Faith then cometh by hearing (Rom. x, 17).

and discovering that the Christian religion is true, than of not making a mistake by believing it to be true.   (241)

37. The true nature of man, his true good, true virtue and true religion are things which cannot be known separately.   (442)

38. *Proofs of religion.*

Morality, Doctrine, Miracles, Prophecies, Symbols.   (290)

39. I blame equally those who take it upon themselves to praise man, those who find fault with him, and those who seek distraction; and I can only approve of those who seek with groans.

(421)

40. *A letter on* The Foolishness of Human Knowledge and Philosophy. This letter to come *before diversion.*

Felix qui potuit . . .

Felix nihil admirari.[1]

Two hundred and eighty different kinds of sovereign good in Montaigne.   (74)

41. The true religion should teach greatness and wretchedness, should make us both respect and scorn the self, love and hate it.

(494)

42. Order. After 'corruption', say: 'It is right that all those who are in this state should be aware of it; those who are satisfied with it as well as those who are not; but it is not right that all should see the Redemption.'   (449)

43. There is nothing on earth which does not reveal either the wretchedness of man, or the mercy of God; or the powerlessness of man without God, or the strength of man with God.   (562)

44. Scepticism. I shall put down my thoughts in any order, but not perhaps in a state of confusion without any pattern: it is the true order and will always reveal my aim by its very disorder. I should be doing my subject too much honour if I treated it in an orderly fashion because I want to show that it is incapable of orderly presentation.   (373)

45. Order. Nature has enclosed each of its truths in itself; our art lies in enclosing them in one another, but it is not natural: each has its prescribed place.   (21)

---

[1] Happy is he who knows the causes of things (*Georgics*, II, 489). Do not be astonished at anything (Horace, *Ep.*, VI, I).

46. *Order.* Why should I divide my moral system into four rather
than into six parts? Why should I divide virtue into four parts
or two, or one? Why into *abstine et sustine* rather than into
'follow nature', or 'carry on his private business without harming anyone', why like Plato, or anyone else?

'But there you are,' you will say, 'everything summed up in
one word.' 'I know, but it is useless unless you explain it; and as
soon as you set out to explain it, and begin with the precept
which contains all the others, they come tumbling out in the
native state of confusion that you were trying to avoid. With the
result that when they are all enclosed in a single one, they are
hidden and useless, as though they were in a chest, and only
appear in their natural state of confusion. Nature has established them all without enclosing them in one another.'   (120)

47. *Order.* I might well have dealt with the disquisition on order
in this way: to show the vanity of all conditions of men, show
the vanity of ordinary lives, then the vanity of philosophical
lives, sceptics as well as stoics; but the order would not be preserved. I know something about it, and how few people understand it. No human knowledge can preserve it. St. Thomas did
not preserve it. Mathematics does, but its profundity is useless.

(61)

48*. *Preface to Part I.* Discuss those who have dealt with self-
knowledge; the divisions of Charron, which sadden and bore
us; the confusion of Montaigne; that he was very conscious of
the lack [of a sound method]; that he avoided it by leaping from
one subject to another, that he tried to be smart.

What a stupid idea his self-portrait was! It was not done
casually in spite of his own principles, in the way that anyone
may come to grief; it was done in accordance with his own
principles and as a basic and fundamental part of his plan. For
to say silly things by accident and through weakness is something that can happen to any of us; but to say them intentionally is intolerable, and to say such things as . . .   (62)

49. *Preface to Part II*:

Say something about those who have dealt with the subject.

I am astonished at the boldness with which such people venture to discuss God.

When addressing themselves to the infidel, their first chapter is devoted to proving the existence of the Divinity from the works of nature. I should not be surprised at the way they set about it if their books were intended for the faithful, because those who have the living faith in their hearts certainly see at once that everything that exists can only be the work of the God whom they worship. But they are intended for those in whom the light of faith has been extinguished and in whom we wish to restore it: those people who are deprived of faith and Grace, and who, with all the insight at their command, concentrate on everything in nature which may lead them to knowledge, and find nothing but obscurity and darkness; to tell such people that they have only to look on the least of the objects which surround them and they will see God openly, to offer them, as the only proof of this great and important subject, the movement of the sun and the planets, and to claim to have completed our proof with such a performance, can only create the impression that the proofs of our religion are very weak; and I can see from reason and experience that nothing is better calculated to make them despise religion.

It is not in this manner that Scripture speaks, which has a better understanding of the things which are God's. On the contrary, it declares that God is a hidden God; and that since the corruption of nature, he has left men in a state of blindness from which they can only emerge through Jesus Christ, without whom they are cut off from all contact with God: *Nemo novit Patrem, nisi Filius, et cui voluerit Filius revelare.*[1]

This is what Scripture means when it says in so many places that those who seek God shall find him. It is not of that light which we speak 'as the noonday sun'. It is not said that those who seek the noonday sun, or water in the sea, will find any; and so it is clearly necessary that the evidence of the

---

[1] And as no one knoweth the Son, but the Father; neither doth anyone know the Father, but the Son and he to whom it shall please the Son to reveal *him* (Matt. xi, 27).

existence of God shall not appear to be of that nature. Therefore, Scripture tells us in another place: *Vere tu es Deus absconditus.*[1]   (242)

2. VANITY

50. Two faces alike, neither of which seems particularly funny
by itself, make us laugh when they are together on account of
their resemblance.   (133)

51. True Christians, however, are obedient to folly; not that they
respect folly, but the command of God which for the punishment of mankind has made them subject to these follies: *Omnis
creatura subjecta est vanitati Liberabitur.*[2] In this way St. Thomas
explains the passage in St. James on giving way to the rich
who, if they do not do it in the sight of God, depart from the
precepts of religion.   (338)

52. *Perseus, King of Macedonia, Paulus-Emilius.*
   People criticised Perseus for not killing himself.   (410)

53. *Vanity.* That something as obvious as the vanity of the world
is so little known that it is considered a strange and surprising
thing to say that it is foolishness to seek greatness is truly a
wonderful thing.   (161)

54. *Inconstancy and oddity.* To live only by one's work and to rule
over the most powerful State in the world are very different
matters. They are united in the person of the Grand Sultan of
Turkey.   (113)

55. A fragment of a cowl is the weapon of 25,000 monks.
                                                              (955)

56. He has four servants.   (318)

57. He lives on the other side of the water.   (292)

58. If we are too young our judgement will not be sound; too
old, same thing.

---

[1] Verily thou art a hidden God . . . (Is. xlv, 15).
[2] For the creature was made subject to vanity . . . the creature shall also
be delivered . . . (Rom. viii, 20-21).

If we do not think about it enough, if we think about it too much, we become obstinate and too infatuated with it.

If we examine our work immediately after finishing it, we are too biased; if too long afterwards, we find that we have lost interest in it.

It is the same if we look at pictures when we are too close or too far away from them; there is only a single indivisible point which is the right place.

The others are too close, too far away, too high, or too low. Perspective decides the matter in painting. But who will decide in the sphere of truth and morality? (381)

59. The power of flies: they win battles, prevent our mind from acting, devour our body. (367)

60. *Vanity of knowledge.* Physical science will not console me for my ignorance of moral philosophy in time of sorrow; but a knowledge of moral philosophy will always console me for being deficient in knowledge of physical science. (67)

61. *Condition of man*: inconstancy, weariness, anxiety. (127)

62. The habit of seeing kings escorted by guards, drums, officers and all the trappings which automatically inspire feelings of respect and awe is the reason why their face, when it is sometimes seen alone and without the trappings, commands feelings of respect and awe from their subjects who do not separate their persons mentally from their suites which they are used to seeing with them. And the world, which does not realise that the effect is the result of habit, believes that it is due to some natural power; hence the words: 'The character of the Divinity is imprinted on his features,' etc. (308)

63. The power of kings is based on reason and on the folly of their people, and much more on folly. The greatest and most important thing in the world is founded on weakness.

And the foundation is admirably solid; for there is nothing more certain than the fact that the people will be weak. Anything that is founded on sound reason is very ill-founded, like a high opinion of wisdom. (330)

64. It is not in man's nature always to go forward; it has its vicissitudes.

Fever has its shivering fits and its burning periods; and the coldness reveals the violence and the heat of the fever as much as the heat itself.

It is the same with the inventions of man from century to century. It is generally the same with the goodness and wickedness of mankind: *Plerumque gratae principibus vices.*[1] (354)

65. *Weakness.* All men's efforts are directed towards the acquisition of wealth; and they could not produce any title proving that they possess it justly, for they have only human whims, and not the strength which gives them a solid hold on it. It is the same with knowledge because illness removes it. We are incapable of the true and the good. (436)

66. *Ferox gens, nullam esse vitam sine armis rati.*[2] They prefer death to peace; other people prefer death to war.

The general opinion may be favourable to life, the love of which appears so strong and so natural. (156)

67. When we choose the captain of a ship, we should not choose the passenger who came from the best family. (320)

68. In the towns through which we pass we do not care whether people think well of us or not. But when we have to stay for a time in one of them we care a great deal. How long do we have to stay for that to happen? A period proportionate to our vain and puny life. (149)

69. *Vanity.* Respect means: To put yourself out for the convenience of others. (317 *bis*)

70*. What most surprises me is to find that everyone is not amazed at his own weakness. We set to work seriously, and each of us follows his profession not because it is a good thing to do so, for that is the fashion; but as though each of us were quite certain where justice and reason lie. We are continually suffering disappointments; and by an amusing form of humility, we think that it is our fault, and not that of the art which we always boast that we possess. But it is a good thing for the fame of scepticism that there are so many people of this kind in the

[1] Changes are usually welcome to the great (Horace, *Odes*, III, *xxix*, 13).
[2] Fierce people who did not believe that life without arms was worth living (Livy, XXXVI, 17).

world who are not sceptics, in order to demonstrate that man is perfectly capable of the most extravagant opinions because he is able to convince himself that he is not in a state of natural and inescapable weakness, and thinks that, so far from it, he is following the path of natural wisdom.

Nothing strengthens Pyrrhonism more than the number of people who are not Pyrrhonists; if they all were, they would be wrong. (374)

71. The sect draws its strength from its enemies rather than from its friends; for the weakness of man is more apparent in those who do not know it than in those who do. (376)

72. *Shoe heel.* 'Oh! how well turned it is! There's a skilful workman for you! How brave that soldier is!' That is the source of our inclinations and our choice of a profession. 'What a lot that man drinks! How little this one drinks!' That is what makes people abstemious and drunkards, soldiers, cowards, etc. (117)

73. Anyone who does not realise the vanity of the world must be very vain himself. Who can fail to see it in the world's amusements and in the thought of the future, except the very young who are all busy kicking up a din? But take away their amusements and you will see them wilt with boredom; they will then become conscious of their nothingness without realising it; for it is a very unhappy position to find ourselves plunged into a state of unutterable sadness the moment we are reduced to scrutinising ourselves, and do not find it amusing. (164)

74. *Trades.* Fame is so sweet that men love it, whatever the object to which it is attached, even death. (158)

75. Too much and too little wine; give him none and he will not discover the truth; give him too much, same result. (71)

76. Men spend their time chasing a ball or a hare; it is the very sport of kings. (141)

77. What vanity is painting which arouses admiration on account of its resemblance to things that we do not admire when we come across them in life. (134)

78*. *Two infinities, middle way.* If we read too fast or too softly, no one understands. (69)

79. How many nations are unaware of our existence! (207)

80. Little things comfort us because little things upset us. (136)

81. Imagination. It is man's dominant faculty, the mistress of error and falsehood, and all the more treacherous because it does not always deceive; for it would be an infallible rule of truth if it were the infallible rule of falsehood. But being mostly false, it gives no indication of its real quality because it sets the same stamp on true and false alike.

I am not speaking of madmen, I am speaking of the wisest of men; and it is among them that imagination carries its greatest power of conviction. Reason protests in vain; it cannot decide the value of things.

This haughty power, which is the enemy of reason, which likes to control and dominate it in order to show what it can accomplish in every sphere, has established in man a second nature. Imagination has its happy men and its unhappy men, its healthy men and its sick men, its rich men and its poor men; it makes people believe in, doubt, deny reason; it suspends the operation of the senses, it makes them feel; it has its fools and its wise men; and nothing exasperates us more than to see that it brings its clients a satisfaction which is fuller and more complete than anything that reason can offer them. People gifted with a lively imagination are far more pleased with themselves than prudent men can reasonably be. They look haughtily at people; they argue boldly and confidently; the others, fearfully and diffidently; and their cheerful countenance often gives them an advantage in the eyes of their listeners; such is the favour that imaginary sages enjoy in the minds of judges of the same stamp. Imagination cannot turn fools into wise men; but it can make them happy and it competes with reason, which can only make its friends wretched; one covering them with glory, the other with shame.

Who creates reputations? Who bestows respect and veneration on people, books, laws, the great, if not the imaginative faculty? How inadequate [are] all the riches of the earth without its co-operation!

Would you not feel inclined to say that the judge whose venerable old age demands the respect of a whole people, is ruled by pure and sublime reason, and that he judges things according to their nature without bothering about trivial circumstances which only offend the imagination of the feeble? Watch him as he goes piously to listen to a sermon, fortifying the solid virtues of his reason by the warmth of his charity. There he is, ready to listen to it with a respect that is an example to the rest of us. Suppose the preacher appears, suppose [that] nature has given him a hoarse voice, a peculiar face, that his barber has shaved him badly, that on top of everything else it so happens that he is scruffier than usual—I'll wager that our senator will lose his gravity. Suppose that the greatest philosopher in the world is standing on a plank which is wider than is necessary for safety: his reason will convince him that he is safe, but if there is a precipice underneath, his imagination will carry the day. Several of them could not bear the thought without growing pale and breaking out into a sweat.

I do not propose to describe all its effects.

Who does not know that the sight of cats, rats, the crushing of a piece of coal, etc., may be enough to unhinge reason? The tone of a voice impresses the wisest among us, and can change a speech into an impromptu poem.

Love or hate alter the course of justice. And how much juster an advocate, who has been well paid in advance, finds his client's cause! How much his bold handling does to make it appear better than it is to the judges who are taken in by appearances! Ridiculous reason which is tossed hither and thither by every wind that blows!

I should have to describe almost all the actions of men, which are only moved by the jolts of imagination. For reason has been compelled to give ground, and the wisest of men accepts as his principles those which the imagination has had the temerity to introduce everywhere.

[Anyone who chose to be guided by reason alone would plainly be regarded as a madman. Having made his choice, he would be obliged to work all day long for rewards which are admittedly imaginary; and when he had been refreshed by sleep after the labours of reason, he would have to leap out of bed at once in order to continue the pursuit of phantoms and submit to the impressions of this mistress of the world. That is one of the principles of error, but not the only one.]

[Man was perfectly right to seek an alliance between those two powers, though in the peace which results imagination enjoys a great advantage; in war it is much more complete. Reason will never succeed entirely in overcoming imagination while the opposite is quite common.]

Our judges are very conscious of the secret power of imagination. Their red robes, the ermine in which they swaddle themselves like furry cats, the courts where they sit, the *fleurs de lys*—all the august display is very necessary; if physicians did not have cassocks and mules and doctors did not have square hats and robes four sizes too large, they would never have fooled people who cannot resist a display which looks so authentic. If the judges possessed true justice and the physicians the true art of healing, there would be no need for square hats; the majesty of their science would be sufficiently imposing in itself. But since their science is purely fictitious, they are obliged to deck themselves out with vain ornaments that strike the imagination which is what they are aiming at; and in this manner, in fact, they win respect. Soldiers alone do not disguise themselves because the part they play is essential: they establish themselves by force, the rest by giving themselves airs.

It is for this reason that our kings have never sought to disguise themselves. They have never dressed up in extraordinary clothes to make themselves look like kings; but they have themselves escorted by guards and cross-bowmen. The armed forces who have neither hands nor strength except for them; the trumpets and the drums which march ahead of them, the legions which surround them make the boldest among us tremble. They do not possess the clothes; they simply have the power. We should need a very purified reason to treat the Grand Sultan of Turkey like any other man when he is in his splendid seraglio, surrounded by forty thousand janissaries.

We cannot even see an advocate in cap and gown without forming a flattering opinion of his abilities.

Imagination is everywhere supreme; it is the source of beauty, justice and happiness, which is everything in the world. I should be glad to see that Italian book which is known to me only by name and alone is worth a whole library: *Dell' opinione regina del mondo*. I approve of what it says without reading it, evil apart if there is any.

Such more or less are the effects of the deceitful faculty which seems to have been bestowed on us on purpose to foster necessary error. We have many other sources of error.

Bygone impressions are not the only ones which are capable of misleading us: the charm of novelty possesses the same power. Hence all the quarrels between men who blame themselves either for being taken in by the false impressions of childhood, or for running recklessly after new ones. Who strikes the happy mean? Let him come forward and prove it. However natural it may appear, there is no principle acquired since childhood, [which cannot] be dismissed as a false impression due either to education or the senses.

'Because,' says someone, 'you have believed since childhood that a chest was empty when you saw nothing in it, you believed that the vacuum was possible. It is an illusion of the senses fostered by habit, which science must correct.' And other people say: 'Because they taught you at school that there was no such thing as a vacuum, they perverted your common sense which understood it so clearly before you were given this misleading impression that it must be corrected by going back to your untutored nature.' Who then is the deceiver? The senses or education?

We have another source of error: sickness. It distorts our judgement and our senses; and if serious illnesses alter them appreciably, I have no doubt that minor ailments do so in proportion to their gravity.

Our personal interest is still a marvellous instrument for closing our eyes to realities in the pleasantest possible manner. It is not permissible for the most equitable man in the world to be judge in his own cause; I know some people who in order to avoid falling victims to this form of pride, have shown themselves the most unjust men in the world in the opposite direction: the surest way of losing a really good case was to persuade near relations of these men to pull strings for you.

Justice and truth are two points which are so delicate that our tools are too blunt to be used on them with any degree of accuracy. If they are used, they blur the point; they slip and slither all over the place and are brought to bear much more on the false than the true.

[Man is therefore so happily fashioned that he possesses no reliable guide to the true and several excellent ones to the false . . . But the most engaging source of his errors is the war between the senses and reason.] (82)

82. That is where we must begin the chapter on the powers of deception. Man is nothing but a creature full of error which is natural and irremovable without grace. Nothing reveals truth to him. Everything misleads him; the two principles of truth, reason and the senses, apart from the fact that each is lacking in sincerity, mislead one another.

The senses mislead reason by deceitful appearances; and the same trick that they play on the soul is played on them in their turn by the soul. It takes its revenge on them. The passions of the soul upset the senses and give them false impressions. They lie and deceive for all they are worth.

But in addition to errors which are the result of accident or lack of understanding be[tween these] heterogeneous faculties . . . (83)

83. *Vanity.* The cause and effects of love: Cleopatra. (163)

84. We never live in the present. We anticipate the future which is felt to be too slow coming, as though to hasten its arrival; or we recall the past to slow it down if it goes too fast: we are so imprudent that we wander through ages which are not ours and never give a thought to the only one that belongs to us; and so frivolous that we think of those that are nothing and thoughtlessly overlook the only one that exists. It is because the present is usually painful. We push it out of sight because it hurts us; and if it is agreeable we are sorry to see it pass away. We try to prop it up by means of the future; and think we can regulate

things that are not in our power for a future which we are by no means sure of reaching.

Let each of us examine his thoughts, and he will find that they are all occupied with the past or the future. We can scarcely think of the present; and if we do think of it, it is only in order to find our bearings for mapping out the future. The present is never our goal; the past and the present are our means; the future alone is our goal. Thus we never live, but we hope to live; and as we are always preparing ourselves to be happy it is inevitable that we never are happy. (172)

85. The mind of the sovereign judge of the world is not so independent that it is not liable to be disturbed by the first sound that makes itself heard anywhere near it. It does not need the boom of a cannon to interrupt its thoughts; it only needs the creaking of a weathercock or a pulley.

Do not be surprised if it does not reason well at the moment; a fly buzzes in its ears; it is enough to make it incapable of giving sound advice. If you want it to discover the truth, drive away the animal which interferes with its thought and upsets its powerful intelligence which rules over towns and kingdoms. What a comic god it is! *O ridicolosissime heroe!* (366)

86. It seems to me that Caesar was too old to amuse himself by conquering the world. This kind of fun was all very well for Augustus or Alexander; they were young men and difficult to stop; but Caesar must have been more mature. (132)

87. The Swiss are offended when they are described as gentlemen, and prove that they are of humble birth in order to be thought worthy of holding high office. (305)

88. 'Why do you want to kill me? You have me at a disadvantage. I'm unarmed.' 'What! Don't you live on the other side of the water? My friend, if you lived on this side I should be a murderer, and it would be criminal to kill you like that; but since you live on the other side, I'm brave and it's right.'

(293-154)

89. *Good sense.* They are compelled to say: 'You're not acting in good faith; we're not asleep', etc. How I love to see that proud reason humbled and playing the part of a suppliant! For that is

not the language of a man who finds his rights challenged and who defends them with arms and the strength of his muscles. He does not waste time saying that someone is not acting in good faith, but punishes bad faith by force. (388)

90. Anyone who wants to appreciate man's vanity to the full need only reflect on the causes and effects of love. The cause is a *je ne sais quoi* (Corneille) and its effects are appalling. The *je ne sais quoi*, which is such a tiny thing that we cannot even recognise it, rocks the world, thrones, armies, the whole of creation to their foundation.

The nose of Cleopatra: if it had been shorter, the face of the earth would have changed. (162)

91. The basest thing in man is his thirst for fame, but that in itself is the clearest sign of his excellence because, whatever possessions he may have on earth, however good his health and however well provided he may be with essentials, he remains unsatisfied unless he enjoys people's good opinion. He sets such high store on reason that, whatever his worldly advantages, unless he is well endowed with it, he is not satisfied. He may have the best place in the world, but nothing can deflect him from this wish, and that is the most indelible quality in the heart of man.

And those who most despise men and put them on the same level as the animals, nevertheless wish to be admired and believed by them, and then contradict themselves by their own feeling; their nature, which is stronger than anything, is more effective in convincing them of man's greatness than reason in persuading them of their baseness. (404)

92. Write against those who probe too deeply into the sciences. Descartes. (76)

93. *On the desire to be thought well of by those whose company we keep.* Pride keeps such a tight hold on us in the midst of our wretchedness, errors, etc. We are delighted to lose our life provided that it makes people talk.

Vanity: gambling, hunting, visiting, the theatre, the false immortality of one's name. (153)

94. Vanity is so deeply rooted in the heart of man that a soldier, a churl, a cook, a picklock, boast and may have admirers; and philosophers expect to have them too; and those who write against them want to enjoy the reputation of writing well; and those who read them want to enjoy the notoriety of having read them; and I, who am writing this, have perhaps the same desire; and perhaps those who will read it . . .   (150)

95. Have you never met people who try to make up for the fact that you do not think much of them, by reeling off the names of important people who have a high opinion of them? I should reply: 'Show me the qualities by which you charmed those people, and I will have the same good opinion of you.'   (333)

96. *Fame.* The animals do not admire one another. A horse does not admire his companion; it is not that there is no spirit of emulation among them during a race, but it is of no consequence; because once they are back in their stables, the heaviest and worst groomed does not give up his oats to the other, as men expect other people to do for them. Their virtue is satisfied with itself.   (401)

97. The whole of men's minds are bent on the acquisition of wealth; and they have neither a title to prove that they have acquired it justly, nor the strength to guarantee security of tenure; so it is with knowledge and pleasure. We possess neither the true nor the good.   (436 *bis*)

98. Good heavens! What foolish talk is this! 'Would God have created the world in order to damn it? Would he ask so much of such feeble creatures, etc?' Scepticism is the remedy for this evil, and will make short work of such vanity.   (390)

99. It is the nature of self-esteem and of the human *self* to love only oneself and to consider oneself alone. But what can a man do? He will not be able to prevent the object of his affection from being full of faults and wretchedness; he wants to be great and finds that he is small; he wants to be happy and finds that he is unhappy; he wants to be perfect and finds that he is riddled with imperfections; he wants to be the object of men's affection and esteem and sees that his faults deserve only their dislike and contempt. The embarrassing position in which he

finds himself produces in him the most unjust and criminal passion that can possibly be imagined; he conceives a mortal hatred of the truth which brings him down to earth and convinces him of his faults. He would like to be able to annihilate it and not being able to destroy it in itself, he destroys it, in so far as he can, in his own mind and in the minds of other people; that is to say, he concentrates all his efforts on concealing his faults both from others and from himself, and cannot stand being made to see them or their being seen by other people.

It is no doubt an evil to be full of faults; but it is a still greater evil to be full of them and to refuse to recognise them, because it is adding still another fault: voluntary blindness. We do not want other people to deceive us; we do not think it right that they should desire us to have a better opinion of them than they deserve: it is therefore also not right that we should deceive them and wish them to think better of us than we deserve.

Thus, when they only discover imperfections and faults which we in fact possess, it is plain that they do us no wrong because they help to deliver us from an evil which is our ignorance of our own imperfections. We ought not to be angry because they know them and despise us: for it is right that they should know us for what we are and despise us if we are despicable.

Those are the feelings which would be found in a heart filled with equity and justice. What therefore are we to say of ours, when we find a completely opposite disposition in it? For is it not a fact that we hate the truth and those who tell us the truth, that we want them to be deceived when it is to our advantage, and that we wish people to think us better than we really are?

Here is a proof of it which horrifies me. The Catholic religion does not compel us to disclose our sins indiscriminately to everybody; it permits us to hide them from everybody else; but it makes an exception in the case of one person to whom we are bidden to reveal the bottom of our heart, and to show ourselves as we really are. There is only this one man in the world whom it orders us to disabuse about ourselves, and it imposes on him an inviolable secrecy with the result that to all intents and purposes the knowledge he has of us does not exist. Can we imagine anything more lenient or more charitable? And yet the corruption of man is such that he still finds this rule a hardship; and it is one of the main reasons which has caused a large part of Europe to rebel against the Church.

How unjust and unreasonable is the heart of man that he should regard it as a bad thing that he is made to do in front of one man what it would, in a way, be just for him to do in front of everybody! For is it right for us to deceive them all?

There are different degrees in this dislike of the truth; but it can be said that it exists to some extent in all of us because it is inseparable from self-esteem. It is this bad kind of delicacy which forces those who feel bound to reprove other people to choose so many devious ways and compromises to avoid shocking them. They are obliged to make light of our faults, to appear to condone them, to throw in praise, protestations of affection and regard. Yet in spite of everything, it remains a bitter pill to our self-esteem. It takes as little of the medicine as it can; it always does so with disgust and often even with a secret ill-feeling towards those who administer it.

It thus happens that if anyone wants to make himself popular with us, he avoids rendering a service that he knows we should find disagreeable; he treats us as we wish to be treated; we hate the truth and people hide it from us; we want to be flattered, and people flatter us; we want to be deceived, and people deceive us.

The result is that each stroke of good fortune, which enables us to rise in the world, takes us further from truth because people are more afraid of wounding those whose friendship is likely to be useful and whose dislike is dangerous. A prince may be the laughing-stock of all Europe, and he will be the only person who does not know it. I am not surprised that it should be so: to speak the truth is useful to the man to whom one speaks it, but disadvantageous to those who do it because they make themselves unpopular. Now, those who live with princes care more about their own interests than those of the prince whom they serve: and so they take care not to do him a good turn at the risk of damaging themselves.

This kind of misfortune is no doubt greater and more common among those who occupy the highest positions, but the lowest are not exempt from it because it is always in our own interest to make people like us. Thus human life is nothing but a perpetual illusion; we do nothing but flatter and deceive one another. No one speaks to us in our presence as he speaks of us behind our backs. The union which exists between men is based entirely on mutual deception; and few friendships would survive if each knew what his friend said about him behind his back, even though he spoke sincerely and dispassionately.

Man is therefore nothing but disguise, deceit and hypocrisy both in himself and in his relations with other people. He does not want people to tell him the truth; he avoids telling it to other people; and all these dispositions which are so far removed from justice and reason have their natural roots in our heart.

(100)

100. Men often mistake their imagination for their heart; and they believe themselves converted as soon as the idea of conversion comes into their heads. (275)

3. WRETCHEDNESS

101. Baseness of man which is pushed to the point of bowing the knee to animals and worshipping them. (42)

102. *Inconstancy*. Things possess different qualities, and the soul different inclinations, for nothing is simple which is presented to the soul, and the soul's approach to an object is never simple. That is why the same thing makes us laugh and cry. (112)

103. *Inconstancy*. We think that we are playing on ordinary organs when we play on man. They are organs to be sure, but odd, fickle, variable [with pipes that do not follow the usual se-

quence]. Those who can only play the ordinary instrument will not produce any chords on them. We need to know the arrangement of the [key] board. (111)

104. We are such a poor lot that we can only enjoy anything provided that we grow angry if it turns out badly; which can and frequently does happen with a thousand things. Anyone [who] discovered the secret of rejoicing over good fortune without growing angry over a corresponding misfortune would have reached the heart of the matter; it is perpetual movement.
(181)

105. It is not a good thing to enjoy too much freedom. It is not a good thing to have all our needs satisfied. (379)

106. Tyranny lies in a desire of domination which is universal and out of order.

There are different assemblies where strong men, handsome men, sensible men and pious men, each hold undisputed sway, but do so nowhere else; and sometimes they meet, and the strong and the handsome come to blows, stupidly, to decide which of them will be the master of the other: for their mastery is different in kind. They do not understand one another, and their mistake is to want to rule everywhere. Nothing can, not even force; it accomplishes nothing in the kingdom of the learned; it is only mistress of external action.

Tyranny. . . . Thus the following sayings are false and tyrannical: 'I am handsome, therefore people should fear me. I am strong, therefore people should love me. I am . . .' And it is equally false and tyrannical to say: 'He isn't strong, therefore I shall not be afraid of him.'

Tyranny is the desire to reach by one path what can only be reached by a different one. We owe different duties to different qualities: the duty to love what is pleasing; the duty to fear power; the duty to believe in knowledge. We ought to perform these duties; it is wrong to refuse, and wrong to demand them from others. (332)

107. When it is a matter of deciding whether it is right to wage war and kill so many men, condemn so many Spaniards to

death, the decision is taken by one man who is an interested party: it ought to be decided by a third and disinterested party.

(296)

108. [In truth he would rid himself of the vanity of laws; it is therefore useful to delude him.]

. . . On what shall a man base the economy of the world that he wants to rule? Will it be on the whim of each individual? What chaos! Will it be on justice? He does not know the meaning of the word.

Certainly, if he had known it, he would not have prescribed this rubric which is the commonest of all those known to men: that each should conform to the customs of his own country; the light of true equity would have brought all nations under its rule, and legislators would not have replaced an enduring conception of justice by taking the whims and fancies of the Persians and the Germans as their models. We should see a model system of justice established in every country in the world in every age, instead of which we see no system of justice or injustice which does not vary from one country to another like the climate. If the temperature at the pole went up by three degrees, it would turn jurisprudence upside down; a meridian determines truth; after a few years' possession, fundamental laws undergo sweeping changes; right has its periods; the entry of Saturn into Leo marks the origin of some crime or other. A comic sort of justice that has a river for its boundary! Truth on this side of the Pyrenees, error on the other.

They admit that justice is not to be sought in custom, but in natural laws which are common to all countries. Certainly, they would stick obstinately to their view if the boldness of chance, which is responsible for human laws, had hit on one that was universal; but the joke is such that human whim is so various that there is none. Robbery, incest, the slaughter of children and fathers have in their time all been regarded as virtuous actions. Can anything be more preposterous than the fact that a man has the right to kill me because he lives on the other side of the ocean and because his prince has a grievance against mine, though I have none against him? There are no doubt natural laws; but once right reason was corrupted, it corrupted everything: *Nihil amplius nostrum est*; *quod nostrum dicimus, artis est. Ex senatus consultis et plebiscitis crimina exercentur. Ut olim vitiis, sic nunc legibus laboramus.*[1]

This confusion leads one man to declare that the essence of justice is the authority of the lawgiver; a second, that it is the comfort of the sovereign; a third, present custom; and that is the safest: according to reason, nothing is just in itself; everything changes with the times. Custom is the whole of equity for the sole reason that it is accepted; that is the mystic foundation of its authority. Anyone who tries to trace it back to its first principles will destroy it. Nothing is so faulty as laws which purport to redress wrongs; anyone who obeys them because they are just, obeys a justice which is the product of his imagination, but not the essence of the law; it is entirely contained within itself; it is law and nothing more. Anyone who wants to examine its structure will find that it is so weak and frivolous that, unless he is in the habit of contemplating the prodigies of human imagination, he will be surprised that in the course of a century it has acquired so much pomp and circumstance. The art of opposition and rebellion lies in undermining established customs by tracing them back to their origins in order to reveal their lack of authority and justice. 'We must,' it is said, 'go back to the primitive and fundamental laws of the State which have been abolished by unjust custom.' It is the surest way of losing everything; nothing will appear just when subjected to a test of that kind. Yet the people easily lend their ears to this kind of talk. They cast off the yoke as soon as they recognise it; and the great take advantage of it to its ruin and that of the curious students of accepted customs. That is why the wisest of legislators said that it is often necessary to deceive men for their own good; and another, who was a sound politician: *Cum veritatem*

[1] There is no longer anything that is ours; what we call ours is a work of convention (Cicero: *De finibus*, v, 21). It is in virtue of the senatus consultus and the plebiscites that crimes are committed (Seneca: *Ep.* xcv). We suffered long ago for our vices: today we suffer for our laws (Tacitus: *Ann.*, III, 25).

qua liberetur ignoret, expedit quod fallatur.[1] He must not know the truth about usurpation: it was introduced in other times without any shadow of reason, and has become reasonable; it is necessary that it should be regarded as authentic, eternal, and its beginnings hidden, unless we desire its imminent collapse.   (294)

109. Justice. Just as fashion determines what is pleasing, so it determines what is just.   (309)

110. [Three guests.] Would anyone who enjoyed the friendship of the King of England, the King of Poland and the Queen of Sweden have felt that he lacked a place of rest and refreshment in the world?   (177)

111. *Fame.* Admiration spoils everything from childhood onwards: 'Oh, well said! Oh, well done! How good he is! etc.'

The children of Port-Royal who are not goaded on by the spur of envy and fame sink into a state of lethargy.   (151)

112. *Mine, thine.* 'The dog's mine,' said these poor children. 'That is my place in the sun.' That is how the usurpation of the whole world began.   (295)

113. *Variety.* Theology is a science, but how many sciences? A man is a whole, but if we dissect him, will he be the head, the heart, the veins, each vein, each fragment of a vein, the blood, each of the blood's humours?

A town and a stretch of country, when seen from afar, are a town and a stretch of country; but as we draw near we see houses, trees, tiles, leaves, grass, ants, the legs of ants, and so on to infinity. All of it is included in the term 'country'.   (155)

114. Injustice. It is dangerous to tell the people that the laws are not just for they only obey them because they believe them to be so. That is why they must be told at the same time that they must obey them because they are laws as they obey their superiors, not because they are just but because they are superiors. If we can make them understand that, every form of sedition can be prevented, which properly speaking is the definition of justice.   (326)

115. Injustice. Jurisdiction is not granted for the benefit of [the]

[1] Since he does not know the truth which gives freedom, it is a good thing for him to be deceived (Augustine: *Civ. dei.* IV, 27).

judiciary, but for the person who is brought to judgement. It is dangerous to say so to the people; but the people have too much trust in you: that will not do them any harm and may help you. It must therefore be published abroad: *Pasce oves meas, non tuas.*[1] You owe it to me to give me food. (879)

116. When I consider the brief span of my life, absorbed in the eternity of time which went before and will come after it, the tiny space that I occupy and even that I see, plunged in the infinite immensity of the spaces which I do not know and which do not know me, I am terrified and astonished to find myself here rather than there, for there is no reason why I should be here rather than there, why now rather than then. Who put me here? By whose order and design were this place and time allotted to me? *Memoria hospitis unius diei praetereuntis.*[2] (205)

117. *Wretchedness.* Job and Solomon. (174 *bis*)

118. If our condition were truly happy, we should not need any form of amusement to keep us from thinking about it. (165 *bis*)

119. *Contradiction.* Pride counter-balancing all forms of misery. Man either hides his misery or, if he reveals it, he prides himself on being aware of it. (405)

120. We must know ourselves; even if it were not sufficient to enable us to reach truth, it would at least serve to regulate our lives, and there is nothing better than that. (66)

121. The sense of the hollowness of present pleasure and ignorance of the vanity of absent pleasure is the cause of inconstancy. (110)

122. *Injustice.* They have not found any way of satisfying their desires without doing wrong to other people. (454)

123. Ecclesiastes shows that the man without God is ignorant of everything, and is condemned to a state of inevitable unhappiness. For to will and be incapable brings unhappiness. Now man wants to be happy and to be assured of some truth; and yet he can neither know nor desire not to know. He cannot even doubt. (389)

---

[1] Feed my sheep not thine.
[2] The hope of the impious is like the memory of the one day guest who passes away (Wisdom v, 15).

124. [But perhaps this is a subject which is beyond the scope of reason. Let us therefore examine its achievements in realms which are within its grasp. If there is anything to which, in its own interest, it must have been applied most seriously, it is the search for the sovereign good. Let us see therefore where powerful and clearsighted minds have placed it, and whether they are in agreement.

One man says that the sovereign good lies in virtue, another finds it in sensual pleasure; another [in] following nature, another in truth: *Felix qui potuit rerum cognoscere causas*[1]; another in total ignorance, another in sloth, others still in resisting appearances, or in not being impressed by anything: *Nihil mirari prope res una quae possit facere et servare beatum*,[2] and the true Pyrrhonists in their ataraxy, their doubt and perpetual dithering; and others again, who are wiser, in the fact that it is not even to be had for the asking. That is something that we have learnt to our cost!

Place after the discussion of the laws the following article.

Thus we must see whether this fine philosophy has achieved any definite results by such long and exacting labour, whether perhaps the soul may at least come to know itself. Listen to the lords of creation on the subject. What conclusions have they come to about its substance? 395

Have they been more successful in housing it? 395

What have they found out about its origins, its length of life, and its departure from the world? 399

Is it therefore a fact that the soul is still too noble for its feeble lights? Let us bring it down to the level of matter, and see whether it knows what the body that it animates is made of, and the other bodies that it contemplates and moves as it chooses. What have the great dogmatists, who are ignorant of nothing, learnt about it? *Harum sententiarum*.[3] 393

That would probably suffice if reason were reasonable. It is

[1] Happy is the man who knows the causes of things.

[2] Not to marvel at anything, that more or less is the only way of finding and keeping happiness (Horace: *Ep.*, I, VI, 1).

[3] Which of these opinions is the true one? Only a god could decide (Cicero: *Tusc.* I, II).

reasonable enough to admit that it has not yet discovered anything definite; but it has not given up hope of succeeding; indeed, it is as ardent as ever in its pursuit, and is convinced that
it possesses within itself the strength necessary for victory. Its
task must therefore be brought to completion, and after testing
its powers by examining their effects, let us study them in themselves; let us see whether it has the powers and grasp which are
necessary to seize truth.] (73)

125. We desire truth, and are dogged by uncertainty.

We seek happiness, and find only wretchedness and death.

We are incapable of not desiring truth and happiness, and
are incapable of certainty or happiness. This desire has been
handed down to us as much to punish as to make us aware of
the state from which we have fallen. (437)

126. Wretchedness. Solomon and Job knew it best, and have
spoken best of the wretchedness of man: one the happiest, the
other the unhappiest of mortals; one knowing the vanity of pleasure from experience, the other the reality of misfortune. (174)

127. Men are so invariably mad, that not to be mad would
amount to being mad in some other way. (414)

128. Wretchedness. The only thing that consoles us for our misery
is distraction, and yet it is the greatest of our miseries. For it is
mainly responsible for preventing us from thinking about ourselves and for our gradual ruin. Without it we should grow
weary, and our weariness would drive us into seeking a much
more solid means of escaping from it. But distractions amuse us
and bring us imperceptibly to death. (171)

129. We are not wretched without being conscious of it; a ruined
house is not wretched. Man alone is wretched. *Ego vir videns.*

(399)

130. I myself admit that as soon as the Christian religion reveals
the principle that human nature is corrupt and separated from
God, it opens our eyes so that wherever we look we discover
evidence of the truth of its teaching; because nature is such that
it bears witness everywhere to a lost God, both in man and
outside him, and a fallen nature. (441)

131. Pride outweighs and banishes every form of misery. It is a strange monster, and an obvious aberration. Now it has fallen from its place; it seeks it uneasily. That is what men do. Let us see who will have found it. (406)

132. *Fallen nature.* Man does not act in accordance with reason which is the source of his being. (439)

133. *Quod crebo videt non miratur, etiamsi cur fiat nescit; quod ante non viderit, id si evenerit, ostentum esse censet.* (90)

Noe iste magno conatu magnas nugas dixerit.

Quasi quicquam infelicius sit homine cui sua figmenta dominantur.[1] (90; 87)

134. Evil is easy; its forms infinite; good almost unique. But a certain kind of evil is as difficult to discover as what is known as good, and in this way people often pass off as good a particular form of evil. It would even require an extraordinary greatness of soul to succeed just as it would to reach the good. (408)

135. The things to which we cling most tenaciously, such as concealing the smallness of our means, are often of practically no importance. It is a molehill which imagination swells into a mountain. Another twist of imagination makes us realise it without difficulty. (85)

136. There are vices which only cling to us through other vices and which, once the trunk is removed, are carried away like branches. (102)

137. When malice has reason on its side, it becomes proud, and makes a display of reason in all its splendour.

When austerity or a hard choice has not led to true good and has to retrace its steps and follow nature, it becomes proud on account of the return journey. (407)

138. Imagination magnifies tiny objects until, by a fantastic appraisal of their worth, it fills our mind with them; and by

---

[1] What he sees frequently does not surprise him even if he is unaware of the reason. But he takes what he has never seen, when that happens, for a prodigy (Cicero: *De div.*, II, 27). There is someone who is going to say with a great effort some very silly things (Terence: *Heaut.*, IV, 1.8). As though there were anything more unfortunate than a man dominated by his imagination (Pliny: II, 7).

its insolent temerity it reduces great things to its own level, as
when speaking of God. (84)

139. They say that eclipses are the heralds of misfortune because
misfortunes are common, and as misfortunes occur so frequently
they are often successful in predicting them, while if they said
that they were the heralds of good fortune they would often be
wrong. They only ascribe good fortune to rare conjunctions of
the stars; so that they are seldom mistaken in their predictions.

(173)

140. *Ne si terrerentur et non docerentur, improba quasi dominatio videre-
tur.* Aug. *Ep.* 48 or 49. IV. vol. *Contra mendacium ad Consentium.*[1]

(186)

141. 'The *self* is hateful: you hide it, Miton, but that doesn't
mean that you can get rid of it; you are therefore always hateful.' 'Not at all, for by behaving, as we all do, obligingly to
everybody, we no longer have any reason to hate ourselves.'
'That would be true if we only hated in the *self* the vexations
which come to us from it.'

But if I hate it because it is unjust, because it makes itself the
centre of everything, I shall always hate it.

In short, the *self* has two qualities: it is unjust in itself because it makes itself the centre of everything; it is disagreeable
to other people because it tries to browbeat them; for each *self*
is the enemy and would like to be the tyrant of all the others.
You remove its unpleasantness, but not its injustice.

You do not make it agreeable to those who hate its injustice,
you only make it agreeable to the unjust who no longer find
their enemy in it; and therefore you remain unjust and are only
acceptable to the unjust. (455)

142. *Injustice.* Add presumption to necessity, and you get extreme injustice. (214)

143. Since nature always makes us unhappy whatever our state
of mind, our desires conjure up a happy state because they introduce into the state in which we are pleasures belonging to a
different state; and even if we managed to satisfy these desires,

---

[1] If one employed terror and not teaching (against the heretics) it would
appear like tyranny.

we should not be happy because we should be filled with still other desires which sprang from our new state.

We must particularise this general proposition.　　(109 *bis*)

144. When we are in good health, we wonder what on earth we should do if we were ill; when we are ill, we cheerfully take medicine: our illness settles the matter for us. We no longer have the appetites or the taste for walks and amusements which good health brings and which we cannot bear to think about when we are ill. Nature therefore imbues us with appetites and tastes which are in keeping with our present state. It is only the fears that we ourselves conjure up, and not nature, which upset us because they introduce into our present state desires properly belonging to a different state.　　(109)

145. [Miton] understands perfectly well that nature is corrupt and that men are the reverse of virtuous: but he does not know why they cannot fly higher.　　(448)

146. A thought sometimes escapes me when I am in the very act of writing it down; but that reminds me of my weakness which I am in constant danger of forgetting; which is as instructive as the vanished thought because I aim only at knowing my own nothingness.　　(372)

147. Not only do we look at things from different angles, but with different eyes; we have no desire to find them alike. (124)

148. We know so little about ourselves that some people think that they are going to die when they are in good health; and some imagine that they are in good health when they are at the point of death, because they do not feel the approaching fever, or the abscess which is about to form.　　(175)

149. Although people may have no interest in what they are saying, we cannot be absolutely certain that they are not lying; for there are people who lie simply for the sake of lying. (108)

150. What a sign of perverted judgement when there is nobody who does not set himself above everybody else; who does not prefer his own good, the continuation of his own happiness and his own life to that of everybody else!　　(456)

151*. *Unusquisque sibi Deum fingit.*[1] Disgust.　　(258)

[1] He maketh a god (Wisdom, xv, 8).

152. *Flux.* It is a horrible sensation to feel that everything we possess is slipping away. (212)

153. Children who are afraid of the face that they have blackened are simply behaving like children; but how can a person who is so feeble when a child become very strong when he is older! We do nothing but change our fantasies.

Everything that is brought to perfection by progress is destroyed by progress. Anyone who has once been weak can never be really strong. It is all very well to say: 'He's grown up; he's changed.' At bottom, he remains the same person. (88)

154. I state as a fact that if everybody knew what they said about each other there would not be four friends left in the whole world. This is apparent from the quarrels caused by the indiscreet disclosures which they sometimes make about one another. [I will go further than that, everyone would be . . .]
(101)

155. The great spiritual efforts that the soul sometimes makes cannot be kept up; it simply makes a leap, not as one might leap on to a throne expecting to stay there for ever, but on to a pinnacle to which one can only cling for a matter of seconds.
(351)

156. *Thoughts. In omnibus requiem quaesivi.*[1] If our condition were truly happy, it would not be necessary to take our minds off it in order to find happiness. (165)

4. ENNUI

157. *Pride.* Curiosity is merely a form of vanity. Usually we only want to know things in order to be able to talk about them. Otherwise, we should go on a sea voyage without ever talking about it, and for the simple pleasure of seeing without any hope of ever being able to tell people what we have seen. (152)

158. Description of man: dependence, desire for independence, need. (126)

159. The weariness we feel when we give up occupations to

[1] In all these I sought rest (Eccles. xxiv).

which we are attached. A man enjoys life at home: he has only
to see a woman who attracts him or have a few days' fun, and
you find him wretched at having to return to his normal
occupation. Nothing is commoner than that.   (128)

160. *Ennui*. Nothing is more intolerable to man than a state
of complete repose, without desires, without work, without
amusements, without occupation. In such a state he becomes
aware of his nothingness, his abandonment, his inadequacy, his
dependence, his emptiness, his futility. There at once wells up
from the depths of his soul weariness, gloom, misery, exasper-
ation, frustration, despair.   (131)

161. Man's dualism is so obvious that there have been people
who thought that we possessed two souls. A simple subject appeared to them to be incapable of such sudden switches from
boundless presumption to a frightful sinking of the heart. (417)

162. The nature of man is pure nature, *omne animal*.

There is nothing which cannot be made natural; there is
nothing natural which we cannot be made to lose.   (94)

162. Movement is the essence of our nature; complete repose is
death to us.   (129)

164. Each of us is a whole to himself; once he is dead, the whole
is dead for him. That is why everyone believes that he is everything to everybody. We must not judge nature according to ourselves but according to itself.   (457)

165. Man is properly speaking *omne animal*.   (94 *bis*)

166. We do not preserve our virtue through our own strength,
but by striking a balance between two contending vices pulling
us in opposite directions, in the same way that we remain upright when caught by cross winds: take away one of these vices,
and we succumb to the other.   (359)

167. What is the *self*?

A man goes over to the window and watches people passing:
if I pass, can I say that he took up his position in order to see
me? No, because he was not thinking of me in particular. But if
a man likes someone on account of his good looks, does he like

the person himself? No, because smallpox, which will destroy his looks without killing the man, will prevent him from liking him any longer.

And if someone likes me because I possess sound judgement or a good memory, does it mean that he is fond of *me*? No, because I can lose both these qualities without myself being lost. Where then is this *self*, if it is not to be found in the body or the mind? And how can we like the body or the mind except on account of their virtues, which are not the ones which constitute the *self* because they are transient? Can we be fond of the substance of a person's soul in an abstract manner and whatever its virtues? That is impossible, and would be wrong. It follows that we are never fond of anyone, but only of his virtues.

Let us therefore no longer make light of those who are honoured for their status and position because we are fond of no one except for their borrowed virtues. (323)

168. The outstanding quality which regulates all the others.

(118)

169. We are not satisfied with the life that is in us and in our own being: we want to live an imaginary life in the minds of other people. For this reason we are anxious to shine. We work continually to embellish and preserve our imaginary being, and neglect the true one. And if we are endowed with tranquillity or generosity or fidelity, we hasten to let everyone know in order to attach those virtues to our other self; we prefer to detach them from our real self and to attach them to the other; we would gladly be cowards in order to win a reputation for valour. Great sign of the nullity of our real self not to be satisfied with one without the other, and often to swap one against the other! For anyone who would not give his life to preserve his honour would be infamous. (147)

5. CAUSE AND EFFECT

170. Deference means: 'Putting yourself to inconvenience.' It may appear pointless, but perfectly just; for it is the same as

saying: 'I would certainly put myself to inconvenience on your account if it were really necessary, because I already do it without being of any assistance to you.' In addition, deference serves to distinguish the great: now, if deference meant sitting in an armchair, we should show deference to everybody, and distinguish nobody; but by being put to some inconvenience, we certainly draw distinctions. (317)

171. The only universal rules are the laws of the country in ordinary matters, and the will of the majority in others. How does that come about? Through the power that is behind them.

And that is why kings, whose power comes from another source, do not follow the advice of the majority of their ministers.

No doubt equality of wealth is right and just; but since force cannot be made to submit to justice, men have made it just to submit to force; and since justice cannot be fortified, we justify force so that justice and force go together and we have peace, which is the sovereign good. (299)

172. Wisdom counsels a return to childhood: *Nisi efficiamini sicut parvuli.*[1] (271)

173. The world is a good judge of things because it is in a state of natural ignorance, which is the true condition of man.

The sciences have two extremes which meet. The first is the state of pure and natural ignorance which is ours at birth. The other extreme is reached by great souls who, after running through the whole gamut of human knowledge, discover that they know nothing.

And they meet in the same state of ignorance in which they began; but it is a knowledgeable ignorance which knows itself. Those among them who have emerged from the state of natural ignorance and have not managed to reach the other kind, have a touch of this sufficient knowledge and pretend to be knowing. They upset people and misjudge everything.

The common people and clever men make up the world; the common folk despise the world and are despised by it. They

[1] Unless you are converted and become as little children (Matt. XVIII, 3).

are bad judges of everything, and are rightly judged by the world.   (327)

174. [*Descartes.* We must say, broadly speaking: 'It is produced by figure and movement,' because it is true. But when it comes to saying what they are and putting the machine together, it is ridiculous because it is useless and uncertain and painful. And if it were true, we do not consider that the whole of philosophy is worth an hour's sweat.]   (79)

175*. Summum jus, summa injuria.

Majority rule is the best because it is plain for all to see, and has the power to make itself obeyed; yet it reflects the opinions of the least competent.

If we had been able to, we should have placed power in the hands of justice; but since power does not allow us to manipulate it as we choose because it is a palpable quality, whereas justice is a spiritual quality which we can use as we wish, justice has been placed in the hands of power; and so we describe as just what we are forced to obey.

Hence the right of the sword because the sword does confer a veritable right.

Otherwise we should see violence on one side and justice on the other (End of the twelfth *Provinciale*).

Hence the injustice of the Fronde which sets up its pretended justice against power. It is not the same in the Church, for there we find true justice and no violence.   (878).

176. *Veri juris.* We no longer have any; if we had, we should not regard submission to the customs of our country as the rule of justice.

It is in this respect that not being able to discover the just, we have found the strong, etc.   (297)

177. The chancellor is grave and is wearing his robes of office.

For his position is false; the king's is not: he has the power; he is not a product of imagination. Judges, doctors, etc., can only rely on imagination.   (307)

178*. . . . It is the result of power and not custom; for those who are capable of originality are rare; the majority only want to follow, and deny fame to those original minds who seek it through their creativeness; and if they are determined to win it, and scorn those who are not original, these people call them by ridiculous names, and feel an urge to beat them. Let us therefore not pride ourselves on our subtlety, or keep our satisfaction to ourselves. (302)

179. *Cause and effect.* It is extraordinary: people do not want me to honour a man covered with brocade who is followed by seven or eight servants! Come! he will have me whipped if I do not salute him. His dress is a form of power. It is precisely the same with a well-harnessed horse compared with another! It is funny that Montaigne cannot see what a difference there is, that he should be surprised at anyone finding any, and ask the reason. 'In truth,' he says, 'whence comes it, etc.' (315)

180. *Cause and effect.* Gradation. The people honour men of noble birth. The half-clever despise them, saying that birth is not an advantage which depends on the person, but on chance. The clever honour them not because they think like the people, but by hindsight. The devout, whose zeal outruns their knowledge, despise them in spite of the consideration which wins them the good opinion of the clever because they judge them by means of a new insight which comes from their piety. But true Christians honour them because they possess another and superior form of insight. So there is an alternation of pros and cons, according to men's lights. (337)

181. *Cause and effect.* We must possess hindsight and judge everything by it, though using the same language as the people. (336)

182. *Cause and effect.* It is therefore true to say that everyone is living in a state of illusion; for though the views of the people are sound, they are not sound in their heads because they imagine that truth is to be found in places where it does not exist. There is certainly truth in their opinions, but not to the extent they imagine. It is true that we should honour the gentry, but not because birth is a practical advantage, etc. (335)

183. *Cause and effect.* Continual reversal of the pro and the con.

We have therefore shown that man is foolish on account of the importance that he attaches to inessentials; and all these opinions fall to the ground.

We went on to show that all these views were very sound, and that as all these forms of vanity have substance, the people are not as foolish as they are said to be; which means that we have demolished the view which demolished that of the people.

But we have now reached the point at which we must demolish the last proposition, and show that it remains true that the people are silly, however sound their opinions; because not seeing truth where it is, which means finding it in places where it does not exist, their views are always very unsound and very misguided. (328)

184. *Sound opinions of the people.* The greatest of evils is civil war. It becomes inevitable if we try to reward merit, because everybody thinks himself meritorious. The evil to be feared from a fool, who succeeds to a position by right of birth, is neither so great nor so certain. (313)

185. *Sound opinions of the people.* It is not altogether pointless to be well turned out; it shows that a large number of people work for you; your hair style shows that you have a valet, a perfumer, etc.; by your bands, ribbons, braid . . ., etc. Now it is not unimportant or a mere matter of outward show to have several pairs of hands at one's disposal.

The more hands you have, the stronger you are. Smartness is a sign of strength. (316)

186. *Cause and effect.* Human frailty is the source of so many things which are reputed to be beautiful, so that [not] being able to play the lute well is only regarded as a bad thing because of our weakness. (329)

187. *Cause and effect.* Lust and power are the springs of all our actions: lust leads to voluntary, power to involuntary action.

(334)

188. Why is it that a lame man does not irritate us and a lame mind does? Because a lame man recognises that we are walking straight and a lame mind says that it is we who are limping; if it were not for that, we should be sorry for him and not angry.

Epictetus asks much more forcibly: 'Why are we not angry if someone says that we have a headache and are angry if someone says that we are arguing badly or making a bad choice?'

The reason is that we are quite certain that we have no headache and that we are not lame; but we are not so certain that we are making the right choice. And since our assurance only rests on the fact that we see a thing with both eyes, when someone else sees exactly the opposite with his two eyes, we are startled and uneasy; this applies still more forcibly when a thousand other people make fun of our choice; for we are bound to prefer our own insight to that of other people, and that is a bold and difficult thing. In the case of a lame man our senses produce no such contradiction. (80)

189. Man is so made that if we are continually telling him that he is a fool, he comes to believe it; and by repeating it to himself he makes himself believe it. For when a man is alone he carries on an interior conversation with himself which should be properly controlled: *Corrumpunt mores bonos colloquia prava.*[1] We should remain silent as much as possible, and only converse with ourselves about God whom we know to be truth; and in this way convince ourselves of it. (536)

190. *Cause and effect.* Epictetus. It is not the same when people say: 'You've got a headache.' We are quite certain about the state of our health, but not about justice; and in fact his was a form of imbecility.

And yet he thought that he had proved it by saying: 'It is either in our power or it is not.' But he did not realise that it is not in our power to regulate our heart, and he was wrong to deduce that we could from the fact that there were Christians.

(467)

191. The people hold very sound views. For example:

1, in choosing amusement and hunting rather than the kill.

Small-time scholars laugh at them and boast at being able to use them to prove the folly of the world; but, for a reason that they do not grasp, the people are right;

2, in judging men by their outward appearance such as birth or wealth. The world triumphs again by showing how unreasonable it is; but it is very reasonable (cannibals laugh at a child-king);

[1] Bad company, they say, can corrupt noble minds (I Cor. xv, 33).

3, in taking offence when someone hits them, or in being so eager for fame.

But it is very desirable on account of the other essential possessions that go with it; and a man who has received a blow without taking offence is overwhelmed by insults and necessities;

4, in working for the uncertain; going on a sea-voyage; walking along a plank. (324)

192. *Justice, power.* It is right that justice should prevail; it is necessary to submit to force. Justice without power is impotent; power without justice is tyrannical. Justice without power is repudiated because there are always wicked men: power without justice is condemned. Justice and power must therefore be brought together, and to that end we must ensure that what is just is strong, or that what is strong is just.

Justice is open to dispute; power is recognisable and cannot be disputed. Thus it has not been possible to give power to justice because power has repudiated justice and declared that it was unjust, and has maintained that power itself was just. And so, being unable to ensure that what is right is strong, people have acted as though what was strong was right. (298)

193. What a great advantage there is in birth which at eighteen places a man in a good position, makes him known and respected as another man might have deserved to be at fifty. It means that you gain a start of thirty years without having to make the slightest effort. (322)

194. We are creatures of habit. Whoever grows accustomed to faith takes it for granted, cannot help being afraid of hell, and does not believe anything else. Whoever grows accustomed to believing that the king is terrible . . . etc.

Who can doubt, therefore, that our soul being accustomed to seeing number, space, movement, believes that and nothing but that? (89)

195. Montaigne is wrong: custom should be followed merely because it is custom, and not because it is reasonable or just; but the people follow it solely because they believe that it is just.

Otherwise, they would not follow it any longer even though it were custom; for we are only prepared to submit to reason or justice. Custom without them would be regarded as tyrannical, but the empire of reason and justice is no more tyrannical than that of pleasure; they are principles which are native to man.

It would therefore be a good thing to obey laws and customs because they are laws; to know that there is no true or just law to be brought in; to realise that we know nothing at all about them, and that for this reason we must simply accept those which are accepted—in this way we should never depart from them. But the people are not susceptible to this doctrine; and since they believe that truth can be discovered and that it lies in law and custom, they believe in them, and regard their antiquity as proof of their truth (and not simply as evidence of their authority without being any guarantee of their truth). For this reason the people obey them; but they are liable to revolt as soon as someone shows them that law and custom are worth nothing; which can happen with them all if they are looked at from a certain angle. (325)

196. We can only imagine Plato and Aristotle in academic garb. They were decent fellows and like the rest of us enjoyed a good laugh with their friends; and when they amused themselves by drawing up their *Laws* and their *Politics*, they regarded it as a joke; it was the least philosophical and least serious part of their lives: the most philosophical was to live simply and quietly.

If they happened to write about politics, it was with the idea of drawing up rules for running a madhouse.

And if they pretended to take it all seriously, they knew perfectly well that the madmen to whom they addressed themselves thought themselves kings and emperors. They humoured them in order to moderate their madness and keep the damage down to a minimum. (331)

197. Power and not opinion is mistress of the world. —But opinion is precisely the thing that makes use of power. — It is power that creates opinion. In our view, gentleness is a fine thing. Why? Because anyone who wants to dance on a tight

rope will find himself on his own; and I will form a more powerful group of people who will say that it is not a becoming sight. (303)

198. Justice is what is established; thus it will be taken for granted that all established laws are necessarily just simply because they are established. (312)

199. To pity the unfortunate does not in any way exclude concupiscence. On the contrary, we are very glad of the opportunity of showing friendship and winning a reputation for kindness without giving anything. (452)

200. An empire founded on opinion and imagination will last for some time, and such an empire is pleasant and easygoing; an empire founded on force will last for ever. Thus opinion is like the queen of the world, but power is its tyrant. (311)

201. *Power.* Why do we submit to the will of the majority? Is it because they have greater right on their side? No, it is because they have more power.

Why do we follow ancient laws and opinions? Is it because they are the soundest? No, it is because they are unique, and remove differences which are rooted in us. (301)

202. Once we have grown accustomed to using bad reasons in order to prove the effects of nature, we are no longer willing to accept good reasons when they are found. The example quoted is the circulation of the blood, which is used to explain why the veins swell below the ligature. (96)

203. Cromwell was on the verge of laying waste the whole of Christendom; the royal family was doomed and his own would have been installed in its place for ever, if it had not been for the tiny particle of sand which got into his bladder. Rome itself was about to succumb; but because of the tiny particle of sand that had got there, he died; his family was brought crashing down; there was peace everywhere and the king was restored. (176)

204. Since duchies and monarchies and magistracies are real and necessary because power rules everything, they are to be found in all countries at all times. But because it is only whim which makes it so, the position is not a stable one and is liable to vary, etc. (306)

205. It is amusing to think that there are people in the world who, having renounced the laws of God and nature, have created their own laws which they observe exactly, as, for example, the soldiers of Mahomet, thieves, heretics, etc. The logicians behave in exactly the same way.

It seems that their licence must be without any bounds or barriers because they have transgressed so many which are very just and very sacred. (393)

206. Time heals sorrows and quarrels because we change; we are no longer the same person. Neither the person offended nor the offender are any longer the same people that they once were. It is like a nation which we have vexed and meet again two generations later. They are still Frenchmen, but not the same Frenchmen. (122)

207. The bonds which preserve people's respect for one another are, in general, bonds of necessity; but there must be different degrees because all men wish to dominate and cannot all do so; only some of them.

Let us imagine therefore that we see the bonds beginning to form. There will undoubtedly be strife until the stronger oppress the weaker, and in the end there will be a dominant party. But when that has once been settled, then the masters, who do not wish strife to continue, give orders that the power which lies in their hands shall be passed on in the way that suits them: some leave it to the people to make their own choice; others decree that it shall be hereditary, etc.

It is at this point that imagination begins to play its part. Until then the issue was decided by power: now power is vested by imagination in a particular party: in France, in the nobility; in Switzerland, in the commoners, etc.

The bonds which attach respect to a particular individual are forged by the imagination. (304)

208. The most unreasonable things in the world become the most reasonable on account of man's unruly nature. What could be more unreasonable than to choose, as the ruler of a State, the eldest son of a queen? We do not choose, as the person best fitted to be the captain of a ship, the passenger who comes from

the best family. Such a rule would be ridiculous and unjust; but because the eldest sons of queens are and always will be chosen, the law becomes reasonable and just. For whom else could one choose? The most virtuous and the ablest? We should at once come to blows: everybody claims to be the most virtuous and the ablest. Let us therefore attach the quality to something which is beyond dispute. It is the eldest son of the king; it is as plain as a pikestaff; there can be no quarrelling. Reason could do no better because civil war is the greatest of all evils.

(320)

6. GREATNESS

209. If an animal did, by the use of its mind, what it does by instinct, and if it used its mind to say what it says by instinct at the hunt to warn its fellows that the prey was found or lost, it would also speak for things that were closer to it such as saying: 'Gnaw through this rope which is hurting me, because I can't reach it.' (342)

210. Greatness. The causes behind the effects are a sign of greatness of man, in that he has extracted from concupiscence such a noble order. (403)

211. The parakeet wipes its beak in spite of the fact that it is perfectly clean. (343)

212. What is it in us that feels pleasure? Is it our hand? Is it our arm? Is it our flesh? Is it our blood? We shall find that it must be something immaterial. (339 *bis*)

213. Against Pyrrhonism. [. . . It is therefore strange that we cannot define these things without obscuring them; we are always talking about them.] We assume that everybody regards them in the same way; but our assumption is entirely gratuitous because we have no proof. I see perfectly well that we use these words on the same occasions and that, whenever two men see a body change places, they both describe the sight of the same object by the same word when the pair of them say that it has moved; and from their use of the identical word we make a large inference about the identity of their ideas; but it is not absolutely and finally conclusive, though we may well wager on the affirmative because we know that the same conclusions are often drawn from different premisses.

That alone is sufficient to breed confusion; not that it completely extinguishes the natural insight which assures us of these things; the academicians would have laid a bet on it; but it makes the dogmatists look dim and confused to the glory of the Pyrrhonist clique, a glory which lies in that ambiguous ambiguity, and in a certain dubious obscurity from which our doubts cannot remove all the light, nor our natural lights banish all the obscurity.   (392)

214. We come to know truth not only by reason, but even more by our heart; it is through this second way that we know first principles, and reason, which has no part in it, tries in vain to undermine them. The Pyrrhonists, whose only object it is, toil away at it fruitlessly. We know that we are not dreaming; however powerless we may be to prove it by means of reason, our powerlessness demonstrates nothing except the feebleness of our reason and not, as they maintain, the uncertainty of the whole of our knowledge. For the knowledge of first principles, such as the existence of space, time, movement, number [is] just as solid as anything produced by reasoning. And reason must trust this instinctive knowledge and base all its arguments on it. [The heart is aware instinctively that space has three dimensions, and that numbers are infinite; and then reason demonstrates that there are not two square numbers, one of which is double the other. Principles are perceived by intuition; propositions are proved; and both methods lead to certainty though by different routes.] And it is just as useless and just as ridiculous for reason to demand of the heart proofs of its first principles in order to concur in them, as it would be for the heart to demand of reason an intuitive knowledge of all its propositions before accepting them.

Its powerlessness should therefore only serve to humiliate reason which would like to be judge of everything, but not to undermine our certainty, as though reason alone were capable of providing us with instruction. Would to God, on the contrary, that we never needed it and that we knew everything by intuition and reasoning! But nature has refused us this gift; so much so that it has only provided us with a very little knowledge of this kind; all the other forms can be acquired only by reasoning.

And that is why those to whom God has given religion by means of intuition are very fortunate. But [to those] who are without it, we can only give it by the use of reason while waiting for God to bestow it on them by insight, without which faith is merely human, and useless for salvation. (282)

215. I can easily imagine a man without hands, feet, head (for it is only experience which teaches us that the head is more necessary than feet). But I cannot imagine a man without thought: he would be a stone or a brute. (339)

216. Instinct and reason, signs of two natures. (344)

217. *Thinking reed.* It is not from space that I must seek my dignity, but from the control of my thought. I should not have more of it through the possession of land. By means of space the universe contains me and swallows me up like a speck; by means of thought I comprehend the universe. (348)

218. The greatness of man is great in so far as he realises that he is wretched. A tree does not know its own wretchedness.

We are therefore wretched when we know that we are wretched; but it is a sign of our greatness to know that we are wretched. (397)

219. *Immateriality of the soul.* Philosophers who have subdued their passions; what material thing has been able to do it? (349)

220. All these miseries are proofs of man's greatness. They are the miseries of a *grand seigneur*, the misfortunes of a fallen monarch. (398)

221. *The greatness of man.* The greatness of man is so evident that it can be deduced even from his wretchedness. What is natural in animals is termed wretchedness in man; from which we recognise that since his nature today resembles that of the animals, he has fallen from a better state which in former times was proper to him.

For who feels unhappy at not being king except a king who has been deposed? Did people think that Paulus-Emilius was unhappy at no longer being consul? On the contrary, they all thought that he was lucky to have been consul at all because it is not an office one holds for life. But people thought that Perseus was very unfortunate in no longer being a king because the natural thing is to be king till the end of one's life, and it seemed strange that he could bear to go on living. Who considers himself unhappy because he only possesses one mouth? And who would not be unhappy if he only possessed one eye? No one perhaps has ever taken it into his head to fret himself over not having three eyes, but a man is inconsolable if he has none.

(409)

222. Greatness of man apparent in his very concupiscence because he has found a way of extracting an admirable code from it and turning it into a veritable picture of charity.   (402)

223. *Greatness of man.* We have such a lofty idea of the soul of man that we cannot bear the idea of being despised or not being esteemed by a single soul; and the whole of human felicity depends on this esteem.   (400)

224. The heart has its reasons which are unknown to reason; we are aware of it in a thousand ways. I maintain that the heart loves the universal being naturally, and itself naturally to the extent that it gives itself to one or the other; and it hardens itself against one or other of them as it chooses. You have rejected one and kept the other: is it through reason that you love yourself?   (277)

225. It is the heart which is aware of God and not reason. That is what faith is: God perceived intuitively by the heart, not by reason.   (278)

226. Man is obviously made in order to think; it is the whole of his dignity and his merit, and his whole duty is to think as he ought. Now the order of thought is to begin with oneself, and with one's author and one's end.

What do people think about? Never about that; but about dancing, playing the lute, singing, writing verse, tilting at the ring, etc., fighting, becoming king without thinking what it means to be king, and to be man. (146)

227. Notwithstanding the spectacle of all our misfortunes, which move us, grip us by the throat, we have a feeling that we cannot repress, which elates us. (411)

228. Memory is indispensable for all the operations of reason. (369)

229. I do not admire a virtue like valour when it is pushed to excess, if I do not see at the same time the excess of the opposite virtue, as one does in Epaminondas, who displayed extreme valour and extreme benevolence. For otherwise it is not an ascent, but a fall. We do not display our greatness by placing ourselves at one extremity, but rather by being at both at the same time, and filling up the whole of the space between them. —But perhaps it is only a sudden leap of the soul from one of these extremes to the other, and it is in fact always at one point like a spark of fire.— Very well, but at least it demonstrates the agility of the soul, even if does not mark its extension. (353)

230. Liancourt's story of the pike and the frog: they are always doing it, and never in a different way, nor with any sign of possessing mental faculties. (341)

231. The calculating machine produces results which come closer to thought than anything animals can do; but it does nothing which can make us say that it possesses will-power like animals. (340)

232. *Thought.* The whole dignity of man lies in his power of thought. But what is this thought? How idiotic it is!

Thought is therefore of its very nature marvellous and incomparable. It would have to have strange faults to be despicable; but it does indeed have such faults that nothing is more ridiculous. How great it is by its nature! How base it is on account of its faults! (365)

233. Thought is the hall-mark of man's greatness. (346)

7. CONTRADICTIONS

234. Contradictions. After demonstrating the baseness and greatness of man. Let man now appreciate himself at his true worth. Let him love himself because there is in him a nature which is capable of good; but let him not on that account love the baseness which is also in him. Let him despise himself because his capacity is sterile; but let him not despise his natural capacity on those grounds. Let him hate and love himself: he possesses within himself the capacity to know truth and be happy; but he has within him no truth which is either constant or satisfying.

I would therefore implant in man the desire to find it, to be free from the thralls of passion and ready to follow truth wherever he finds it, knowing how much his knowledge is clouded by his emotions; I would that he hated concupiscence in itself which of its nature determines his actions, so that it will not blind him when he comes to make his choice, and will not hold him back when he has chosen. (423)

235. We are so presumptuous that we should like to be known all over the world, even by those who will come when we are no longer there; and so vain that we are pleased and flattered by the good opinion of half a dozen people who happen to be standing round us. (148)

236. It is dangerous to let a man see too clearly how much he has in common with the animals without at the same time making him realise his greatness. It is also dangerous to let him see his greatness too clearly without realising his baseness. It is more dangerous still to leave him in ignorance of both. But it is very advantageous to draw attention to both. (418)

237. At P.-R. Greatness and wretchedness. Since wretchedness can be deduced from greatness and greatness from wretchedness, some people have laid more stress on wretchedness because they have taken it as a proof of greatness; and since others have emphasised wretchedness all the more strongly because they have deduced it from greatness, all that has been said to demonstrate greatness has only served to induce some people to settle for wretchedness, for we are all the more wretched because we have fallen from a higher state; and others the contrary. They have both been operating in a closed circle: because it is certain that in so far as men possess insight they find both greatness and wretchedness in man. In a word, man knows that he is wretched; he is therefore wretched because he is so; but he is very great because he knows it.   (416)

238. Contradiction: contempt for our own life; die for nothing; hatred of our own life.   (157)

239. *Contradictions.* Man is naturally credulous, sceptical, timid, bold.   (125)

240. What are our natural principles if not our normal principles, and in children those which they have derived from the habits of their fathers like the habit of hunting in animals?

We know from experience that different habits will produce in us different natural principles; and if there are some which cannot be eradicated by habit, there are others that derive from habit which are contrary to nature and cannot be removed by nature, or by secondary habits. That depends on a man's character.   (92)

241. Fathers fear that the natural love of their children may vanish. What then is this nature which is likely to be obliterated?

Habit is a second nature which destroys the first. But what is nature? Why is habit not natural? I am very much afraid that nature is only a first habit, as habit is a second nature.   (93)

242. The nature of man can be considered from two points of view: one according to his end and there he is great and incomparable; the other according to opinion, as we judge the nature of the horse or the dog in a popular fashion by their speed *et animum arcendi*; and there man is abject and vile. And those are the two ways which make us judge him differently, and lead to such squabbles among the philosophers.

For one denies the supposition of the other; one says: 'He is not born for that end because all his actions are repugnant to it.' The other says: 'He moves away from his end when he is guilty of these base actions.' (415)

243. Two things teach man everything about his own nature: instinct and experience. (396)

244. *Trade. Thoughts.* All is unity, all is diversity. How many natures in that of man! And how many vocations! And what a matter of chance! Usually each of us selects the thing he has heard commended. Well turned heel. (116)

245.   If he boasts, I humiliate him,
         If he is humble, I vaunt him;
         And contradict him always,
         Until he comes to understand
         That he is an incomprehensible monster. (420)

246. The main contentions of the sceptics—I am leaving out the minor ones—are, that we cannot be certain of the truth of these principles apart from faith and revelation, except in [so far] as we feel them naturally in ourselves. Now, natural feeling is not a convincing proof of their truth because if, apart from faith, we are uncertain whether man is created by a good God, a wicked devil or by chance, we remain doubtful whether these innate principles are true, false or uncertain; the answer must depend on our origin.

What is more, apart from faith, nobody knows for certain whether he is awake or asleep, for while we are asleep we are firmly convinced that we are as wide awake as we are now; we believe that we see space, shapes and movements; we feel time passing, we measure it; in fact we behave in exactly the same way as in our waking state; so that as half our life, on our own admission, is spent in sleep in which, however it may appear to us, we have no idea of truth because all our feelings are mere illusions,—who knows if the other half of life, when we think that we are awake, is not another form of sleep which is a little different from the first from which we wake when we think that we are asleep?

[And who can doubt that, if we dreamt in company with other people, if by chance we had the same dreams, which is not uncommon, and that if we stayed awake by ourselves, we should not imagine that the roles were reversed? In short, since we often dream that we are dreaming, piling one dream upon another, is not life itself a dream on to which other dreams are grafted from which we awake at death,—a dream during which we are just as far from being in possession of the principles of the true and the good as during natural sleep; the different thoughts which agitate us being perhaps no more than illusions like the passing of time and the nebulous phantoms of our dreams?]

Such are the main contentions on both sides.

I shall leave out of account the lesser ones, such as the sceptics' pronouncements against the impressions left by habit, education, manners, countries and other things of the same kind which, though they affect the great majority of ordinary men who only dogmatise on these illusory foundations, are blown away by the lightest breath of scepticism. You have only to glance at their books if you are not already convinced; you very soon will be convinced, perhaps too much so.

I shall say something about the dogmatists' only strong point, which is that when speaking in good faith and sincerely, we cannot doubt natural principles.

The sceptics have only one objection to this: the uncertainty of our origins which includes that of our nature; to which the dogmatists have been busy replying since the world began.

So it is open warfare between men in which each of us must inevitably take sides, and throw in his lot either with the dogmatists or the sceptics. For anyone who imagines that he can remain neutral will find that he is the sceptic *par excellence*; neutrality is the fundamental tenet of the sect: whoever is not against them is well and truly for them. They are not for themselves: they are neutral, indifferent, doubting everything, including themselves.

What then shall man do in such a state of affairs? Will he doubt everything? Will he doubt whether he is awake, if someone pinches or burns him? Will he doubt whether he doubts? Will he doubt whether he exists? It is impossible to come to such a pass as that, and I take it as axiomatic that there has never been a completely dyed-in-the-wool sceptic. Nature lends its support to tottering reason and prevents it from pushing its lunacy to such lengths as that.

Will he then declare that, on the contrary, he is certainly in possession of truth—the man who when subjected to slightest pressure, is unable to appeal to any authority and is obliged to give in?

What sort of a monster then is man? What a novelty, what a portent, what a chaos, what a mass of contradictions, what a prodigy! Judge of all things, a ridiculous earthworm who is the repository of truth, a sink of uncertainty and error; the glory and the scum of the world.

Who shall unravel such a tangle?

[It is certainly beyond the powers of dogmatism and scepticism, and all human philosophy: man transcends man. Let us therefore grant to the sceptics what they have so often proclaimed: that truth is not within our reach nor is it our prey, that it does not dwell on earth, that it is the familiar of heaven, that it lodges in the bosom of God, and that it can only be known in so far as it pleases him to reveal it. Let us learn about our true nature from uncreated and incarnate truth.]

Nature confounds the sceptics, and reason confounds the dogmatists. What then will become of you, O men, who seek to discover your true condition through your natural reason? You cannot avoid one of these sects, or live with any of them.

Know then, proud man, what a paradox you are to yourself. Humble yourself, impotent reason; be silent, dull-witted nature, and learn from your master your true condition which you do not know. Listen to God.

For in the last resort, if man had never been corrupted, he would in his innocence be secure in his enjoyment of both truth and happiness; and if man had never been anything but corrupt, he would have no conception of either truth or blessedness. But, unhappy wretches that we are, and more unhappy than if there were no element of greatness in us, we have a vision of happiness and are unable to attain it; we are aware of the reality of truth and possess only the shadow: incapable alike of complete ignorance and certain knowledge, so obvious it is that we once possessed a high degree of perfection and have unhappily fallen from it!

It is an astonishing thing, however, that the mystery which is furthest removed from our knowledge—the mystery of the transmission of sin—is something without which we can have no knowledge of ourselves!

For there is no doubt that there is nothing that shocks our reason more than to say that the sin of the first man was the cause of the guilt of those who were so far from the source of infection that it seems impossible that they should have been contaminated by it. The transmission of sin seems to us not only impossible, it even seems very unjust; for what could be more contrary to the rules of our sorry justice than the eternal damnation of a child incapable of will-power for a sin in which he seems to have played so small a part, and which was committed six thousand years before he was born? Nothing, to be sure, is more of a shock to us than such a doctrine, and yet without this mystery, which is the most incomprehensible of all, we should be incomprehensible to ourselves. The tangled knot of our condition acquired its twists and turns in that abyss; so that man is more inconceivable without the mystery than the mystery is to man.

Whence it seems that God, desiring to make the mystery of our nature intelligible to us, hid the knot so high up, or better, so low down, that we are quite incapable of reaching it, so that it is not through the proud exertions of our reason, but by the simple submission of reason that we can truly come to know ourselves.

These foundations, solidly established on the inviolable authority of religion, enable us to understand that there are two truths of faith of equal permanence: one, that man in his native state, or state of grace, is raised above the whole of nature and made like God, participating in his divinity; the other, that in his state of corruption and sin he has fallen from this estate and become like the animals. These two propositions are both equally sound and certain.

Scripture declares it plainly when it states in some places: *Deliciae meae esse cum filiis hominum. Effundam spiritum meum super omnem carnem. Dii estis*, etc., and when it says in other places: *Omnis caro foenum. Homo assimilatus est jumentis insipientibus, et similis factus est illis. Dixi in corde meo de filiis hominum.*[1]

[Whence it appears clearly that, by means of grace, man is made like God and participates in his divinity, and that without grace, he resembles the beasts of the field.]   (434)

247. If man is not made for God, why is he happy only in God? If man is made for God, why is he so opposed to God?
                                                                                          (438)

248. All these contradictions, which seem to carry me further from the knowledge of any religion, are what have led me soonest to the true religion.   (424)

249. This interior war between reason and passion means that those who desired peace have divided into two sects. Some wished to renounce the passions and become gods; others wished to renounce reason and become brute-beasts (Des Barreaux). But neither have been able to do so; reason always remains, which denounces the baseness and injustice of the passions and disturbs the peace of mind of those who abandon themselves to them; and the passions are always alive in those who wish to renounce them.   (413)

250. Contradictions. Infinite wisdom and folly of religion.
                                                                                  (588 *bis*)

251. Nature [cannot] . . . [Nature has placed us so neatly in the middle state that, if we tamper with one side of the scales, we necessarily tilt the other: *Je fesons, zôa trékei*. That makes me think that there are springs in our head which are so arranged that anyone who releases one also releases its opposite.]   (70)

---

[1] And my delights were to be with the children of men (Prov. VIII, 31); I will pour out my spirit on all flesh (Joel II, 25); You are gods (Ps. XLVIII, 13); All flesh is grass (Is. XLI, 6); Man is compared to the senseless beasts, and is become like to them (Ps. XLVIII, 13); I said in my heart concerning the sons of men . . . (Eccl. III).

252. *Greatness, wretchedness.* In so far as we possess light, we discover more greatness and more baseness in man.

The common run of men.

Those who stand highest.

The philosophers.

They astonish the common run of men.

The Christians astonish the philosophers.

Who then will feel surprised to see that religion simply understands thoroughly what we recognise all the more clearly because we possess more insight? (443)

253. Internecine war in man between his reason and his passions.

If he only had reason without passions . . .

If he only had passions without reason . . .

But since he has both, he is bound to be in a state of interior conflict, because he can only be at peace with one by being at war with the other: therefore he is always divided and at odds with himself. (412)

254. The most important thing in life is the choice of a profession: it is decided by chance.

Habit produces masons, soldiers, roofers. 'He's an excellent roofer,' people say; and when talking about soldiers: 'They're completely mad,' they say; but others take a very different view: 'Nothing is great but war; the rest of mankind are rogues.' Through hearing these trades praised when we were children and all the others spoken of with contempt, we make our choice; for we are naturally inclined to love virtue and hate folly; the words themselves will be the deciding factor: we are only at fault in our application of them.

So great is the force of habit that we produce many different kinds of men out of those whom nature has simply made men.

In some parts of the country men are all masons; in others, all soldiers, etc. No doubt nature is not as methodical as that. Habit is therefore responsible because it brings pressure to bear on nature; and sometimes nature overcomes it and makes a man follow his inclination in spite of every habit, good or bad. (97)

255. Lectures on modesty are a source of pride to the vain-glorious, and humility to the humble. Thus lectures on scepticism encourage believers to lay down the law; few people speak humbly of humility; few chastely of chastity; few doubtingly of scepticism. We are nothing but lies, duplicity, contradictions; and we conceal and disguise ourselves from ourselves. (377)

256. It is natural for the mind to believe and for the will to love so that when deprived of legitimate objects they are bound to attach themselves to false. (81)

257. Man is neither angel nor beast, and it is a misfortune that whoever tries to play the angel ends by playing the beast. (358)

258. Great and small are prone to the same accidents and the same annoyances and the same passions; but one is on the rim of the wheel, the other near the hub, and therefore less disturbed by the same movements. (180)

259. We should fear death when we are out of danger, and not when we are exposed to it; for we must be men. (215)

260. Scripture contains passages which are intended to console people of all conditions, and to frighten people of all conditions.

Nature seems to have accomplished the same result with its two infinites, natural and moral: for there will always be higher and lower, more and less astute, people who are more elevated and more wretched, in order to lower our pride and raise us from our state of abjection. (532)

261. If we dreamt about the same thing every night, it would affect us as much as the things we see every day. And if an artisan were certain to dream for twelve hours every night that he was king, I think that he would be almost as happy as a king who dreamt for twelve hours every night that he was an artisan.

If we dreamt every night that we were pursued by enemies and harassed by these painful phantoms, and that we spent every day in different occupations as when we go on a journey, we should suffer almost as much as though it were real, and we should be as afraid of going to sleep as we are of waking up when we apprehend that we are really going to become involved in such misfortunes. And, indeed, it would be nearly as painful as the reality.

But because dreams are all different and a single dream undergoes variations, what we see in them affects us far less than what we see when we are awake on account of its continuity, though it is not so continuous or so smooth that it does not change too; but except on rare occasions as, for example, when we are travelling, it changes less abruptly than dreams; and then we say to ourselves: 'I must be dreaming'; for life is slightly less fickle than our dreams. (386)

262. Nature possesses forms of perfection in order to show that it is the image of God, and faults to show that it is only his image. (580)

263. Men, not being accustomed to create merit but only to reward it where they find it already in existence, judge God by themselves. (490)

264. [A single thought occupies our minds; we cannot think about two things at the same time: this is a piece of good fortune for us in the eyes of the world, but not in the eyes of God.] (145)

8. DIVERSIONS

265. Diversion. If man were happy he would be all the happier if he amused himself less, like the saints and God. —Yes, but is not the pleasure we derive from amusements a way of being happy? —No, because they come from somewhere else and from outside us; which means that man is dependent and nevertheless exposed to a thousand accidents that inevitably lead to affliction. (170)

266. . . . Notwithstanding these miseries he wants to be happy, and only to be happy, and cannot wish not to be happy, but how is he to set about it? In order to make a good job of it, he would have to make himself immortal, but since he is unable to do so, he tries to stop thinking about it. (169)

267. *Diversion.* Since they are unable to cure death, misery, ignorance, men imagine that they can find happiness by not thinking about such things. (168)

268. I feel that it would have been possible for me not to have existed because the essence of the self lies in thought; thus I who think might not have existed if my mother had been killed before giving me life; therefore I am not a necessary being. I am not therefore eternal or infinite; but I see clearly that in nature there is a being who is necessary, eternal and infinite.   (469)

269*. Diversion. Sometimes when I have sat down and thought about the fuss and worry of men's lives, the perils and hardships to which they are exposed at the court and in war, which are the source of so many quarrels, so much violence, bold and often evil adventures, etc., I have often felt that men's unhappiness is due solely to the fact that they are incapable of sitting down quietly in a room and relaxing. If he were capable of staying at home and enjoying it, a man who has enough to live on would not abandon his home in order to go on a sea voyage or take part in the siege of a fortified city. We only pay a high price for a commission in the army because we find it intolerable not to leave town; and we only look round for people to talk to and compete against one another at games because we are incapable of deriving any pleasure from staying quietly at home.

But when I thought about it with more concentration, when I had arrived at the source of all our misfortunes, and wanted to discover the reason, I came across a very convincing one: it lies in the natural misfortune of our feeble and mortal state which is so wretched that when we give it serious thought, nothing can console us for it.

Whatever position we imagine for ourselves, and if we allow our minds to dwell on all the good things that it is possible to possess, royalty remains the finest position in the world; and yet, if we picture a man occupying it with all the good things that go with it, if he is without any form of amusement and is left to think about himself and his position, the tepid satisfaction that he derives from it will not be sufficient to keep him going; he will of necessity brood over the opinions which are a threat to his office, the revolts which may occur, death and sickness which are inevitable; with the result that if he is without what is known as amusements he will be unhappy and [more] unhappy than the least of his subjects who plays and amuses himself.

[Men's sole good therefore lies in the discovery of some form of distraction which will stop them from thinking about their condition; some business which takes their minds off it; some novel and agreeable pursuit which keeps them occupied, such as gambling, hunting, or an entertaining show: in a word, what is known as amusement.]

That is why gambling, women's conversation, war, great positions, are so sought after. It is not, indeed, because they bring happiness, or because anyone imagines that true bliss lies in the possession of the money that you may win at cards or in the hare that you hunt: we wouldn't accept them if someone made us a present of them. We do not seek the soft and easy life, which leaves us time to brood over our unhappy lot, the hazards of war, or the labour which goes with high office; we seek the fuss and flurry which stop us from brooding and keep us amused.

That is the reason why we prefer the hunt to the kill.

That is why men are so fond of din and disturbance; why imprisonment is such a frightful punishment; why the pleasures of solitude are something incomprehensible; why the best thing of all about being a king is that people spend their time trying to entertain him and organising an unending round of pleasure for him.

The king is surrounded by people whose only task is to keep the king amused, and prevent him from thinking about himself. For king though he be, he is unhappy the moment he begins to think about himself.

That is all that men have been able to devise to make themselves happy. Those who use it as a pretext to play the philosopher, and think that it is very unreasonable of people to spend the whole day chasing a hare that they would not have bothered to buy, have a poor knowledge of human nature. The hare would be no guarantee against the spectacle of death and unhappiness; but the hunt, which takes our mind off them, is.

The advice given to Pyrrhus, to enjoy the rest that he was seeking through so much labour, created many difficulties.

[To tell a man to live quietly is the same as telling him to live happily; it is to advise him to live in a state which is completely happy and which he can think over at leisure without coming across anything to distress him; it is the equivalent of [advising] him . . . It means that those who give it do not understand human nature.

[Therefore, men who are naturally aware of their condition avoid rest like the plague; there is nothing that they will not do in order to find something to fret about. It is not that they are without the instinct which tells them that true blessedness . . . The vanity, the pleasure of showing it to others.

[Thus it is a mistake to blame them; there is nothing wrong in seeking excitement provided that it is only regarded as a distraction; what is wrong is that they seek it as though possession of the things they seek would make them truly happy, and it is in this respect that we are right in taxing their search with futility; so that, taken all round, those who blame and those who are blamed do not understand man's true nature.]

If, therefore, when we criticised them on the grounds that what they pursued with such relish would be totally unable to satisfy them, they had replied, as they should, if they had given the matter serious thought, that they were simply seeking violent headstrong action which would take their minds off themselves, and that it was for this reason that they chose a charming and attractive object which draws them rapturously towards it, their adversaries would have no answer. But they do not give this answer because they do not know themselves. It does not occur to them that it is only the pursuit and not the kill which they are after.

Dancing: we have to think carefully where we are going to put our feet. —The country gentleman sincerely believes that hunting is a great and royal sport: but that is not the view of his huntsman.

They imagine that if they had been given the appointment, they would have proceeded to enjoy a rest; they are quite una-

ware how insatiable their greed is. They sincerely believe that
they are seeking rest when in fact all they want is turmoil.

They possess a secret sense which impels them to seek amusement or occupation outside themselves and comes from the
consciousness of their perpetual unhappiness; they have another
secret sense which is a legacy of the greatness of our first nature
and brings with it the realisation that happiness is to be found
only in repose and not in turmoil; and through these two conflicting senses they come to formulate a confused plan which
lies hidden from their sight in the depths of their soul, which
leads them to seek repose through turmoil, and to imagine always that the contentment which is lacking will come to them if,
by overcoming one or two obstacles, they succeed in opening
the door to repose.

That is how the whole of our life slips away. We seek repose
by battling against a few obstacles; and if we overcome them,
repose becomes unbearable because of the boredom it generates.
We have to get away from it and go round begging for excitement. No state is pleasant without fun and noise, and every state
is agreeable in which we can enjoy some sort of distraction. But
think what sort of a happiness it is that consists in being diverted
from thinking about ourselves!

For we either think of the miseries which are ours, or of those
which threaten us. And even if we found ourselves adequately
protected all round, boredom would, of its own accord, soon
come welling up from the depths of our heart, where it has its
natural roots, and fill the mind with its poison.

Thus man is so wretched that, owing to his peculiar disposition, he would still be bored even if he had no cause for boredom; and he is so frivolous that though he has scores of genuine
reasons for unhappiness, the smallest thing like a game of
billiards or hitting a ball is sufficient to take his mind off them.

'But,' you will ask, 'what is the object of it all?' It is to be
able to boast tomorrow among friends that he has played better
than someone else. Thus other people sit sweating in their
studies in order to convince scholars that they have solved a
problem of algebra which no one before them had been able to

solve; and so many others expose themselves to the direst perils in order to be able to boast later on of some position that they have captured, and in my opinion they are just as stupid.

Finally, others still wear themselves out by poring over such subjects, not in order to become wiser, but simply to show that they know, and they are the most foolish of the lot because they are aware of their foolishness, whereas we may think that the rest might cease being foolish if they realised their folly.

So-and-so gets through life without boredom by gambling a little every day. Give him the same amount of money every morning that he is likely to win during the day's play on condition that he does not gamble, and you will make him thoroughly unhappy. It will perhaps be said that he only cares about the fun of gambling and not about his winnings. But make him play for nothing; he will not get any excitement out of it at all and will merely be bored. This means that he is not looking for entertainment alone: a vapid amusement which rouses no passion will weary him. He must grow excited and fool himself into believing that he would be delighted to win the money that he would hate to be given to him on condition that he does not gamble, so that he can find something that rouses his passion, that he can use to excite his desires, his wrath, his fear of the object that he has constructed, like children who are frightened of a face which they have blackened.

How does it happen that a man who has lost his only son a few months ago, who is overwhelmed by lawsuits and disputes, was worried about them this morning and now no longer gives them a thought? Do not be surprised: he is completely absorbed in trying to decide which way the game will come that his dogs have been pursuing with such ardour for the past six hours. Nothing further is necessary. No matter how unhappy he is, if we can persuade him to take up some pastime man will be happy as long as the game lasts; and no matter how happy he is, unless his mind is occupied by some passion or pastime which keeps away boredom, he will soon become gloomy and wretched.

Without amusements, there is no joy; with amusements there is no sadness. And it is that, too, which creates the happiness of people of high estate, because they have a number of persons who are busy entertaining them, and they have the means of remaining in that state.

Take care. What does being a superintendent of finance, a chancellor, a judge mean, except that from morning to night a large number of people come from all over the place and do not leave them a single hour of the day in which they can brood about themselves? And when they are disgraced and banished to their country houses, where they have plenty of money and servants to minister to their needs, they soon become lonely and unhappy because there is no one at hand to prevent them from thinking about themselves. (139)

270. Diversion. Is not the prestige of royalty great enough in itself to make its possessor happy by the mere contemplation of what he is? Must he be prevented from thinking about himself like ordinary men? I realise that we make a man happy by taking his mind off his domestic worries and encouraging him to concentrate on becoming a good dancer. But will it be the same with a king? Will he be a happier man because he devotes his mind to frivolous occupations rather than to his own greatness? And what more satisfying object could be found for his mind? Would it not spoil his pleasure to concentrate on keeping time to a tune, or the skilful placing of a [ball] instead of enjoying the peaceful contemplation of the splendour and majesty that surround him? Let someone put it to the test: let him leave the king all by himself without anything to occupy him, without a care in his head, without company, so that he can think about himself at leisure; and we shall see that a king without pastimes is a man bowed down by misery. For this reason people are careful to avoid doing it; they go out of their way to ensure that kings are surrounded by a crowd of people whose job it is to see that amusements follow business and who devote their leisure to devising pastimes and games, so that there is no vacuum; that is to say, that they are surrounded by people who take marvellously good care to see that the king is not left alone to brood, knowing very well that, king though he be, he will be wretched if he does.

In saying this, I am not speaking of Christian kings in so far as they are Christians, but only in so far as they are kings. (142)

271. *Diversion.* It is easier to accept death without thinking about it than the idea of death when we are in no danger of dying.

(166)

272. *Diversion.* Men are responsible from childhood for preserving their honour, their wealth, their friends, and also the wealth and honour of their friends. They are overburdened with business, with the study of languages and exercises; they are made to understand that they could not expect to be happy unless their health, their honour, their wealth and that of their friends are in good shape, and that the lack of a single thing would make them unhappy. Thus they are given positions and employment which harass them from morning till night. 'That,' you will say, 'is a strange way of making them happy! What could be better calculated to make them unhappy?' 'What are you talking about! What else could one do?' It would merely be necessary to relieve them of all these cares; for then they would see themselves in their true colours, brood over the sort of people they were, whence they came and whither they were going; and so one cannot do too much to occupy them and take their minds off such things. And that is why, when so much has been found for them to do, if they have a short respite, they are advised to spend it amusing themselves, in gambling, and keeping themselves always fully occupied.

How hollow is the heart of man and how full of vileness!

(143)

273. *Excitement.* When a soldier complains of the hardness of his lot, or a labourer, etc., leave them with nothing to do. (130)

274. Without examining all the different occupations in detail, it is sufficient to include them all under the heading of distractions. (137)

275. [Why is it that a man, who is so grief-stricken over the

death of his wife and only son, who has an important lawsuit on his hands which is worrying him, is not sad at the moment, and appears to be completely free from all painful and disturbing thoughts? We must not be surprised; someone has just served a ball to him and he has to return it; he is busy taking it in order to win the game, when the roof collapses; how do you expect him to think about his business when he has this other matter to attend to? There's something that is worthy of occupying this great soul, and blotting out every other thought from his mind. This man was born to know the universe, to be judge of all things, to rule over a whole State, and yet we see him entirely taken up with the business of coursing a hare! And if he does not stoop to this and wants always to be upright, the more fool he, because he will be trying to raise himself above humanity though in the last resort he is only a man, that is to say, capable of little and much, of everything and nothing: he is neither angel nor beast, but man.] (140)

276. There is nothing we enjoy more than the struggle, but we do not care a fig for victory: we like to see battles between animals, not the victor flinging himself passionately on the vanquished. What would there be left for us to wish for except the end of the victory? And as soon as it comes, we are intoxicated with it. It is the same with gambling, with the search for truth. During an argument, we enjoy watching the clash of different opinions; but as for contemplating the truth which emerges from the encounter—not much; in order to enjoy it, we must see it actually emerge from the debate. It is the same with the passions: it is pleasant to see two opposing passions come into collision; but when one of them is the master, it becomes a mere exhibition of brutality. We never seek things, but the pursuit of things. At the theatre we care nothing for tranquil scenes which are devoid of pity or terror, or extremes of unhappiness without hope, or brutal love affairs, or the harsh measures which follow. (135)

277. Men are naturally roofers and can turn their hand to any job except when they are alone in their room. (138)

9. PHILOSOPHERS

278.* Even if Epictetus had seen the path perfectly clearly, he would still have said to mankind: 'You're on the wrong track'; he shows that there is another, but does not tell us how to get there. It is to will what God wills; Jesus Christ alone can lead us to it: *Via, veritas*.

 The vices of Zeno himself.   (466)

279. *Philosophers*. A fine thing to yell at a man who does not even know himself to find the way to God alone! And a fine thing to say it to a man who does know himself!   (509)

280. [*Against the philosophers who believe in God without Jesus Christ.*]

 Philosophers. They believe that God alone is worthy to be loved and admired, and have themselves desired to be loved and admired of men; they are not aware of their own corruption. If they are filled with a desire to love and worship him and find their principal delight in him, let them feel pleased with themselves, and good luck to them! But if they are repelled by it all, if their one aim is simply to make men think well of them and if their idea of perfection is simply to make men think (though without forcing them) that happiness is to be found in liking them, then I declare that this form of perfection is horrible. What! they have come to know God and have not been moved solely by the desire that men should love him, but that men should stop short at them! They have desired to be the object of men's unthinking delight!   (463)

281. *Philosophers*. We are full of things which take us out of ourselves.

 Our instinct makes us feel that we must seek our happiness outside ourselves. Our inclinations drive us outwards even in the absence of any object calculated to excite them. External objects are in themselves a temptation to us and lure us on even when we are not thinking about them. And the philosophers are wasting their time when they say: 'Go back into yourselves; you will find the good life there.' We do not believe them; and those who do believe them are the emptiest and silliest of all. (464)

282. What the Stoics propose is so difficult and so futile!

The Stoics say: All those who have not reached the highest degree of wisdom are just as foolish and vicious as those who stand in two inches of water. (360)

283. The three forms of concupiscence have created three sects, and the philosophers have done nothing but indulge in one of these three forms. (461)

284. *Stoics.* They believe that we can always do what we can sometimes do, and that since the desire for fame makes those whom it possesses do something well, the others will be able to do it too. They are feverish impulses which good health cannot reproduce.

Epictetus infers from the fact that there are some devout Christians, that each of us can very well be devout. (350)

285. The philosophers did not prescribe sentiments which were in keeping with the two states.

They inspired a sense of undiluted greatness, and that is not man's estate.

They inspired a sense of undiluted lowliness, and that is not man's estate either.

A sense of lowliness and humility is necessary but it should be the result of penance and not of natural feeling; not in order that we may cling to it, but in order that we may achieve a sense of greatness. A sense of greatness is necessary, but it should be due to grace and not to a belief in our own merit; it should follow from the sense of our own lowliness. (525)

286. The Stoics say: 'Go back into yourselves; it is there that you will find peace.' It is not true.

Others say: 'Go out of yourselves: seek happiness by amusing yourselves.' And that is not true. We are a prey to disease.

Happiness is neither outside nor inside us; it is in God, and outside and inside us. (465)

287*. Instinct. Reason. There is an incapacity to prove things which is impervious to all forms of dogmatism. We have an idea of truth which is impervious to scepticism. (395)

288. Falseness of philosophers who did not discuss the immortality of the soul. Falsity of their dilemma in Montaigne. (220)

289. *Scepticism.* The man of extreme views is accused of foolishness which is regarded as the supreme weakness. Nothing is good but mediocrity. This has been settled by the majority which goes for anyone who escapes it, whichever end he chooses for his escape. I shall not insist on the point; I am perfectly content to find myself classed with the mediocre, and refuse to be placed at the bottom end, not because it is low, but because it is the end; for I should refuse equally to be placed at the top. We separate ourselves from humanity if we diverge from the mean.

The greatness of the human spirit lies in being able to stay there; so far from its being a sign of greatness to separate ourselves from humanity, greatness lies in not being separated from it. (378)

290. [I spent a great part of my life in the belief that justice existed; and in that I was not mistaken; for there is justice according as God has chosen to reveal it to us. But I did not look at it in this way, and that was my mistake; because I believed that our justice was essentially just, and that I was in a position to know and pronounce upon it. But I so often found myself lacking in right judgement that I ended by coming to distrust myself and others. I have seen all countries and men changing; and so, after many changes of opinion about the nature of true justice, I came to realise that our nature was simply a process of unending change, and I have not altered my mind since; and if I did, I should merely confirm my own opinion.

The sceptical Arcesilaus who reverted to dogmatism.] (375)

291. [It may be that there are genuine demonstrations; but it is not at all certain. Thus, it proves nothing except that it is not certain that everything is uncertain, to the glory of scepticism.] (387)

292. It cannot be doubted that the mortality or immortality of the soul makes a vital difference to morality. And yet philosophers have worked out their moral systems independently of it: they deliberate in order to pass the time.

Plato, for preparing people for Christianity. (219)

293. All their principles are true whether they are Pyrrhonists, stoics or atheists, etc. But their conclusions are false because the opposite principles are also true. (394)

294. *Conversation.* Big words: religion—I deny it.

Conversation. Scepticism serves the cause of religion. (391)

295. Scepticism is true. For, after all, before Jesus Christ men did not know where they stood, nor whether they were great or small. And those who said one thing or the other knew nothing about it; they guessed without using their reason and relied on chance; and what is more, they were always wrong because they excluded one or the other.

Quod ergo ignorantes quaeritis, religio annuntiat vobis.[1] (432)

296. Scepticism spells obstinacy. (51)

297. Descartes useless and unreliable. (78)

298. *Scepticism.* Everything to do with it is partly true and partly false. Essential truth is not like that; it is completely pure and completely true. A mixture dishonours and destroys it. Nothing is pure truth; with the result that nothing is true if we understand it in the sense of pure truth. It will be argued that it is true that homicide is a bad thing; yes, because we are well acquainted with the bad and the false. But what can we describe as absolutely good? Chastity? I reply that it is not because it would bring the world to an end. Marriage? No. Continence is better. Not to kill? No, because the disorders would be appalling and the wicked would kill the good. To kill? No, because it destroys nature. We only enjoy partial possession of the true and the good, which are mixed with the bad and the false. (385)

[1] What therefore you worship, without knowing it, that I preach to you (Acts XVII, 23).

10. THE SOVEREIGN GOOD

299. The sovereign good. Argument about the sovereign good. Ut sis contentus temetipso et ex te nascentibus bonis.[1] There is a contradiction in it, for in the end they advise you to kill yourself. Oh, what a happy life from which we deliver ourselves as though it were the plague! (361)

300. Second part. That without faith man cannot come to a knowledge of true good, or justice. All men seek happiness; there are no exceptions; however different the means used, they all tend towards this goal. What makes some men go to war and others not is the same desire, which is common to both of them, and is prompted by different views. The will never makes the slightest move except in the direction of this object. It is the impulse behind all human actions, even those of men who go and hang themselves.

And yet for so many years no one without the faith has ever reached the point at which all are constantly aiming. All lament: princes, subjects, nobles, commoners; old, young; strong, weak; learned men, ignorant men; the healthy, the sick; from all countries, at all times, at every age and all conditions.

An ordeal which has been so protracted, so unremitting, so unchanging, should certainly convince us of our powerlessness to reach the good by our own efforts; but we profit little from examples. They are never so completely alike that there is not some very slight difference; that is why on each occasion we are sure that our hopes will not be disappointed as they were on the previous one. And so, since the present never satisfies us, experience tricks us and leads us from one misfortune to the next until we reach death, which is the crowning misfortune.

[1] In order that you may find satisfaction within yourself and in the good things which proceed from you (Sen. *Ep.* xx).

What then are avidity and impotence crying out to us if not that in other days true happiness existed for man, that all that remains of it is man's empty shell which he is trying in vain to fill up with anything that comes to hand, seeking from absent things the help that he does not obtain from present things; but they are equally incapable of helping him because the bottomless gulf can only be filled by an infinite unchanging object, that is to say by God himself?

He alone is man's true good; and since man has abandoned him, there is, strange to say, nothing in nature which has been able to take his place: stars, sky, earth, elements, plants, cabbages, leeks, animals, insects, calves, serpents, fever, pest, war, famine, vices, adultery, incest. And since he lost the true good, everything may appear to him to be equally the true good down to his own destruction, though it is contrary to the law of God, to reason and to nature all in one.

Some seek true good in authority, others in scientific research or in sensual delight. Others still, who in fact have come closer to it, have thought that the universal good, which all men desire, is not to be found in particular objects, which can only be possessed by a single person, and which once they are shared cause the possessor more distress by their incompleteness than the satisfaction which comes from the enjoyment of what really does belong to him. They have realised that the true good must be such that all could possess it at the same time without diminution and without envy, and that no one could lose it against his will. And after arguing that since this desire is natural to man because it is necessarily in all of us, and because he cannot be without it, they go on to conclude . . .

(425)

301. Since the loss of true nature, everything becomes its own nature; just as true good being lost, everything becomes its own true good. (426)

302. The God of Christians is a God who makes the soul feel that he is its only good, that its whole peace lies in him, that it will only find joy in loving him; and at the same time makes it abhor the obstacles which hold it back and prevent it from loving God with all its strength: self-love and sensual pleasure, which stop it, are intolerable to it. God makes it feel that there is still a residue of self-love in it and that he alone can cure it. (544)

303. For the philosophers, two hundred and eighty sovereign goods. (74 *bis*)

304. *Ex senatus-consultis et plebiscitis scelera exercentur*. Sen.

Nihil tam absurde dici potest quod non dicatur ab aliquo philosophorum. Divin.

Quibusdam destinatis sententiis consecrati quae non probant coguntur defendere. Cic.

Ut omnium rerum sic litterarum quoque intemperantia laboramus. Senec.

Id maxime quemque decet, quod est cuiusque suum maxime. Sen.

Hos natura modos primum dedit. Georg.

Paucis opus est litteris ad bonam mentem.

Si quando turpe non sit, tamen non est non turpe quum id a multitudine laudetur.

Mihi sic est, tibi ut opus facto, fac. Ter.[1] (363)

305. *Search for the true good*. The common run of men believe that the good lies in wealth and in material possessions, or at least in amusements. The philosophers have demonstrated the vanity of it all, and have placed it where they could. (462)

306. It is a good thing to be worn out and exhausted by the unsuccessful pursuit of true good in order to hold out one's arms to the Saviour. (422)

---

[1] It is in virtue of the senatus-consultus and plebiscites that crimes are committed.

There is nothing so absurd that it has not been said by one philosopher or another.

Committed to certain settled opinions they are forced to defend what they do not approve.

We suffer from an excess of literature as from any other form of excess.

What suits each of us best is what is most natural to him.

Nature first of all imposed on them these limits.

It does not require very much literature to form a good mind.

A thing which is not shameful in itself becomes so when it is approved by the masses.

That is what I do with it; you do as you think best.

307. Those who, when things go wrong, are always full of hope and rejoice over strokes of good fortune, if they are not equally downcast by misfortune, are suspected of being glad because the deal has gone wrong; they are overjoyed at discovering excuses for hoping in order to show that they are concerned over the outcome, and to conceal by their pretended satisfaction the real satisfaction they feel at seeing that the deal has fallen through.   (182)

308. . . . But it is impossible that God should ever be the end unless he is the beginning. We turn our eyes upwards, but build our foundations on sand: the earth will give way, and we shall fall with our eyes gazing up to heaven.   (488)

11. AT PORT-ROYAL

309. At P.-R. (*Beginning, after explaining incomprehensibility.*)

The greatness and wretchedness of man are so evident that true religion must necessarily teach us both that there is some deeply-rooted principle of greatness in man, and that there is also a deeply-rooted principle of wretchedness.

It must go on to explain the reasons for these astonishing contradictions.

In order to make man happy religion must show him that there is a God; that we are bound to love him; that our true happiness lies in being in him, and that our only sorrow is to be separated from him; must recognise that we are filled with darkness which prevents us from knowing and loving God; and that since our duty impels us to love God and our concupiscence turns us away from him, we are full of injustice. It must explain the reasons for our opposition to God and to our own good. It must provide us with a remedy for our infirmity and the means of obtaining it. Let us examine all the religions of the world from this point of view and see whether there is any other except the Christian religion which satisfies these conditions.

Shall we find it in the philosophers who offer us, as our sole good, those forms of good that are within us? Is that the true good? Have they found the remedy for our ills? Is the cure for man's presumption to place him on the same level as God? Have those who reduce us to the level of animals, have the Mahommedans, who offer us the pleasures of the world as the sole good, even in eternity, found the cure for our sensual appetites? What religion then will teach us how to cure pride and lust? What religion, in short, will teach us the nature of our good, our duty, the weaknesses that deflect us from them, the cause of those weaknesses, the remedies that may cure them, and the means of obtaining those remedies?

All the other religions have failed to do it. Let us see what the wisdom of God will do.

'Do not expect, O men,' it says, 'either truth or comfort from men. I am that which created you, and alone can tell you who you are. But you are now no longer in the state in which I created you. I created man holy, innocent, perfect; I filled him with light and intelligence; I showed him my glory and my wonders. The eye of man then beheld the majesty of God. He was not at that time surrounded by the darkness which blinds him or the victim of mortality and wretchedness which afflict him. But he was unable to bear so much glory without giving way to presumption. He wanted to be his own centre and to be independent of my help. He withdrew from my dominion; and when he made himself equal to me by his desire to find his happiness in himself, I abandoned him to his own devices; and calling on the creatures who had been placed under him to rebel against him I turned them into his enemies; so that today man has become like the beasts and so far removed from me that he scarcely retains even a confused image of his author: to such an extent has his knowledge been extinguished or dimmed! The senses, which are independent of reason and often its masters, have snatched him away in the pursuit of pleasure. All creatures are a source of temptation or affliction; tyrants who reduce him by force or seduce him by gentleness, which is a much more terrible and more damaging form of enslavement.

'That is the state of men today. There remains in them some faint desire for happiness, which is a legacy of their first nature, and they are plunged into the miseries of their blindness and lust, which have become a second nature to them.

'From this principle which I am revealing to you, you can recognise the cause of so many contradictions which have been a source of bewilderment to all mankind, and which have awakened in them such mixed feelings. Observe now all the stirrings of greatness and glory which the ordeal of so many miseries cannot stifle, and see whether the cause may not lie in another nature.'

At Port-Royal for tomorrow (Prosopopoeia). 'It is in vain, O men, that you seek within yourselves the cure for your miseries. All your insight only leads you to the knowledge that it is not in yourselves that you will discover the true and the good. The philosophers promised them to you, and have not been able to keep their promise. They do not know what your true good is, or what your true state is. How should they have provided you with a cure for ills which they have not even understood? Your principal maladies are pride, which cuts you off from God; sensuality, which binds you to the earth; and they have done nothing but foster at least one of these maladies. If they have given you God for your object, it has only been to pander to your pride: they have made you think that you were like him and resembled him by your nature. And those who have grasped the vanity of such a pretention have cast you down into the other abyss by making you believe that your nature was like that of the beasts of the field, and have led you to seek your good in lust, which is the lot of the animals.

'That is not the way to cure you of your evil doing which was unknown to these sages. I alone can make you understand who you are, to . . .'

Adam, Jesus Christ.

If you are one with God, it is through grace, not nature.

If you have been humbled, it is through penance, not nature.

Thus, this dual capacity . . .

You are not in the state in which you were created.

Since these two states have once been revealed, it is impossible for you not to recognise them.

Follow your own impulses, observe yourselves, and see if you do not find the living characteristics of these two natures in you.

Are so many contradictions to be found in a simple subject?

'Incomprehensible?' 'Everything that is incomprehensible nevertheless exists. Infinite number. An infinite space equal to a finite space.'

'Unbelievable that God should unite himself to us?'——This opinion is simply derived from the spectacle of our baseness. But if you hold it sincerely, push it as far as I do, and realise that we are in fact so low that we are incapable of discovering for ourselves whether his mercy can make us capable of knowing him. For I should like to know what gives this creature, which realises that it is so weak, the right to measure the mercy of God and impose whatever limits on it that fancy suggests. He has so little idea of what God is that he does not know what he himself is; and thoroughly upset as he is by the sight of his own state, he has the audacity to declare that God cannot make him capable of communion with him.

But I should like to ask him whether God expects anything else of him except that he should love him and know him; and why he thinks that God is unable to make himself known and the object of love since man is by nature capable of loving and knowing. There is no doubt that he knows this at least: that he is and that he loves something. Therefore, if he sees something in the darkness in which he is plunged, and if he finds some object of love among the things of the earth, why, if God reveals to him some glimmer of his essence, should he not be capable of knowing and loving him in the manner in which it pleases God to communicate himself to us? Although it seems to be based on an apparent humility, there is therefore an intolerable presumption in this type of argument which is neither sincere nor reasonable unless it forces us to admit that, not knowing of ourselves who we are, we can only learn it from God.

'I do not mean you to submit and believe in me without a reason, and I do not claim the right to reduce you by force. Nor do I claim to explain the reasons for everything. And in order to reconcile these contradictions, I intend to show you clearly, by unassailable proofs, by signs of divinity in me, which will convince you of the fact that I exist, and invest me with authority by wonders and proofs which you cannot reject; and that afterwards I intend you to believe the things which I teach you when you find no other reason for rejecting them except that you cannot know of yourself whether they exist or not.

'God wished to redeem mankind and open the way of salvation to those who sought it. But men have shown themselves so unworthy of it, that it is right that God should refuse to some on account of the hardness of their hearts, what he grants to others by a mercy to which they are not entitled. If he had wished to overcome the stubbornness of the most hardened of them, he could have done so by revealing himself so openly to them that they would not have been able to doubt the truth of his existence, as it will appear on the last day with such a blaze of lightning and such an upheaval of nature that the dead will rise and the blindest will see him for themselves.

'It is not in this manner that he chose to appear in the gentleness of his coming; because since so many men had become unworthy of his clemency, he wished them to suffer the privation of the good that they did not want. It would not have been right therefore for him to appear in a way that was plainly divine and absolutely bound to convince all mankind; but it was not right either that he should come in a manner so hidden that he could not be recognised by those who sought him sincerely. He chose to make himself perfectly knowable to them; and thus, wishing to appear openly to those who seek him with all their heart, and hidden from those who flee him with all their heart, he tempered the knowledge of himself, with the result that he has given signs of himself which are visible to those who seek him, and not to those who do not seek him.

'There is light enough for those who desire only to see, and darkness enough for those of a contrary disposition.'   (430)

310. Instead of complaining that God has hidden himself, you must thank him for revealing so much of himself; and you must thank him again for not revealing himself to the proud and the wise who are unworthy to know so holy a God.

There are two kinds of people who know: those who are humble of heart and love lowliness however high or low their degree of intellect; or those who have sufficient intelligence to perceive truth, whatever opposition they encounter. (288)

311. When we want to think of God, is there nothing which distracts us, tempts us to think about other things? It is all bad and is native to us. (478)

312. Man does not know what rank to claim for himself. He is plainly bewildered, and falls from his true position without being able to find it again. He seeks it everywhere, humbly and uneasily, in the impenetrable darkness which surrounds him.
(427)

313. It is untrue that we deserve to be loved by other people; it is unjust that we should desire it. If we were born reasonable and detached people, knowing ourselves and others, we should not give this twist to our will. We are born with it, however; we are therefore born unjust, for everything tends towards itself. It is contrary to all order; we must tend towards the general; and the inclination towards oneself is the beginning of every sort of disorder; in war, in policy, in economy, in the body of the individual man. The will is therefore depraved.

If the members of natural and civil communities tend towards physical well-being, the communities themselves must tend towards another and more general body of which they are members. We must therefore tend towards the general. We are therefore born unjust and depraved. (477)

No religion except ours has taught that man is born in sin; none of the philosophical sects has admitted it: none therefore has spoken the truth.

No sect or religion has always been on earth except the Christian religion. (606)

314. Let us imagine a number of men in irons, and all condemned to death, some of whom are slaughtered each day in the sight of the others, so that the survivors see their own state in that of their fellows, and, looking at one another in sorrow and without hope, await their turn. It is the image of the human condition. (199)

315. It therefore follows that everything speaks to man of his condition, but he must understand it correctly: for it is not true that everything reveals God, and it is not true that everything conceals the presence of God. But it is true that he hides himself from those who tempt him, and that he reveals himself to those who seek him because men are at one and the same time unworthy and capable of God: unworthy on account of their corruption, capable in virtue of their first nature. (557)

316. What conclusion shall we draw from all our darkness except our unworthiness? (558)

317. If there had been no mystery, man would not be aware of his corruption; if there were no light, man would not expect any remedy. Thus it is not merely right, but useful for us that God should be partly hidden and partly revealed because it is equally dangerous for man to know God without being aware of his own wretchedness, and to be aware of his own wretchedness without knowing God. (586)

318. The conversion of the heathen was reserved for the grace of the Messiah only. The Jews had struggled against them for a long time without success: everything that had been said of them by Solomon and the prophets had proved a waste of time. The sages like Plato and Socrates could not convince them.
(769)

319. If nothing of God had been revealed, our eternal privation would have been equivocal, and might just as well be attributable to the absence of any divinity as to man's unworthiness to know it; but the fact that he reveals himself sometimes though not always removes any form of ambiguity. If he reveals himself once, he is always there; so that we can only conclude that there is a God and that men are unworthy of him.
(559)

320. Greatness. Religion is so great a matter that it is right that those who do not want to be bothered to explore it because it is obscure should go without it. For what have they to complain about if it is to be had for the asking? (574)

321. Everything down to the obscurities of Scripture turns to the advantage of the elect; because they honour them through divine illumination. And everything, down to divine illumination, turns out badly for the others because they blaspheme against it on account of obscurities which they do not understand. (575)

322. [From those who are in the unhappy position of being without faith we see that God does not give them understanding; but with the others we see that there is a God who darkens their understanding.] (202)

323. Original sin is foolishness in the eyes of men, but we are the first to admit it. You are therefore not entitled to blame me if the doctrine appears devoid of reason because I put it forward as being without rational foundation. But this foolishness is wiser than the wisdom of men, *sapientius est hominibus*. Because without it what shall we say that man is? His whole state depends on this invisible point. And how would he have come to know it through reason if it is contrary to reason, and because reason, so far from inventing it by its own methods, moves off as soon as it is faced with it? (445)

324. *Clarity, obscurity.* There would be too much obscurity if truth were not accompanied by visible signs. It is a marvellous sign that it is always present in one Church and one visible community of men. There would be too much light if there were only one opinion in the Church; the one that has always been preserved is the true one because truth has always existed, and no falsehood has always been in existence. (857)

325. Incomprehensible that God exists, and incomprehensible that he does not exist; that the soul is in the body, that we have no soul; that the world was created, that it was not created, etc.; that original sin exists, and that it does not exist. (230)

12. BEGINNING

326. The infidels who profess to follow reason must be unusually strong in reason. What have they got to say?

'Do we not see,' they say, 'animals living and dying like men, Turks like Christians? They have their ceremonies, their prophets, their doctors, their saints, their religious like ourselves, etc.' (Is that contrary to Scripture? Does not Scripture say precisely that?)

If you do not bother much about discovering truth, that is enough to leave you in peace. But if you desire with all your heart to know it, it is not enough; look at the details. It would be all right if it were a mere problem of philosophy; but here where everything is at stake . . .

And yet, after a frivolous reflexion of this kind, we go off and amuse ourselves, etc.

Let us ask religion itself whether or not it can give some reason for its obscurity; perhaps it will provide us with an answer. (226)

327. We are foolish to depend on the company of our fellows: they are wretched and feeble like ourselves, and will be of no help to us; we shall die alone. We must therefore behave as though we were on our own; would it then be sensible to spend our time building splendid houses? We should unhesitatingly set to work to discover truth, and if we refuse to, it shows that we care more about public opinion than the search for truth.

(211)

328. Between us and hell or heaven, there is only life, which is the most fragile thing in the world. (213)

329. What do you promise me, in addition to inescapable anxieties, but ten years of self-esteem (for ten years is the span), trying hard to please and never succeeding. (238)

330. *Choices.* Our life in this world would vary according to these different suppositions:

1. If we could be here for ever;

2. [If it is uncertain whether we shall be here for ever or not];

3. [If it is certain that we shall not be here for ever];

4. [If it is certain that we shall not be here for ever and uncertain whether we shall be here for a long time; —false];

5. If it is certain that we shall not be here for long, and uncertain whether we shall even be here for an hour.

This last supposition is ours. (237)

331. Heart, instinct, principles. (281)

332. Pity the atheists who seek, for are they not unhappy enough? Denounce those who boast of their unbelief. (190)

333. Atheism is a sign of a powerful mind, but up to a certain point only. (225)

334. According to the different courses which are open to you, you must take the trouble to seek truth; for if you die without worshipping the true principle you are lost. 'But,' you reply, 'if he had wished me to worship it, he would have given me some sign of his wishes.' So he has, but you neglect them. Seek them then; it is well worth it. (236)

335. If we ought to spend a week of our life on the job, we ought to spend a hundred years. (204)

336. There are only three kinds of person: those who have found God and serve him; those who spend their time seeking him without finding him; and the third kind who live without seeking or having found him. The first are reasonable and happy; the last crazy and unhappy; those in the middle group are unhappy and reasonable. (257)

337. Atheists should say things that are perfectly clear; now it is not perfectly clear that the soul is material. (221)

338. Begin by commiserating with the unbelievers; they are already unhappy enough owing to their state. We ought not to abuse them unless it would do them some good; but it does them harm. (189)

339. Imagine a man in a dungeon not knowing whether sentence has been passed on him or not, with only an hour in which to find out, because if he finds out that it has been

passed, an hour would be sufficient to have it set aside: it would be contrary to nature if he spent that hour not in finding out whether sentence has been pronounced or not, but in playing piquet. Thus it is supernatural that man, etc. It is the weight of the hand of God.

So it is not only the zeal of those who seek him that proves God's existence, but the blindness of those who do not seek him. (200)

340. *Beginning. Dungeon.* I think that it is a good thing not to probe the opinion of Copernicus: but this . . .

It is important for one's whole life to know whether or not the soul is immortal. (218)

341. The final act is bloody, however fine the rest of the play: you end by throwing earth on to the head, and that is the end for ever. (210)

342. We rush carelessly over the edge of the precipice after putting something in front of us to prevent our seeing it. (183)

343. *Infinite. Nothing.* Our soul is tossed into the body where it finds number, time, dimensions. It argues about them, calls them nature or necessity, and cannot believe in anything else.

Unity joined to infinity does not add anything to it, any more than a foot to a measure which is infinite. The finite is annihilated in the presence of the infinite, and becomes pure nothingness. Thus it is with our mind in the presence of God; thus our justice in face of divine justice.

There is not such a great disproportion between our justice and God's as between unity and infinity.

The justice of God must be immense like his mercy. Now justice shown to the damned is less overwhelming and must be less shocking, than mercy towards the saved.

We know that there is an infinite, but are ignorant of its nature. Since we know that it is untrue that numbers are finite, it follows that there is infinity in number. But we do not know what it is: it is untrue to say that it is even, untrue to say that it is odd; for the addition of unity does not alter its nature; yet it is a number and every number is odd or even (it is true that this applies to all finite numbers). Thus we may be sure that there is a God without knowing what he is.

Is there not one substantial truth, since there are so many true things which are not truth itself?

We therefore know the existence and nature of the finite because we are finite and like it consist of extension in space. We know the existence of the infinite and do not know its nature because it possesses extension like ourselves, but not limits like us. But we do not know either the existence or the nature of God because he has neither extension nor limits.

But through faith we know that he exists; through glory we shall come to know his nature. Now, I have already shown that we can perfectly well know the existence of something without knowing its nature.

Let us now speak according to our natural lights.

If there is a God, he is infinitely incomprehensible because having neither dimensions nor limits, he has no relation to us. We are therefore incapable of knowing either what he is, or whether he exists. That being so, who will be bold enough to attempt the solution of the problem? Not we who have no communication with him.

Who then will blame Christians for not being able to give reasons for their beliefs since they profess belief in a religion which they cannot explain? They declare, when they expound it to the world, that it is foolishness, *stultitiam*; and then you complain because they do not prove it! If they proved it, they would not keep their word; it is through their lack of proofs that they show they are not lacking in sense.

'Yes, but even if it excuses those who present it in such a way, and if it excuses them for presenting it without giving reasons, it does not excuse those who accept it.'

Let us consider the point and say: 'Either God exists, or he does not exist.' But which of the alternatives shall we choose? Reason can determine nothing: there is an infinite chaos which divides us. A coin is being spun at the extreme point of this infinite distance which will turn up heads or tails. What is your bet? If you rely on reason you cannot settle for either, or defend either position.

Do not therefore accuse those who have made their choice of falseness because you know nothing about it.

'No, I do not blame them for their choice, but for making a choice at all because he who calls heads and he who calls tails are guilty of the same mistake, they are both wrong: the right course is not to wager.' 'Yes, but we have to wager. You are not a free agent; you are committed. Which will you have then? Come on. Since you are obliged to choose, let us see which interests you least. You may lose two things: the true and the good; and there are two things that you stake: your reason and your will, your knowledge and your beatitude; and your nature has two things from which to escape: error and unhappiness. Your reason is not more deeply wounded by choosing one rather than the other because it is bound to choose. That disposes of one point. But what about your beatitude? Let us measure the gain and the loss by saying: "Heads God exists." Let us compare the two cases; if you win, you win everything; if you lose, you lose nothing. Don't hesitate then. Take a bet that he exists.'

'That's fine. Yes, I must take a bet; but perhaps I am staking too much.'

'Come. Since there is an equal chance of gain and loss, if you were only to win two lives for one, you could still wager; but if there were three to be won, you would have to gamble (since you are bound to gamble), and it would be imprudent, when you are obliged to gamble, not to risk your life in order to win three lives at a game in which there is such a chance of loss and gain. But there is an eternity of life and happiness at stake. And since it is so, if there were an infinite number of chances of which only one was for you, you would still be right to risk one to win two; and you would be taking the wrong road if, being forced to gamble, you refuse to stake one life against three in a game in which, out of an infinite number of chances, one is for you, if the prize were an infinity of life which was infinitely happy. But in this game you can win eternal life which is eternally happy; you have one chance of winning against a finite number of chances of losing, and what you are staking is finite. That settles it: wherever there is infinity, and where there is not an infinity of chances of losing against the chance of winning, there is no room for hesitation: you must stake everything. And so, since you are forced to gamble, you must abandon reason in order to save your life, rather than risk it for the infinite gain which is just as likely to turn up as the loss of nothing.'

For it is useless to say that it is doubtful whether we shall win, that it is certain that we are running a risk, and that the infinite distance which lies between the *certainty* of what we stake and the *uncertainty* of what we shall win, is equal to the finite good which we certainly stake against the uncertain infinite. It is not like that; every gambler risks something that is certain in the hope of winning something which is uncertain; and nevertheless he risks a finite certainty in order to win a finite uncertainty without committing a sin against reason. There is not an infinite distance between the certainty of the risk and the uncertainty of a win; that is untrue. There is, to be sure, an infinite distance between the certainty of winning and the certainty of losing. But the uncertainty of winning is proportionate to the certainty of what we risk, depending on the proportion between the chances of gain and loss. Thus if there are as many chances on one side as on the other, the odds are equal; and then the certainty of the stake is equal to the uncertainty of the prize: it is far from being true that the distance between them is infinite. And so our argument is of overwhelming force, when the finite must be staked in a game in which the chances of gain and loss are equal, and the infinite is the prize. That can be demonstrated; and if men are capable of grasping any truth, that is one.

'I confess, I admit it. But is there still no means of seeing the reverse side of the cards?' 'Yes, Scripture and the rest, etc.'

'Yes, but my hands are tied and my lips sealed; I am forced to gamble and am not free; they will not let go of me. And I am made in such a way that I cannot believe. What do you expect me to do?'

'That's true. But at any rate, you must realise that since your reason inclines you to believe and yet you cannot believe, your inability to believe comes from your passions. Try then, not to convince yourself by multiplying the proofs of the existence of God, but by diminishing your passions. You want to find faith but you do not know the way; you want to cure yourself of unbelief, and you ask for the remedies: learn from the examples of those who like yourself were in bondage and who now stake their whole fortune: they are people who know the path that you would like to follow, and who have been cured of an ill of which you wish to be cured. Follow the method by which they began: it is by behaving as though they did believe, by taking holy water, by having masses said, etc. That will naturally make you inclined to believe and will calm you.'

'But that's just what I'm afraid of.' 'But why? What have you got to lose?'

'But in order to prove to you that it works, it will diminish the passions which for you are the great stumbling-block.'

End of the address. 'Now, what harm will you come to if you adopt this course? You will be faithful, honest, humble, grateful, beneficent, a true friend, genuine. In truth, you will no longer find yourself submerged in poisonous pleasures, such as lust and desire for fame: but will you have no others? I tell you that you will gain in this life; and that with every step you take along this path, you will see such certainty of gain and so much of the worthlessness of what you risk, that you will have gambled on something that is certain, infinite and has cost you nothing.'

'Oh, these words delight and ravish me, etc.'

If the argument appeals to you and appears well founded, you must know that it was composed by a man who went down on his knees, before and after it, to pray to the Infinite Indivisible Being to whom he submitted the whole of his being that God might grant the submission of the whole of your being for your own good and for his glory, and that in this way strength might be given to lowliness. (233)

344. 'Do you think that it is impossible for God to be infinite and indivisible?' 'Yes.' 'Then I will try to show you something that is infinite and indivisible.'

It is a point moving everywhere at an infinite speed.

For it is one wherever it is and exists as a whole wherever it is.

May this effect of nature, which previously seemed to you to be impossible, make you realise that there might be others which you do not yet know. Do not assume that after your apprenticeship there is nothing left for you to learn; you still have an infinite amount to learn. (231)

345. *Fascinatio nugacitatis.*[1] In order to prevent passion from doing harm, let us behave as though we only had a week left to live. (203)

346. If it were unnecessary to do anything except when dealing with certainties, we should do nothing for religion because it is not a certainty. But how many things we do in fact do when dealing with the uncertain, such as going on sea voyages and into battle! I maintain therefore that we should do nothing at all because nothing is certain; and that there is more certainty in religion than in the belief that we shall live to see tomorrow: for it is not certain that we shall see tomorrow, but it is certainly possible that we shall not. We cannot say the same of religion. It is not certain that it is true; but who will dare to say that it is certainly possible that it is not true?

Now, when we labour for tomorrow and for the uncertain, we are acting reasonably because we have to work for the uncertain in accordance with the doctrine of chance, as we have shown above.

St. Augustine saw that we work for the uncertain on sea, in battle, etc.; but he did not understand the doctrine of chance which shows that we are compelled to do so. Montaigne saw that we are put off by a limping mind, and that habit can achieve anything; but he did not understand the reason.

[1] The bewitching of vanity (Wisdom, IV, 12).

All these people saw the effects, but they did not see the causes; compared with those who discovered the causes they are like people who have eyes compared with those who possess intelligence; for the effects are, so to speak, tangible, and the causes are only perceptible to the mind. And though the effects can be perceived by the mind, compared with a mind that perceives the causes such a mind is like the physical senses compared with the mind. (234)

347. Nature repeats the same things over and over again: the years, the days, the hours; it is the same with space, while numbers are placed end to end, one after the other. Thus a kind of infinite and eternal is created. It is not that there is anything which is infinite and eternal about it, but these finite objects multiply indefinitely. Thus it seems to me, that the number which multiplies them is infinite. (121)

348. *Infinite movement.* Infinite movement, the point which fills the whole, the moment of rest: infinite without quantity, indivisible and infinite. (232)

349. *Objection.* Those who hope for salvation are happy in that respect, but it is counterbalanced by the fear of hell.

Reply. Who has the greater reason to fear hell, the man who does not know whether there is a hell and who is certain of damnation if there is one; or the man who is to a certain extent convinced that there is a hell, and hopes to be saved if there is?

(239)

350. 'I should soon have given up pleasure,' they say, 'if I had had faith.' But I tell you: 'You would soon have had the faith if you had given up pleasure.' Now it is up to you to begin. If I could, I would give you faith; I cannot do so, and for that reason I cannot test the truth of what you are saying. But you can very well give up pleasure and test the truth of what I am saying. (240)

351. Superstition, —and sensual pleasure.

Scruples, —evil desires.

Evil fear.

Fear, not the fear which comes from the fact that we believe in God, but the fear which comes from doubting whether he exists or not. The right kind of fear comes from faith: the wrong kind from doubt. The right kind linked to hope because it is born of faith, and because we hope in the God in whom we believe: wrong kind linked to despair because we fear the God in whom we do not believe. Some fear to lose him, —others fear to find him. (262)

13. SUBMISSION AND USE OF REASON

352. Submission and use of reason which is the secret of true Christianity. (269)

353. How I hate all this nonsense, not believing in the Eucharist, and that sort of stuff! If the Gospel is true. If Jesus Christ is God, where is the difficulty? (224)

354. I should not be a Christian without the miracles, says St. Augustine. (812)

355*. Submission. We must know when to doubt, when to feel certain and when to submit. Anyone who does otherwise does not understand the power of reason. There are some who break these three rules, either by assuring us that everything can be proved because they understand nothing about the nature of proof; or by doubting everything because they do not know when it is necessary to submit; or by submitting in everything because they do not know when we must use our judgement.

Sceptic, mathematician, Christian; doubt, certainty, submission. (268)

356. *Susceperunt verbum cum omni aviditate, scrutantes Scripturas, si ita se haberent.*[1] (696)

357. It is the way of God, who orders all things with gentleness, to implant religion in the mind by means of arguments, and in the heart by grace. But people who are determined to place it in our mind and heart by force and threats, do not implant religion but terror, *terrorem potius quam religionem.* (185)

358. If we submit everything to the test of reason, our religion

[1] They welcomed the word with all eagerness, and examined the Scriptures, day after day, to find out whether all this was true (Acts XVII, II).

will have nothing mysterious or supernatural about it. If it shocks the principles of reason, our religion will be absurd and ridiculous. (273)

359. St. Augustine: Reason would never submit unless it considered that there were occasions on which it must submit.

It is therefore right that reason should submit when it decides that it ought to submit. (270)

360. One of the things that will bring confusion to the damned will be the discovery that they are condemned by their own reason by which they claimed to condemn the Christian religion. (563)

361. Those who do not love truth make use of the excuse that it is contested, and that vast numbers of people deny it altogether. With the result that their error is due simply to the fact that they do not love truth or charity; and therefore they have no excuse. (261)

362. Contradiction is an ill sign of truth:

> several things which are certain are challenged;
> several things that are false pass without contradiction.

Contradiction is not a sign of falsity, nor absence of contradiction a sign of truth. (384)

363. Note the two kinds of men mentioned under the heading Perpetuity. (747 *bis*)

364. There are very few real Christians, even as regards faith. There are many who believe, but out of superstition: there are many who do not believe, but because they are libertines: few are half-and-half.

I do not include those who are truly pious, or all those who believe by intuition. (256)

365. Jesus Christ performed miracles and the Apostles after him, and the first saints in great numbers; because, as the prophecies were not yet fulfilled and were being fulfilled by them, there was no testimony except miracles. It was foretold that the Messiah would convert the nations. How could this prophecy be fulfilled without the conversion of the nations? And how would the nations have been converted to the Messiah without witnessing the final fulfilment of the prophecies which

proved his claims? It was not until he had died, risen from the dead and converted the nations that all the prophecies were fulfilled; and miracles were therefore necessary during the whole of this period. Now they are no longer necessary against the Jews because the fulfilment of the prophecies is a continuing miracle. (838)

366. Piety is different from superstition.

To push piety to the point of superstition is to destroy it.

Heretics criticise us for our superstitious submission, which means that they are doing the very thing for which they criticise us. . .

Impiety of not believing in the Eucharist because we do not see it. (255)

Superstition of believing in the propositions. Faith, etc.

367. There is nothing which is so much in conformity with reason as the rejection of reason. (272)

368. Two forms of excess: to exclude reason, and not to admit anything but reason. (253)

369*. It would have been no sin not to have believed in Jesus Christ without the miracles.

Videte an mentiar. (811)

370. Faith does indeed tell us what the senses do not tell, but does not contradict their findings. It transcends, but does not contradict them. (265)

371. You abuse the faith that the people have in the Church and delude them. (947)

372. It is by no means uncommon for us to have to reprove people for being too docile. Superstition is a natural vice like unbelief, and just as pernicious. (254)

373. Reason's last step is the recognition that there are an infinite number of things which are beyond it; it is merely feeble if it does not go so far as to grasp that.

If natural things are beyond it, what are we to say about supernatural? (267)

374. *Authority.* So far from making it a rule to believe a thing

because you have heard people say it, you must not believe anything without behaving as though you had never heard it.

It is your own assent to yourself, and the unceasing voice of your own reason, not of other peoples', which should make you believe.

Belief is so important!

A hundred contradictions would be true.

If antiquity were the rule of faith, does this mean that the ancients were without a rule?

If assent were general, would men have perished?

False humility, pride.

Lift the curtain.

In vain; you must either believe, or deny, or doubt.

Does this mean that there is no rule?

We judge animals by the fact that what they do they do well.

Is there no rule for judging men?

To deny, to believe and to have serious doubts are to men what running is to the horse.

Punishment of those who sin, error. (260)

375. There is a universal and essential difference between the actions of the will and all others.

The will is one of the principal organs of belief; not because it forms belief, but because things are true or false according to the angle from which we look at them. The will, which finds one more agreeable than another, diverts the mind from the consideration of the qualities of those which it does not like to see; and so the mind, marching in step with the will, stops to examine the side that appeals to it; and so it judges by what it finds there. (99)

376. Faith is a gift of God; do not imagine that we are saying that it is the fruit of reasoning. The other religions do not say that of their faith: they only proposed reasoning as a means of reaching it, which does not bring them to it anyway. (279)

377. Reason commands us far more imperiously than a master because by disobeying the one we are unhappy, and by disobeying the other we are fools. (345)

378. There are two ways of convincing people of the truths of our religion: one by the power of reason, the other by the authority of the person who speaks. We do not use the second but the first. We do not say: 'You must believe it because Scripture, which says so, is divine'; but we say that it must be believed for this or that reason, which are feeble arguments because reason can be bent in any direction one chooses.   (561)

379. The only form of knowledge which is opposed to common sense and nature is the only one which has always existed among men.   (604)

14. EXCELLENCE OF THIS METHOD OF PROVING THE EXISTENCE OF GOD

380. *God through Jesus Christ.* We only know God through Jesus Christ. Without the Mediator all communication with God is removed; through Jesus Christ we know God. All those who have claimed to know God and to prove his existence without Jesus Christ had to make do with very inadequate proofs. But as proofs of the claims of Jesus Christ, we have the prophecies, which are solid, palpable proofs. And as the prophecies were fulfilled and proved true by events, they are a sign of the certainty of these truths, and are therefore proofs of the divinity of Jesus Christ. Thus we know God in him and by him. Without him, without Scripture, without original sin, without the necessary Mediator who was promised and came, we cannot prove the existence of God absolutely, or teach either sound doctrine or sound morality. But through Jesus Christ and in Jesus Christ we can prove the existence of God, and we teach morality and doctrine. Jesus Christ is therefore the true God of men.

But at the same time we become aware of our own wretchedness. Thus we cannot come to a proper knowledge of God without knowing our own iniquities.

Therefore, those who have known God without knowing

their own wretchedness have not glorified him, but have glorified themselves.

Quia .. non cognovit per sapientiam ... placuit Deo per stultitiam praedicationis salvos facere.[1]   (547)

381. *Preface.* The metaphysical proofs of the existence of God are so remote from men's methods of reasoning and so involved that they produce little impact; and even if they did help some people, the effect would only last for a few moments while they were actually watching the demonstration, but an hour later they would be afraid that they had made a mistake.

Quod curiositate cognoverint superbia amiserunt.[2]

That is the result of a knowledge of God which is reached without Jesus Christ, which is communication without a mediator with the God whom we have known without a mediator.

Instead of which those who have known God through a mediator are aware of their own wretchedness.   (543)

382. It is not only impossible, but useless to know God without the intermediary of Jesus Christ. They are not removed from, but brought closer to him; they are not brought lower, but ...

Quo quisque optimus eo pessimus, si hoc ipsum, quod optimus sit, abscribat sibi.[3]   (549)

383. Man's knowledge of God without an awareness of his own wretchedness leads to pride.

An awareness of his wretchedness without the knowledge of God leads to despair.

The knowledge of Jesus Christ represents the middle state because we find in it both God and our wretchedness.   (527)

---

[1] The world, with all its wisdom, could not find its way to God; and now God would use a foolish thing, our preaching, to save those who will believe in it (I Cor. i, 21).

[2] What they had gained by their curiosity would be lost through pride (St. Augustine, Sermons, CXLI).

[3] The better we are, the worse we become by taking credit for our own excellence (St. Bernard: *In Cantica Sermones*, 84).

15. FROM THE KNOWLEDGE OF MAN TO A KNOWLEDGE OF GOD

384. *Prejudice leading to error.* It is deplorable to find that everybody is concerned about means alone, and never about the end. Everyone thinks about the way that he will acquit himself in his profession; but when it comes to the choice of profession and fatherland, the question is settled by chance.

It is a pitiful thing to see so many Turks, heretics, infidels, following in the footsteps of their fathers for the sole reason that they have each been advised that it is the best course. And that is what induces each of us to adopt a particular profession, such as locksmith, soldier, etc.

That is why savages care nothing for Provence. (98)

385. Why is my knowledge limited? My height? My span of life to a hundred rather than a thousand years? What was nature's reason for making me like that, for choosing this number rather than that, because out of the infinity of numbers that exist there is no reason for choosing one rather than another, because no one of them is more tempting than another? (208)

386. *A little of everything.* [Since we cannot become universal minds by knowing all that can be known about everything, we must know a little about everything. For it is much better to know something about everything than everything about one subject; this form of universality is the best. If we could possess both it would be better still, but if we have to choose we must choose the second; the world knows it and does so because the world is often a sound judge.] (37)

387. [Some whim makes me dislike croakers and people who snort when they eat. Whims carry great weight. What benefit do we derive from this? That we are carried along by the weight because it is natural? No, but because we shall resist it . . .] (86)

388. [There is no better proof of human vanity than to contemplate the causes and effects of love: for the whole universe is changed by it. (The nose of Cleopatra.)] (163 *bis*)

389. H.5. When we behold the blindness and wretchedness of man, when we look on the whole dumb universe, on man without light, abandoned to his own devices and appearing as though lost in some corner of the universe, without knowing who has placed him there, what he is supposed to be doing, what will become of him when he dies, incapable of all knowledge, I am overcome by fear like a man who has been carried off during sleep and deposited on some terrifying desert island, who wakes up without knowing where he is and without any means of escape. And I am amazed that people do not fall into despair over such a wretched state. I find myself surrounded by other people of the same kind: I ask them whether they are better informed than myself; they tell me that they are not; and at that the wretched, wandering creatures look round, and catching sight of a few pleasant objects, abandon themselves to them and become attached to them. But I myself cannot become attached, and considering how strongly appearances suggest that there are other things besides the ones I see, I have sought to discover whether God might not have left some signs of himself.

I come across several conflicting religions, yet without exception all of them are false. Each of them wishes to be believed on its own authority and uses threats against unbelievers. I do not believe in them on that score. Each of us can say the same, can proclaim himself a prophet. But I see the Christian religion in which I find prophecies, and that is not something that everyone can do.   (693)

390. H.9. *Disproportion of man.* [This is as far as innate knowledge takes us. If it is not true, there is no truth in man; if it is true, he finds it a great source of humiliation which compels him to lower himself in one way or another.

And, since he cannot exist without accepting that knowledge, I wish that, before embarking upon a deeper study of nature, he would consider it seriously for once and at his leisure, that he would also examine himself, and realising what a disproportion there is . . .]

Let man therefore contemplate all nature in her full and

lofty majesty; let him turn his eyes away from the lowly objects which surround him. Let him look upon the dazzling light, placed like an eternal lamp to illuminate the universe; let the earth appear like a point compared with the vast circle that the orb describes, and let him be filled with amazement that the vast circle itself is only a tiny point in relation to the course traced by the stars revolving in the firmament.

But if our eye comes to a halt there, let imagination go further; it will be more likely to grow weary of forming ideas than nature of providing material. The whole of the visible world is no more than an imperceptible speck in the ample bosom of nature. None of our ideas comes anywhere near it. We waste our time in pushing our ideas beyond the imaginable confines of space; we produce only atoms compared with the reality of things. Nature is an infinite sphere whose centre is everywhere, whose circumference is nowhere. In short, it is the greatest tangible sign of the omnipotence of God that our imagination boggles at the thought of him.

Let man, when he recovers himself, consider what he is compared with what is; let him look upon himself as though he had strayed into a backwater of nature; and from the little dungeon where he is housed—I mean the universe—let him learn to judge the earth, kingdoms, towns and himself at their proper value. What is a man in face of the infinite?

But in order to show him another minute and equally astonishing prodigy, let him seek out the tiniest of objects known to him. Suppose, for example, a mite with its body presents him with the spectacle of incomparably smaller parts, minute legs with joints, veins in its legs, blood in its veins, humours in its blood, drops in the humours, vapours in the drops until, dividing them again, his mind reels at such ideas, and let the last object which he is able to reach be the one of which we are speaking; he will think perhaps that it is the ultimate example of minuteness in nature. I will show him a fresh abyss in it. I will describe for him not only the visible universe, but the whole inconceivable vastness of nature enclosed in this abridgement of an atom. Let him see in it an infinity of universes, each of which has its firmament, its planets, its earth in the same proportion as the visible world: in this earth animals and finally mites, in which he will find again what he found in the first; and still finding in the others the same thing without end or rest, let him stand speechless before these wonders, which are as astonishing in their minuteness as the others in their vastness; for who will not marvel to find that our body, which a moment ago was not visible in the universe, which was itself imperceptible in the bosom of the whole, is at present a colossus, a world, or rather a whole, compared with the void which lies beyond our ken?

Anyone who regards himself in this way will be terrified at himself, and seeing himself sustained in the body that nature has given him, between the two abysses of the infinite and the void, will tremble at the sight of these wonders; and I think that, as curiosity changes to wonder, he will be more disposed to contemplate them in silence than to presume to question them.

For after all, what is man in nature? A void in comparison with the infinite, a whole in comparison with the void, a middle term between nothing and all. Infinitely far from grasping the extremes, the end of things and their origin are completely hidden from him in impenetrable mystery; he is equally incapable of seeing the void whence he comes, and the infinite in which he is engulfed.

What will he do but catch some fleeting glimpse of the middle of things, in an eternal despair of ever knowing their origin or their end? All things come from the void and are carried onwards to the infinite. Who will follow these astonishing processes? The author of these wonders understands them. No one else can.

Through their failure to contemplate these infinites, men have rashly set to work to examine nature, as though there were any proportion between them and it. It is strange that they have desired to understand the origin of things, and from that to reach an understanding of everything through a presumption which is as infinite as their object. For there is no doubt that one could not embark on such a project without infinite presumption or a capacity which is infinite like nature herself.

When we have learnt a little about it, we realise that, as nature has set her image and that of her author on all things, they almost all share her twofold infinity. Thus we see that all the sciences are infinite in the range of their researches. For who can doubt that geometry, for example, has an infinity of infinities of problems which await a solution? They are as infinite as the number and subtlety of their principles, for who does not see that those which are presented as final are not independent, and that they rest on others which by resting on others still, to support them, can never be final? But we treat the last which are perceptible to reason as we treat material things when we describe as indivisible a point beyond which our senses perceive nothing more, though it is of its nature infinitely divisible.

Of the two infinites of the sciences, that of largeness is much more apparent, and that is why few people have ventured to claim that they know everything. 'I am going to speak of everything,' said Democritus.

But infinite smallness is far less perceptible. Philosophers have been much more inclined to claim that they have reached it, and it is here that they have all come to grief. It is this that has given rise to such commonplace titles as these: *First Principles*, *Principles of Philosophy*, and the like, which are as pretentious in fact, though less in appearance, as this one which hits us in the eye: *De omni scibili*.

We naturally believe ourselves to be far more capable of reaching the centre of things than of embracing their circumference. The visible expanse of the world visibly exceeds our capacities; but since it is we ourselves who are greater than small things, we believe ourselves more capable of comprehending them; and yet it requires no lesser capacity for reaching the nothing than the whole: the capacity for doing either must be infinite, and it seems to me that anyone who had understood the ultimate principles of things might also succeed in reaching the infinite. One depends on the other, and one leads to the other.

These extremes meet and combine on account of their very distance from one another; they are to be found again in God, and in God alone.

Let us therefore understand our limitations; we are something and we are not everything; what life we possess conceals from us the knowledge of first principles which are born of the void; and the little life that we have hides from us the sight of the infinite.

Our intelligence occupies the same position in the realm of intelligible things as our body in the realm of nature.

Limited in every direction, this middle state between two extremes is characteristic of all our faculties. Our senses do not register extremes; too much noise deafens us; too much light dazzles us; too great or too short a distance impedes our view; too long or too short an address makes it obscure; too strong a dose of truth staggers us (I know people who cannot understand that four from nought leaves nought); first principles are too obvious for us; too much pleasure incommodes us; too many harmonies are displeasing in music, and too many benefactions are a source of irritation: we want the means to overpay the debt: *Beneficia eo usque laeta sunt dum videntur exolvi posse; ubi multum antevenere, pro gratia odium redditur.*[1] We do not feel either extreme heat or extreme cold. Qualities which are excessive are inimical to us and not perceptible; we do not feel them; we suffer them. The extremes of youth and age stultify the mind, like too much or too little learning. In short, extremes do not exist for us, or we for them: they escape us, or we them.

That is our veritable condition. It is that which makes us incapable either of certain knowledge or of absolute ignorance. We float over a vast expanse, always uncertain and drifting, tossed hither and thither. Whatever the point to which we seek to attach ourselves to consolidate our position, it shifts and leaves us; and if we follow it, it eludes our grasp, slips away and flies from us in unending flight. Nothing stops for us. It is the

[1] Benefactions are agreeable so long as we think we can repay them; if they go very far beyond this limit, gratitude gives way to hatred (Tacitus, *Ann.*, IV, 18).

state which is natural to us, and at the same time the one most contrary to our inclinations; we burn with the desire to find a stable position, a solid base for building a tower which will rise to infinity; but our entire foundations crack; the earth opens like a vast abyss.

Therefore, let us not look for security and stability. Our reason is always cheated by deceitful appearances; nothing can stabilise the finite between the two infinites which enclose it, and fly from it.

Once this is clearly understood, I think that we can remain at peace in ourselves, each of us in the state to which nature has called him. Since the middle state which has fallen to our lot is always far from the extremes, what does it matter if one [man] has a little more understanding than another? If he has, it simply means that he is a little quicker in grasping them. Is he not always an infinite distance from the end, and is not the span of our life equally tiny in the bosom of eternity, whether or not it lasts another ten years?

In the sight of these infinites all finite things are equal; and I do not see why I should fix my imagination on one rather than on the other. The mere comparison between ourselves and the finite is painful to us.

If man studied himself first, he would see how incapable he is of going further. How could a part come to know a whole? —But he may perhaps try to get to know at least the parts when there is some proportion between him and them? But the parts of the world are so inter-related and their connection with one another such that I believe that it is impossible to know one without the other and without the whole.

There is, for example, a relation between man and everything that he knows. He needs space to contain him, time in which to exist, motion in order to live, warmth and food to nourish [him], air to breathe; he sees light; he feels bodies; in short, he has a relationship with everything. In order to know man, therefore, we must know why he needs air to breathe; and, to understand air, to understand why it plays the part it does in man's life, etc.

Flame cannot exist without air; thus in order to know one it is necessary to know the other.

It follows that as all things are caused and causing, supported and supporting, mediate and immediate, and all held together by a natural and imperceptible link which joins the most distant and diverse, I am convinced that it is impossible to know the parts without knowing the whole, any more than we can know the whole without a detailed knowledge of the parts.

[The eternity of things in itself or in God must still be a source of astonishment in our little life. The fixed and unchanging immobility of nature compared with the changes continually taking place in ourselves ought to produce on us the same effect.]

And what crowns our incapacity to know things is that they are simple in themselves and that we are composed of two opposite natures which are different in kind: soul and body. For it is impossible that the part of us which reasons should be other than spiritual; and if it were claimed that we were simply corporeal, it would exclude us all the more completely from the knowledge of things because there is nothing so inconceivable as saying that matter knows itself; it is not possible for us to say how it could know itself.

And so, if we [are] purely material we can know nothing at all, and if we are composed of spirit and matter, we cannot know simple things perfectly, whether spiritual or corporeal.

That is why almost all philosophers confuse the ideas of things, speaking in spiritual terms of material things, and in material terms of spiritual things. For they declare boldly that bodies fall, that they aspire towards their centre, that they flee destruction, that they fear the void, that [they have] inclinations, sympathies, antipathies, which are all attributes belonging only to minds. And in speaking of minds, they treat them as being localised in a particular place, and ascribe to them the faculty of moving from one place to another, which are qualities that belong only to bodies.

Instead of perceptions being received in their pure form, they are coloured by our own attributes, and we set the stamp

[of] our composite being on all the simple things which confront us.

Who would not imagine, when he saw us endow everything with mind and body, that such a mixture would be perfectly comprehensible to us? It is nevertheless the thing that we understand least. In his own eyes, man is the most marvellous object in the world; for he cannot grasp what a body is, still less what a mind is, and least of all how a body can be joined to a mind. That is his supreme difficulty, and yet it is the essence of his being: *Modus quo corporibus adhaerent spiritus comprehendi ab hominibus non potest, et hoc tamen homo est.*[1]

Finally, in order to complete the demonstration of our weakness, I will close by these two observations . . .   (72)

391. H.3. Man is only a reed, the feeblest thing in nature; but he is a thinking reed. It is not necessary for the entire universe to take up arms in order to crush him: a vapour, a drop of water is sufficient to kill him. But if the universe crushed him, man would still be nobler than the thing which destroys him because he knows that he is dying; and the universe which has him at its mercy, is unaware of it.

All our dignity therefore lies in thought. It is by thought that we must raise ourselves, and not by space or time, which we could never fill. Let us apply ourselves then to thinking well: that is the first principle of morality.   (347)

392. The eternal silence of these infinite spaces terrifies me. (206)

393. Take comfort! It is not from yourselves that you must expect it, but on the contrary by expecting nothing from yourselves that you must hope for it.   (517)

394. No other [religion] has understood that man is the most excellent of creatures. Some, which have fully recognised how real his excellence is, have regarded the unworthy sentiments which are natural to him as a sign of cowardice and ingratitude;

---

[1] The manner in which the spirit is united to the body cannot be understood by man, and yet it is the essence of man (St. Augustine: *De Civ. Dei*, XXI, 10).

and others which have been well aware how real his unworthiness is, have treated with lofty ridicule his sense of his own greatness, which is just as natural to man.

Lift up your eyes to God, say some; look on him whom you resemble, and who has made you so that you may worship him. You can make yourself like him; wisdom will make you equal to him if you choose to follow him. 'Lift up your heads, free men,' said Epictetus. And others say to him: Look down, miserable worm that you are, look at the animals who are your true companions.

What then will become of man? Will he be the equal of God or of the beasts of the field? What an appalling distance between the two! What will become of us then? Who does not see from this that man has gone astray, that he has fallen from his rightful place, that he is seeking the way back to it uneasily, that he cannot find it again? And who will show him the way? The greatest men have failed to do so. (431)

395. Concupiscence has become natural to us, and is a second nature. Thus there are two natures in us: one good, the other bad. Where is God? He is where you are not, and the Kingdom of God is within you. Rabbis. (660)

396. There are three ways of acquiring faith: reason, habit, grace. The Christian religion, which alone has reason for its ally, does not recognise as its true children those who believe without grace; it is not that it excludes reason and habit—far from it; but we must approach the proofs with an open mind, be confirmed in them by habit, and respond in a spirit of humility to the promptings of grace which alone is capable of bringing true and lasting faith: *Ne evacuetur crux Christi.*[1] (245)

[1] Lest the Cross of Christ be robbed of its force (I Cor. 1. 17).

16. FALSENESS OF THE OTHER RELIGIONS

397. Mahomet without authority.

His arguments must therefore have been extremely cogent because they had no authority but their own force.

What does he say? That we must believe in him!   (595)

398. *Falseness of the other religions.* They have no witnesses. The Jews have. God defies the other religions to produce such signs as ours: Is. XVIII; 9; XLIV, 8.   (592)

399. If there is a single principle behind all things, everything has a single end, everything by him, everything for him. It is necessary therefore that the true religion should teach us to worship only him and to love only him. But since we find that we are incapable of worshipping what we do not know and of loving anything but ourselves, the religion which teaches us these duties must also make us understand our own incapacity, and provide us with a remedy. It teaches us that through one man all was lost, the link between God and man broken, and that through one man the link was restored.

We are born so unresponsive to the love of God and it is so necessary, that we must be born in guilt, or God would be unjust.   (489)

400. *Rem viderunt, causam non viderunt.*[2]   (235)

401. *Against Mahomet.* The Koran is no more Mahomet's than the Gospel of St. Matthew for it is quoted by a number of authors in the course of the centuries; its enemies themselves, Celsus and Porphry, never denied it.

The Koran says that St. Matthew was a good man. Therefore he was a false prophet either through calling good people bad, or through not agreeing with what they have said of Jesus Christ.   (597)

[2] They see the thing, but do not see its cause (St. Augustine, *Contra Pel.*, *IV*, 60).

402. Without this divine knowledge, what could men have done except become elated by the inward sense of their past greatness which remains to them, or collapse at the sight of their present weakness?

Because they do not see truth in its wholeness, men have been unable to attain perfect virtue. Since some regard nature as uncorrupted and others as beyond redemption, they have not escaped either pride or laziness, which are the twin sources of all the vices; and [they] can do nothing except abandon themselves to them out of cowardice or escape from them through pride. For, if they recognised the excellence of man, they were ignorant of his corruption; so that they succeeded in avoiding sloth, but gave way to pride; and if they recognised the infirmity of nature, they were unaware of its dignity: with the result that they were certainly able to avoid vanity, but only at the price of plunging into despair.

Whence come the different sects of stoics and epicureans, dogmatists and academicians, etc.

The Christian religion alone has been able to cure these two vices, not by using one to drive out the other through worldly wisdom, but by driving both out with the simplicity of the Gospel. For it teaches the righteous—whom it raises to the level of participating in the divinity itself—that even in this sublime state, they still bear within them the seed of all corruption which throughout their lives makes them the victims of error, misery, death, sin; and it cries aloud to the most impious that they are capable of the grace of their Redeemer. Thus, making those whom it justifies tremble, and comforting those whom it condemns, it so justly tempers fear with hope through the double capacity which is common to us all of grace and sin, that it humbles us infinitely more than reason alone, but without reducing us to despair, and it is infinitely more elevating than natural pride, but without puffing us up: making us realise that being alone exempt from error and vice, only the Christian religion has the right to instruct and correct mankind.

Who therefore can refuse to believe in and worship the

heavenly light? For is it not clearer than daylight that we are aware of indestructible signs of excellence in us? And is it not also true that at every moment of the day we are aware of the deplorable effects of our condition? What then does this chaos, this monstrous confusion, proclaim if not the truth about these two states, with a voice so powerful that it is impossible to resist it? (435)

403. *Difference between Jesus Christ and Mahomet.*

Mahomet was not foretold; Jesus Christ was.

Mahomet slew; Jesus Christ caused the death of his own followers.

Mahomet forbade reading; the Apostles ordered it.

In short, they are so opposed that if Mahomet, humanly speaking, chose the path of success, Jesus Christ, humanly speaking, chose that of death; and instead of concluding that, since Mahomet succeeded, Jesus Christ could have succeeded, we must say that, since Mahomet succeeded, Jesus Christ was bound to die. (599)

404. All men hate one another instinctively. They have used concupiscence as best they could for the general good; but it is nothing but a pretence and a false image of charity; for at bottom it is simply a form of hatred. (451)

405. Men have used concupiscence as a foundation and have extracted from it some admirable rules of policy, morality and justice.

But at bottom, the vile bottom of man's soul, that *figmentum malum*, is only veiled: it is not eradicated. (453)

406. Jesus Christ is a God whom we approach without pride, and before whom we humble ourselves without despair. (528)

407. *Dignior plagis quam osculis non timeo quia amo.*[1] . (551)

408. It is the sign of true religion that it should make man love his God. That is fair enough, and yet none of the other religions have prescribed it; ours alone has done so.

It must also have known lust and frailty; ours has.

It must have provided cures for them; one is prayer. No

---

[1] More deserving of blows than kisses, I fear nothing because I love (St. Bernard: *In Cantica Sermones*, 84).

other religion has asked God to teach man to love and follow
him.   (491)

409. *After reaching an understanding of the whole nature of man.* For
a religion to be true, it must have understood our nature. It
must have grasped its littleness and its greatness, and the
reasons for both. What religion but the Christian has done so?
                                                                                          (433)

410. True religion teaches us our duties and our weaknesses
(pride and concupiscence); and the remedies (humility and
mortification).   (493)

411. There are some symbols which are clear and compelling;
but there are others which seem to be too fine spun, and only
convince those who are already convinced by some other source.
They are similar to the Apocalyptics. But the difference is that
they have none which are absolutely convincing; so much so
that there is nothing so unfair as when they argue that theirs are
as well-founded as some of ours, for none of theirs is conclusive
as some of ours are.

The odds therefore are not even. We must not equate and
confuse things because they happen to appear alike in one respect when they are so different in others; when this form of
illumination is divine in origin, it is right that we should respect
the obscurities which go with it.

[It is like people who make use of a certain obscurity of
language: those who did not understand it would interpret it
foolishly.]   (650)

412. It is not by what is obscure in Mahomet, which can be
passed off as having a hidden meaning, that I wish him to be
judged, but by what is clear in him, by his paradise, and the
rest. It is that which makes him ridiculous. And that is why it is
not right to take his obscurities for mysteries, considering that
what is clear in him is ridiculous.

It is not the same with Scripture. I agree that it has obscurities which are just as odd as Mahomet's; but there are
things which are admirably clear, prophecies which are plain
and have been fulfilled. The odds therefore are not even. We
must not confuse and treat as equal things which are only alike

on account of their obscurity and not their clarity, which demands respect for the obscurities. (598)

413. The other religions like the pagan religions are more popular because their essence lies in externals; but they are not intended for clever people. A purely intellectual religion would be more suitable for clever people; but it would be of no use to ordinary people. The Christian religion alone is suitable for everybody because of its blend of inward and outward. It elevates people inwardly, and humbles the proud outwardly; it is not perfect without both elements because the people must understand the spirit of the letter, and the clever must submit to the letter. (251)

414. No other religion has suggested hatred of self. No other religion therefore can appeal to those who hate themselves, and who seek a truly gracious being. And even if they had never heard anyone speak of the religion of a humiliated God, they would unhesitatingly embrace it. (468)

415. Antiquity of the Jews. What a difference there is between one book and another! I am not surprised that the Greeks produced their *Iliad*, or the Egyptians and the Chinese their histories. We only need to see how it happened. Their fabled historians were not contemporary with the events of which they write. Homer wrote a novel which was offered and accepted as such; for no one supposed that Troy and Agamemnon had existed any more than the golden apple. He had no idea either of presenting it as history; it was simply intended as an entertainment; he was the only man to write about his own time, and the beauty of the book has made it immortal; everybody studies it and talks about it; we have to know it, and indeed everyone knows it by heart. Four hundred years later the people who witnessed the events are no longer living; there is no one who knows from personal experience whether it is fact or fiction; it has simply been handed down from generation to generation and might easily pass for fact.

All history which is not contemporary is suspect; it so happens that the books of the sybils and Trismegistus, and many others which have enjoyed a great reputation for veracity, are false and are seen to be false with the passing of time. The position of contemporary authors is not the same.

There is a great difference between a book written by an individual and tossed to the people, and a book which is itself written by a people. We cannot doubt that the second kind of book is as old as the people. (628)

416. *Against the history of China.* The historians of Mexico, the five suns, the last of which was only eight hundred years ago.

Difference between a book which is accepted by a nation, and one which creates a nation. (594)

417. If there is a God, we must love only him, and not transient creatures. The argument of the unbelievers in the Book of Wisdom is simply based on the assumption that there is no God. 'Now we've got that settled,' they say, 'let us take our pleasure with creatures.' It is a *pis-aller.* If there were a God to love, they would not have settled for that, but for the opposite. And that is the conclusion of the wise: 'There is a God, let us not therefore seek our pleasure with creatures.'

Thus everything that encourages us to attach ourselves to creatures is bad because it prevents us either from serving God, if we have found him, or seeking him if we have not found him. Now we are full of sensual desires, therefore we are full of evil; therefore we should hate ourselves and anything which encourages any form of attachment except to God alone. (479)

418. Anyone who does not hate in himself his self-love and the impulse which drives him to turn himself into God, is very blind indeed. Who can fail to see that nothing is more contrary to justice and truth? For it is false to say that we deserve to be; and it is unjust and impossible to achieve God because all men demand the same thing. It is therefore a patent injustice in which we are born, from which we cannot escape, and from which we must escape.

No other religion, however, has pointed out that a sin was committed, that we were born in it, that we are obliged to resist it, nor thought of providing us with remedies. (492)

419. On the fact that the Christian religion is not unique. So far from this being a reason for not believing that it is the true religion, it is the very thing that makes us see that it is.   (589)

420. The ordinary man has the faculty of not thinking about things that he does not wish to think about. 'Don't think about the passages on the Messiah,' said the Jew to his son. Our own people often do the same. In this way false religions are preserved, and for many people even the true one. But there are some who do not possess the ability to prevent themselves from thinking, and who think all the more because they are forbidden to do so. These people put away both false religions and the true religion, unless they can find solid arguments for it.   (259)

421. *History of China.* I only believe histories whose witnesses are ready to let themselves be torn to pieces.

[Which is the more credible of the two, Moses or China?]

It is not a question of a rough estimate. I tell you that there is something to confuse and something to enlighten us.

With this one word I destroy all your arguments. 'But China obscures things,' you say; and I reply: 'China obscures the issue, but the light is there to be found; look for it.'

Thus everything you say strengthens one of the arguments and does nothing to destroy the other. Therefore it is useful and does no harm.

For this reason we must look at it closely; we must produce the documents.   (593)

422. Every religion is false which does not, as part of its creed, worship a God as the principle of all things, and which in its moral system does not love one God as the object of all things.

(487)

17. A GRACIOUS RELIGION

423. Jesus Christ for all. Moses for a single people.

The Jews blessed in Abraham: 'I will bless all who bless thee.' But: 'All nations are blessed in his seed,' *Parum est ut*, etc. *Lumen ad revelationem gentium.*[1]

Non fecit taliter omni nationi, said David, when speaking of the law.[2] Isaiah. Therefore it is Jesus Christ who is universal; the Church herself only offers the sacrifice for the faithful: Jesus Christ offered up the sacrifice of the Cross for all men.　(774)

424. The carnal Jews and the heathen have their misfortunes; so do Christians. There is no Redeemer for the heathen because they do not hope for one. There is no Redeemer for the Jews; they wait for him in vain. There is only a Redeemer for Christians (*see Perpetuity*).　(747)

425. In matters of religion we must be sincere: true heathen, true Jews, true Christians.　(590)

426. Jesus Christ never condemned anyone without a hearing. To Judas: *Amice, ad quid venisti?* The man who did not have the wedding garment was addressed in the same manner.

(780)

427. If we do not see that we are a mass of pride, ambition, lust, weakness, misery and injustice, we must be very blind. And if, once we do know it, we do not seek deliverance from them, what can we say of a man . . . ?

How then can we have anything but a good opinion of a religion which understands the failings of human nature so well, and what can we do but wish that a religion, which promises such desirable remedies, should be true?　(450)

428. The style of the Gospels is admirable in many ways, among them the fact that they never use invective against the murderers and enemies of Jesus Christ. For in none of the historians

---

[1] I have appointed thee to be the light of the Gentiles (Is. XLIX, 6).
[2] Not such his dealings with any other nations (Ps. CXLII, 20).

is there any invective against Judas, Pilate or any of the Jews.

If the modesty of the historians of the Gospels had been assumed, as well as their many other admirable qualities, if they had only assumed it in order to draw attention to it, and if they had not been bold enough to remark on it themselves, they would not have failed to gain friends whose comments would have been flattering to them. But since in fact they were devoid of affectation and completely disinterested, they did not draw anyone's attention to it. And I think that up to the present a number of other qualities of the same kind have gone unnoticed, and that is a sign of the detachment with which the job was done. (798)

429. It is all very fine. We have to admit that there is something astonishing about the Christian religion. 'It is because you were born in it,' someone will say. Far from it; I set my face against it for this very reason, because I was afraid that prejudice would influence me; but though I was born in it, I soon found that it was astonishing. (615)

18. FOUNDATIONS OF RELIGION AND REPLY TO OBJECTIONS

430. We must transfer what we have said about the nature of symbols from the chapter on *Symbolic Writing* to the chapter on *The Foundations*: why Jesus Christ's first coming was foretold; why foretold in an obscure manner. (570)

431. Unbelievers are the most credulous of people. They believe in the miracles of Vespasian so that they will not have to believe in those of Moses. (816)

432. Just as Jesus Christ remained unknown among men, so truth remains buried beneath conventional opinions without any outward difference. It is the same with the Eucharist and ordinary bread. (789)

433. The whole of faith lies in Jesus Christ and in Adam; and the whole of morality in concupiscence and in grace. (523)

434. What objection have they got to the Resurrection, or to a Virgin giving birth? Is it more difficult to produce a man or an animal than to reproduce them? And if they had never seen a particular kind of animal, would they be able to say whether they could be produced without one another? (223)

435. What do the prophets say about Jesus Christ? That he will manifestly be God? No; they say that he is truly a hidden God; that he will not be recognised; that none will think that it is he: that he will be a stumbling block which will cause the fall of many, etc. Therefore, let no one criticise us for want of clarity since we make profession of it.

'But,' someone will say, 'there are obscurities.' And without them, Jesus Christ would have caused no one to stumble, and it is one of the formal pronouncements of the prophets: *Excaeca . . .'* (751)

436. Religion teaches children things that men have learnt as the fruit of their profoundest insights. (444)

437. Not everything that is incomprehensible is non-existent.

(430 *bis*)

438. If we choose to say that man is too insignificant to deserve communion with God, we must be very great to judge the matter. (511)

439. We shall understand nothing about the works of God unless we accept the principle that he wished some people to be blind to them and others to understand them clearly. (566)

440. Jesus Christ does not say that he is not from Nazareth in order to leave the wicked in their state of blindness, nor that he is not the son of Joseph. (796)

441. God prefers to mould the will rather than the mind. Perfect clarity would be a help to the mind and harmful to the will. Humble the proud. (581)

442. Jesus Christ came to bring blindness to those who saw clearly, and to give sight to the blind; to cure the sick, and leave the healthy to die; to call sinners to repentance and justify them, and leave the righteous to their sins; to give to the needy, and leave the rich empty. (771)

443. There is sufficient light to enlighten the elect and sufficient

darkness to humiliate them. There is sufficient darkness to blind the damned, and sufficient light to condemn them and make them unpardonable. St. Augustine, Montaigne, *Sebonde*.

The genealogy of Jesus Christ in the Old Testament is mixed up with so many others which are pointless that it cannot be distinguished from them. If Moses had simply kept a record of the ancestors of Jesus Christ, it would have been too obvious. If he had not stressed that of Jesus Christ sufficiently, it would not have been plain enough. But after all, anyone who looks into the matter carefully enough can see that Jesus Christ is clearly distinguished by Thamar, Ruth, etc.

Those who ordered sacrifices were aware of their uselessness, and those who asserted that they were useless did not hesitate to perform them.

If God had only allowed a single religion, it would have been too easy to recognise; but when we examine it carefully, we can easily distinguish what is true beneath the confusion.

Principle: Moses was a clever man. If therefore he was guided by his intellect, he would not say anything which was directly contrary to the intellect.

Thus all the more obvious weaknesses are a source of strength. Example: the two genealogies in St. Matthew and St. Luke. What could be plainer than the fact that they did not put their heads together? (578)

444. If Jesus Christ had only come to sanctify, the whole of Scripture and everything else would emphasise the point, and it would be perfectly easy to convince unbelievers. If Jesus Christ had only come to make them blind, the whole of his behaviour would be a muddle and we should have no means of convincing the unbeliever. But as he came in *sanctificationem et in scandalum*, as Isaiah says,[1] we cannot convince unbelievers and they cannot convince us; but for that very reason, we do convince them because we say that in the whole of his behaviour there is nothing to convince either side. (795)

445. *Symbols.* God wishing to deprive his people of perishable

[1] Let the hour of peril consecrate you to him; for the rest . . . it will be a stone to trip men's feet, a boulder that catches them unawares (Is. VIII, 14).

gifts, created the Jewish people in order to show that it was not
through lack of power.   (645)

446. Man is not worthy of God, but he is not incapable of being
made worthy of him.

It is unworthy of God to unite himself to man in his misery;
but it is not unworthy of God to rescue him from his misery.

(510)

447. *Proof.* Prophecies and their fulfilment; what preceded and
what followed Jesus Christ.   (705)

448. *Source of contradictions.* A God humiliated to the point of
death on a cross; a Messiah triumphing over death by his death.
Two natures in Jesus Christ, two comings, two states of the
nature of man.   (765)

449. *That God chose to hide himself.* If there were only one religion,
God would be plainly revealed in it.

It would be the same if our religion were the only one to
have martyrs.

Since God has so hidden himself, every religion which does
not declare that God is a hidden God is not true; and every
religion which does not give the reason is not a teaching religion.
Ours does both: *Vere tu es Deus absconditus.*[1]   (585)

450.* [*Foundation of our faith.*] The pagan religion is [today] without any foundations. [It is said that at other times its foundations were provided by the oracles. But what books are there
which contain any proof that they spoke? Does their authorship
make them worthy of credence? Have they been preserved with
such care that we can be certain that the text has not been
tampered with?]

The foundations of the Mahommedan religion are Mahomet
and the Koran. But had the coming of the prophet, who was
supposed to be the last hope of the world, been foretold? What
is there about him that is not to be found in anyone who wants
to be regarded as a prophet? What miracles does he himself
claim to have performed? What mysteries is he supposed by his
followers to have taught? What moral system and what form
of happiness?

[1] Truly . . . thou art a God of hidden ways (Is. xlv, 15).

The Jewish religion must be considered differently according to the tradition of the Sacred Books and that of the people. Its moral system and its conception of happiness are ridiculous according to the tradition of the people; but admirable according to that of [the] Sacred [Books] (and it is the same with every religion: for there is a great difference between the way in which the Christian religion is presented in the Sacred Books and in the works of the casuists). The foundations are admirable: it is the oldest book in the world and the most authentic; and whereas Mahomet tried to preserve his book by forbidding people to read it, Moses tried to preserve his by ordering everybody to read it.

Our religion is so divine that another divine religion has merely provided it with a foundation. (601)

451. Objection of atheists: 'But we possess no light.' (228)

452. The truth of religion is apparent from its very obscurity, from the small amount of information that we have about it, from our indifference in finding out about it. (565)

453. If he once existed, the Eternal Being exists always.

(559 *bis*)

454. All the objections advanced on both sides simply militate against one another, and not against religion. Everything that the infidels say ... (201)

455. They go all the more astray because each of them pursues a single aspect of truth. Their mistake does not lie in following something which is false, but in not following another form of truth. (863)

456. If it is a sign of weakness to prove the existence of God by the argument from nature, do not despise Scripture; if it is a sign of strength to have been aware of these contradictions, give Scripture credit for it. (428)

457. [*Baseness.*] God used the blindness of the Jewish people for the benefit of the elect. (577)

458. As the creation of the world was beginning to recede into the distance, God provided a unique contemporary historian and entrusted a whole people with the preservation of his book, so that his history should be the most authentic in the world, and everyone might learn from it something which it is so necessary to know and which could only be learnt in that way. (622)

459. Proofs. —1. The Christian religion, by its foundation, by establishing itself so firmly, so gently, though so contrary to nature. 2. The holiness, loftiness and humility of a Christian soul. 3. The wonders of Holy Scripture. 4. Jesus Christ in particular. 5. The apostles in particular. 6. Moses and the prophets in particular. 7. The Jewish people. 8. The prophets. 9. Perpetuity: no religion possesses perpetuity. 10. Doctrine, which provides us with a reason for everything. 11. The holiness of the law. 12. By the behaviour of the world.

There can be no doubt that, once we have come to see what life is and what religion is, we cannot refuse to follow our inclination and embrace it, if it comes into our heart; and it is certain that there are no grounds for making fun of those who do so. (289)

460. Two conflicting reasons. We must begin by that: otherwise we shall understand nothing, and everything will be heretical; and it should be added that with each truth we come upon, we must remind ourselves of the truth which is opposed to it. (567)

461. *General behaviour of the world towards the Church: God wishing to bring darkness and light.* Since events have proved the divine nature of the prophecies, everything else they say must be taken on trust. And so we see the order of the world in this manner.

When the miracles of the creation and the flood had been forgotten, God sent the law and the miracles of Moses, the prophets who foretold particular things; and in order to prepare the way for an abiding miracle, it was preceded by the prophecies and their fulfilment; but as the prophecies might be suspect, he took steps to ensure that they would be free from suspicion, etc. (576)

462. The Church has always been attacked by opposing errors, but never before, perhaps, simultaneously, as she is today. And if she suffers more on account of the large number of errors, she also has this advantage—that they are mutually destructive.

She complains of both, but far more of the Calvinists because they were responsible for the schism.

There is no doubt that a number belonging to the two opposing sects have been duped; we must disabuse them.

The faith contains several truths which appear to contradict one another. 'Time for laughter, time for tears, etc.' *Responde. Ne Respondeas*, etc.

Their origin is the union of two natures in Jesus Christ.

And also two worlds (the creation of a new heaven and a new earth; new life, new death; all things duplicated, and the same names remaining).

And finally, the two persons who are in the nature of the righteous man (for they are two worlds, and a member and image of Jesus Christ. And thus all names are applicable to them: righteous, sinners; dead, living; saved, damned, etc.)!

There are therefore a great number of truths both of faith and morals which appear repugnant, and which all exist in wonderful order.

The origin of all heresy is the exclusion of one or other of these truths.

And the origin of all the objections that heretics bring against us is ignorance of some aspect of truth.

And what usually happens is that not being capable of perceiving the relation between two opposing truths and believing that the admission of one implies the rejection of the other, they accept one and reject the other, and think that we do the opposite. Now rejection is the cause of their heresy; and their ignorance of the fact that we hold the other is the cause of their objections.

First example: Jesus Christ is God and man. The Arians, being unable to see the connection between these two things which they thought incompatible, declared that he was man: in that they were Catholics. But they denied that he was God: in that they were heretics. They claimed that we denied his humanity: in that they showed that they were ignorant.

Second example: on the subject of the Blessed Sacrament. We believe that the substance of the bread is changed, and transubstantiated into the Body of Our Lord, that Jesus Christ is really present. That is one of the truths. Another is that the

Sacrament is also a symbol of the Cross and of glory, and a commemoration of the two. That is the Catholic faith which includes two truths which appear to conflict.

Contemporary heresy, not realising that the Sacrament contains together both the presence of Jesus Christ and a symbol of him, and that it is both a sacrifice and a commemoration of a sacrifice, believes that for this reason we cannot admit one of these truths without denying the other.

They insist on this one point—that the Sacrament is symbolical; and in that they are not heretical. They think that we reject this truth; whence it comes that they bring so many objections against us over the passages in the Fathers which say that it is symbolical. Finally, they deny the Presence; and in that they are heretical.

Third example: indulgences.

That is why the quickest method of preventing heresy is to give instruction about all these truths; and the surest way of refuting all heresies is to bring them out into the open. For what will the heretics say?

In order to discover whether an opinion belongs to one of the Fathers . . . (862)

463. The cunning are people who recognise truth, but who only support it in so far as it is in their interest to do so; and apart from that, reject it. (583)

464. *Objection.* Scripture is evidently full of things which were not dictated by the Holy Spirit. *Reply.* In that case, they do no harm to the faith. *Objection.* But the Church has declared that the whole of it is by the Holy Spirit. *Reply.* I answer two things: one, that the Church has never said that; the other, that, if she had said it, it could be upheld. (568)

465. Against those who misuse passages from Scripture and who take advantage of any which appear to support their error. The office of Vespers, Passion Sunday, the prayer for the king.

Explanation of these words: 'Who is not for me is against me.' And of these others: 'Who is not against you is for you.' To a person who says: 'I am neither for nor against,' we should reply . . . (899)

238

466. For this reason I reject all the other religions.

In that way I find an answer to all the objections.

It is right that a God who is so pure should only reveal himself to those whose hearts have been purified.

For this reason I find religion gracious, and for me it is sufficiently authenticated by such a divine system of morality; but I find more besides.

I find that in fact, as far back as human memory stretches, there has been in existence a people who are older than any other people.

Men are constantly being told that they are in a state of universal corruption, but that a Redeemer will come.

That it is not one man who says so, but an infinite number of men, and a whole people foretelling him and doing so deliberately for four thousand years; their books dispersed for four hundred years.

The more I study them, the more truths I find in them; a whole people foretell him before his coming, a whole people worship him after his coming; and what came before and went after; and the synagogue which preceded him; finally the people without idols, or kings, wretched and without prophets, who follow him and who, all being enemies, are admirable witnesses to the truth of the prophecies in which their wretchedness and blindness were foretold.

The darkness of the Jews was appalling and foretold.

Eris palpans in meridie.

Dabitur liber scienti litteras, et dicet: 'Non possum legere'.[1]

The sceptre still in the hands of the first foreign usurper.

The rumour of the coming of Jesus Christ.

Thus I hold out my arms to my *Saviour* who, after being foretold for a period of four thousand years, came to suffer and die for me on earth at the time and in exactly the circumstances which had been predicted; and by his grace I await death in peace of mind, in the hope of being eternally united to him;

---

[1] And mayst thou grope at midday (Deut. xxviii, 29). A book, shall be given to one who is learned . . . and he shall say: 'I cannot read' (Is. xxix, 11).

and yet I live joyfully either among the good things which it pleases him to bestow upon me, or amid the ills which he sends me for my own good, and has taught me to suffer by his example. (737)

467. The two oldest books in the world are Moses and Job, one a Jew, the other a heathen, who both regard Jesus Christ as their common centre and object; Moses by recording God's promises to Abraham, Jacob, etc., and his prophecies; and Job: *Quis mihi det ut*, etc. *Scio quod redemptor meus vivit*, etc.[1] (741)

468. Suppose that an heir finds the title deeds of his house. Will he say: 'They may be false!' without bothering to examine them? (217)

469. Our religion is wisdom and foolishness. Wisdom because it is the most knowledgeable, and the most firmly based on miracles, prophecies, etc. Foolishness because it is not these things that make us cling to it; it is a good reason for condemning those who do not belong to it, but not for making those who do belong to it believe. What makes them believe is the Cross, *ne evacuata sit crux*.[2]

And so St. Paul, who came with wisdom and signs, said that he had not come with wisdom or signs: for he came to convert. But those who only come to convince can say that they come with wisdom and signs. (588)

470. The two foundations, one inward, the other outward: grace, miracles; both supernatural. (805)

471. *Atheists*. What grounds have they for saying that we cannot rise from the dead? Which is more difficult, to be born or to rise from the dead, that something which has never happened should happen, or that something which has happened should happen again? Is it more difficult to come into being than to return to being? Custom makes one easy for us, the absence of custom makes the other impossible: popular method of judging!

Why cannot a virgin give birth? Does not a hen lay eggs without a cock? What distinguishes them outwardly from one

[1] Who will grant me, etc. For I know that my Redeemer liveth. (Job XIX, 23-25.)
[2] Lest the Cross of Christ should be made void (I Cor., I, 17).

another? And how do we know that the hen cannot form the germ just as well as the cock? (222)

472. Religion is adapted to every sort of mind. The first stop at its foundation alone, and our religion is such that its foundation alone is sufficient to prove its truth. The others go back as far as the apostles. The most fully instructed go back to the beginning of the world. The angels have a still better view and from a greater distance. (285)

473. It is not possible to base the rejection of miracles on reasonable grounds. (815)

474. 'A miracle,' people say, 'would strengthen my faith.' They say that sort of thing when they do not see one.

The reasons which, when seen from a distance, seem to impede our view, but when we come closer we begin to see beyond them. Nothing puts a stop to the volubility of our minds. There is no rule, it is said, without an exception, and no truth so general that it does not have some aspect which is defective. It is sufficient for it not to be absolutely universal to provide us with an opportunity of applying the exception to the present subject, and to say: 'It is not invariably true; there are therefore some instances in which it is not true.' It only remains to show that this is one of them; and it is in this respect that we must be either very clumsy or very unfortunate if we do not find some light. (263)

475. *Miracle.* The people come to that conclusion of their own accord; but if you have to give a reason for it . . .

It is annoying to be an exception to the rule. Nonetheless, as there are undoubtedly exceptions to the rule, they must be judged strictly but fairly. (833)

476. The prophecies were equivocal: they are no longer so. (830)

477. *Title: Why we believe so many liars who tell us that they have seen miracles and do not believe any of those who claim to possess the secret of making man immortal or rejuvenating him.* After considering why we place so much faith in so many impostors who claim to possess powers of healing, to the extent sometimes of placing our lives

in their hands, it appeared to me that the real reason is that some of them are genuine: for it is not possible that there should be so many who are frauds and that we should place so much faith in them, if there were not some who are genuine. If there had never been any remedy for any illness and if all illnesses had been incurable, it is impossible that men should have imagined that they could provide cures; and still more that so many others should have believed those who boasted that they did know of remedies: in the same way that, if a man boasted that he could prevent us from dying, no one would believe him because there has never been a case of its happening. But as there were a large number of remedies which were found to be genuine and acknowledged by the greatest men, human belief bowed to them; and since it was known to be possible, people came to the conclusion that it was a fact. For people usually argue in this way: 'A thing is possible, therefore it is a fact'; for if a thing cannot be denied out of hand because there happen to be particular effects which are genuine, the people, who are unable to distinguish which of these particular effects is genuine, believe in them all. In the same way, what makes us believe in many of the illusory effects of the moon is that some of them are genuine like the tides of the sea.

It is the same with prophecies, miracles, sorcery, spooks, etc. For if there had never been anything authentic in that sort of thing, no one would ever have believed any of it: and so instead of deciding that there are no genuine miracles because there are so many spurious ones, we should adopt the opposite point of view and argue that there are certainly some genuine miracles because there are spurious ones, and that there are only spurious ones because there are some genuine ones.

We must use the same arguments with religion; because it would not have been possible for men to invent so many false religions if there were not one true one. The objection to that is that even savages have a religion: but the answer is that they have heard people talk about religion, as we can see by the flood, circumcision, the cross of St. Andrew, etc.   (817)

478. After asking myself why there are so many bogus miracles, false revelations, spooks, etc., I came to the conclusion that it is because there are some genuine ones, since the existence of so many spurious miracles would not be possible if there were no genuine ones, or so many false religions if there were not a true one. For if there had never been anything in it, it is impossible that men should have imagined that there had and still more impossible that so many others should have believed it. But, as there have been some very great miracles which were genuine and for this reason were believed by great men, the impression they made means that nearly everybody has become liable to believe in the spurious ones as well. And so, instead of coming to the conclusion that there are no genuine miracles because there are so many spurious ones, we should argue that there are some genuine miracles because there are so many spurious ones, that the only reason that there are spurious ones is that there are some genuine ones, and that in the same way there are only false religions because there is a true religion.

The objection is that savages have a religion; but it is because they have heard people speak of the true religion as we can see from the cross of St. Andrew, the flood, circumcision, etc. This is due to the fact that when the human mind finds itself bound to accept something as true, by the same token it becomes so gullible that it swallows every kind of bogus story of the . . .   (818)

19. THE SYMBOLIC LAW

479. That the law was symbolical.   (647)

480. *Symbols.* The Jewish and Egyptian peoples plainly foretold by the two individuals whom Moses met: the Egyptian beating the Jew, Moses avenging him by killing the Egyptian, and the Jew being ungrateful for it.   (657)

481. *Symbolism.* 'Make everything according to the pattern which was shown there on the mountain.' Whereupon St. Paul said that the Jews represented heavenly things.   (674)

482. *Symbols.* The prophets using the symbols of the girdle, the beard, the burnt hair, etc. (653)

483. *Symbolical.* Key of the cipher: *Veri adoratores.* —*Ecce agnus Dei qui tollit peccata mundi.*[1] (681)

484. *Symbolical.* The term sword, *écu. Potentissime.* (667)

485. Anyone who wishes to explain the meaning of Scripture and does not take it from Scripture is the enemy of Scripture. Augustine: *De doctrina christiana.* (900)

486. Two kinds of error: 1. To interpret everything literally; 2. to interpret everything in a spiritual sense. (648)

487. *Symbols.* Jesus Christ opened their minds so that they might understand the Scriptures.

Two great openings are as follows: 1. Everything came to them in the form of symbols: *vere Israelitae, veri liberi*, true bread from heaven; 2. a God humiliated to the extent of dying on the Cross: Christ had to suffer in order to enter into his glory: 'that, through death, he might destroy the empire of death'. Two comings. (679)

488. Attack those who use too many symbols. (649)

489. In order that the Messiah should be accepted by good men and rejected by bad, God had his coming foretold in this manner. If the way of the Messiah had been clearly foretold, there would have been no obscurity, even for the wicked.

If the time had been foretold obscurely, there would have been obscurity even for the good; because the [goodness of their hearts] would not have enabled them to understand, for example, that the closed *mem* signifies six hundred years. But the time had been clearly foretold, and the manner by means of symbols.

In this way, the wicked, assuming that the promised riches meant material riches, went astray in spite of the fact that the time had been clearly foretold, and the righteous did not go astray.

For knowledge of the promised riches depends on the heart which describes what it loves as 'good'; but knowledge of the

[1] True worshippers. —Look this is the Lamb of God . . . who takes away the sin of the world (John IV, 23; I, 29).

promised time does not depend on the heart. And so the clear prediction of the time and the obscure prediction of riches only deceived the wicked. (758)

490. The materialist Jews did not understand the greatness or the lowliness of the Messiah whose coming had been foretold by their prophets. They failed to recognise in him the greatness which had been foretold, as when it is said that the Messiah will be David's Lord though his son, that he is before Abraham and has seen him; they did not believe him to be so great that he was eternal. And they failed to recognise him in his lowliness and death: 'The Messiah,' they said, 'abideth for ever, and this man says that he will die.' They did not believe therefore either that he was eternal or mortal: they only looked for worldly greatness in him. (662)

491. Contradiction. We can only give ourselves a good countenance by reconciling the conflicting elements in ourselves, and it is not enough to display a succession of harmonious qualities without reconciling opposites. In order to grasp the meaning of a writer, we must reconcile all the conflicting passages.

Thus, in order to understand Scripture there must be an interpretation which reconciles all the conflicting passages. It is not enough to have one which fits a number of passages that happen to agree: there must be one which reconciles even the contradictory passages.

Every writer has a meaning to which all conflicting passages are subordinated, or his work is meaningless. We cannot say that Scripture and the prophets are meaningless; they undoubtedly had too much good sense. We must therefore seek one interpretation which reconciles all the contradictions.

The true meaning is not therefore that of the Jews; but in Jesus Christ all the contradictions are reconciled.

The Jews would not be able to reconcile the end of the royal and princely line predicted by Osee with the prophecy of Jacob.

If we accept the law, the sacrifices, and the kingdom as

realities, we cannot reconcile all the passages. It therefore follows that they must only be regarded as symbols. We should not even be able to reconcile the different passages of the same writer, or of the same book, or sometimes the same chapter, which shows only too clearly what the author meant; as when Ezechiel, Chapter xx, says that we shall and shall not live according to the commandments of God. (684)

492. It was not permissible to sacrifice outside the city of Jerusalem, which was the place that the Lord had chosen, or even to eat the first fruits anywhere else. Deut., xii, 5, etc.; Deut., xiv, 23, etc.; xv, 20; xvi, 2, 7, 11, 15.

Osee foretold that they would be without kings, without princes, without sacrifices, without idols; which is what has happened today because no lawful sacrifice can be offered outside Jerusalem. (728)

493*. Symbols. If the law and the sacrifices are the truth, they must be pleasing to God and not displeasing to him. If they are symbols, they must be pleasing or displeasing.

Now all through Scripture they please and displease.

It is said that the law will be changed, that the sacrifice will be changed, that the people will be without law, without princes and without sacrifices; that a new covenant will be made; that the law will be renewed; that the precepts which they have received are not good; that their sacrifices are abominable; that God did not ask for them.

On the other hand, it is said that the law shall last for ever; that the covenant shall be for ever; that the sacrifice shall be everlasting; that the sceptre shall never depart from them because it must not depart from them until the coming of the everlasting King.

Are all these passages intended literally? No. Are they intended symbolically? No, they are intended literally or symbolically. But the first, which exclude a literal interpretation, show that they must only be understood symbolically.

All these passages when taken together cannot be said to be true in the literal sense; they can all be described as symbolic: therefore they do not apply to reality, but to symbolism.

Agnus occisus est ab origini mundi juge sacrificium.[1]   (685)

494. *Symbols*. A portrait involves absence and presence, pleasure and pain. Reality excludes absence and pain.

In order to find out whether the law and the sacrifices are reality or symbol, we must see whether the prophets, when speaking of them, allowed their mind and thought to dwell on them, whether they saw only the old covenant, or if they saw something else of which it was a representation; for in a portrait we see a representation of the object. In order to discover the answer, all we need to do is to ask ourselves what they say about it.

When they proclaim that the covenant will be everlasting, are they speaking of the same covenant which they say will be changed; and the same with sacrifices, etc.?

A cipher has a double meaning. When we come across a key letter which has a clear meaning, and which says nevertheless that the meaning is veiled and obscure, that it is hidden, so that we see the letter without seeing it and understand without understanding it—what conclusions shall we draw except that it is a cipher with a double meaning, the more so because the literal meaning contains manifest contradictions?

The prophets said clearly that God would always cherish Israel, and that the law would be everlasting; they also said that their meaning would not be understood, that it would be veiled.

How highly therefore should we esteem those who decode the message for us and help us to understand its hidden meaning, particularly when the principles that they extract from it are completely clear and simple! That is what Jesus Christ and the Apostles did. They broke the seal, tore aside the veils and revealed the spirit. In this way they taught us that the enemies of man are his passions; that the Redeemer would be spiritual and his reign spiritual; that there would be two comings: one in poverty in order to humiliate the proud, the other glorious to exalt the humble; that Jesus Christ would be God and man.

(678)

---

[1] The Lamb slain in sacrifice ever since the world was made (Apoc., xiii, 8).

495. The time of the first coming was deliberately foretold; the time of the second was not because the first was to be hidden, the second dazzling and so manifest that his enemies themselves would be forced to recognise him. But his first coming was to be shrouded in obscurity, and to be known only to those who had probed the Scriptures. (757)

496. What could his enemies, the Jews, do? If they had accepted him, their acceptance would have been proof of his claims, because he would have been accepted by those to whom the expectation of the Messiah had been entrusted; if they rejected him, they proved the truth of his claims by their rejection. (762)

497. *Contradictions.* The sceptre until the coming of the Messiah, —without king or prince.

Everlasting law—changed.

Everlasting covenant,—new covenant.

Good laws,—bad precepts. Ezech., xx. (686)

498. The Jews were accustomed to great and striking miracles, and after the great miracles of the Red Sea and the land of Canaan, which were an epitome of the splendid deeds of their Messiah, they expected even more striking events of which the miracles of Moses were no more than a foretaste. (746)

499. A symbol involves absence and presence, pleasure and pain.

A cipher with a double meaning: one clear, and one in which the meaning is said to be hidden. (677)

500. We might perhaps think that when the prophets predicted that the sceptre would not depart from Juda before the coming of the everlasting king, they spoke in order to flatter the people, and that their prophecy was proved false by Herod. But to show that this was not what they meant and that on the contrary they knew that the temporal kingdom would come to an end, they said that for many years the people would be without king and without prince. Osee, III, 4. (719)

501. *Symbols.* Once the mystery has been revealed, it is impossible not to see it. Let us read the Old Testament, and let us see if the sacrifices were true, if the fatherhood of Abraham was the true cause of the friendship of God, if the promised land

was the true place of rest? No; therefore they were symbols.

Let us look, in the same light, at all the ceremonies which were prescribed, all the commandments which were not for charity, and we shall see that they were symbols.

All the sacrifices and ceremonies were therefore symbols or absurdities. Now there are things which are clear and too sublime to be dismissed as absurdities.

See whether the vision of the prophets was confined to events in the Old Testament, or whether they saw other things in it.

(680)

502. *Symbols*. The letter kills.

Everything came in the form of symbols.

It was necessary that Christ should suffer.

A humiliated God. That is the cipher that St. Paul gives us.

Circumcision of the heart, true fasting, true sacrifice, true temple. The prophets showed that it all had to be spiritual.

Not the meat which perishes, but the meat which does not perish. 'You will be truly free.' Therefore the other freedom is only a symbol of freedom.

'I am the true bread from heaven.'   (683)

503. There are some who understand clearly that man has no enemy except concupiscence, which makes him turn away from God and not from the . . . and no good except God, and not fertile land. Those who believe that man's good lies in the flesh, and evil in the things which induce him to turn his back on the pleasures of the senses, deserve to become glutted with them and to die of them. But let those be comforted who seek God with all their heart, who have no sorrow except being deprived of the sight of him, whose only desire is to possess him, who have no enemies except those who detach them from God, and who are distressed to find themselves surrounded and dominated by such enemies, for I bring them good news: they have a Saviour; I will show him to them; I will show them that there is a God for them; I will not show others. I will show them that a Messiah was promised who would deliver them from their enemies; that one came who delivered them from iniquity, but not from their enemies.

When David foretold that the Messiah would deliver his people from their enemies, we may believe that according to the flesh he meant the Egyptians, and then I should not be able to show that the prophecy was fulfilled. But we may also very well believe that he meant iniquities, for, in truth, the Egyptians were not enemies, but iniquities are. The word enemies is therefore ambiguous.

But if he says, as he does, in another place like Isaiah and the rest, that he will deliver his people from their sins, the ambiguity is removed, the double sense of enemies reduced to the simple sense of iniquities. For if he had in mind sins, he could very well have referred to them as enemies, but if he was thinking of enemies he could not have described them as iniquities.

Now, Moses, David and Isaiah used the same terms. Who then will argue that they did not mean the same thing, and that the meaning of David, which is clearly iniquities when he speaks of enemies, was not the same as [that of] Moses when speaking of enemies.

Daniel (ix) prays for the deliverance of the people from the captivity of their enemies; but he was thinking of sins, and, to prove it, he said that Gabriel came and told him that his prayer was granted and that there were no more than seventy weeks to wait, after which the people would be delivered from iniquity, that sin would come to an end, and that the saviour, the Saint of saints, would bring *everlasting* justice, not legal but everlasting justice. (692)

504. A. *Symbols.* The Jews had grown old in these earthly thoughts: that God loved their father Abraham, that he loved his flesh and what was born of it; that for this reason he had caused them to multiply and set them apart from all other peoples without permitting them to mix with them; that, when they were languishing in Egypt, he brought them forth with the aid of all those great signs; that he fed them with manna in the desert; that he led them to a very fertile land; that he gave them kings and a well-built temple for offering up their sacrifices of animals; that by shedding the blood of animals they were puri-

fied; that in the end he would send them the Messiah to make
them masters of the whole world, and he foretold the time of his
coming.

When the world had grown old in these materialistic errors,
Jesus Christ came at the time which had been foretold, but not
with the blaze of glory which had been expected; and therefore
they did not think that it was he. After his death, St. Paul came
to teach men that all things had happened symbolically; that
the kingdom of God did not belong to the flesh, but the spirit;
that men's enemies were not the Babylonians, but their passions; that God did not delight in temples made with hands but
in a pure and humble heart; that the circumcision of the body
was pointless and that it was the circumcision of the heart
which was necessary; that Moses had not given them bread
from heaven, etc.

But since God did not wish to reveal these things to his
people who were unworthy of them, and nevertheless wished to
foretell them so that they would be believed, he foretold the
time of their fulfilment clearly; and sometimes expressed them
clearly, but much more often by means of symbols, so that
those who liked things expressed symbolically would linger over
them, and that those who liked the things symbolised would
see them.

All that does not tend towards charity is symbolical.

The sole object of Scripture is charity.

All that does not refer directly to the only good is a symbol
of it. For since there is only one goal, everything that does not
refer to it literally is a symbol of it.

God thus lends diversity to the one precept of charity in
order to satisfy our curiosity, which seeks diversity through that
form of diversity which always leads us to the one thing necessary. For one thing alone is necessary, and we love diversity;
and God satisfies both by these forms of diversity which lead
to the one thing necessary.

The Jews so loved symbolical things and waited so patiently
for them, that they mistook the reality when it came at the time
and in the manner which had been foretold.

The rabbis took the breasts of the Spouse for symbols, and everything that did not express their one goal, which was worldly goods.

And Christians even take the Eucharist for a symbol of the glory towards which they strive. (670)

505. Jesus Christ did nothing but teach men that they only loved themselves, that they were slaves, blind, sick, unhappy and sinful; that he had come to deliver them, bring them light, sanctify and heal them; that this would come about through their hating themselves and following him to misery and death on the cross. (545)

506. *Symbols*. When the word of God, which is true, is false in a literal sense, it is true in a spiritual sense. *Sede a dextris meis* is untrue in the literal sense; therefore true in the spiritual sense.

In expressions like this God is spoken of in human terms; and it does not mean anything except that God will have the same intention as men when they invite someone to sit on their right hand; it is therefore a sign of God's intention and not of the way in which he will carry it out.

Thus, when it is said: 'God liked the fragrance of your perfumes and will reward you with rich land,' it means that his intention is the same as a man's who, if he liked your perfume, would give you in return a piece of fertile land: so God will have the same intention towards you because you have the same intention towards [him] as a man has towards the person to whom he gives perfume.

Thus, *iratus est*, 'jealous God', etc. For since the things of God are inexpressible, they cannot be said in any other way, and the Church still uses them today: *Quia confortavit seras*,[1] etc.

It is not permissible to read into Scripture meanings that it has not been shown to possess. Thus to argue that the closed *mem* in Isaiah means 600 is something which has not been revealed. It is not said that the final *tsades* and the *he deficientes* stood for mysteries. It is therefore not permissible to say so, still

---

[1] He has given fresh strength to his people (Ps. cxlviii, 13).

less to argue that it is the manner of the philosopher's stone. But we maintain that the literal sense is not the true sense because the prophets themselves have said so. (687)

507. Those who find difficulty in believing give as a reason the fact that the Jews did not believe: 'If it was so clear,' they say, 'why did they not believe?', and almost wished that they did believe in order not to be held back by the example of the refusal of the Jews. But it is their very refusal that is the foundation of our own belief. We should feel much less disposed to believe if they were in our camp. We should then have a much more plausible pretext. It is a wonderful thing to have turned the Jews into great connoisseurs of prophecies, and great enemies of their fulfilment. (745)

508. *Proof of the two Testaments at the same time.* In order to prove the truth of both at the same time, we only need to see whether the prophecies of one are fulfilled in the other.

In order to examine the prophecies we must understand them.

For, if we believe that they only have one meaning, it is certain that the Messiah has not come; but if they have two meanings, it is certain that he came in the person of Jesus Christ.

The whole question is therefore to discover whether or not they have two meanings.

The proofs that Scripture has two meanings which were given by Jesus Christ and the Apostles are as follows:

1. Proof from Scripture itself;

2. Proof by the rabbis: Moses Maymon says that it has two faces, and that the prophets only foretold Jesus Christ;

3. Proofs by the Kabbala;

4. Proofs by the mystical interpretation that the rabbis themselves give to Scripture;

5. Proofs from the principles of the rabbis that there are two meanings, that there are two advents of the Messiah, glorious or lowly, according to their merit, that the prophets only spoke of the Messiah—the law is not everlasting but must change at the coming of the Messiah—that when he comes no one will remember the Red Sea, that Jews and Gentiles will mingle;

6. [Proofs by means of the key that Jesus Christ and the Apostles have provided.]   (642)

509. *A. Symbols*. Is. LI. The Red Sea, symbol of the Redemption. *Ut sciatis quod filius hominis habet potestatem remittendi peccata, tibi dico: Surge.*[1]

God, wishing to show that he could create a holy people with an invisible holiness and endow them with everlasting glory, created visible things. As nature is an image of grace, he created among the good things in the order of nature what he was going to create in the order of Grace, so that men would understand that he could create invisible things because he created visible things. Thus, he saved the people from the flood; he caused them to be born of Abraham, he delivered them from their enemies, and gave them rest.

God's aim was not to save a whole people from the flood or cause them to be born of Abraham simply to lead them into the promised land.

And even Grace is only a symbol of glory because it is not the final end. It was prefigured by the law, and is itself a symbol of [glory]: but it is the symbol of it, and its origin or cause.

The ordinary life of man is like that of the saints. They all seek their own satisfaction, and only differ in the object in which they locate it; they regard as their enemies those who keep them from it, etc. God has therefore shown his power of bestowing invisible rewards by bestowing visible ones.   (643)

510. Suppose that there were two people relating improbable stories, one with a double meaning which was only intelligible to a clique, the other with only one meaning: anyone not in the know who heard them talking would judge them alike. But if, in what followed, one said angelic things while the other continued to say flat and commonplace things, he would decide that one spoke of mysterious things, but not the other because one would have shown that he was incapable of such silliness and was capable of mystery; the other that he was incapable of mystery and capable of silliness.

---

[1] But that you may know that the Son of man hath power on earth to forgive sins . . . I say unto thee: Arise (Mark II, 10).

The Old Testament is a cipher. (691)

511. Why did not Jesus Christ come openly instead of basing his credentials on earlier prophecies?

Why did he have his coming foretold in symbolical terms?

(794)

512. *Symbols.* Since God wished to create for himself a holy people whom he would separate from all the other nations of the earth, whom he would deliver from their enemies, whom he would lead to a place of rest, he promised that he would do it, and foretold by his prophets the time and manner of his coming. And yet in order to strengthen the hopes of his elect, he showed them his image at all times, never leaving them without a guarantee of his power and his desire for their salvation. For at the creation of man Adam was his witness, and the recipient of a promise of the Saviour who was to be born of woman when men were still so close to the creation that they could not yet have forgotten their creation and their fall.

When those who had known Adam were no longer in this world, God sent Noah and saved him, and drowned everybody else by a miracle which was a sufficient sign of his power to save the world, and to bring to birth from the seed of woman Him whom he had promised.

This miracle was sufficient to strengthen [men's] hopes.

While the memory of the Flood was still fresh in men's minds and Noah still alive, God made his promises to Abraham, and when Sem was still living God sent Moses, etc. (644)

513. Hypothesis of crooked apostles.—The times clearly, the manner obscurely.—Five Symbolical proofs

$$2{,}000 \left\{ \begin{array}{l} 1{,}600 \text{ prophets.} \\ 400 \text{ Scattered.} \end{array} \right.$$

(572)

514. The veil which hides the meaning of the books of the Bible from the Jews does the same for bad Christians, and for all those who do not hate themselves. But how well disposed we are to

understand them and to know Jesus Christ, when we truly hate ourselves! (676)

515. I do not say that the *mem* is mysterious. (688)

516. Is., I, 21. Changing of good into evil and vengeance of God. —Is., X, 1; XXVI, 20; XXVIII, 1.

Miracles: Is. XXXIII, 9; XXXIII, 10; LX, 26; XLIII, 13.

Jer. XI, 20-21; XVII, 9: that is to say, who will know the evil of it, for it is already known that he is wicked; —trust in external sacraments; —VII, 16; VII, 22; VII, 23; VII, 24: the essential does not lie in the external sacrifice; —XI, 13; XI, 14.

Is., XLIV, 20; XLIV, 21-22; XLIV, 23-24; LIV, 8; LXIII, 12; LXIII, 14; LXIII, 16; LXIII, 17; LXIV, 17.

Jer., II, 35; IV, 22; IV, 23-27; V, 4-6; V, 29; V, 30; V, 31; VI, 16-17; multiplicity of doctrines, XXIII, 15-17. (682)

517. *Symbols.* The arguments against the view that the Old Testament is purely symbolical and that by temporal goods the prophets meant other goods are:

First, that it would be unworthy of God;

Secondly, that their pronouncements express very clearly the promise of temporal goods, and that they say nevertheless that their pronouncements are obscure, and that their meaning will not be understood. Whence it appears that the secret meaning was not the one that they voiced openly and that, as a result, they meant other sacrifices, another saviour, etc. They say that we shall only understand it at the end of time. Jer., XXX, *ult.*

The second proof is that their pronouncements are contradictory and cancel out, so that, if we assume that by the words law and sacrifice they did not mean anything different from Moses, there is an obvious and flagrant contradiction. Therefore they meant something else, sometimes contradicting themselves in the course of the same chapter.

Now, in order to grasp an author's meaning . . . (659)

518. *Reason for Symbols.* [They had to deal with a carnal people, and make it the repository of a spiritual Testament]; in order to create faith in the Messiah, it was essential that there should have been earlier prophecies, and that the authors of them should have been people who were not suspect; whose diligence,

fidelity and zeal were outstanding, and known throughout the world.

In order to ensure success, God chose a nation of materialists to whom he entrusted the prophecies which foretold the Messiah who was to appear in the role of saviour and dispenser of those worldly goods which the people loved. And so they showed an exceptional regard for their prophets and brought the books which foretold the Messiah to the notice of everybody, assuring all nations that he would come in the manner foretold in the books which were there for everyone to read. Thus the people, who were disappointed by the poor and lowly coming of the Messiah, were his bitterest enemies. With the result that the people who in all the world were least likely to favour us, showed themselves the most scrupulous and zealous for his law and his prophets, and preserved them uncorrupted.

And the people who rejected and crucified Jesus Christ, because he was a scandal to them, were the people who were in possession of the books which bear witness to him, and say that he will be rejected and a scandal; so that their very rejection proved that it was he, and his claims were proved alike by the righteous Jews who accepted him and the unrighteous who refused him, for both were foretold.

That is why the prophecies have a hidden meaning, a spiritual meaning, to which the people were hostile, underlying the materialistic meaning which appealed to them. If the spiritual meaning had been discovered, they would not have been capable of cherishing it; and since they could not bear it, they would not have had the zeal necessary for preserving their books and ceremonies; and if they had cherished the spiritual promises and had preserved them uncorrupted until the coming of the Messiah, their testimony would have carried no weight because they would have been his friends.

That is why it was a good thing that the spiritual meaning was hidden; but, on the other hand, if the meaning had been so completely hidden that there was no trace of it, it would have been useless as a proof of the claims of the Messiah. What then became of it? It was hidden beneath the temporal meaning in many passages and revealed so clearly in others; besides the fact that the time and the state of the world had been so plainly foretold that they were clearer than the sun; and this spiritual meaning is so transparent in some places that it needed a blindness equal to that which the flesh inflicts on the mind when it is a slave to it for people not to understand it.

That was the way in which God acted. In countless places, the spiritual meaning is hidden by another meaning and revealed in very few places though nevertheless in such a way that the passages in which it is hidden are equivocal and can be interpreted in both ways; whereas the passages in which it is revealed are unequivocal and can only be interpreted in a spiritual sense.

Hence it could not lead to error, and only a people who were as materialistic as the Jews could be mistaken about it.

For when good things were promised in abundance, what prevented them from understanding that they were truly good things except their greed which made them think that the promise referred to worldly goods? But those who found their good in God alone saw that this promise related only to God. For there are two principles which battle for control of the human will: greed and charity. It is not that greed is incompatible with belief in God, or charity with worldly goods; it is that greed makes use of God and takes pleasure in the world; but not charity.

Now the final end is what gives things a name. Everything that prevents us from attaining it is called an enemy. Thus creatures though good are enemies of the righteous when they turn them away from God; and God himself is the enemy of those whose covetousness is frustrated.

Thus, since the meaning of the word enemy depends on the final end, the righteous understand it to mean their passions, and the worldly understand it to mean the Babylonians; and so the terms were obscure only to the unrighteous.

And that is what Isaiah says: *Signa legem in electis meis*, and that Jesus Christ will be a stumbling block. But 'Blessed is he that shall not be scandalised in him!'

Osee, *ult.*, puts it perfectly: 'Where is the wise man and he shall understand what I say. The righteous shall understand it: for the ways of the Lord are just and the righteous shall walk in them; but the transgressors shall fall in them.'   (571)

519* . . . will stumble. And yet the Covenant, which was designed to darken the understanding of some and bring light to others, was a sign, even in those whose understanding was darkened, of the truth which should have been known to the others. For the visible blessings which they received from God were so great and so divine that it was apparent that he was able to bestow on them invisible blessings and a Messiah.

For nature is a symbol of grace, and visible miracles symbols of invisible ones. *Ut sciatis . . . tibi dico: Surge.*[1]

Isaiah says that the Redemption will be like the crossing of the Red Sea.

God therefore has shown by the exodus from Egypt, the crossing of the Sea, the defeat of the kings, the manna and the whole of the genealogy of Abraham that he was capable of saving, of making bread come down from heaven, etc.; so that the hostile people are the symbol and the image of the same Messiah whom they did not know, etc.

He therefore taught us that ultimately all these things were only symbols, and what is meant by 'truly free', 'true Israelite', 'true circumcision', 'true bread from heaven', etc.

In these promises each of us discovers what lies in the depths of his heart; temporal and spiritual blessings, God or creatures; but with this difference, that those who seek creatures in them will find them though with many contradictions; with the prohibition against loving them and the command to worship only God and to love only him, which is one and the same thing, and that finally no Messiah has come for them; instead of which those who seek God in them will find him, without any contradiction, with the command to love only him, and will find that a Messiah came at the appointed time to give them the blessings for which they asked.

[1] To convince you . . . I tell thee, rise up (Mark II, 10-11).

Thus the Jews witnessed miracles and the fulfilment of the prophecies; their faith taught them to worship and love only one God; and it was eternal. It therefore possessed all the signs of the true religion: therefore it was the true religion. But we must draw a distinction between the teaching of the Jews and the teaching of the law of the Jews. Now the teaching of the Jews was not true though it had the support of miracles, the prophecies and perpetuity because it did not possess the other precept, which is to worship and love only God. (675)

520. The synagogue was not destroyed because it was a symbol; but because it was only a symbol, it fell into a state of servitude. The symbol lasted until the coming of truth so that the Church would always be visible, either in the image which promised it, or in the reality. (646)

521. *Extravagances of the Apocalyptics and Pre-Adamites. Millenarians,* etc. Anyone who wishes to base extravagant theories on Scripture will be able to do so with this for an example.

It is said that 'this generation shall not pass until all these things be done'. About which I shall say that after this generation will come another, and so on.

II. Paralipomena speaks of Solomon and the king as though they were two different persons. I shall say that there were two of them. (651)

522. Change symbols because of our weakness. (669)

523. Adam *forma futuri.* Six days to create one, six ages to create the other; the six days that Moses speaks of for the creation of Adam are merely a symbol of the six ages needed for the creation of Jesus Christ and the Church. If Adam had not sinned, and Jesus Christ had not come, there would only have been a single covenant, one age of men, and the creation would have been represented as though it had all happened at the same time. (656)

524. *Symbols.* Saviour, father, sacrificer, host, nourishment, king, sage, legislator, man of sorrows, poor man, who was to produce a people whom he was to lead and feed, and bring into his land . . . (766)

525. *Symbolical.* God used the concupiscence of the Jews to serve

the purposes of Jesus Christ [who brought the remedy for con-
cupiscence]. (664)

526. *Symbolical.* Nothing resembles charity so closely as covetousness, and nothing is so contrary to it. Thus the Jews, amply provided with goods which flattered their covetousness, were very
like Christians and at the same time very unlike them. And by
this means they possessed the two qualities which they needed
to be like the Messiah in order to symbolise him, and very unlike him in order not to be suspect witnesses. (663)

527. *Fascinatio . . . Somnum suum. Figura huius mundi.*

The Eucharist. *Commedes panem* tuum. *Panem* nostrum.

Inimici Dei terram lingent, sinners lick the ground, that is to
say, love worldly pleasures.[1]

The Old Testament contained symbols of future joy, and the
New describes the means of reaching it.

The symbols were representations of joy; the means, penance; and nevertheless the paschal lamb was eaten with wild
lettuces, *cum amaritudinibus.*

Singularis sum ego donec transeam, before his death Jesus Christ
was almost the only martyr.[2] (666)

528. John, VIII: *Multi crediderunt in eum. Dicebat ergo Jesus: 'Si
manseritis . . .* VERE *mei discipuli eritis et* VERITAS LIBERABIT *vos.'
Responderunt: 'Semen Abrahae sumus, et nemini servimus unquam.'*[3]

There is a great difference between disciples and *true* disciples. He recognises them by saying that the truth will make
them free; for if they reply that they are free and have it in
them to escape from the bondage of the devil, they are certainly
disciples but not true disciples. (519)

529. 'Victory over death.'

'What shall it serve a man to gain the whole world if he lose
his soul?'

---

[1] Witchery evil . . . Their sleep. The fashion of this world (Wisdom, IV,
12: Ps. LXXV, 6; I Cor. VII, 31). Eat thy bread (Deut. VIII, 9).

[2] And I pass on in safety (Ps. CXL, 10).

[3] Many believed in him. Then Jesus said . . . If you continue in my
word, you shall be my disciples indeed . . . and the truth shall make you
free. They answered him: We are the seed of Abraham: and we have never
been slaves to any man. (John VIII, 31-33.)

'Whoever wishes to keep his soul will lose it.'

'I have not come to destroy the law but to fulfil it.'

'The lambs did not take away the sins of the world, but I am the lamb who takes away sins.'

'Moses gave you not bread from heaven. Moses did not bring you out of captivity, and did not make you really free.'

(782)

530. *Fac secundum exemplar quod tibi ostensum est in monte.*[1]

The religion of the Jews was therefore based on its resemblance to the truth of the Messiah; and the truth of the Messiah was recognised by the religion of the Jews, which was a symbol of it.

With the Jews, truth was only symbolical: in heaven, it is manifest.

In the Church it is hidden, and recognised by means of the symbol.

The symbol is founded on truth and truth is recognised by means of the symbol. (673)

531. The Jews, who were called upon to subjugate nations and kings, were the slaves of sin; and Christians, whose vocation it was to serve and be subjects, are the children of freedom. (671)

532. Charity is not a symbolical precept. It is a horrible thing to say that Jesus Christ, who came to replace symbols by reality, only came to provide a symbol of charity, to remove the reality which existed before his coming.

'If then the light that is in thee be darkness: the darkness how great shall it be?' (665)

533. Penance was the only one of the mysteries which was clearly revealed to the Jews, and by St. John the forerunner; and then the other mysteries as a sign that in each man, as throughout the entire world, the command must be obeyed.

(661)

534. 20 V. In the Gospels the symbols of the sick soul are sick bodies; but because a body cannot be sick enough to express it properly, there had to be several of them. Thus there are the

---

[1] Look and make it according to the pattern, that was shown thee in the mount (Exodus xxv, 40).

deaf, the mute, the blind, the paralytic, the dead Lazarus, the man possessed of a devil. Everything is to be found together in the sick soul. (658)

535. Difference between dinner and supper.

In God the word does not differ from the meaning because it is true; nor the word from the effect because it is powerful; nor the means from the effect because he is wise. Bern., *ult. sermo in Missus.*

Augustine, *de Civ. Dei.* v. 10: The rule is general: God can do everything with the exception of those things which, if he could do them, he would not be omnipotent: die; be deceived, lie, etc.

Several Evangelists as a confirmation of truth; the useful differences between them.

Eucharist after the Last Supper: the reality after the symbol.

Ruin of Jerusalem: symbol of the ruin of the world, forty years after the death of Jesus.

Jesus does not know, as man or as ambassador. Matt., XXIV, 36.

Jesus condemned by Jew and Gentile.

Jews and Gentiles represented by the two sons. Aug., *de Civit.*, XX, 29. (654)

20. RABBINISM

536. *Chronology of Rabbinism.* (The page references come from the book known as *Pugio*.)

Page 27, R. Hakadosch (year 200), author of the *Mischna* or oral law, or second law.

Commentaries on the *Mischna* (year 340): One *Siphra*

> *Barajetot.*
> *Talmud.*
> *Hierosol.*
> *Tosiphtot.*

Bereschit Rabba, by R. Osaia Rabah, commentary on the *Mischna.*

Bereschit Rabba, *Bar Nachoni*, are subtle, agreeable, historical and theological disquisitions. The same author wrote some books called *Rabot*.

A hundred years after (440) the *Hierosol Talmud*, the *Babylonian Talmud* was written by R. Ase with the universal consent of the Jews who are necessarily obliged to observe everything set out in it.

The addition of R. Ase is called *Gemara*, that is to say, the 'commentary' on the *Mischna*.

And the *Talmud* contains both the *Mischna* and the *Gemara* together.   (635)

537. *On original sin. Ample tradition of original sin according to the Jews.*

On the word in Genesis VIII: the nature of man's heart is bad from childhood. *R. Moses Haddarschan:* The bad leaven is placed in man the moment that he is conceived.

Massechet Succa. The bad leaven has seven names in Scripture; it is called *evil, foreskin, unclean, enemy, scandal, heart of stone, icy blast*; all this means the malignity which is hidden and engraved in the heart of man.

Misdrach Tillim says the same thing, and that God will deliver man's good nature from his bad.

The malignity is renewed every day against man, as it is written in Psalm XXXVI: 'The wicked man watched the just man, and seeketh to put him to death, but the Lord will not leave him in his hands.' Wickedness tempts the heart of man in this life, and will accuse him in the other. This is all found in the *Talmud*.

Misdrach Tillim on Psalm IV: 'Be angry and sin not. Be angry and frighten your concupiscence and it will not lead you into sin.' And on Psalm XXXVI: 'The unjust man has said within himself that he would sin: there is no fear of God before his eyes'; that is to say, the wickedness which is native to man said that to the infidel.

Misdrach el Kohelet: 'Better is a child that is poor and good than a king who is old and foolish and cannot foresee the hereafter.' The child is the virtue, the king the evil which is in man.

It is called king because all his members obey it, and old because it is in the heart of man from infancy to old age, and foolish because it leads man into the way of [*perdition*] which he does not foresee.

The same thing is in *Misdrach Tillim*.

Bereschit Rabba on Psalm XXXV: 'Lord, all my bones shall bless thee Who delivered the poor from the hand of them that are stronger than he'; and is there a greater tyrant than the evil leaven?—And on Proverbs XXV: 'If thy enemy be hungry, give him to eat'; that is to say, if the evil leaven is hungry; give him the bread of wisdom of which it is spoken in Proverbs IX; and if he is thirsty, given him the water of which it is spoken in Isaiah LV.

Misdrach Tillim says the same thing; he also says that when it speaks of our enemy, Scripture means the evil leaven; and that in [*giving*] him bread and water, we heap coals of fire on his head.

Misdrach el Kohelet on Ecclesiastes IX: 'A great king has besieged a little town.' The great king is the evil leaven, the vast machines with which he is surrounded are temptations, and he has found a wise and poor man whom he has delivered, that is to say, virtue.

And on Psalm XLI: 'Blessed is he that understandeth concerning the needy and the poor.'

And on Psalm LXXVIII: 'The spirit goes away and does not return': which has led to erroneous views on the immortality of the soul, but the meaning is that the spirit is the evil leaven which remains with man until death, and will not return at the resurrection.

And on Psalm CIII, the same thing.

And on Psalm XVI.

Principles of the Rabbis: two Messiahs. (446)

21. PERPETUITY

538. *Perpetuity.* A saying of David or of Moses such as 'God will circumcise their heart', enables us to judge their minds. While all their other sayings may be equivocal and only doubtfully philosophical or Christian, a saying of this kind finally determines the meaning of all the others, just as a saying of Epictetus governs all the rest in the opposite sense. Up to that point there is ambiguity, but not afterwards. (690)

539. States would perish if the law were not frequently made to yield to necessity. But religion never suffered such a thing, and never made use of it. For this reason compromises are essential, or miracles. It is not unusual for a thing to be preserved when it yields, but it is not properly speaking a method of preservation; and in the end the things that yield are completely destroyed: none of them has lasted a thousand years. But the fact that religion has always been preserved and has remained unbending is a sign of its divinity. (614)

540. *Perpetuity.* Our religion, which lies in believing that man has fallen from a state of glory and communion with God into a state of sadness, penance and estrangement from God, but that after this life we shall be restored by a Messiah who was to come, has always existed on earth. All things have passed away, and religion has remained for which all things exist.

In the first age of the world, men were carried away by every sort of disorder, and yet there were saints like Enoch, Lamech and others, who waited patiently for the Christ who had been promised since the beginning of the world. Noah witnessed extreme examples of the wickedness of men: and he deserved to save the world in person through the hope of a Messiah of whom he was the symbol. Abraham was surrounded by idolaters when God made known to him the mystery of the Messiah whom he hailed from afar. In the time of Isaac and Jacob, abominations were rife throughout the world;

and Jacob, who died blessing his children, cried out in an ecstasy which interrupted his speech: 'I await, O my God, the Saviour whom you have promised: *Salutare tuum expectabo, Domine.*'

The Egyptians were infected with idolatry and magic; even the people of God were led astray by their example; but nevertheless, Moses and others believed him whom they did not see, and worshipped him in looking to the eternal gifts which he was preparing for them.

Then came the Greeks and Romans who were responsible for the reign of false gods; the poets created a hundred different theologies; the philosophers were divided into a thousand different sects; and yet there were always, in the heart of Judaea, chosen men who foretold the coming of a Messiah which was known only to them.

He came at last in the fulness of time; and since his coming we have seen the birth of so many schisms and heresies, the disruption of so many states, so many changes in every sphere, and this Church, which has always worshipped him who has always been worshipped, has existed without a break. And what is wonderful, what is incomparable and wholly divine, is that this religion, which has always remained, has always been attacked. A thousand times it has been on the verge of total destruction, and every time God has restored it by some extraordinary manifestation of his power. For what is amazing is that it was preserved without yielding or bending under the will of tyrants. It is not surprising that a state should continue to exist when its laws are sometimes made to yield to necessity, but that . . . (See the circle in Montaigne.)   (613)

541*. *Perpetuity.* People have always believed in the Messiah. The tradition of Adam was still fresh in the time of Noah and Moses. The prophets have since foretold him though always when predicting other things; and when, from time to time, the things that they predicted came to pass, for all men to see, they were a sign of the truth of their mission, and in consequence of their promises of the Messiah Jesus Christ performed miracles, as the apostles did, which converted the heathen: and in that manner

all the prophecies were fulfilled, and the Messiah's claims
proved once for all. (616)

542. The six ages, the six fathers of the six ages, the six wonders
at the beginning of the six ages, the six orients at the beginning
of the six ages. (655)

543. The only religion which is against nature, against common
sense, and hostile to our pleasures, is the only one that has always existed. (605)

544. If the ancient Church had been in error, the Church would
have fallen. If she were in error today, it would not be the same:
for she can always appeal to tradition, to the faith of the
ancient Church; and so her submission and conformity to the
ancient Church prevails and acts as a corrective to everything.
But the ancient Church did not pre-suppose the Church of the
future and did not regard her, as we take for granted and regard
the ancient Church. (867)

545. Two kinds of men in each religion: among the heathen the
worshippers of the beasts of the field, and the others, the worshippers of the one God of natural religion; among the Jews,
sensual men and spiritual men who were the Christians of the
old law; among Christians, the crude men who are the Jews of
the new law. The worldly Jews expected a worldly Messiah; the
gross Christians think that the Messiah has dispensed them
from loving God; true Jews and true Christians worship a
Messiah who teaches them to love God. (609)

546. Anyone who judges the religion of the Jews by its cruder
adherents has little knowledge of it. It is obvious in the Holy
Books and in the tradition of the prophets, who have shown
clearly that they did not interpret the law in a literal sense.
Thus our religion is divine in the Gospels, the Apostles and
tradition; but it is ridiculous in those who treat it badly.

According to materialistic Jews, the Messiah was to be a
great temporal prince. According to materialistic Christians,
Jesus Christ came to dispense them from the need of loving God
and to give us the sacraments which do everything without our
co-operation. Neither are genuine representatives of the Christian or the Jewish religion.

True Jews and true Christians have always awaited a Messiah who would make them love God, and through the love of God triumph over their enemies. (607)

547. Moses (Deut. xxx) promises that God will circumcise their hearts in order to make them capable of loving him. (689)

548. The materialistic Jews occupy an intermediate position between Christians and heathen. The heathen do not know God, and only love the earth. The Jews know the true God, and do not love the earth. The Jews and the heathen enjoy the same good things. The Jews and the Christians know the same God.

The Jews were of two kinds: some only had pagan, the others had Christian dispositions. (608)

549. Maccabees, since they have had no more prophets. The Masorah since Jesus Christ. (630)

550. Perpetuity. Let us remember that from the beginning of the world the expectation or worship of the Messiah has never ceased to exist; that there have been men who said that God had revealed to them that a Redeemer would be born who would be the saviour of his people; that Abraham came afterwards and said that he would be born of him by a son of his; that Jacob declared that, among his twelve children, the Messiah would be born of Judah; that Moses and the prophets followed and announced the time and manner of his coming; that they said that the law they had would only last until that proclaimed by the Messiah; that until then it would be perpetual, but that the other law would endure for ever; that therefore their law, or the law of the Messiah, of which it was only a pledge, would always be on earth; that in fact it has always been there; that in fact Jesus Christ came precisely in the way which had been foretold. This is a wonderful thing. (617)

551. When the creation and the Flood were past, and since God was never again to destroy the world any more than to recreate it or give any of those great signs of himself, he began to rear a people on earth, whom he created specially for this purpose, and who were destined to last until the coming of the people whom the Messiah would fashion after his own spirit.

(621)

552. *Advantages of the Jewish people.* In this search the Jewish people first attract my attention by a number of admirable and unexpected qualities.

I see first of all that they are a people consisting wholly of brothers and that, while all other peoples are composed of an infinite number of families, the Jewish people though strikingly fertile are all descended from a single man and, since they are all of one flesh and members of one another, [they] form a powerful State built out of a single family. That is unique.

This family, or this people, is the most ancient known to man: which seems to me to call for special veneration, particularly in the study in which we are engaged, because if God has at all times been in contact with man, it is this people whom we must consult in order to learn about tradition.

The people is important not only on account of its antiquity; it is also peculiar owing to the manner in which it has survived and has always gone on existing from its beginnings until the present time. For unlike the peoples of Greece and Italy, Lacedemonia, Athens, Rome and others who came much later and disappeared long ago, the Jews always remain and despite the attacks of so many powerful kings who attempted a hundred times to destroy them, as their historians show and as it is easy to judge from the natural order of things during such a long period of time, they have nevertheless been preserved (and this preservation was prophesied); and, extending from the earliest to the most recent times, their history contains all our histories [though they were so far in advance of us].

The law by which the Jewish people are governed is at once the oldest law in the world, the most perfect and the only one which has been preserved uninterruptedly in any State. That is what Josephus has so admirably demonstrated *against Apion*, and Philo the Jew, in different places where they show that it is so ancient that the very name of law was not known to the most ancient of the other peoples until more than a thousand years later; so that Homer, who wrote the history of many nations, never used it. And it is easy to gauge its perfection from merely reading it, which shows that every contingency has been provided for with such wisdom, such equity, such judgement that the earliest of the Greek and Roman legislators, when they gained some knowledge of it, borrowed their principal laws from it; all of which is apparent from what they call the Twelve Tables and the other proofs which are given by Josephus.

In so far as it deals with the practice of religion, their law is the strictest and most rigid of all laws; in order to keep them to the path of duty, it compels them to submit, on pain of death, to a thousand special and onerous observances. It is therefore a very remarkable thing that it should always have been preserved unchanged through so many centuries by a rebellious and impatient people like the Jews, while all the other States have changed their laws from time to time though their laws were altogether more lenient.

The book which contains the law, the first of all laws, is itself the oldest book in the world because those of Homer, Hesiod and others only came six or seven hundred years later. (620)

553. *Sincerity of the Jews.* They have preserved, with loving care, the book in which Moses declares that they have been ungrateful to God all their lives; that he knows that they will be still more ungrateful after his death; but that he calls heaven and earth to bear witness against them, and that he has impressed it on them sufficiently.

Finally, he declares that God will grow angry with them, will scatter them among all the peoples of the earth; that, as they have angered him by worshipping gods which were not their God, so he will provoke them by calling them a people who are not his people; and wishes all his sayings to be preserved for ever, and his book to be placed in the ark of the covenant so that it will serve for ever as a witness against them.

Isaiah says the same thing, xxx, 8. (631)

554. *To show that true Jews and true Christians have one and the same religion.*

The religion of the Jews appeared to consist essentially in the fatherhood of Abraham, in circumcision, in sacrifices, in ceremonies, in the ark, in the temple, in Jerusalem; in short, in the law and the covenant of Moses.

I say:

That it did not consist in any of these things, but only in the love of God, and that God rejected all other things;

That God will not accept the posterity of Abraham;

That if they offend him the Jews will be punished by God as though they were strangers. Deut. VIII, 19: 'But if thou forget the Lord thy God, and follow strange gods, and serve and worship them: behold now I foretell thee that . . . as the nations, which the Lord destroyed at thy entrance, so shall you perish';

That if they love him, strangers shall be received by God like the Jews.

Isaiah, LVI, 3: 'And let not the son of the stranger speak saying: The Lord will divide and separate me from his people . . . And the children of the stranger that adhere to the Lord, to worship and to love his name . . . I will bring them into my holy mount . . . Their holocausts and their victims shall please me upon my altar: for my house shall be called a house of prayer . . .';

That the true Jews could only consider their merit as coming from God, and not from Abraham.

Isaiah, LXIII, 16: 'For thou art our father: and Abraham hath not known us, and Israel hath been ignorant of us. Thou, O Lord, art our father, our redeemer . . .'

Even Moses told them that God will not accept persons.

Deut., x, 17: 'God, he said, accepteth no person nor taketh bribes.'

The sabbath was only a sign. Ex. XXXI, 13; and in memory of the exodus from Egypt, Deut., v, 15. Thus it is no longer necessary because we must forget Egypt.—Circumcision was only a sign, Gen., XVII, 11. And that is why, during the time that they were in the wilderness, they were not circumcised because they could not be confused with other peoples, and because after the coming of Jesus Christ, it is no longer necessary;

That the circumcision of the heart is a command. Deut., x, 16; Jer., iv, 4: 'Circumcise therefore the foreskin of your heart; and stiffen your neck no more. Because the Lord your God he is the God of gods, and the Lord of lords and mighty and terrible who accepteth no person';

That God said that he would do it one day. Deut., xxx, 6: 'The Lord thy God will circumcise thy heart; and the heart of thy seed: that thou mayest love the Lord thy God with all thy heart';

That those whose heart is uncircumcised shall be judged. Jer., ix, 26: for God will judge the uncircumcised peoples, and all the people of Israel because 'they are uncircumcised in their heart';

That the exterior is worth nothing without the interior, Joel, ii, 13: *Scindite corda vestra*, etc. Is., lviii, 3, 4, etc. The love of God is commanded all through Deuteronomy.

Deut., xxx, 19: 'I call heaven and earth to witness this day, that I have set before you life and death, blessing and cursing. Choose therefore life, that both thou and thy seed may live. And that thou mayest love the Lord thy God, and obey his voice and adhere to him (for he is thy life and the length of thy days)';

That the Jews, because they are lacking in this love, will be condemned for their offences, and the heathen chosen in their place. Os., i, 10.

Deut., xxxii, 20: 'And he said: I will hide my face from them, in the sight of their crimes, and will consider what their last end shall be. For it is a perverse generation, and unfaithful children. They have provoked me with that which was no god, and have angered me with their vanities. And I will provoke them with that which is no people. They are a nation without counsel, and without wisdom.' Is., lxv, 1;

That temporal goods are false, and that true good is to be united with God, Psalm, cxliii, 15;

That their feasts are displeasing to God. Amos, v, 21.

That the sacrifices of the Jews are displeasing to God. Is., lxvi, 1-3; i, 11. Jer., vi, 20. David. *Miserere*.—Even those of the good. *Expectavi*. Psalm XLIX, 8, 9, 10, 11, 12, 13 and 14;

That he did not choose them on account of their hardness of heart. Micheas, admirably, VI, 6-8; I Kings, XV, 22; Os., VI, 6;

That the sacrifices of the Gentiles will be accepted by God, and that God will take no pleasure in the sacrifices of the Jews. Malach., I, 11;

That God will make a new covenant by the Messiah, and that the old ones will all be rejected. Jer., XXXI, 31: *Mandata non bona*; Ezech., XX, 25;

That the old things will be forgotten. Is., XLIII, 18, 19; LXV, 17, 18;

That the ark shall no longer be remembered. Jer., III, 15, 16;

That the temple shall be cast down. Jer., VII, 12, 13, 14;

That their sacrifices will be rejected and other pure sacrifices introduced in their place. Malach., I, 11;

That the order of Aaron's priesthood shall be condemned, and that of Melchisedech introduced by the Messiah. Psalm, *Dixit Dominus*;

That this order of sacrifice shall be eternal. *Ibid.*;

That Jerusalem shall be condemned, and Rome admitted. Psalm, *Dixit Dominus*;

That the name of the Jews shall be condemned, and a new name given. Is., LXV, 15;

That the last name would be better than that of Jew, and would endure for ever. Is., LXII, 5.

That the Jews would be without prophets (Amos), without king, without princes, without sacrifices, without idols;

That the Jews would nevertheless always survive as a people. Jer., XXXI, 36. (610)

555. I see the Christian religion founded on an earlier religion, and that is what I find convincing.

I am not speaking here of the miracles of Moses, Jesus Christ and the Apostles, because they do not at first sight appear convincing, and because I only wish to put in evidence at this stage the fundamentals of the Christian religion which are beyond doubt and cannot be called in question by anybody.

It is certain that in a number of places on earth we see a peculiar people who are separated from all other peoples, and are called the Jewish people.

At all times therefore I see people inventing religions in different parts of the world, but they do not possess either a morality which appeals to me, or proofs which can convince me. The result is that I should have rejected equally the religions of Mahomet, China, the ancient Romans, and the Egyptians for this one reason: since it cannot be said that one of them is truer than any other, or possesses anything which necessarily convinces me, my reason cannot induce me to accept one rather than another.

But when I go on to consider the strangely variegated assortment of creeds and moral systems which have existed at different periods, I find in one corner of the earth a peculiar people, who are set apart from all other peoples and are the most ancient of all peoples whose history is older by several centuries than the oldest known to us.

I therefore find a great people in very large numbers who are descended from a single man, who worship one God and who live by a law which they say was given to them by his hand. They maintain that they are the only people in the world to whom God has revealed his mysteries, that all men are fallen and disgraced in the sight of God, that they have all abandoned themselves to sensual pleasures and their own wayward spirit, instead of remaining steadfast in their conduct, which produces strange errors and continual changes of religion and custom; but that God will not always leave the other peoples in their state of darkness, that a deliverer will come for all men, that the Jews are in the world in order to proclaim his coming to men, that they were created specially to be the forerunners and heralds of the great event, and to call on all the peoples to unite with them in their expectation of the saviour.

The encounter with this people fills me with amazement; and seems to me to be worth attention.

I examine the law which they boast that they have received from God, and I find it admirable. It is the first of all laws, and of such a kind that the Jews had received it and observed it without a break for nearly a thousand years before the word 'law' was used by the Greeks. And it seems strange that the first law in the world turns out to be the most perfect, so that the greatest legislators have borrowed their own laws from it, as we can see from the law of the Twelve Tables of Athens, which was later adopted by the Romans as could easily be shown if Josephus and others had not already dealt adequately with the subject.   (619)

556. This is plain fact. While the philosophers are all divided into different sects, we find in one corner of the world a people who are the oldest people in the world, declaring that everyone is living in error, that God had revealed the truth to them, that it will always exist on earth. Indeed, all the other sects vanish while this one always remains, and has done for 4,000 years.

They declare that their ancestors have taught them that man has fallen from communion with God into a state of complete estrangement from him, but that God has promised to redeem him, that this doctrine would always exist on earth; that their law has a double meaning; that for sixteen hundred years they had people whom they believed to be prophets who foretold the time and the manner;

That four hundred years later they were scattered over the face of the earth because the coming of Jesus Christ was to be proclaimed throughout the world;

That Jesus Christ came in the manner and at the time foretold;

That since then the Jews have been scattered and are everywhere under a curse, and nevertheless continue to exist.   (618)

557. *The Sincerity of the Jews.* After the cessation of the prophets, Machab.

Since Jesus Christ, Masaroth.

'This book shall be your witness.'

The defective final letters.

Sincere against the interests of their honour, and dying for it; it has no parallel in the world, nor its roots in nature. (630)

558.

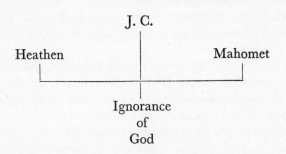

(591)

559. If the Jews had all been converted by Jesus Christ, we should no longer have any but suspect witnesses. And if they had been exterminated, we should have none at all.　(750)

560. *Jesus Christ. Offices.* He and he alone would produce a great people, an elect, a holy and chosen people; guide them, nourish them, bring them into a place of peace and holiness; make them holy for God; make them the temple of God, reconcile them with God, save them from the wrath of God, deliver them from the bondage of sin which clearly reigns in the heart of man; give his people laws, engrave the laws in their hearts, offer himself to God for them, sacrifice himself for them, be a victim without blemish and himself the high priest: having to offer up himself, his body and blood, and nevertheless offer bread and wine to God . . .

Ingrediens mundum.

'Stone upon stone.'

What preceded, what followed. All the Jews survivors and wanderers.　(766)

561. It is a pleasure to be in a vessel buffeted by a storm when we are certain that we shall not perish.

The persecutions directed against the Church are of this kind.　(859)

562. The history of the Church should, properly speaking, be described as the history of truth.　(858)

563. Gen., XVII, *Statuam pactum meum inter me et te foedere sempi-terno . . . ut sim Deus tuus . . .*

Et tu ergo custodies pactum meum.[1]   (612)

564*. On Esdras. Argument: The books were burnt at the same time as the temple. Forged by the Macchabees: 'Jeremiah gave them the law.'

Argument: that he recited it all by heart. Josephus and Esdras show that *he read the book.* Baron., *An.* p. 180: *Nullus penitus Hebraeorum antiquorum reperitur qui tradiderit libros periisse et per Esdram esse restitutos, nisi in* IV *Esdrae.*[2]

Argument: that he changed the letters.

Philo, *in Vita Moysis*; *Illa lingua ac character quo antiquitus scripta est lex sic permansit usque ad* LXX.[3]

Josephus maintains that the law was in Hebrew when it was translated by the Seventy.

Under Antiochus and Vespasian, when people wanted to demolish the books and when there was no prophet, they could not do it; and under the Babylonians, when there was no persecution and when there were so many prophets, would they have allowed the books to be burnt? . . . Josephus laughs at the Greeks who would not suffer . . . Tertull.: *Perinde potuit abolefactam eam violentia catalysmi in spiritu rursus reformare, quemadmodum et Hierosolymis Babylonia expugnatione deletis, omne instrumentum judaicae litteraturae per Esdram constat restauratum.*[4]

He says that Noah could just as well have reconstructed in his mind the book of Enoch, lost in the Flood, as Esdras was able to reconstruct the Scriptures lost during the Babylonian captivity.

---

[1] And I will establish my covenant between me and thee . . . by a perpetual covenant to be a God to thee . . . and thou therefore shall keep my covenant.

[2] No one among the ancient Hebrews can be found who relates that the books were destroyed and were reconstructed by Esdras except in the Fourth Book of Esdras.

[3] The language and letters in which of old the law was written remained the same until the Septuagint (Philo, Bk. II).

[4] [Noah] could very well have reconstructed in his mind the book (of Enoch) which was destroyed by the violence of the cataclysm, as it is certain that Esdras was able to do for the entire collection of the Hebrew books which was destroyed during the capture of Babylon (Tertullian: *De Cultu femin.*, Bx., I, c. 3).

(Θεός) ἐν τῇ ἐπὶ Ναβουκοδόνοσορ αἰχμαλωσίᾳ τοῦ λαοῦ, διαφθαρεισῶν τῶν γραφῶν . . . ἐνέπνευσε Ἐσδρᾷ τῷ ἱερεῖ ἐκ τῆς φυλῆς Λευὶ τοὺς τῶν προγεγονότων προφητῶν πάντας ἀνατάξασθαι, λόγους καὶ ἀποκαταστῆσαι τῷ λαῷ τὴν διὰ Μωυσέως νομοθεσίαν.[1]

He alleges this in order to show that it is not incredible that the Seventy explained the Sacred Scriptures with the consistency that we admire in them. And he found it in St. Irenaeus.

St. Hilary, in his preface to the Psalms, says that Esdras arranged them in order.

This tradition originated in the fourteenth chapter of the Fourth Book of Esdras: *Deus glorificatus est, et Scripturae vere divinae creditae sunt, omnibus eamdem et eisdem verbis et eisdem nominibus recitantibus ab initio usque ad finem, uti et praessentes gentes cognoscerunt quoniam per inspirationem Dei interpretatae sunt Scripturae, et non esset mirabile Deum hoc in eis operatum: quando in ea captivitate populi quae facta est a Nabuchodonosor, corruptis Scripturis et post 70 annos Judaeis descendentibus in regionem suam, et post deinde temporibus Artaxercis Persarum regis, inspiravit Esdrae sacerdoti tribus Levi praeteritorum prophetarum omnes rememorare sermones, et restituere populo eam legem quae data est per Moysen.*[2]   (632)

565. *Against the argument of Esdras,* II, *Mach.,* II;—Josephus, *Ant.,* II, 1. *Cyrus* used the prophecy of Isaiah for setting the people free. The Jews held their property in peace under Cyrus in Babylon; therefore they might well have had the law.

Josephus, in the whole of the history of Esdras, does not say a word about its reconstruction.—IV Kings, XVIII, 27.   (633)

[1] During the captivity of the people under Nabuchodonosor, when the Scriptures had been destroyed, (God) inspired Esdras, the priest of the tribe of Levi, to recover all the utterances of the former prophets, and to renew the Law which Moses had given to the people.

[2] God has been glorified and the truly divine writings were believed, that everybody recited in exactly the same terms from the beginning to the end, so that the present-day people should know that the Scriptures had been interpreted by the inspiration of God, and that it was not surprising that God should have accomplished this work in them, since, during the captivity of the people under Nabuchodonosor, the Scriptures were destroyed, and seventy years later when the Jews returned to their own country and then in the time of Artaxerxes, king of the Persians, he inspired Esdras, a priest of the tribe of Levi, with the idea of recalling the ancient prophecies and restoring to the people the law which had been given by Moses.

566. If the story of Esdras is credible, we must believe that Scripture is Holy Scripture because the story is only based on the authority of those who rely on that of the Seventy, which shows that Scripture is holy.

If therefore the tale is true, it gives us what we want; if not, we can find it somewhere else. And so those who desire to ruin the truth of our religion, founded on Moses, establish it by the very authority which they use to attack it. Thus through providence it exists always. (634)

22. PROOFS OF MOSES

567. *Another circle.* The length of life of the patriarchs, instead of leading to the disappearance of the history of the past, helped on the contrary to preserve it. The reason why we are sometimes not sufficiently well informed about the history of our ancestors is that we have scarcely spent any part of our lives with them, and that they are often dead before we have attained the age of reason. For when men lived to such a great age the children spent many years with their fathers, and were able to talk to them a great deal. Now, what would they have talked about except the history of their ancestors, since all history comes down to that, and since they had no studies or science or art which account for a considerable part of our own conversation in life? Therefore, we can see that in those days the people took particular care to preserve their genealogies. (626)

568. This religion so rich in miracles, in saints, in the pure, the irreproachable, in scholars, in famous witnesses and martyrs; in reigning monarchs, (David); Isaiah, a prince of the blood;— so rich in knowledge, after displaying all its miracles and all its wisdom, brushes them all aside and declares that it offers neither wisdom nor signs, but simply the folly of the Cross.

For those who by these signs and this wisdom have deserved your belief, who have proved their character to you, give you notice that none of it can change us, or make us capable of knowing and loving God except the power of the folly of the

Cross, without wisdom or signs; and not the signs without this power.

Thus, our religion is foolishness when we look at its effective cause, and wisdom when we look at the wisdom which prepared the way for it. (587)

569. *Proof of Moses.* Why does Moses make men's lives so long, and their generations so few?

Because it is not the length of the years, but the generations which make for obscurity. Truth is only altered by change in men. And yet Moses brings two events, the most memorable events that have ever been imagined, the Creation and the Flood, so close together that they almost seem to touch. (624)

570. If we ought to devote a week, we ought to devote the whole of our lives to the search. (204 *bis*)

571. As long as the prophets were there to uphold the law, the people were careless; but once the prophets disappeared, they became filled with zeal. (703)

572. Josephus conceals the shame of his people. Moses does not hide his own shame, or . . .

Qui mihi det ut omnes prophetent.[1]

He was sick of the people. (629)

573*. Sem, who saw Lamech, who saw Adam, also saw Jacob, who saw those who had seen Moses; therefore the accounts of the Flood and the Creation are true. That is conclusive for many people who have a proper understanding of the matter. (625)

574. Zeal of the Jewish people for their law, and chiefly since the cessation of the prophets. (702)

23. PROOFS OF JESUS CHRIST

575. *Order. Reply to the objection that Scripture has no order.* The heart has its own order; the intellect has its own order which operates by means of principle and demonstration; the heart has a different one. We cannot prove that we ought to be loved by set-

[1] For myself I would have the whole people prophesy (Numbers XI, 29).

ting out in their proper order the causes of love: that would be absurd.

Jesus Christ and St. Paul possess the order of charity, not of intellect; because they wished to warm the hearts of the people, not to instruct them. It is the same with St. Augustine. This order consists mainly in a disquisition on each point which relates to our final end, so that it will always be kept in view. (283)

576. The Gospels only speak of the virginity of the Virgin up to the birth of Jesus Christ. Everything in relation to Jesus Christ. (742)

577. Jesus Christ in an obscurity (as people understand the term) which was such that historians writing only of matters which were politically important barely noticed him. (786)

578. *Holiness. Effundam spiritum meum.*[1] All nations had succumbed to unbelief and sensuality: all the earth was on fire with charity, princes laid aside their greatness, their daughters suffered martyrdom. Whence came this strength? It was because the Messiah had come; those are the effects and signs of his coming. (772)

579. The combinations of miracles. (809)

580. An artisan who talks about wealth, a procurator who talks about war, royalty, etc.; but the rich man speaks well of wealth, the king speaks casually about a great gift that he has just bestowed, and God speaks well of God. (799)

581. *Proofs of Jesus Christ.*

Why was the book of Ruth preserved?

Why the story of Thamar? (743)

582. *Proofs of Jesus Christ.* It was no captivity when you were certain that you would be liberated in seventy years. But now they are prisoners without any hope of deliverance.

God promised them that though he would scatter them to the ends of the earth, if they remained faithful to his law, he would nevertheless unite them again. They have indeed remained faithful to it, and they are still oppressed. (638)

583. The Jews, by trying to discover whether he was God, have shown that he was man. (763)

---

[1] I will pour out my spirit.

584. The Church has had just as much trouble in proving that Jesus Christ was man, in the face of those who denied it, as in proving that he was God; and the appearances were just as great.   (764)

585. The infinite distance between bodies and minds symbolises the infinitely more infinite distance between minds and charity; for charity is supernatural.

The blaze of fame has no attraction for people who are engaged in intellectual pursuits.

The greatness of men of intellect is invisible to kings, to the rich, to captains, to all those who are great according to the flesh.

The greatness of wisdom, which is nothing if it does not come from God, is invisible to the sensual and to the men of intellect. They belong to three different orders.

The great geniuses have their empire, their splendour, their greatness, their victory, their glamour, and have no need of greatness according to the flesh with which they have no connection. They are seen not with eyes, but with minds; it is sufficient.

The saints have their empire, their splendour, their victory, their glamour; and have no need of material or intellectual greatness with which they have no connection, for they neither add nor take away anything. They are seen by God and the angels, and not by bodies or inquisitive minds: God is sufficient for them.

Archimedes, without any outward show, would be held in the same veneration. He did not stage any visible battles, but he made his discoveries available to all minds. O how he burst upon men's minds!

Jesus Christ, without possessions and without any outward display of knowledge, stands in his order of holiness. He made no discoveries; he did not reign; but he was humble, patient, holy, holy, holy unto God, terrible to devils, and without sin. O with what great pomp and vast magnificence he came in the eyes of the heart, which perceives wisdom!

It would have been pointless for Archimedes, prince though he was, to play the prince in his mathematical works.

It would have been pointless for Our Lord Jesus Christ to come as a king, in order that his reign of holiness should dazzle; but he certainly came with the splendour which belongs to his order!

It is quite ridiculous to take offence at the lowliness of Jesus Christ, as though his lowliness were of the same order as the greatness which he came to reveal. When we consider the greatness that he showed in his life, in his Passion, in his obscurity, in his death, in the choice of his disciples, in their desertion, in his secret resurrection, and the rest, we shall see that it is so great that there is no reason to be scandalised by a lowliness which is not there.

But there are some who are only impressed by worldly greatness, as though there were no spiritual greatness; and others who only admire spiritual greatness, as though there were no other forms of greatness which stand infinitely higher in the order of wisdom.

All bodies, the firmament, the stars, the earth and its kingdoms, are not equal to the least among minds, for the mind knows it all and itself; and bodies, nothing.

From all the bodies put together we should not be able to extract one little thought: it is impossible and belongs to another order. From all the bodies and minds we should not be able to extract a single spark of true charity: it is impossible and belongs to another order which is supernatural.

(793)

586. *Proofs of Jesus Christ.* Jesus Christ said things so simply that it seems that he did not think them, and yet so clearly that we see quite well that he did think them. Such clarity joined to such simplicity is marvellous. (797)

587. *Proof of Jesus Christ.* The hypothesis that the Apostles were frauds is absurd. Let us follow it to its logical conclusion: let us imagine those twelve men coming together after the death of Jesus Christ and conspiring to say that he had risen from the dead. It would have been an attack on all the powers. The heart

of man is strangely prone to levity, to change, to promises, to wealth. If a single one of them had denied it under the influence of these seductions or, more probably, under the pressure of imprisonment, torture and death, they would have been lost. Follow that to its conclusion. (801)

588. It is an amazing thing, and worthy of special attention, to find the Jewish people surviving after so many years, and to see them always in a state of wretchedness; but in order to prove the claims of Jesus Christ it was essential that they should both survive and be wretched because they crucified him; and though to be wretched and to survive is a contradiction they nevertheless still survive in spite of their wretchedness. (640)

589. *Prodiga lege.—Impleta cerne.—Implenda collige.*[1] (607)

590. *Canonical.* The existence of heretical writings in the early years of the Church serves to authenticate the canonical writings. (569)

591. When Nabuchodonosor led the people away, out of fear that it might be thought that the sceptre had been taken away from Juda they were told beforehand that they would only be there for a short time, and that they would be released.

They were always comforted by the prophets; their kings continued. But the second destruction carried no promise of restoration, was without prophets, without kings, without consolation, without hope, because the sceptre had departed from them for ever. (639)

592. Moses was the first to teach the doctrines of the Trinity, original sin, the Messiah.

David, great witness: king, good, forgiving, noble soul, fine mind, powerful; he prophesied and his miracle took place; it is infinite.

He would only have needed to say that he was the Messiah if he had been vain: for the prophecies about him are more definite than about Jesus Christ.

[1] Read the prophecies; see what has been accomplished; collate what is still to be accomplished (Pascal).

Same with St. John. (752)

593. Who taught the Evangelists the qualities which belong to a completely heroic soul to enable them to depict it so perfectly in Jesus Christ? Why were they weak during his agony? Did they not know how to describe constancy in death? Yes, for the same St. Luke describes St. Stephen's death which was more powerful than Jesus Christ's.

Therefore, they show him as being capable of fear before the necessity to face death had come, and afterwards as completely steadfast.

But the occasions on which they show him in such a state of distress are those when he is distressed of his own accord; and when men cause him distress he is seen to be very strong.

(800)

594. Zeal of the Jews for their law and their temple (*Josephus and Philo the Jew ad Caïum*).

What other people have shown such zeal? They needed it.

The advent of Jesus Christ foretold both as to the time and the state of the world: the bone taken from the thigh and the fourth dynasty.

How fortunate we are to have this light in our darkness!

How marvellous it is to see with the eyes of faith Darius and Cyrus, Alexander, the Romans, Pompey and Herod, working without realising it for the glory of the Gospel! (701)

595. The apparent discordance of the Gospels. (755)

596. The synagogue preceded the Church; the Jews, the Christians. The prophets foretold the Christians; St. John, Jesus Christ. (699)

597. Macrobius: the innocents slain by Herod. (178)

598. Every man can do what Mahomet did; for he performed no miracles; his coming was not foretold. No one can do what Jesus Christ did. (600)

599. The Apostles were either deceived or deceivers; either is difficult to accept because it is not possible to imagine that a man has been raised from the dead . . .

While Jesus Christ was with them, he could give them support; but if he did not appear to them, who gave them the strength to act afterwards? (802)

600. Jesus Christ, whom both Testaments regard, the Old as its hope, the New as its model, both as their centre. (740)

601. *Nature is corrupt.* Without Jesus Christ man necessarily finds himself condemned to a life of vice and misery; with Jesus Christ he is exempt from vice and misery. The whole of our virtue and our happiness are in him; outside him there are only vice, misery, error, darkness, death, despair. (546)

602. We not only do not know God except through Jesus Christ, but we only know ourselves through Jesus Christ. We only know life and death through Jesus Christ. Except in Jesus Christ, we do not know the meaning of our life or our death, or God or ourselves.

Thus without Scripture, which has only Jesus Christ for its object, we know nothing and see only darkness and confusion in the nature of God and in nature itself. (548)

603. Jews witnesses of God, Is. XLIII, 9; XLIV, 8. (714)

604. They are plainly a people who were created expressly to bear witness to the Messiah (Is., XLIII, 9; XLIV, 8). They were the possessors of the books; they loved them, and did not understand them. And it was all foretold: that the judgements of God were entrusted to them, but as a sealed book. (641)

605. What man ever had greater fame? The entire Jewish people foretold his coming before he came. The Gentiles worshipped him after his coming. Both peoples, Jews and Gentiles, regarded him as their centre.

And yet what man ever enjoyed his fame less? Of his thirty-three years, thirty were spent without any public appearance. In three years he passed for an impostor; the priests and the leaders of the people rejected him; his friends and closest relatives scorned him. Finally, he died, betrayed by one of his own disciples, denied by another, and deserted by all of them.

What share had he then in this fame? Never has a man had greater glory, never has a man suffered greater ignominy. All his fame was for our sake, to enable us to recognise him; and he himself got nothing out of it. (792)

606. Marvellous to see with the eyes of faith the story of Herod, Caesar. (700)

607. Jesus Christ did not desire the testimony of devils or those who had no vocation, but that of God and John the Baptist.

(784)

608. Jesus Christ symbolised by Joseph: innocent, beloved of his father, sent by his father to see his brothers, was sold by his brothers for twenty pieces of silver, and through that became their lord, their saviour, the saviour of strangers, and saviour of the world; which would never have happened without the plot to bring about his undoing, without their selling him into slavery and their rejection of him.

In prison the innocent Joseph between two criminals; Jesus Christ crucified between two thieves. Joseph foretold the salvation of one and the death of the other according to the same omens. Jesus Christ saves the elect and condemns the lost souls for the same crimes. Joseph only prophesied; Jesus Christ acted. Joseph asked the man who was saved to remember him when he came in glory; and the one whom Jesus Christ saved asked him to remember him when he entered into his kingdom. (768)

609. The corruption of reason is apparent from so many different and extravagant forms of behaviour. It was necessary for truth to come so that man no longer went on living inside himself.

(440)

610. 'I will leave me seven thousand.' I like these worshippers who are unknown to the world, and to the prophets themselves.

(788)

611. *On the fact that neither Josephus nor Tacitus and the other historians mention Jesus Christ.*

So far from being an argument against, it is on the contrary an argument in favour. For it is certain that Jesus Christ existed, that his religion caused a great stir, and that these men were not unaware of it. It is therefore clear that they could only have concealed it intentionally; or that they spoke of it and that what they said was suppressed or altered. (787)

612. When Augustus learnt that his own son was among the children below the age of two whom Herod had had put to death, he said that it was better to be Herod's hog than his son. Macrobius, Book II, *Sat.*, chap, IV. (179)

613. [Either the Jews or the Christians must be wicked.] (759)

24. PROPHECIES

614. Ruin of the Jews and the heathen by Jesus Christ: *omnes gentes venient et adorabunt eum. Parum est ut,* etc. *Postula a me. Adorabunt eum omnes reges. Testes iniqui. Dabit maxillam percutienti. Dederunt fel in escam.*[1] (773)

615. . . . That idolatry would then be overthrown: that the Messiah would cast down all idols, and lead men to the worship of the true God.

That the temples of idolatry would be demolished and that, among all the nations and in all places throughout the world, a pure victim would be offered up to him, and not animals.

That he would be King of the Jews and the Gentiles. And so we see the King of the Jews and the Gentiles persecuted by both Jew and Gentile who plot his death; the ruler of both, destroying both the worship of Moses in Jerusalem, which was its centre, where he founded his first Church, and the worship of idols in Rome, which was its centre, where he established his principal Church. (730)

616. That he would teach men the way of perfection.

And no man has come, either before or after him, who taught anything divine which was comparable to that. (733)

617. . . . And what crowns it all is the prophecy, so that it cannot be said to have happened by chance.

Anyone who had only a week to live would not think that

---

[1] All the races of the heathen will worship before him. Use thee I will. Ask thy will of me. All kings must needs bring their homage. Perjured witnesses. Cheek buffeted in scorn, bravely endured. They gave me gall to eat. (Ps. XXI, 28; Is. XLIX, 6; Ps. II, 8; LXXI, 11; XXXIV, 11; Lamentation III, 30; Ps. LXVIII, 22.)

the best course was to assume that it was all a matter of chance!

Now, if we were not in the clutches of our passions, a week or a hundred years would come to the same thing.   (694)

618. After many people had come before him Jesus Christ ended by coming and saying: 'Here I am, the time is fulfilled. I tell you that what the prophets said would come to pass in the fulness of time will be accomplished by my disciples. The Jews will be rejected; Jerusalem will shortly be destroyed; and the heathen will come to the knowledge of God. My disciples will accomplish it after you have killed the heir to the vineyard.'

And then the Apostles said to the Jews: 'You will be accursed' (*Celsus laughed at them*); and to the heathen: 'You will come to know God'. And that is what happened.   (770)

619. '... That at that time no one will teach his neighbour saying: Here is the Lord, *for God will make himself felt by all.*'—'Your sons shall prophesy.'—'I will implant my law in their innermost thoughts, engrave it in their hearts' (Jer. XXXI, 33).

It all comes to the same thing. To prophesy is to speak of God, not in terms of external proofs, but by an *immediate* inward feeling.   (732)

620. .... That Jesus Christ would be small in his beginnings and grow later. Daniel's little stone.   (734)

If I had never heard anyone speak of the Messiah at all, nevertheless after the admirable prophecies about the order of the world which I have seen fulfilled, I should see that he is divine. And if I knew that these same books foretold a Messiah, I should feel sure that he would come; and seeing that they put the time before the second destruction of the temple, I should say that he had come.   (734)

621. *Prophecies.* The conversion of the Egyptians (Is. XIX, 19); an altar in Egypt to the true God.   (725)

622. In the time of the Messiah the people were divided. The spiritual men accepted the Messiah; the grosser elements remained to bear witness to him.   (748)

623. *Prophecies.* If a single man had compiled a book of prophecies about Jesus Christ, pointing both to the time and the manner of his coming and if Jesus Christ had come in the

manner foretold, it would have been a source of infinite strength.

What we find is much more than that. There was a succession of men who one after another, over a period of four thousand years, consistently and unwaveringly foretold this same coming. It was a whole people who proclaimed it, and who had been in existence for four thousand years in order to bear witness as a body to their certainty about it from which they could not be diverted by the few threats and persecutions to which they were subjected: this is something far more impressive. (710)

624. *Prophecies.* The time foretold by the state of the Jewish people, by the state of the heathen, by the state of the temple, by the number of years. (708)

625. Os., III.—Is., XLII, XLVIII, LIV, LX, LXI, and lastly: 'I foretold it of old so that they might know that it is I'. Jaddus to Alexander. (716)

626*. The most convincing of the proofs of Jesus Christ are the prophecies. They are also the ones with which God was most lavish; because the central event is a miracle which exists from the birth of the Church until the end. Therefore, God raised up prophets for a period of sixteen hundred years; and for four hundred years afterwards he scattered all the prophecies with the Jews who were their bearers to the four corners of the earth. Such was the preparation for the birth of Jesus Christ, and since his Gospel had to be believed by the whole world it was essential, not only that there should be prophecies to make people believe it, but that the prophecies should be spread all over the world, so that the Gospel should be believed by the whole world. (706)

627. You have to be bold to foretell the same event in so many different ways: the four dynasties, whether idolatrous or heathen, the end of the reign of Juda, and the seventy weeks all had to happen at the same time, and everything before the second destruction of the temple. (709)

628. Herod believed in the Messiah. He had wrested the sceptre from Juda, but he was not from Juda. It represented a large sect. And Barcosba and another accepted by the Jews. And the

rumours which were going round everywhere at that time. Suetonius. Tacitus. Josephus.

Curse of the Greeks on those who count the years.

How could it be the Messiah when it was assumed that through him the sceptre would remain in Juda for ever, and that at his coming the sceptre would be taken away from Juda.

Nothing could have been better calculated to ensure that in seeing they did not see, and that in hearing they did not understand. (753)

629. *Predictions.* That during the fourth dynasty before the second destruction of the temple, before the overlordship of the Jews was taken from them, in the seventieth week of Daniel, during the period when the second temple was standing, the heathen would be instructed and brought to the knowledge of the God worshipped by the Jews; that those who loved him would be delivered from their enemies, and filled with the fear and love of God.

And it happened that during the fourth dynasty before the second destruction of the temple, etc., the heathen in the mass worshipped God and led an angelic life; the girls consecrated their virginity and their lives to God; the men renounced all forms of pleasure. What Plato could not persuade a handful of chosen and educated men to accept, was accepted by a hundred million ignorant men through the secret power of a few words.

The rich abandoned their fortunes, the children left the comfortable homes of their fathers to live in the austerity of the desert, etc. (See Philo the Jew.) What did it all mean? It was what had been foretold long ago. For two thousand years no heathen had worshipped the God of the Jews; and at the time predicted, vast numbers of them went over to this one God. The temples were destroyed; the kings themselves bowed the knee to the Cross. What did it all mean? It was the spirit of God which extended over the face of the earth.

No heathen from Moses to Jesus Christ, according to the rabbis themselves. After the coming of Jesus Christ, large numbers of the heathen believed in the books of Moses, conformed to them in substance and in spirit, and only rejected what was useless in them. (724)

630. As the prophecies had spoken of different signs which would all come to pass at the advent of the Messiah, it was necessary that all the signs should occur at the same time. Thus it was necessary that the fourth dynasty should have come when the seventy weeks of Daniel were accomplished and when the sceptre was taken away from Juda, and it all happened without any hitch; that the Messiah should come at that time, and Jesus Christ came who said that he was the Messiah, and there was still no hitch, which is clearly a sign of the truth of the prophecies. (738)

631. *Non habemus regem nisi Caesarem.*[1] Therefore, Jesus Christ was the Messiah because they no longer had a king except a stranger, and they would not have any other. (720)

632. *Prophecies.* Daniel's seventy weeks is ambiguous so far as the beginning is concerned owing to the terms of the prophecy; and so far as the end is concerned owing to the divergencies of the chronologists. But the entire difference does not amount to two hundred years. (723)

633. *Prophecies.* The dynasty was not interrupted by the Babylonian captivity because the return was prompt and had been foretold. (637)

634. Prophecies. Great Pan is dead. (695)

635. What can we feel except veneration for a man who clearly foretells events which in fact occur, who announces his intention both to make people blind and to enlighten them, and who mingles obscurities with things which are clear and came to pass? (756)

636. Parum est ut . . . Vocation of the Gentiles through Jesus Christ (Is., LII, 15). (727 *bis*)

637. *Predictions.* It was foretold that when he came the Messiah would establish a new covenant which would make men forget the exodus from Egypt, Jer., XXIII, 5; Is., XLIII, 16; that he would place his law not in externals, but in men's hearts; that he would place fear of himself, which had only been external,

[1] We have no king but Caesar.

in the depths of the heart. Who does not discern the Christian faith in all these things? (729)

638. *Prophecies*. That the Jews would reject Jesus Christ and be rejected by God because the chosen vine would only produce sour fruit. That the chosen race would be unfaithful, ungrateful and unbelieving, *populum non credentem et contradicentem*. That God would strike them with blindness, and that they would stumble in broad daylight like blind men. That a precursor would come before him. (735)

639. The eternal reign of the house of David, ii. Chron., viii, 18., according to all the prophecies, and with vows. And not fulfilled from a temporal point of view: Jer., xxiii, 20. (718)

640. But it was not enough for the prophecies to exist; they had to circulate everywhere and be preserved at all times. And to prevent people from regarding his coming as a matter of chance, it had to be foretold.

It is much more glorious for the Messiah that the Jews were the spectators and even the instruments of his glory apart from the fact that God had reserved them for it. (707)

641. 'If it was so clearly foretold to the Jews, how is it that they did not believe it? Or how was it that they were not exterminated for resisting something which was so transparent?'

I reply: In the first place, it was foretold that they would not believe something so transparently clear, and that they would not be exterminated. And nothing is more glorious for the Messiah; for it was not enough that there were prophecies, they had to be preserved from any taint of suspicion. Now, etc. (749)

642. . . . Then Jesus Christ came to tell men that they had no enemies except themselves, that it was their passions which cut them off from God, and that he had come to destroy them and bring them his grace in order to transform them all into one holy Church, that he had come to bring the heathen and the Jews into the Church, that he had come to destroy the idols of the heathen and the superstitions of the Jews.

All men were opposed to it, not merely through the instinctive opposition of concupiscence; but, on top of everything, the kings of the earth joined forces in order to destroy this religion in its beginnings, as had been foretold (Proph.: *Quare fremerunt gentes . . . reges terrae . . . adversus Christum*).[1]

All that is great on earth united, the scholars, the sages and the kings. Some wrote, others condemned, others slew. And notwithstanding all this opposition, simple, powerless people resisted all those powers, compelled the kings, the scholars, the sages to submit, and banished idolatry from the face of the earth. And it all happened by means of the power which had foretold him.   (783)

643. [*Prophecies.* Promise that David would always have descendants. Jer.]   (717)

644. Sophonias, III, 9. 'I will send my word to the Gentiles so that all will serve me as one man.'

Ezech., XXVII, 25: 'David, my servant, that rules over them for ever'.

Exodus, IV, 22. 'Israel is my first-born son.'   (713 *bis*)

645. The prophets foretold and were not themselves foretold. The saints were foretold, but were not foretellers. Jesus Christ prophesied and prophesying.   (739)

646. *Predictions of particular events.*

They were strangers in Egypt without any possessions of their own, either in that country or anywhere else. [There was not the slightest sign either of royalty, which was there so long afterwards, or of the sovereign council of the seventy judges whom they called the *sanhedrin* which after being instituted by Moses lasted until the time of Jesus Christ: all these things were as far removed as they could be from their situation at that time] when Jacob, dying and blessing his children, declared that they would be the possessors of a great land, and foretold in particular that the kings who would one day rule over the tribe of Juda would belong to their family and that all their brothers would be its subjects [and that even the Messiah,

[1] What means this turmoil among the nations? . . . See how the kings of the earth, how its rulers make common cause against the Lord (Ps. II, 1-2).

whose coming all nations must await, would be born of it, and that the sceptre would not depart from Juda, or the governor or legislator from his descendants until the expected Messiah was born into his family].

This same Jacob, disposing of the future land as though he were master of it, gave one more share of it to Joseph than to the others: 'I am giving you,' he said, 'one more share than your brothers.' And blessing his two children, Ephraim and Menasse, whom Joseph had presented to him, the elder, Menasse, on his right, and Ephraim, the younger, on his left, he crossed his arms, and placing his right hand on the head of Ephraim and his left hand on the head of Menasse, he blessed them in that way; and when Joseph suggested that he preferred the younger, he answered with admirable firmness: 'I know it perfectly well, my son, I know it perfectly well; but Ephraim will grow up quite different from Menasse.' (Which turned out to be so true in what happened later that being by himself almost as fertile as the two whole families which together constituted an entire kingdom, they were generally known together simply by the name of Ephraim.)

This same Joseph, when he came to die, advised his children to take his bones with them whenever they went into the land, which did not happen for two hundred years.

Moses himself, who wrote down all these things so long before they happened, allotted shares in the land before they reached it, as though he had been its ruler [and ended by declaring that God would raise up from their people and their family a prophet of whom he had been a symbol, and foretold precisely what would happen to them in the land which they would enter after his death, the victories that God would send them, their ingratitude to God, the punishments that would fall upon them and all their other adventures]. He gave them arbiters for dividing up the land; he prescribed in detail the political regime under which they would live there, the cities of refuge that they would build, etc. . . . . (711)

647*. *During the life of the Messiah. Aenigmatisa.* Ezech., XVII.

His precursor. Malach., III.

He will be born a child. Is., ix.

He will be born in the town of Bethlehem. Mich., v. He will be seen mainly in Jerusalem, and will be born of the family of Juda and David.

He will make the wise men and the learned blind, Is., vi, viii, xxix, etc., and preach the Gospel to the poor and the weak, Is., xxix, restore the sight of the blind, heal the sick, and bring light to those who languish in darkness. Is., lxi.

He will show men the way of perfection, and be the teacher of the Gentiles. Is., lv, xlii, 1-7.

The prophecies will be unintelligible to the infidel. Dan., xii; Os., *ult.*, 10, but intelligible to those who are properly instructed.

The prophecies which represent him as a poor man, also represent him as ruler of the nations. Is., lii, 14, liii, etc.; Zach., ix, 9.

The prophecies which foretell the time, only foretell him as ruler of the Gentiles and suffering, and not sitting in the clouds in judgement. And those which represent him as sitting in judgement and coming in glory do not foretell the time.

That he must be the victim sacrificed for the sins of the world. Is., xxxix, liii, etc.

He will be the corner stone, the precious stone. Is., xxviii, 16.

He will be the stumbling block and a scandal. Is., vii. Jerusalem will be flung against the stone.

The builder will reject the stone, Ps., cxvii, 22.

God will make this stone the headstone of the corner.

And the stone will grow into a huge mountain, and fill all the earth. Dan., ii.

That in this way he will be rejected, unrecognised, betrayed. Ps., cviii, 8, sold, Zach., xii, spat upon, buffeted, mocked, afflicted in countless ways, and given vinegar to drink, Ps. lxv, iii; stabbed, Zach., xii; his feet and hands pierced, slain, and lots drawn for his clothing.

That he would rise from the dead, Ps., xv, the third day, Os., vi, 3.

That he would ascend into heaven and sit on the right hand. Ps., cix.

That the kings would take up arms against him. Ps., ii.

That being on the right hand of the Father, he would be victorious over his enemies.

That the kings of the earth and all the people would worship him, Is., lx.

That the Jews will continue to exist as a nation. Jer.

That they will be wanderers, without kings, etc., Os., iii, without prophets, Amos, awaiting salvation and not finding it. Is., lix.

Vocation of the Gentiles through Jesus Christ. Is., lii, 15; lv, 5, lx, etc. Ps., lxxxi.

Os., i, 9: 'For you are not my people, and I will not be your God. And the number of the people of Israel shall be as the sand of the sea that is without measure and shall not be numbered from the dispersal. The places where my people are not called, I will call it my people.' (727)

648. *Prophecies fulfilled.*—iii Kings, xiii, 2. iv Kings, xxiii, 16.—Jos., vi, xxvi.—iii Kings, xvi, 34.—Deut., xxiii.

Malach., i, ii. The sacrifice of the Jews rejected, and the sacrifice of the heathen (even outside Jerusalem) and in every place.

Moses foretold the vocation of the Gentiles before he died, Deut., xxxii, 21, and the reprobation of the Jews.

Moses foretold what was to happen to each tribe. (714)

649. *Prophecies.* 'Your name shall be execrated by my people and I will give them another name.' (714)

650. 'Their hearts hardened.' How? By flattering their concupiscence and holding out hopes to them of gratifying it.

(714)

651. We have no king but Caesar. (721)

652*. *Prophecies.* Amos and Zachary: They sold the just one, and for that will never be recalled.—Jesus Christ betrayed.

They will no longer remember Egypt; see Is., xliii, 16, 17, 18, 19; Jer. xxiii, 6, 7.

Prophecies. The Jews shall spread everywhere. Is., xxvii, 6.—The new law. Jer., xxxi, 32.

Malachy, *Grotius*.—The second glorious temple. Jesus Christ will come to it. Agg., II, 7, 8, 9, 10.

Vocation of the Gentiles. Joel., II, 28; Os., II, 24; Deut., XXXII, 21; Malachy, I, 11.   (715)

653. *Omnis Judaea regio, et Jerosolomytae universi, et baptizabantur.*[1] On account of all the conditions of men who came to him.

Stones *can* be children of Abraham.   (778)

654. The devil upset the zeal of the Jews before Jesus Christ because it was salutary for them, but not afterwards.

The Jewish people, mocked by the Gentiles; the Christian people persecuted.   (704)

655. The Jews rejected him, but not all of them: the saints accepted him, and not the worldly. So far from that detracting from his glory, it was the crowning mark of it. Since their reason for it, and the only one to be found in all their writings, in the Talmud and in the Rabbis, was because Christ did not subdue the nations by force of arms, *gladium tuum, potentissime.*[2]

[Is that all they have to say? Jesus Christ was killed, they say; he succumbed; he did not subdue the heathen by his strength; he did not give us their spoils; he did not give us riches. Is that all they have to say? It is because of that that I find him lovable. I should have no use for the person whom they expected him to be.]

It is evident that it was only vice which prevented them from accepting him and by their rejection they are witnesses without reproach, and, what is more, in that way they fulfilled the prophecies.

The fact that the people did not receive him produced this marvel: the prophecies were the only lasting miracles which could be performed, but they were subject to refutation. (760)

656. *Prophecies. Transfixerunt*, Zach, XII., 10.[3]

That a saviour would come who would crush the devil's head, who would deliver his people from their sins, *ex omnibus*

---

[1] And all the country of Judaea and all those who dwelt in Jerusalem went out to see him, and he baptised them (Mark I, 5).

[2] Gird on thy sword at thy side, great warrior (Ps. XLIV, 4).

[3] Towards me shall they look, me whom they have pierced through.

iniquitatibus;[1] that there would be a New Testament which would be everlasting; that there would be another priesthood according to the order of Melchisedech; that it would be eternal; that Christ would be glorious, powerful, strong, and nevertheless so wretched that he would not be recognised; that he would not be taken for what he is; that he would be rebuffed, that he would be slain; that his people, who had denied him, would no longer be his people; that he would be accepted by the idolaters who would appeal to him; that he would leave Sion and reign in the centre of idolatry; that nevertheless the Jews would go on existing; that he would come from Juda where there was no longer a king. (736)

657. *Prophecies.* That Jesus Christ shall be on the right hand while God shall make his enemies subject to him.

Thus he will not make them submit himself. (731)

658. You imagine that the prophecies quoted in the Gospels are reported in order to make you believe? Not at all: it is to prevent you from believing. (568)

659. The prophecies of particular events are mixed with those relating to the Messiah, so that those foretelling the Messiah would not be without proofs, and particular prophecies would not be without point. (712)

660. We only understand the prophecies when we see the things happen: thus the proofs of retreat, of discretion and of silence, etc., only convince those who know and believe in them.

St. Joseph so interior in a law which is wholly external.

External penance disposes us to interior penance, as humiliations incline us to humility. Thus the . . . (698)

661. *Prophecies.* [In Egypt, *Pugio Fidei*], p. 659, *Talmud*: 'It is a tradition among us that when the Messiah comes, the house of God, destined for the propagation of his teaching, will be full of filth and impurity, and that the wisdom of the scribes will be corrupt and rotten. Those who fear to sin will be rejected by the people and treated as fools and madmen.'

Is., XLIX: 'Listen, remote islands; pay heed to me, nations from far away. Ere ever I was born, the Lord sent me his sum-

---

[1] He it is who will ransom Israel from all his iniquities (Ps. CXXIX, 8).

mons, kept me in mind, when I lay in my mother's womb. Word of mine is sword of his, ready sharpened, under cover of his hand; arrow he has chosen out carefully, hidden yet in his quiver. Thou art my servant, he whispers, thou art the Israel I claim for my own. To me, all my labour seemed useless, my strength worn out in vain; his to judge me, he, my God, must reward my work as he would. But now a new message he sends me; I am his servant, appointed ever since I lay in the womb, to bring Jacob back to him. What if Israel will not answer the summons? None the less, the Lord destines me to honour; none the less, he, my God, protects me. Use thee I will, he promises, nor with thy service be content, when the tribes of Jacob thou hast summoned, brought back the poor remnant of Israel; nay, I have appointed thee to be the light of the Gentiles, in thee I will send out my salvation to the furthest corners of the earth.

'A message from the Lord, Israel's ransomer, Israel's Holy One, to the despised one, to the nation that is abhorred, to the slave of tyrants, when they see this, shall rise up from their thrones, princes too, and fall down to worship, in honour of the Lord, that keeps his promise so faithfully, the Holy One of Israel, that claims thee still.

'Thus says the Lord, Here is a time of pardon, when prayer of thine shall be answered, a day of salvation, when I will bring thee aid. I have kept thee in readiness, to make, by thy means, a covenant with my people. Thine to revive a ruined country, to parcel out the forfeited lands anew, men that are bound in darkness restoring to freedom and to the light. There shall be pasture for my flock by the wayside, feeding-grounds they shall have on all the barren uplands; they will hunger and thirst no more, noonday heat nor sun overpower them; theirs is a merciful shepherd, that will lead them to welling fountains and give them drink. And I will turn all these mountains of mine into a highroad for you; safe through the uplands my path shall lead. See how they come from far away! Exiles from north and west, exiles from the south country return. Ring out, heaven, with praise; let earth keep holiday, and its mountains echo that praise again; the Lord brings consolation to his people, takes pity on their need.

'Did Sion complain, the Lord has forsaken me, my own Master gives me never a thought? What, can a woman forget her child that is still unweaned, pity no longer the son she bore in her womb? Let her forget; I will not be forgetful of thee. Why, I have cut thy image on the palms of my hands; those walls of thine dwell before my eyes continually. Here are craftsmen ready to build thee again; vanished, now, the spoilers that plundered thee. Look about thee, and see thy children met together, coming back to thee; as I am living God, the Lord says, all these shall be a robe to deck thee, shall ring thee round like a bride's jewels; the silent homes, the lonely places of a ruined countryside, shall have no room, now, for thy many inhabitants, when all that robbed thee of thy lands have fled far away. Sons born to thee in the days of thy barrenness shall cry out, Here all is confined, give me room to live! Who has begotten me these? thou wilt ask. Barren days of exile, when I could not give birth; who has reared me these, when I was left solitary? Where were these all the while? Even now, says the Lord God, I will beckon to the nations, lift up a signal for all the world to see; son and daughter of thine shall be nursed in their arms, carried on their shoulders. Thou shalt have kings to foster them, queens to nurse them for thee; kings and queens shall bow to earth before thee, kissing the dust thy feet have trodden. And thou shalt know at last what a Lord I am, a Lord none ever trusted in vain.

'Shall the strong be robbed of his spoil? Who shall deliver the captives from a warrior's hand? Captives of the strong, the Lord says, shall be taken away from him, the valiant warrior shall lose his spoil. I will pass judgement on the men who have been thy judges, and thy own children shall escape. I will feed thy enemies on their own flesh, give them their own blood to make them drunk, and all mankind shall know that I, the Lord, have delivered thee, that I, the Prince of Israel, have brought thee rescue.'

Is., L: 'Thus says the Lord, Who can shew writ of separation your mother had from me when I sent her away? Was I in debt, that I must needs sell you as slaves? Nay, if I sold you, it was for your disobedience; it was wanton wife I thrust out of doors. And now must I come to you, and find none to greet me, call you, and hear no answer to my call? What, has arm of mine grown shrunk and shrivelled, lost its power to save? Have I strength no longer to set men free? Nay, with a word I can yet turn sea into desert, dry up rivers, till the fish lie rotting on the banks, dead of thirst; I can yet cover the heavens with darkness, and give them mourning weeds to wear.

'Ever the Lord schools my tongue to utterance that shall refresh the weary; awakes my dull ears, morning after morning, their Master's bidding to heed. An attentive ear the Lord has given me; not mine to withstand him; not mine to shrink from the task. I offered my body defenceless to the men who would smite me, my cheeks to all who plucked at my beard; I did not turn away my face when they reviled me and spat upon me. The Lord God is my helper; and that help cannot play me false; meet them I will, and with a face unmoved as flint; not mine to suffer the shame of defeat; here is One stands by to see right done me. Come, who pleads? Meet me, and try the issue; let him come forward who will, and accuse me. Here is the Lord God ready to aid me; who dares pass sentence on me now? One and all they shall be brought to nothing, like garment the moth has eaten!

'Who is here that fears the Lord, listens to his servant's message? Who would make his way through the dark places, with no glimmer of light? Let him trust in the name of the Lord, and lean upon his God. For you others, with brand at girdle, that your own fire would make, with fire your own brands have kindled light the path if you can; this is all the gift I have for you, a bed of anguish.'

Is., LI: 'Listen to me, then, you who follow the true path, you that have recourse to the Lord. Think of the rock you were quarried from, of the hidden depths whence you came, of Abraham that begot you, of Sara that was your mother; he was a childless man when I called him, and blessed him, and granted him a posterity. And has the Lord no pity for Sion, left desolate, no pity on her ruined state? Doubt not he will turn that wilderness into a garden of delight, that loneliness into a paradise; in her, too, mirth and gladness shall be found, there shall be thanksgiving and songs of praise. People of mine, men of a chosen race, give heed and hearing! Henceforth, my law shall be promulgated, my decrees be ratified, for a whole world's enlightening.'

Amos, VIII: 'By Jacob's ancient renown the Lord swears it, crimes of yours shall remain for ever unforgotten. Well may the earth quake over such doings, to the hurt of all that dwell in it; everywhere mount up, and shift, and sink, like Egypt's river in flood. Day of doom, says the Lord God, when there shall be sunset at noon, and earth shall be overshadowed under the full light! All your feasting turned into lament, all your songs to dirge and dole; not a loin but goes clad in sackcloth, not a head but is shaved bald; never was such mourning made, though it were for an only son; bitter the day, bitter its ending.

'A time is coming, says the Lord God, when there shall be great lack in the land, yet neither dearth nor drought. Hunger? Ay, they shall hunger for some message from the Lord, yet go they from eastern to western sea, go they from north to south, making search for it everywhere, message from the Lord they shall have none. Thirst, ay, they shall thirst, fair maid and brave warrior both. Fools, that by the shame of Samaria take their oaths, pin their faith to Dan's worship or Bersabee pilgrimage! Here is fall there is no amending.'

Amos, III, 2: 'Nation is none I have claimed for my own, save you.'

Daniel, XII, 7, after describing the whole span of the reign of the Messiah says: 'Strength of God's holy people must be broken utterly; when that is over, all is over and done.'

Aggaeus, II, 4: 'To Zorobabel, and Josue, and all the people with them his word was: Tell me, those of you who saw this house in its former brightness, what make you of it now? It is no better in your eyes than a very nothing. Take heart, Zorobabel; Josue, son of Josedec, take heart! And you, too, people of the land, the Lord of hosts bids you put heart into the work; is not he, the Lord of hosts on your side?

'. . . the promise I gave you when you escaped from Egypt; my own spirit shall be among you, do not be afraid.

'A little while now, the Lord of hosts says, and I mean to set heaven and earth, sea and dry land rocking; stirred all the nations shall be, hither shall come the prize the whole world treasures, and I will fill this temple with the brightness of my presence, says the Lord of hosts.

'Silver or gold, what matters it? the Lord of hosts says. Both are mine! Bright this new temple shall be, he tells you, as never the first was; here, he tells you, his blessing shall rest.'

Deut., XVIII, 16: 'Was it not thy own plea, that day when all were publicly assembled at mount Horeb, that thou mightest hear the voice of the Lord thy God no longer, have sight of that raging fire no longer, lest it should be thy death? And the Lord told me, All that they have said is well said. I will raise up for them a prophet like thyself, one of their own race, entrusting my own message to his lips, so that he may instruct them at my bidding. Whoever refuses obedience to these commands which he gives in my name, shall feel my vengeance.'

Genesis, XLIX: 'But thou, Juda, shalt win the praise of thy brethren; with thy hand on the necks of thy enemies, thou shalt be reverenced by thy own father's sons. Juda is like a lion's whelp; on the hills, my son, thou roamest after thy prey; like a lion couched in his lair, a lioness that none dares provoke. Juda shall not want a branch from his stem, a prince drawn from his stock, until the day when he comes who is to be sent to us, he, the hope of the nations.' (726)

662*. Daniel, II: 'Never wizard or sage, never diviner or prophet, that can give the king's grace an answer! But there is a God in heaven, king Nabuchodonosor, that makes hidden things plain; he it is that has sent thee warning of what must befall long hence. Let me tell thee what thy dream was, what visions disturbed thy sleep. As thou wast lying there abed, my lord king, thy thoughts still turned on future times; and he that makes hidden things plain revealed to thee what the pattern of those times should be. If the secret was disclosed to me also, it is not that I have wisdom beyond the wont of living men; I was but the instrument by which the meaning of it was to be made known, and a king's thoughts unravelled.

'A vision thou hadst of a great image; what splendour, how terrible an aspect it was that confronted thee! of fine gold the head, breast and arms of silver, belly and thighs of bronze; of iron the legs, and of the feet, too, part was iron, part was but earthenware. And as thou wert watching it, from the mountain-side fell a stone no hands had quarried, dashed against the feet of yonder image, part iron, part clay, and shattered them. With that, down came iron and clay, down came bronze and silver and gold; chaff of the threshing-floor was never so scattered on the summer breeze. They were gone, none knew whither; and stone that had shattered image grew into a high mountain, filling the whole earth.

'So much for the dream, and now we that know the secret of it will tell the king's grace what it means. Thou hast kings for thy vassals; royalty, power, dominion and great renown the God of heaven has bestowed on thee; every haunt of man and wild beast and flying bird he has given over to thee, all alike he has made subject to thee; the head of gold, who else but thou? Another and a lesser empire must follow thine, one of silver, then another of bronze, still wide as the world; then a fourth, of iron, breaking down and crushing all before it, as iron has power all-conquering, all-subduing. But feet and toes of the image were part iron, part clay; this fourth empire will be divided within itself. Foundation of iron there shall yet be, from which it springs; sure enough, in the feet thou sawest, earthenware was mixed with true steel. Yet was true steel mixed with base earthenware, token that this empire shall be in part firmly established, in part brittle. Iron and clay mingled; race of the conquerors shall be adulterated with common human stock; as well mix clay with iron!

'And while those empires yet flourish, another empire the God of heaven will bring into being, never to be destroyed, never to be superseded; conqueror of all these others, itself unconquerable. This is that stone thou sawest none ever quarried, that fell from the mountain-side, bringing clay and iron and bronze and silver and gold to nothing; this was a revelation the king's grace had from the most high God himself of what must come about; true was thy dream, and this, past doubt, the meaning of it.

'With that, king Nabuchodonosor bowed down face to earth,' etc.

Daniel, VIII, 8: Daniel has seen the battle between the ram and the goat that vanquished it. 'So now it was the goat's turn to enjoy dominion; yet no sooner had he reached his full strength, than the great horn was broken, and four other horns must grow up in place of it, fronting the four winds of heaven.

'It was from one of these a single horn now sprang; a little horn that grew till it outrivalled south and east, aye, and the armies . . . For the armies of heaven itself it proved a match, bringing heavenly powers down to earth, and trampling them underfoot; a match even for the captain of those armies, that must lose the daily sacrifice offered to him, and look on at the destruction of his sanctuary.

'But for me, for Daniel, that saw the vision, understanding of it was none, till one appeared to me that had the semblance of a man, and a voice hailed him from between the Ulai gates; For thee it is, Gabriel, to make the vision clear. And Gabriel said: Horned ram of thy vision rules over the Medes and the Persians; buck-goat over the realm of Greece, and the great horn between his eyes is first of the Greek kings. Those four others that grew after its breaking are four kings that shall arise, fellow-countrymen of his, but not his peers. These reigning, the world shall go from bad to worse, till a new king comes to the throne, brazen-faced, a master of riddles. Great power shall he wield, though of that first king not the peer, making havoc beyond belief, thriving and prospering. Strength of arms nor holiness of life shall rescue peoples from his will; all shall go well with crafty scheming of his, till his heart grows proud, and he deals death about him, when peril is none. And at last with the Prince of princes he shall try conclusion; no human hand it shall be that crushes him down at last.'

Daniel, IX, 20: 'Thus prayed I, thus did I confess my own sins, and the sins of my fellow Israelites, pouring out supplication, there in the presence of my God, for that holy mountain which is his dwelling-place. And I was still at prayer, when the human figure of Gabriel, as I had seen it at the beginning of my vision, flew swiftly to my side; it was the hour of the evening sacrifice when he reached me. And with these words he enlightened me: Daniel, my errand is to instruct thee and give thee discernment. Even as thy prayer began, a secret was disclosed, and I am here to make it known to thee, so well heaven loves thee. Mark well, then, the message, and read the revelation aright. It is ordained that this people of thine, that holy city of thine, should wait seventy weeks before guilt is done away, sin ended, wrong righted; before God's everlasting favour is restored, and the visions and the prophecies come true, and he who is all holiness receives his anointing. (After which the people will no longer be your people, nor the city the holy city. The time of wrath will have passed, the years of grace will have come.)* Be assured of this, and mark it well; a period of seven weeks must go by, and another period of sixty-two weeks, between the order to rebuild Jerusalem and the coming of the Christ to be your leader. (The Jews were accustomed to divide numbers and to put the small one first; these 7 and 62 make 69; of these 70 there will therefore remain the 70th; that is to say, the last 7 years of which he will speak later.)*

'Street and wall will be built again, though in a time of distress; and then sixty-two weeks must pass before the Christ is done to death; the people will disown him and have none of him. Then the army of an invading leader will destroy both city and sanctuary, so that his taking away will mean utter destruction; only a ruin is to be left when that war is ended. High covenant he shall make, before another week is done (which is the 70th that remains*), and with folks a many; but when that week has run half its course (that is to say, the last three and a

* Gloss by Pascal.

half years*), offering and burnt-sacrifice shall be none; in the temple all shall be defilement and desolation, and until all is over, all is fulfilled, that desolation shall continue.'

Daniel, XI: The angel said to Daniel: 'And now (after, Cyrus under whom we find ourselves*) a king shall rise in Persia, the fourth from this (Xerxes—the others were Cambyses, Smerdis, Darius*) rich in great revenue beyond all the others; in the power such wealth gives him, he will set the whole world in motion against the realm of Greece . . .

'And a warrior king (Alexander*) shall arise, winning such empire that there is no resisting his will. Divided that empire shall be, as soon as it is established, between the four quarters of heaven (as it had said before, VI, 6; VIII, 8*); not sons of his they shall be that rule it, nor peers of his; besides these, foreign lords shall part his dominions between them (these four principal successors).*

'The southern kingdom a strong ruler shall have, but of his vassals one shall be mightier than he (Egypt, Ptolemy, son of Lagus*); and in dominion excel him; wide, wide his domain (Seleucus, king of Syria. Appianus tells us that he was the most powerful of the successors of Alexander*); until at last these two make terms between them, and, to seal their amity, daughter of Egyptian king (Berenice, daughter of Ptolemy Philadelphus, sons of the other Ptolemy*) to Syrian king must pass (to Antiochus Deus, king of Syria and Asia, nephew of Seleucus Lagidas.*)

'Yet thrive she may not, nor dynasty of hers endure; herself in due time, with retinue of hers, faction of hers, must be a victim (Berenice and her son were killed by Seleucus Callinicus).*

'Not unavenged; scion of her own father's stock (Ptolemeus Evergetes will be born of the same father as Berenice*) shall march on Syria, and do battle, and prevail; shall carry off to Egypt the images of Syria's gods, its treasures of silver and gold (if he had not been recalled to Egypt for domestic reasons, he would have despoiled Seleucus in a very different manner, says

* Gloss by Pascal.

Justin*). Then his rival mastered, with that inroad he shall be content, and to his own kingdom return.

'To Syria's heirs the quarrel is left; and now there are great hosts a-mustering (Seleucus Ceraunus, Antiochus Magnus*), under a new king that must ever be hurrying on, like a river in flood, returning with spirit to the charge, throwing all his forces into the assault. See with what fury the Egyptian king takes the field against him (Ptolemeus Philopator against Antiochus Magnus at Raphia*), rallies a great host of his own, and over Syria's host gains the mastery! Captives a many, dead warriors a many, to gladden his heart, but all to no purpose (Ptolemeus profaned the temple: Josephus*); back Syria comes (Antiochus Magnus*), in greater force than ever, ranks filled and treasures swollen, with the years. All the world will be for picking a quarrel with Egypt then (the young Ptolemeus Epiphanes was reigning*); hot-heads there will be among thy own people who think to fulfil the old prophecies thus, but to their cost (those who had abandoned their religion to please Evergetes when he sent troops to Scopas, for Antiochus will retake Scopas and defeat them*). On marches he, younger Syrian king, raises a mound, and makes fortified cities his own; Egypt's vigour is all spent, never a halt, though its best warriors engage him, irresistible he comes, to impose terms on his enemy, sets foot in a noble land and crushes it under his heel. How to secure possession of the whole kingdom? (despising the youthfulness of Epiphanes, says Justin*). A bargain must be struck; gift of a royal bride shall be the land's undoing! (Cleopatra, so that she would betray her husband; whereupon Appianus says that, abandoning the idea of making himself master of Egypt by force on avowal of the protection of Rome, he decided to do it by finesse*). But no, that will not serve, never shall it be his. To the sea-coasts he turns and conquers lands a many (that is to say, maritime country*); but a great leader opposes him (Scipio the African who halted the progress of Antiochus Magnus because he offended Rome in the persons of her allies*) puts to silence the author of his own disgrace, and covers him with disgrace in his turn. But at last,

* Gloss by Pascal.

to his own province turning back, he totters to his fall, and the fame of him is heard no more.

'To a vile creature his throne must pass, of a throne (which is the people*) unworthy.

'(Seleucus Philopator or Soter, sons of Antiochus Magnus*); soon shall his end come, and yet no blow struck in anger, or in battle. And after him a man little thought of; royal investiture he has none, yet see how stealthy his approach, what shifts he uses to win a throne! Down go strong armies, crushed before him, down goes covenanted chief; treaty first, and then treachery; of armed following he needs but little. So he makes his way into rich cities that suspect no harm, outdoes father and grandsire both in havoc, so much wealth to plunder and to squander; into strong cities, too, by crafty devices, while fortune serves.'

(722)

663. The Jews by killing him, so that they would not have to accept him as the Messiah, bestowed on him the final mark of the Messiah.

And by persisting in their refusal to recognise him they made themselves into unimpeachable witnesses; and by killing him and persisting in their denial of him, they fulfilled the prophecies (Is., LX; Ps., LXX). (761)

664. *Unending captivity of the Jews*. Jer., XI, II: 'And now, the Lord says, I mean to visit (Juda) with punishment inevitable, punishment inexorable.'

Symbols. Is., v. The Lord 'had a vineyard in a corner of his ground . . . Then he waited for grapes to grow on it, and it bore wild grapes instead . . . I mean to make waste-land of it; no more pruning and digging; only briars and thorns will grow there, and I will forbid the clouds to water it. Alas, it is the house of Israel that the Lord called his vineyard; the men of Juda are the plot he loved so. He looked to find right reason, and all was treason.'

Is., VIII. 'Not for thee and thine to go in fear, dismayed like these others; enthrone the Lord of hosts above all else, him you must fear, of him stand in awe. Let the hour of peril consecrate

* Gloss by Pascal.

you to him; for the rest, both in Israel and in Juda, it will be a stone to trip men's feet, a boulder that catches them unawares. A trap, a fine snare, for the citizens of Jerusalem; and there are many of them that will stumble, and fall, and bruise themselves, caught in its meshes. (Now to guard the prophetic record close, now to seal up these instructions, in the keeping of my disciples! What though the Lord hide his face from the men of Israel? To him will I look and wait patiently for him; here stand I and these children . . .)'

Is., xxix: 'Ay, gape and gaze as you will; hum and haw you, bemused ere you lifted cup, besotted ere you have been at your wine, besotted with never a taste of drink! So deep a lethargy the Lord instils, blinding the prophets that should be your eyes, muffling with a veil the wise heads that should see visions for you.' Dan., xii: 'And still there are sinners that will not leave their sinning, The riddle, for these others, a riddle must remain, but wise counsellors there be that will find the clue to it.' After pronouncing many earthly blessings, the last verse of the last chapter of Osee says: 'All this the wise discern, the thoughtful understand', etc. 'What is revelation to you, but a sealed book, offered as vainly to a scholar that finds it sealed, as to yonder simpleton, that vows he never learned his letters?

'This people, the Lord says, makes profession of worshipping me, does me honour with its lips, but its heart is far from me. If they fear me, it is a lesson they learned from human precepts. What remains but some great, some resounding miracle, to strike awe into such hearts as these? Bereft of wisdom their wise men shall be, cunning of their counsellors vanish.'

Prophecies. Proofs of divinity. Is., xli: 'Let them come forward, these other gods, and tell us the future. So read the past for us, that study of it may disclose what needs must follow; coming events make known. Foretell you what is yet to be, we shall know you are gods indeed. Then, if you have the power, grant good or ill fortune to mankind; confer we, and pass judgement on it! Why, you are all empty air, a nothing that nothing can effect; he courts his own shame, that makes choice of you.

Which of you foretold (by contemporary authors*) this from the first? Let us recognise it. Which of you knew it from the beginning? We needs must say, His plea is just. But no, none gave tidings of it, none foretold it; there was no word came from you.'

Is., xlii: 'I am the Lord, whose name tells of power; I will not let the boast that is mine pass to another, or share my renown with graven gods. What I told you long since, has proved true under your eyes; I tell you now what is still to be; you shall hear of it before ever it comes to light. Sing the Lord a new song; let his praise sound from end to end of the earth.'

Is., xliii: 'Bring them out, then, into the light of day, this people of mine that have eyes, and still cannot see, have ears, and cannot hear. Round about us, all the nations of the world are gathered, all its tribes assemble. And now, which among you (and your gods*) can make this claim, give us an account of the events foretold long ago? Let them produce witnesses to justify their claim, so that all may listen and say, It is the truth. I call you to witness, the Lord says, you and this servant of mine, on whom my choice has fallen; will you not recognise the truth, and believe me? Will you not learn to understand that I am the God you seek? None ever came into being before me, or will after me.

'It is I, I, the Lord; no other can bring deliverance. It was I who promised that deliverance, I who brought it; I told you of it, when there was no alien god worshipped among you; you are my witnesses to that, the Lord says. I am God, and what I was, I am; from my power there is no escaping; when I execute my designs, none can avert them. If I send my emissaries to Babylon, casting down all its barriers, casting down the Chaldeans, with all the pride of their navies, it is for their sakes, I, the Lord, am your Holy One, I, the maker of Israel, am your king. A message to you from that same Lord, who could once lead you through the sea, make a passage for you through foaming waters; could bring out chariots and horses, rank and file and chieftain together in pursuit, to fall there and never to rise again,

* Gloss by Pascal.

313

crushed like a wick, and their light quenched. Do not remember those old things, he says, as if you had eyes for nothing but what happened long ago; I mean to perform new wonders; even now they are coming to the birth; surely you will understand at last? I mean to make a causeway over the desert, with streams flowing beside it in the waste. The wild things will do me honour, the serpents and the ostriches, for thus giving them water in the desert, streams in the waste; but it was for my people's sake that I did it, to give drink to my chosen people. I made them for myself, surely they too will have praise to give me, etc.

'It was I, ever I, that must be blotting out thy offences, for my honour's sake, effacing the memory of thy sins. Time, now, thou shouldst remember me; come, let us settle the matter by arbitration, thou and I; tell me what plea thou hast to bring forward. For the guilt of thy first father, for the rebellions of thy spokesmen against me.'

Is., XLIV: 'I am before all; there is no other God but I. What other is like me? Let him expound the history of the past, ever since I established the primal race of man; then let him make known the future that is yet to come. Do not be afraid, or bewildered; you can bear me witness that from the first I proclaimed it in your hearing, there is no other God but I, no other Powers to rival me.'

Prediction of Cyrus. Is., XLV, 4: 'Know by this that it is I, the Lord God of Israel, who am calling upon thee by thy name; and that I do it for love of my servant Jacob, of Israel, my chosen people.'

Is., XLV, 21: 'Tell us your thoughts, come, take counsel among yourselves; who was it that proclaimed this from the first, prophesied it long ago? Was it not I, the Lord?'

Is., XLVI: 'Remember the lesson of times long since, that I am God, and there is no other, none to rival me; did I not tell you from the first the events of the latter days, from the beginning what had not yet come to be? My purpose, I promised, should not fail, my whole will must needs be done.'

Is., XLII: 'What I told you long since, has proved true under your eyes; I tell you now what is still to be; you shall hear of it before ever it comes to light.'

Is., XLVIII, 3: 'What happened in times past, I had foretold long before; warning was uttered, and in the public ear; then, suddenly, I would set to work, and the prophecy was fulfilled. I knew what an untamed creature thou art, neck as stubborn as an iron hawser, forehead intractable as bronze; I would warn thee from the first, tell thee what was coming before it came; never shouldst thou say this was the work of thy false gods, the will of idols thou didst carve and cast.

'Consider closely the things I warned thee of, was there any foretelling them? Ever I reveal to thee, long before, things kept secret from thy knowledge; events that are coming about now, unheard of then. When they are yet beyond knowledge, I reveal them; not thine to boast, it was no news to thee. And still thou wouldst not listen, thou wouldst be ignorant still; when I prophesied to thee in times past, I could get no hearing; what hope from the traitor but of treason? I know thee a rebel from thy birth.'

Reprobation of the Jews and conversion of the Gentiles. Is., LXV: 'So ready I to answer, and ask they will not; so easy to be found, and search for me is none! A people that will not call on my name; else my own voice should whisper, I am here, I am close at hand. Outstretched these hands of mine, all the day long, to a nation of rebels, straying this way and that as the mood takes them, openly defying me. Shrines hidden away in gardens, altars of brick! See how they lodge in tombs, pass the night in the precincts of strange gods: eat swine's flesh, and stew themselves broth of forbidden things, etc. What marvel, if my indignation smoulders yet? Nay, fire it is that burns continually . . . I will take vengeance, pour it out into their laps. Sin of yours, the Lord says, sin of your fathers, worshipped on the hill-sides in defiance of me; for all these I must repay due measure, poured out into the lap; that is my first task.

'Thus says the Lord: If one sound grape is found in a cluster, the cry is, Do not destroy it, there is a blessing in it. And I, for the sake of my true servants, will not destroy root and branch; I will leave Jacob a stock to breed from, settlers enough in Juda for these mountains of mine; the men of my choice shall have their portion, my servant shall dwell there. Flocks there shall be, folded on the Plain, and cattle resting in the valley of Achor; of my people none shall be disappointed that had recourse to me. But you that forsook the Lord, left his mountain sanctuary forgotten, spread a table for the Powers of Fortune, and poured out wine at it, fortune that awaits you is the sword, you shall bow down to death. My call unanswered, my voice unheard, you did ever what I forbade, chose ever what I hated.

'This, then, is the sentence the Lord God pronounces; you shall be hungry, while my servants have food, you shall be thirsty, while my servants drink, you shall be disappointed, while my servants are glad. My servants shall be light-hearted and sing, while you, with sad hearts, cry aloud, groan in the heaviness of your spirits.

'A name you shall leave behind you to serve my chosen people as a curse; the Lord God takes full toll. For his own servants he will have a new name instead; by the God of truth shall be the blessing men invoke, by the God of truth shall be the oath men take, in this land of mine henceforward. Forgotten, the sorrows of past days, hidden away from my eyes. See where I create new heavens and a new earth; old things shall be remembered no longer, have no place in men's thoughts. Joy of yours, pride of yours, this new creation shall be; joy of mine, pride of mine, Jerusalem and her folk, created anew. I will rejoice in Jerusalem, take pride in my people, and the sound of weeping and lament shall be heard no more . . .

'Answer shall come ere cry for help is uttered, prayer find audience while it is still on their lips. Wolf and lamb shall feed together, lion and ox eat straw side by side, and the serpent be content with dust for its food; all over this mountain, my sanctuary, there shall be no hurt done, the Lord says, no life shall be forfeit.'

LVI, 3: 'Keep right order, the Lord says, faithful to your duty still; ere long I will send deliverance, my own faithful shall be revealed. Blessed, every man that so lives, every mother's son that by this rule holds fast, keeps the sabbath holy, and his own hands clear of mischief.

'And so it shall be with the alien born, will they but throw in their lot with the Lord's worshippers, that cherish the love of his name; the Lord's servants that keep the sabbath inviolate, and are true to his covenant. Free of the mountain that is my sanctuary, welcome guests in the house where men pray to me, not vainly to my altar they shall bring burnt-offering and sacrifice. Claimed my house shall be, for a house of prayer, by all the nations. Such promise the Lord God makes, that now brings home the exiled sons of Israel: I have others to bring, that must yet rally to thy side.'

Is., LIX, 9: 'Guilt of yours has estranged him that he denies you audience. . . . What wonder if redress is still far from us, if reprieve linger on its way? Crave we light, and nothing see but darkness, hope we for dawn, and walk in dusk. Blind men that grope along a wall, hands, not eyes, to shew the way, stumble we at noonday as though benighted; we are dead men in a world of shadows.

'No better than growling bears, or doves that moan and mourn, still we hope for the redress that never comes, the deliverance that is far away.'

Is., LXVI, 18: 'Trust me, I will hold assize upon all such deeds and devices of theirs; ay, upon all nations and races. All must come and see my glory revealed, and I will set a mark upon each of them. What of those that find deliverance? I have an errand for them, to be my messengers across the sea; to Africa, and to Lydia where men draw the bow, to Italy, and to Greece, and to the Islands far away. They shall go out where men never heard my name, never saw my glory among the nations. And out of all nations they shall bring your brethren back . . .'

Jer., VII. *Reprobation of the temple.* 'Go and visit that sanctuary of mine at Silo, where of old my power rested; look well, what havoc I have made of it, to punish the misdeeds of Israel, that was my people too. Because of so much done amiss, the Lord says; because you would not listen when I cried early at your doors, or answer any call of mine; this house, shrine of my name and centre of your hopes, this home I gave to you and to your fathers, shall fare as Silo fared. (For I have rejected it and made a temple for myself in another place.)

'All those brethren of yours, the whole stock of Ephraim, I banished from my presence, and you shall be banished in your turn (banished without return*). Nor do thou, Jeremias, think to plead for this people of mine.'

Jer., VII, 22: 'No more be at pains to distinguish between burnt-sacrifice and offering; use for your own eating the flesh of all alike! Burnt-sacrifices, offerings, not of these was my theme when I gave commandments to your fathers at the time of their deliverance from Egypt; my word of command to them was, Obey my bidding, if I am to be your God, you my people. (It was only after they had sacrificed to the golden calf that I commanded sacrifices to me to bring good from a bad habit.)'

Jer., VII, 4: 'Trust never in the false assurances that proclaim this place The Lord's Temple, The Lord's Temple, The Lord's Temple, are . . .' (713)

25. PARTICULAR IMAGES

665. *Particular images.* Double law, double tables of the law, double temple, double captivity. (652)

666. [The genealogy begins with Japhet.] Joseph crosses his arms and prefers fasting. (623)

* Gloss by Pascal.

26. CHRISTIAN MORALITY

667. Christianity is strange. It bids man recognise that he is base, even abominable; it also bids him desire to be like God. Without such a counterweight, his elevation would make him vain, or his abasement would reduce him to a terrible state of abjection. (537)

668. Wretchedness encourages despair.

Pride encourages presumption.

The Incarnation reveals to man the greatness of his wretchedness by the greatness of the remedy which was necessary.

(526)

669. . . . . Not an abasement which makes us incapable of good, or a holiness which is free from evil. (529)

670. No teaching is better suited to man than the one which enables him to understand his dual capacity for receiving and being deprived of grace on account of the twofold danger to which he is continually exposed: despair or pride. (524)

671. Of all that is on earth, he only participates in what is unpleasant and not in what is pleasant. He is fond of his relatives, but his charity is not confined within these limits; it extends to his enemies, then to the enemies of God. (767)

672. What is the difference between a soldier and a Carthusian when it comes to obedience? For they are both equally obedient and dependent, and the exercises imposed on them equally disagreeable. But the soldier is always hoping to reach a higher rank and never does so because captains and even princes are always in a state of servitude and dependence on others; yet he goes on hoping and struggles to get where he wants; whereas the Carthusian takes a vow never to be anything except in a state of dependence. Thus there is no difference in the servitude which is their common lot save the hope which is always to be found in one and never in the other. (539)

673. No one is as happy as a true Christian, or as reasonable, virtuous or lovable. (541)

674. How little the Christian prides himself on the belief that he is united to God! How little sense of abjection he feels in comparing himself to an earthworm!

A fine way of meeting life and death, good and ill fortune! (538)

675. The example set by the noble deaths of the Lacedemonians and others scarcely moves us. What meaning can it possibly have for us? But we are touched by the deaths of the martyrs because they are 'members of us'. We are on common ground; their resolution can help to build up our own, not only on account of their example, but perhaps because their resolution deserves our own. There is nothing of the sort in the examples of the heathen, and we have nothing in common with them; just as one does not become rich by seeing a stranger who is, but through seeing one's father or husband who is. (481)

676. *Beginning of thinking members. Morality.* When God had created heaven and earth, which were not aware of their happiness, he wanted to create beings who would be, and who would form, a body of thinking members. For our limbs do not feel the happiness of their union, their admirable understanding, nature's care in pouring spirits into them, and making them grow and endure. How happy they would be if they felt and knew it! But they would need to possess intelligence in order to be aware of it, and the good will to consent to the will of the universal soul. And if, after receiving the gift of intelligence, they used it to retain nourishment instead of allowing it to pass to the other limbs, they would not only be unjust; they would also be wretched, and would hate rather than love themselves; because their happiness no less than their duty lies in accepting the guidance of the whole soul to which they belong, and which loves them better than they love themselves. (482)

677. Are you less of a slave because your master is fond of you and flatters you? You're lucky, slave. Your master flatters you now; he will soon start beating you. (209)

678. The will itself will never be satisfied, even if it had power over everything it wished; but we are satisfied the moment we

abandon our own will. Without it, we could not be discontented; with it, we shall never be satisfied.　　　　(472)

679. They give free rein to concupiscence and stifle scruples, when the right thing is to do the opposite.　　　　(914)

680. It is a sign of superstition to place one's hopes in formalities; but it is a sign of pride not to conform to them.　　(249)

681. Experience enables us to recognise the enormous difference between piety and goodness.　　　　(496)

682. Two kinds of men in each religion (see *Perpetuity*): Superstition—Concupiscence.　　　　(747 *ter*)

683*. *Not formalists*. When St. Peter and the Apostles thought of abolishing circumcision where it was a question of acting against the law of God, they did not consider the prophets, but simply the reception of the Holy Spirit by uncircumcised persons.

They decided that it was more certain that God approved those whom he filled with his Spirit than the observance of the law. They knew that the sole aim of the law was the Holy Spirit; and that since people could very well have it without circumcision, circumcision was not necessary.　　(672)

684. *Members. Begin with that*. In order to regulate the love that we should have for ourselves, we must imagine a body consisting of thinking members because we are members of everything, and see how each member ought to love itself, etc.　　(474)

685. *Republic*. The Christian republic, and even the Jewish, has only had God for its master, as Philo the Jew remarks, *On Monarchy*.

When they fought it was only for God; and their main hope was in God; they only considered their towns as belonging to God, and preserved them for God. *I* Paralip., XIX, 13.　(611)

686. In order to ensure the happiness of the members, they must possess a will, and see that it conforms to the body.　(480)

687. Imagine a body composed of thinking members.　(473)

688. To be a member means to have life, being and movement only through the spirit of the body and for the sake of the body.

The severed member, no longer seeing the body to which it

belongs, no longer has anything but a wasting, moribund existence. Yet it believes itself to be a whole, and not seeing the body on which it is dependent, it comes to believe that it is only dependent on itself, and wants to transform itself into a centre and a body. But since it has no principle of life in itself, it merely goes astray and is bewildered by the uncertainty of its existence, because it is very conscious that it is not a body and yet does not see that it is a member of a body. Finally, when it comes to know itself, it has, so to speak, returned home, and no longer loves itself except for the sake of the body. It laments its past errors.

It could not of its own nature love another thing except for its own sake and in order to subjugate it, because each thing loves itself more than anything in the world. But by loving the body, it loves itself because it has no being except through and for the sake of the body: *qui adhaeret Deo unus spiritus est.*[1]

The body loves the hand; and the hand, if it had a will of its own, ought to love itself in the same way that the soul loves it. All love in excess of this is wrong.

Adhaerens Deo unus spiritus est. We love ourselves because we are members of Jesus Christ. We love Jesus Christ because he is the body of which we are members. All is one; one is in the other like the three Persons of the Trinity. (483)

689. We must love only God and hate only ourselves.

If the foot had always been unaware of the fact that it belonged to the body and that there was a body on which it was dependent, if it had only known and loved itself, and it came to know that it belonged to a body on which it was dependent, what sorrow, what shame it would feel over its past life because it had been useless to the body which had poured life into it, which would have destroyed it if it had rejected and separated it from itself, as the foot had separated itself from the body! What supplication to be allowed to remain where it was! What submissiveness to the will which governed the body even to the point of allowing itself to be amputated or deprived of membership of the body if necessary! For every limb must be prepared

[1] But he who is joined to the head is one spirit (I Cor. VI, 17).

to die for the body, which is the one thing for which each part exists. (476)

690. If the feet and hands had a will of their own, they would never function properly in their own order except when submitting their individual wills to the primary will which governs the whole body. Without that they would fall into a state of disorder and collapse; but by desiring only the good of the body they achieve their own salvation. (475)

691. The philosophers have consecrated the vices by attributing them to God himself; Christians have consecrated the virtues. (503)

692. Two laws are more effective in regulating the entire life of the Christian Republic than all political laws put together. (484)

693. We owe a great debt to people who point out our faults because they mortify us; they make us realise that we have earned the contempt of our fellows; they do not prevent it from happening again in the future because we possess many other failings which arouse contempt. They set in motion the machinery which leads to the correction and removal of one fault. (535)

694. The meaning of the words good and evil. (500)

695. God (and the Apostles), foreseeing that the needs of pride would give birth to heresies and not wishing to nurture them by providing them with the correct terminology, placed in Scripture and in the prayers of the Church contradictory words and phrases so that they would produce their fruit in due time.

In the same way that he tempered morality with charity, which produced fruits that countered sensuality. (579)

696. 'Everything to be found in the world is concupiscence of the flesh, or concupiscence of the eyes, or pride of life: *libido sentiendo, libido sciendi, libido dominandi.*' Unhappy is the land of malediction which these three rivers of fire consume instead of irrigating! Happy those who, being on the rivers, are not submerged, are not carried away, but stand immovably firm; not

upright but seated on a low, firm base from which they do not rise before daybreak but, enjoying their rest, stretch out their hands to him who will raise them and enable them to stand upright and firm in the porches of Jerusalem, where pride will no longer be able to wrestle with them and bring them down; and who nevertheless weep not at the sight of fragile things passing, as they are swept away by the current, but in memory of their beloved fatherland, the celestial Jerusalem which is continually in their minds during their long exile! (458)

697. The elect will be ignorant of their virtues, and the damned of the greatness of their crimes: 'Lord, when was it that we saw thee hungry, and fed thee, or thirsty, etc.' (515)

698. If we were converted, God would heal and forgive us. *Ne convertantur et sanem eos, et dimittantur eis peccata.*[1] (779)

699. The true and only virtue is therefore to hate oneself (for we are hateful on account of our concupiscence), and to seek a being who is truly lovable and to love him. But since we cannot love him who is outside us, we must love a being who is within us, and who is not ourself, and that is true of each and every man. Now, there is only the universal Being who answers to this description. The kingdom of God is within us: the universal good is within us, is ourself, and is not we. (485)

700. There are only two kinds of men: the good who believe themselves to be sinners; the sinners who believe themselves to be good. (534)

701. Abraham took nothing for himself, but only for his servants; and so the righteous man takes nothing from the world for himself nor accepts its applause; he takes only for his passions which he uses like a master, saying to one: 'Go, and [to another]: Come.' *Sub te erit appetitus tuus.*[2] Once mastered, his passions become virtues: avarice, jealousy, wrath. Even God attributes them to himself, and they are just as much virtues as mercy, pity, fortitude, which are also passions. We must make use of them as though they were slaves, and by providing them

[1] Lest at any time they should be converted and their sins forgiven them (Mark IV, 12).
[2] Meanwhile he is at thy mercy (Gen. IV, 7).

with nourishment prevent the soul from feeding on them; because when the passions are our master they are vices, and then they give the soul their sustenance and the soul lives on it and is poisoned by it. (502)

702. If it is a form of supernatural blindness to live without seeking to know what we are, it is a terrible form to lead a wicked life while believing in God. (495)

703. Fine actions which are kept secret are the most praiseworthy. When I come across some of them in history (as p. 184), they fill me with delight.[1] This means that they have not been kept completely secret because they are known; and though people have done what they could to hide them, the small amount of information which leaked out spoilt everything; for the finest thing of all is the desire to hide them. (159)

704. Must we kill to prevent the existence of wicked men? To do so is to make two wicked men instead of one: *Vince in bono malum*, St. Aug.[2] (911)

705. The conditions in which it is easiest to live according to the world are the most difficult in which to live according to God; and the reverse: nothing is more difficult in the eyes of the world than the religious life; nothing is easier in the sight of God. Nothing, according to the world, is easier than to hold a great office and to enjoy a great fortune; nothing, according to God, is more difficult than to live like that, without participating in it and developing a taste for it. (906)

706. Those whose lives are disorderly say to those whose lives are well-ordered that they are the people who are turning their back on nature, and are convinced that they themselves are following nature: as those who are on board ship have the impression that those on shore are receding. Language is the same everywhere. We must have a fixed point from which to judge it. The haven judges those who are on board ship; but where shall we find a haven in morality? (383)

707. When everything moves at an even pace nothing appears to move at all, as when we are on board ship. When everyone

---

[1] Reference is to Montaigne, *Essais* I, 14 (Ed. 1635, p. 184).
[2] Disarm malice by kindness (Rom. XII, 21).

stoops to debauchery, no one appears to be indulging in it. The man who comes to a halt draws attention to the fury of the rest, like a fixed point. (382)

708. *Grace*. The movements of grace, hardness of heart; external factors. (507)

709. It is not absolution alone that remits sins in the sacrament of penance, but contrition which is not genuine unless it seeks the sacrament.

Thus it is not the nuptial blessing which prevents procreation from being a sin, but the desire to conceive children for God which is only genuine in marriage.

And just as a contrite man without the sacrament is fitter for absolution than an impenitent one who has received the sacrament, so the daughters of Lot, for example, who only desired children, were purer without being married than married people who do not desire children. (923)

710. *Universal*. Morality and language are particular forms of knowledge, but they are universal. (912)

711. What a man's virtue is capable of achieving should not be measured by the special efforts he makes, but by his everyday standard of performance. (352)

712. First stage: to be blamed for doing wrong and praised for doing right. Second stage: not to be praised or blamed.

(501)

713. All the principal forms of amusement are a danger to the Christian life; but of all those invented by the world, none is more to be feared than the theatre. Its representation of the emotions is so natural and delicate that it awakens them in our hearts; and more than all others the emotion of love; this applies with particular force when love is shown as being very chaste and very proper. For the more innocent it appears to innocent minds, the more capable they are of being influenced by it; its violence is agreeable to our self-esteem which at once conceives the desire of producing the same effects as those which we see so well acted; and at the same time we form an opinion of it which is based on the propriety of the feelings which we see, and that removes fear from pure minds who imagine that there

is nothing to offend purity in loving with a love which seems to them so moral.

Thus we leave the theatre with our hearts so filled with the charm and beauty of love, and our soul and mind so convinced of its innocence, that we are very well prepared to receive its first impress, or rather to seek an opportunity of awakening it in someone's heart in order to enjoy the same pleasure and the same sacrifices that we have seen so admirably portrayed on the stage. (11)

714. The example of Alexander's chastity has not produced anything like so many continent men as the number of drunkards produced by his drunkenness. No one need be ashamed at not being as virtuous as he, and it seems excusable not to be more vicious than he. We imagine that we are not really succumbing to the vices of ordinary people when we find ourselves indulging in the vices of great men without realising that in this matter they are no different from the common man. We cling to that side of them by which they themselves stoop to the tastes of the common people; for however lofty their position, there is something in them which creates a bond between them and the least of mortals. They are not suspended in mid air without any contact with our society. Far from it. If they are greater than we, it is because they carry their heads higher, but their feet are planted on the ground like our own. At this point they are all on the same level, and supported by the same earth; and at this extremity they are as low as we, as the most insignificant of people, as children, as the animals. (103)

715. *Against those who, on the strength of their confidence in God's mercy, remain in a state of apathy without undertaking good works.* Since the twin sources of our sins are pride and sloth, God has revealed to us two qualities in him for curing them: his mercy and his justice. The proper function of justice is to crush pride, however holy its works, *et non intres in judicium*, etc., and the proper function of mercy is to combat sloth by encouraging good works as we can see from this passage: 'Dost thou not know that God's kindness is inviting thee to repent?'; and the other one about the men of Nineveh: 'Forsake, each of you, his

327

sinful life, his wrongful deeds! God may yet relent and pardon.'
Thus, so far from authorising laxity, mercy is the quality which
is most definitely opposed to it; and instead of saying: 'If there
were no mercy in God, we should have to make every effort to
be virtuous', we must say on the contrary, that it is because
there is mercy in God that we must spare no effort.   (497)

716. Men cannot be taught to be real men, but they can be
taught everything else; and they never boast so much of knowing nothing about everything else as of being real men. They
only boast of knowing the one thing that cannot be learnt. (68)

717. Will it be argued that because they asserted that justice had
departed from the earth men have known original sin?—*Nemo
ante obitum beatus*.[1] Does that mean that they have known that
eternal and essential bliss begins with death?   (447)

718. St. Paul himself says that people will forbid marriage and
he speaks of it in the Epistle to the Corinthians in a manner
which is a trap.

For if a prophet had said one thing and St. Paul another,
he would at once have been attacked.   (673)

719. *Comminuentes cor* (St. Paul).[2]—such is the character of the
Christian.

'Albe vous a nommé, je ne vous connais plus' (Corneille).

That is the inhuman character. The human character is the
reverse of it.   (533)

720. The rivers of Babylon flow, and fall, and carry away. O holy
Sion, where all is solid and nothing falls!

We must sit on the rivers, not under them or in them, but
above; and not stand upright but sit; in order to be humble
because we are seated, and in safety, because we are above.
But we shall be standing upright in the porches of Jerusalem.

Let us see whether our pleasure is lasting or transient: if it
vanishes, it is like one of the rivers of Babylon.   (459)

721. *Concupiscence of the flesh, concupiscence of the eyes, pride*, etc.

There are three orders of things: the flesh, the mind, the
will.

---

[1] Call no man happy till he's dead (Ovid: *Met.*, iii, 135).
[2] Falling in with the common folk (Rom. xii, 16).

The carnal are rich men, kings: their object is the body.

The inquisitive and scholarly: their object is the mind.

The sages: their aim is justice.

God must reign over everything, and everything must tend towards him.

In the realm of the flesh, it is, properly speaking, lust which reigns.

In intellectual men, it is really curiosity.

In wisdom, it is really pride.

It is not that one cannot become famous for goodness or knowledge, but it is not the place of pride; for in granting to a man that he is learned, we shall not fail to convince him that he is wrong to be proud.

The proper sphere of pride is wisdom; for we cannot admit to a man that he has acquired wisdom and that he is wrong to boast of it; because that is only right.

Therefore God alone gives wisdom, and that is why: *Qui gloriatur, in Domino glorietur.*[1]   (460)

722. The outer must be joined to the inner in order to obtain anything from God; that is to say, we must go down on our knees, pray with our lips, etc., so that the proud man, who did not want to humble himself before God, must now humble himself before the creature. To expect help from externals is superstitious; not to wish to unite outer and inner is a sign of pride.

(250)

723. When a blind urge impels us to do something, we forget our duty: so that if we like a book we read it when we ought to be doing something else. But in order to remind ourselves of duty, we must set to work to do something that we dislike; and then we make excuses for ourselves on the grounds that we have something else to do, and by this means we are reminded of our duty.   (104)

724. According to Scripture, every condition of man, even the martyrs, has reason to fear.

The greatest punishment of purgatory is the uncertainty of the sentence.

[1] If anyone boasts, let him make his boast in the Lord (I Cor. 1, 31).

Deus absconditus. (518)

725. We do not grow tired of eating and sleeping day after day, because hunger and fatigue return; without them we should be bored. It would be the same without hunger for spiritual things: we should be bored. Hunger for justice: eighth beatitude. (264)

726. The Christian religion alone makes a man *amiable and happy* at the same time. In the case of mere uprightness, one cannot be amiable and happy at the same time. (542)

27. CONCLUSION

727. What a vast distance there is between knowing God and loving him! (280)

728. 'If I had seen a miracle,' they say, 'I should be converted.' How can they be so certain that they would do something of which they are ignorant? They assume that conversion is a form of worship which is conducted as they imagine they would conduct a business transaction or a conversation. True conversion consists of self-annihilation before the universal Being whom we have often angered, and who may legitimately damn us at any moment; in recognising that we can accomplish nothing without him, and that we deserve nothing of him but disfavour. It means knowing that there is an invincible barrier between God and us, and that without a mediator, there can be no contact with him. (470)

729. Miracles do not help to convert, but to condemn (*Sum. Theol.* Q. 113, A. 10. *Ad.* 2). (825)

730. Do not be surprised at the sight of simple people who believe without argument. God makes them love him and hate themselves. He inclines their hearts to believe. We shall never believe with a vigorous and unquestioning faith unless God touches our hearts; and we shall believe as soon as he does so. That is what David realised so clearly: *Inclina cor meum, Deus, in (testimonia tua).*[1] (284)

---

[1] Incline my heart unto thy testimonies (Ps. cxviii, 36. Douai version).

731. Those who believe without reading the Testaments, do so because they possess an innate holiness, and because what they hear of our religion is in keeping with it. They feel that a God made them; they want to love only God; they want to hate only themselves. They feel that in themselves they do not possess the necessary strength; that they are incapable of going to God; and that, if God does not come to them, they are incapable of any communion with him. And they hear it said that in our religion we must love only God, and hate only ourselves; but that since we all are fallen beings and incapable of God, God became man in order to unite himself to us. Nothing more is needed to convince men who possess such a disposition, and who have a conscious knowledge of their duty and their incapacity.   (286)

732*. Those who are plainly Christians without knowing anything about the prophecies and the proofs, are just as well able to judge them as those who possess a knowledge of them. They judge according to their hearts as others judge with their minds. It is God himself who induces them to believe, and so they are very effectively convinced.

[It will be said that this manner of judging the matter is not reliable, and that by adopting it heretics and infidels go astray.

It will be replied that infidels will say the same thing, but my answer to that is that we have proofs that God truly inclines the hearts of those whom he loves to believe in the Christian religion, that the infidels have no proof of what they say, with the result that though they employ similar terms our propositions differ in so far as one is without proof and the other convincingly proved.]

I freely admit that a Christian who believes without proofs may not possess the ability to convince an unbeliever who will say as much of his own accord. But those who are familiar with the proofs of religion will have no difficulty in proving that the believer is truly inspired by God though he could not prove it himself.

For since God said through his prophets (who were undoubtedly prophets) that, during the reign of Jesus Christ, he

331

would pour out his spirit over the peoples, and that the sons and daughters and the children of the Church would prophesy, there is no doubt that the spirit of God is with them, and that it is not with the others.

[*Eorum qui amant.*]

[God inclines the hearts of those whom he loves.]

[*Deus inclinat corda eorum.*]

[He who loves him. He whom he loves.] (287)

733. Since God's mercy is so great that he gives us a salutary lesson, even when he hides himself, what light must we not expect of him when he reveals himself? (848)

734. The world exists for the exercise of mercy and judgement, not as though men were in the same condition as they were on leaving the hands of God, but as the enemies of God to whom he gives by grace sufficient light to return, if they choose to seek and follow him, but to punish them if they refuse to seek or follow him. (584)

735. One of the antiphones of the vespers of Christmas:

Exortum est in tenebris lumen rectis corde.[1] (847)

736. The prophecies, even the miracles and the proofs of our religion, are not of such a nature that we can assert that they are absolutely convincing. But they are nevertheless of such a kind that we cannot say that it is unreasonable to be convinced by them. Thus, there is evidence and obscurity to enlighten some and obscure the minds of others. But the evidence for is such that it surpasses, or at any rate it equals, the evidence against religion; and since it is not reason which makes us mistrust it, it can only be concupiscence or the evil in our hearts. Thus there is sufficient evidence to condemn and not sufficient to convince, so that it may be apparent that those who accept it do so by grace and not reason; and that those who turn their backs on it, do so through concupiscence and not reason.

Vere discipuli, vere Israelita, vere liberi, vere cibus. (564)

[1] To the righteous a light is risen up in darkness (Ps. cxi, 4. Douai version).

PART TWO

1. PERSONAL NOTES
†

737.　　　　The year of grace 1654,
　　Monday 23 November, Feast of St. Clement, Pope and
　　　　martyr,
　　And others belonging to the martyrology.
　　Vigil of St. Chrysogonos, martyr, and others,
　　From about half past ten in the evening until about half
　　　　past twelve midnight.

　　　　　　　　Fire.
　　'God of Abraham, God of Isaac, God of Jacob'
　　　　not of the philosophers and the scholars.
　　Certitude, Certitude, emotion, joy, peace.
　　　　　　God of Jesus Christ
　　　　　Deum meum et deum vestrum
　　　　'Thy God shall be my God.'
　Oblivion of the world and of everything, except God.
He can only be found by the ways taught in the Gospel.

　　　　Greatness of the human soul.
　'Righteous Father the world has not known thee, but I
　　　have known thee.'
　　　　Joy, Joy, Joy, tears of joy.
I have separated myself from him.
Dereliquerunt me fontem aquae vivae.
Lord, wilt thou forsake me?
Let me not be separated from him eternally.
'This is eternal life, that they should know that thou art
the only true God and him whom thou has sent, J. C.'

333

Jesus Christ
Jesus Christ

I have cut myself off from him; I have fled from him,
    denied him, crucified him.
Let me never be separated from him.
We can only keep him by the ways taught in the Gospel.

Total and delicious renunciation.
Etc.

Total submission to Jesus Christ and to my spiritual
director.
Eternal joy in return for one day of travail in this life.

Non obliviscar sermones tuos. Amen. (—)

738. We make an idol of truth itself; for truth without charity
is not God, and is his image and an idol which we must not love
or worship; and still less must we love or worship his opposite,
which is a falsehood.

I may well love total darkness; but if God leads me to a path
which is in semi-darkness, this touch of darkness which is there
is disagreeable to me, and because I do not appreciate the
value of complete darkness, I find it unpleasing. It is a fail-
ing, and a sign that I have made an idol of darkness, separated
from the divine order. Now we must only worship his order.

(582)

739. *The Mystery of Jesus Christ.* In his passion Jesus suffered the
torments inflicted on him by mankind; but in his agony he
suffered the torments which he inflicted on himself: *turbare
semetipsum*. It was torture inflicted by a hand which was not
human, but all-powerful, and it was necessary to be all-powerful to support it.

Jesus sought some consolation at any rate in his three dearest friends, and they were asleep; he begged them to watch with
him for a while, and they unthinkingly abandoned him because

they felt so little compunction for him that it did not even prevent them from dropping off to sleep for a few minutes. And so Jesus was left alone with the wrath of God.

Jesus was alone on earth not merely without anyone to feel and share his suffering, but even to know of it: heaven and he were alone in this knowledge.

Jesus was in a garden, not of delight like the first Adam when he fell and the whole of the human race with him, but in a garden of torture, where he saved himself and the whole of the human race.

He suffered this anguish and abandonment amid the terrors of the night.

I believe that Jesus never uttered a complaint except on this one occasion; but this time he did complain because he could no longer contain his anguish: 'My soul is sad unto death.'

Jesus sought the companionship and comfort of men. This was unique in his whole life, it seems to me. But he did not receive any because his disciples were asleep.

Jesus will be in agony until the end of the world: we must not sleep during that time.

In the midst of this universal abandonment, when he found the friends whom he had chosen to watch with him asleep, Jesus grew angry over the peril to which they had exposed not him, but themselves; he spoke to them of their own salvation and well-being with gentle affection while they showed such ingratitude, and remarked that the spirit was willing and the flesh weak.

When he found them still asleep, untroubled by any consideration either for him or themselves, Jesus showed his goodness by not waking them, and let them sleep on.

Jesus prayed in his uncertainty over the will of the Father, and was afraid of death; but when he knew his Father's will, he went to meet death and offer himself to it: *Eamus. Processit* (Joannes).

Jesus prayed to men, and his prayer was not answered.

While his disciples slept, Jesus wrought their salvation. He did it for each of the righteous while they were asleep, and in the void before they were born, and in their sins after they were born.

He only once prayed that the cup might pass from him, and did so in a spirit of submission, and twice that it might come if it were necessary.

Jesus in a state of weariness.

Jesus, seeing all his friends asleep and all his enemies on the watch, put his trust completely in his Father.

Jesus did not see hostility in Judas, but the command of God which he loved; so little was he aware of it, that he addressed Judas as friend.

Jesus tore himself away from his disciples in order to enter into his agony; we have to tear ourselves away from our nearest and dearest in order to follow his example.

Since Jesus is in agony and is undergoing the greatest suffering, let us pray longer.

We implore God's mercy not in order that he will leave us to indulge our vices undisturbed, but so that he will deliver us from them.

If God gave us masters with his own hand, O how gladly we should obey them! Events are infallibly determined by necessity.

'Be comforted. You would not seek me if you had not already found me.'

'I thought of you in my agony. I shed those drops of blood for you.'

'It is tempting me rather than proving yourself to ask whether you should do something when there is no call to do it: I will do it in you if the occasion arises.'

'Be guided by my precepts: see how well I led the Virgin and the saints who allowed me to act on them.'

'The Father loves everything that I do.'

'Do you want me always to pay with the blood of my humanity without your shedding a single tear?'

'Your conversion is my business; do not be afraid, and pray trustingly as though it were for me.'

'I am present to you by my word in Scripture, by my spirit

in the Church and by inspiration, by my power in the priests, by my prayer among the faithful.'

'The doctors will not heal you; for in the end you will die. But I heal and make the body immortal.'

'You must bear physical bonds and servitude; I shall only free you from spiritual bondage here and now.'

'I am more of a friend to you than this man or that because I have done more for you than they, and they would not bear what I have borne from you, and would not die for you at the time of your infidelity and cruelty, as I have done, as I am ready to do and do, in my elect and in the Blessed Sacrament.'

'If you knew your sins, you would lose heart.'

'I shall lose it then, Lord, for I believe in their wickedness on the strength of your words.'

'No, because I, who am speaking to you, can cure you of them, and what I have said is a sign that I wish to cure you. While you are doing penance for them, you will come to know them, and it will be said to you: "See your sins which are remitted. Do penance, therefore, for your hidden sins and for the hidden evil of those which you do know." '

'Lord, I give you everything.'

'I love you more fervently than you love your depravity, *ut immundus pro luto*.'

'Let mine be the glory, not yours, worm and clay.'

'Confess to your director that my words are an occasion of evil in you, and of vanity or curiosity.'

'I see the depths of my pride, my curiosity, my sensuality. I have no communion with God, or Jesus Christ. But he was made sin by me; all your plagues have fallen on him. He is more hateful than I, and far from loathing me, he feels honoured that I should go to his aid.'

But he healed himself, which is all the more reason why he should heal me.

My wounds must be added to his; I must unite myself to him; and he will save me by saving himself. But none must be added in the future.

Eritis sicut dii scientes bonum et malum.[1] Everyone plays the role of a god when he passes judgement and says: 'That is good or bad'; and by being too distressed or too jubilant over what happens.

Do small things as though they were great because of the majesty of Jesus Christ who does them in us, and who lives our life; and great things as though they were small and easy because of his omnipotence.

The false justice of Pilate serves only to make Jesus Christ suffer, because he had him scourged through his false justice and then slew him. He would have done better to have slain him straight away. So much for the falsely just: they do good and evil in order to please the world and show that they do not belong entirely to Jesus Christ; for they are ashamed of him. And finally, on great occasions and in great temptations, they kill him.   (553)

740. . . . another reason: that charity regards it as a privation of the spirit of God and an evil action as a result of the suspension or interruption of the spirit of God in him; and he repents of it and grieves over it.

The righteous man acts according to the precepts of religion in the smallest things: when he rebukes his servants, he desires their amendment through the spirit of God; he prays to God to make them better, expects as much from God as from his own scolding, and prays to God to bless his rebukes. It is the same with his other actions.   (504)

741. 25 Bb. Reflect on the role of Jesus Christ in everybody, and in ourselves: Jesus Christ as father in his Father, Jesus Christ as brother in his brothers, Jesus Christ as a poor man in the poor, Jesus Christ as rich in the rich, Jesus Christ as doctor and priest in priests, Jesus Christ as sovereign in princes, etc. For he is by his glory all that is great, being God, and is by his mortal life all that is stunted and abject. That is why he assumed this unhappy condition, that he might be in all people, and serve as a model for all conditions of men.   (785)

742. 24 AA. It seems to me that Jesus Christ allowed men to

[1] You yourselves will be like gods, knowing good and evil (Gen. III, 5).

touch only his wounds after his resurrection: *Noli me tangere*. We must only unite ourselves with him in his sufferings.

He gave himself as a mortal in communion at the Last Supper, as risen from the dead to the disciples at Emmaus, as ascended into heaven to the whole Church. (554)

743. *On miracles*. As God has made no family happier, may he grant that none will be found which is more grateful. (856)

744. It is true that the entry into the devout life is painful. Now the pain does not come from the piety which is stirring in us, but from the impiety which still remains in us. If our senses did not resist penance and our corruption were not the reverse of the purity of God, we should find nothing painful in it. We only suffer to the extent that vice, which is natural to us, resists supernatural grace. Our heart feels torn between conflicting impulses; but it would be very unjust to attribute the violence to God, who draws us to him, instead of to the world which holds us back. It is like a child whom its mother snatches from the arms of robbers, and who in the midst of the pain it suffers is bound to love the tender and legitimate violence of the woman who obtains its freedom, and only hates the injurious and tyrannical violence of those who hold on to it with criminal intent. The cruellest war that God can wage against men in this life is to leave them without the war that he came to bring. I came, he said, to bring war; and, as instrument of this war: 'I came to bring you sword and fire.' Before him, the world lived in a state of spurious peace. (498)

745. We only desert God by deserting charity.

Our prayers and our virtues are abominable in the sight of God if they are not the prayers and virtues of Jesus Christ. And our sins will never be the object of the [mercy], but of the justice of God, if they are not [the sins of] Jesus Christ.

He took our sins upon himself and [admitted us to his] covenant because virtues are [natural], [and] sins alien to him, while our sins are natural to us.

Let us change the rule, on which we have relied up to [the present], for deciding what is good. Our rule was our will; let us now take the will of [God]: whatever he wills is right and good for us; anything that he does [not] will is [bad and wrong].

Whatever is not willed by God is forbidden. Sins are forbidden by the general declaration that God has made, that he did not will them. The other things which he has left without a general prohibition and which for this reason are described as permissible, are nevertheless not always permitted. For when God takes one of them from us and when by that fact, which is a manifestation of God's will, it appears that God does not wish us to have a thing, it then becomes forbidden to us as a sin, because it is God's will that we are not to have one any more than the other. But so long as God does not wish it, we are bound to regard it as a sin; while the absence of God's will, which alone is all goodness and all justice, makes it wrong and wicked. (668)

746. Jesus Christ did not wish to be put to death without a show of justice, because it is far more ignominious to be justly put to death than to be slain in an unjust uprising. (790)

747. The Christian hope of possessing an infinite good is mixed with actual enjoyment as well as with fear; for Christians are not like those who hope for a kingdom from which they would gain nothing because they are subjects; they hope for holiness, deliverance from injustice, and they possess something of it.

(540)

748. [I love all men as my brothers because they are all redeemed.] I love poverty because He loved it. I love wealth because it offers the means of helping the poor. I keep faith with everybody; I do [not] return evil for evil; but I wish those who do me ill a condition like my own in which we receive neither good nor evil at the hands of men. I have tried to be just, true, sincere and faithful to all men; I feel affection for those with whom God has united me closely; and whether I am alone or in company, in all my actions I have my eye on God who will judge them, and to whom I have offered them all.

Such are my feelings, and every day of my life I bless my Redeemer who placed them in me and who has turned a man riddled with frailties, sorrows, sensual desires, pride and ambition into a man who is free from these failings by the power of

his grace to which all glory is due because wretchedness and
error are my only contribution.   (550)

749. Everything may have fatal consequences for us, even the
things done to help us; as, in nature, walls may kill us, or steps
unless we walk carefully.

The slightest movement affects the whole of nature; a stone
can change the entire surface of the sea. Thus in the order of
Grace, the least action counts because its results affect the whole.
Therefore everything is important.

In every action we must consider, apart from the action itself, our present, past and future state, and others whom it may
affect, and see the connection between all these things. And
then we shall keep ourselves firmly under control.   (505)

750. *Outward works*. Nothing is more dangerous than what is
pleasing to God and to men; for states which please God and
men have one element which pleases God and another which
pleases men; like the greatness of St. Teresa; what pleases God
is her profound humility in her revelations; what pleases men
are her visions. With the result that people destroy themselves
by their attempts to imitate her discourses in the belief that
they are reproducing her state; and in that way to love what
God loves and to place themselves in a state which is pleasing
to God.

It is better not to fast and to be ashamed of the fact than to
fast and be complacent about it.

Pharisee, publican.

What would be the point of my remembering it, if it can
equally well harm and help me, and if everything depends on
God's blessing which he only bestows on actions done for him,
and according to his rules and ways, because the manner is as
important as the matter, perhaps more so since God can bring
good out of evil, and since without God we bring evil out of
good?   (499)

751. 'Do not compare yourself to others, but to me. If you do
not find me in those with whom you compare yourself, you are
comparing yourself to someone who is hateful. If you find me,
compare yourself with me. But with whom shall you compare

yourself? With yourself, or with me in you? If with yourself, it is with someone hateful. If it is with me, you compare me with myself. Now I am God in all things.

'I often speak to you and give you advice because your own guide cannot speak to you, and I do not want you to be without a guide.

'And perhaps I do it in answer to his prayers, and so he guides you without your noticing it.

'You would not seek me if you had not already found me.

'Therefore, be not troubled.' (555)

752. *Sepulchre of Jesus Christ.* Jesus Christ had died, but in the sight of men, on the Cross. He was dead and hidden in the sepulchre.

Jesus Christ was buried only by saints.

Jesus Christ performed no miracles in the sepulchre.

It was the saints alone who entered it.

It was there that Jesus Christ began a new life, not on the Cross.

It is the final mystery of the Passion and Redemption.

Jesus Christ had nowhere on earth to rest except the sepulchre.

His enemies did not cease to harry Him until he was in the sepulchre. (552)

753. *Lustravit lampade terras.*[1] There is little connection between the weather and my mood; I have my fogs and my fine weather inside me; my success or lack of success in business, indeed, plays little part in it. I sometimes pit myself against chance; the glory of mastering it makes me tackle it lightheartedly; instead of which I am sometimes overcome with disgust when my luck is in. (107)

754. [When I was small, I put my book away; and because it sometimes happened . . . by thinking that I had put it away, I deceived myself.] (371)

755. It is wrong for anyone to attach himself to me even though it is done gladly and spontaneously. I should be deceiving those

[1] Such is the light with which Jupiter lighted the world (*Odyssey*, XVIII, 136. Quoted after Montaigne, II, 12).

in whom I aroused the desire because I am no man's end, and do not possess what is necessary to satisfy them. Am I not about to die? And so the object of their attachment will die. Therefore, as I should be guilty of making them believe something false, even though I persuaded them of it by gentle means, and they believed it gladly, and so gave me pleasure; in the same way I should be to blame if I made myself loved. And if I encourage people to attach themselves to me, whatever advantage it might have for me, I must warn those who are ready to consent to an untruth that they must not believe it, and, for the same reason, that they must not attach themselves to me, because they must devote their lives and their efforts to pleasing God or seeking him. (471)

756. I had spent a long time in the study of the abstract sciences; and the little contact that one can have left me with a feeling of disgust. When I began the study of man, I saw that the abstract sciences are not proper to man, and that I had strayed further from my path by delving into them than others by being ignorant of them. I have forgiven other people for knowing little about them. But at least I expected to find many associates in the study of man because it is the true study and is proper to him. I was mistaken; there are even fewer who study man than mathematics. It is only through lack of the knowledge necessary for the study of man that we go in for other things; but is it not a fact that it is not yet a form of knowledge for which man is fitted, and that it is better for him to be ignorant of his own nature in order to be happy? (144)

757. One day a man told me that he was filled with joy and trust when he left the confessional. Another told me that he remained a prey to fear. This made me think that the two of them together would have made one good man, and that each of them lacked something in so far as he did not possess the feeling of the other. The same thing often happens in other spheres. (530)

758. It is not in Montaigne, but in myself that I find everything that I see there. (64)

759. May God not impute our sins to us, that is to say, all the

consequences and effects of our sins, which are appalling, down to the least faults, if he chooses to count them against us without mercy! (506)

760. Chide Miton for not bestirring himself, when God reproaches him. (192)

2. NOTE FOR THE *TRAITÉ DU VIDE* (1651)

761. (Part. I, L. 2, C. i, S. 4.) [Conjecture. It will not be difficult to bring it down another peg and make it look ridiculous.]

What is more absurd than to say that inanimate bodies are subject to passions, fears, feelings of horror, that bodies without feeling, without life, which are even incapable of life, have feelings, which pre-supposes at least a sentient soul to harbour them? What is more, that the object of their horror was the vacuum? What is there to be afraid of in the vacuum? What is baser or more ridiculous?

Nor is that all. That they have within them a principle of movement to enable them to escape the vacuum?

Do they have arms, legs, muscles, nerves? (75)

3. NOTES FOR THE *ÉCRITS SUR LA GRÂCE*

762. Law has not destroyed nature, but has informed it; grace has not destroyed the law, but has led to its application.

Faith received in baptism is the source of the whole of the life of the Christian and of converts. (520)

763. Why God established prayer:

    1. To bestow on his creatures the dignity of causation.

    2. To teach us from whom we derive virtue.

    3. To enable us to deserve the other virtues through work.

But, in order to preserve the first of them for himself, he bestows the gift of prayer on whom he chooses.

Objection: But we may believe that prayer comes to us from ourselves.

That is absurd; if we cannot have the virtues even though we have faith, how could we obtain faith? Is there a greater distance between unbelief and faith than between faith and virtue?

Deserved: the word is ambiguous.

Meruit habere Redemptorem.

Meruit tam sacra membra tangere.

Digno tam sacra membra tangere.

Non sum dignus.

> *Qui manducat indignus.*
>
> *Dignus est accipere.*
>
> *Dignare me.*[1]

God only owes according to his promises. He has promised to grant justice in answer to prayer; never did *he* promise prayer except to the children of his promise.

St. Augustine said definitely that strength would be taken away from the righteous. But he said it by chance; because the opportunity of saying it might not have occurred. Yet it is clear from his principles that, since the opportunity did occur, it was impossible for him not to say it, or to say the opposite. It therefore gains greater weight from the fact that he was obliged to say it because the opportunity occurred than if he had said it when the opportunity occurred: one implied necessity, the other chance. But the two together are the most we can ask for.

(513)

764. He who knows the will of his master will receive the greater number of blows,

On account of the power given to him by knowledge.

---

[1] He deserved to have a Redeemer (Office of Holy Saturday).
He deserved to touch limbs which were so sacred (Office of Good Friday).
Worthy to touch limbs which are so sacred (*Vexilla regis*).
I am not worthy (Luke VII, 6).
Whoever eats unworthily (I Cor. XI, 29).
Thou art worthy to receive (Apoc. IV, 66).
Find me worthy (Office of Our Lady).

Qui justus est, justificetur adhuc,[1]

On account of the power that comes to him through justice.

From him who has received most the strictest account will be demanded,

Because of the power derived from God's grace.   (531)

765. Grace will always be in the world—in nature, too,—so that in a way it is natural. And therefore there will always be Pelagians, and always Catholics, and always strife;

Because the first birth creates the former, and the grace of second birth the latter.   (521)

766. Rom., III, 27. Glory excluded: by what law? Works? No, but by faith. Therefore faith is not in our power like the operations of law, and it is given to us in a different manner.   (516)

767. The law compelled obedience to something which it did not give. Grace gives what it imposes.   (522)

768. '*Humilibus dat gratiam; an ideo non dedit humilitatem?*

Sui eum non receperunt; quotquot autem non receperunt an non erant sui?'[2]   (901)

769. It requires grace to turn a man into a saint, and anyone who doubts it does not know what a saint or what a man is.

                                                                                      (508)

770. The images of the totality of the Redemption, such as the sun shining on all men, are merely a sign of totality; but the images of exclusion, such as the Jews chosen to the exclusion of the Gentiles, are a sign of exclusion.   (781)

771. 'Jesus Christ the Redeemer of all . . .' Yes, because he made his offer as a man who redeemed all those who were willing to come to him. As for those who die on the way, that is their misfortune; but so far as he is concerned, he offered them redemption.—It is a good example, where he who redeems and he who prevents death are two, but not in Jesus Christ who did both.—No, because Jesus Christ, in his role of Redeemer, is not

---

[1] The righteous man shall be justified (Apoc. XXII, 11).

[2] God gives the humble man his grace (James IV, 6). Does that mean that he has not given humility? (Pascal).

He came to what was his own, and they who were his own gave him no welcome (John I, 11). But were all those who did not welcome him not his own? (Pascal).

perhaps master of all; and therefore, in so far as it is in him, he is the redeemer of all. (781)

772. When people say that Jesus Christ did not die for all men, they encourage the weakness of men who at once regard themselves as exceptions, which fosters despair; instead of turning them away from despair to hope. For in this way we grow accustomed to inward virtues by [outward observances]. (781)

773. *If* is not a sign of indifference; Malachy, Isaiah.

Is., *Si volueris,* etc.

In quacumque die. (636)

774. 'Work out your salvation with fear' (Phil., II, 12).

The poor men of grace.

Petenti dabitur.[1]

Therefore, it is in our power to ask. On the contrary, it is not: because what is asked for is granted, the [power] to pray is not there. For because salvation is not in our power, and the power of obtaining it is, prayer is not in our power.

The Righteous Man should therefore no longer hope in God because he must not hope, but set to work to obtain what he is asking for.

Let us then conclude that since man is now incapable of using proximate power, and since it is not God's will that he should cling to him by this means, it is only through an effective power that he cleaves to God.

Therefore, those who abandon God are without the power without which we do not detach ourselves from him, and those who do not detach themselves possess effective power.

Therefore, if those who have persevered for a certain time in prayer through effective power, stop praying, they are without this effective power.

And yet, in this sense, it is God who detaches himself first.

(514)

---

[1] To him that asks shall be given.

NOTES FOR *LES PROVINCIALES*

775. Examine the reasons behind the vote of censure as they appear from the facts.

Work out a hypothesis which fits them all.

The habit of an order determines its teaching.

You shrive so many people who only go to confession once a year.

I thought that it was one opinion against another.

When someone is so wicked that he no longer feels any remorse, he no longer commits sins. Therefore you are persecuting M. Arnauld without remorse.

I distrust this doctrine because it is too easy, considering the spite which is said to be in me.

I distrust the alliance between them on account of their particular differences of opinion.

I will wait for them to reach agreement before taking sides: for a friend I should have too many enemies; I am not sufficiently learned to reply to them.

Why not choose some really great heresy.

The wager.

I certainly thought that one would be damned for not having good thoughts, but the idea that no one has any is new to me.

What is the use of that? To comfort the righteous and save them from despair? No, because no one can be in a state in which he believes himself to be righteous.

M. Chamaillard would rank as a heretic, which would obviously be wrong because he has written in support of M. Arnauld.

Those who think that they are doing good when they are committing sins.

In 1647 grace was universal; in 1650 it was less common, etc.

The grace of M. Cornet, M. . . .

Luther, miles from the truth.

As though there had not been similar incidents in the Church! But I take my parish priest's word for it!

One alone speaks the truth.

However small the inconvenience it causes; they devise other [forms of grace] because they are at their disposal like their own handiwork; on each occasion, a grace for each person, grace for the nobility, grace for rogues.

In short, M. Chamaillard is so close to it that, if there are steps leading down into the void, sufficient grace is now close at hand.

Amusing to be called a heretic on that account.

There was nobody who was not surprised, because no one had ever come across it in Scripture or the Fathers, etc. . . .

How long is it, Father, since it became an article of faith? It can only be since the words 'proximate power'; I really believe that its birth created the heresy, and that it was born simply for that.

The censure merely forbids us to speak of St. Peter like that, and nothing more.

I am very much obliged to them. They are clever people; they were afraid that the letters written to provincials. . . .

It was not worth while just for one word. Childish naïveté, praised without being known. Wicked creditors. I think that they are sorcerers. Luther, miles from the truth. Heretical member. *Unam sanctam.*

The *Enluminures* have done us a lot of harm.

A proposition may be sound in one writer and unsound in another. I know, but there are other unsound propositions.

There are people who submit to censure; others to arguments, and all to reasons. I am therefore surprised to find that you have adopted the general and not the particular practice, or at any rate that you have not brought the two together.

What a relief! No Frenchman is a good Catholic!

The litanies—Clement VIII, Paul V—the censure.

God is obviously watching over us.

Man is certainly out of his mind. He cannot create a mite ...

Not God, but the grace to get there. Plurality of graces.

Jansenist translators.

St. Augustine has the most because of the divisions among his enemies. Besides, a thing to be considered is an unbroken tradition of 12,000 popes, councils, etc.

M. Arnauld must therefore have a very bad disposition if he infects his friends.

The censure has done this much for them: when they are condemned they will fight it by saying that they are following the example of the Jansenists. (925)

776. If they have not succeeded in making their judgement right by suborning the bishops and the Sorbonne, they have managed to make their judges guilty of injustice. And so, when they are condemned for it in the future, they will argue *ad hominem* that they were unjust, and in this way will repudiate their judgement. But it will not do them any good. Since they cannot argue that the Jansenists have been properly condemned merely because they have been condemned, they will not be able to argue that they themselves have been improperly condemned because it was done by venal judges. For their condemnation will be just, not because it is pronounced by judges who are always just, but by judges who are just on this point; which will be demonstrated by other proofs. (948)

777. 'When I heard the rumour from the Feuillants, I went to see him,' said my old friend. 'When discussing religion, he thought that I had some feeling for it, that I might become a Feuillant and could help by writing, particularly at that time, against the innovators.'

'We recently acted against our general chapter, which took the line that the bull should be signed.'

'That he hoped that God would inspire me.'

'Father, ought one to sign?' (902 *bis*)

778. 'I am afraid that it is by no means certain,' said the Feuillant; 'because opposition is a sign of uncertainty (St. Athanasius, St. Chrysostom; morality, the infidels).'

The Jesuits have not cast doubts on truth, but they have shown that there is no doubt about their own impiety.

There have always been contradictions in order to prevent the wicked from seeing, because everything that shocks truth or charity is evil; that is the true principle.   (902)

779. Have you the right ideas about our order?

The Church has lasted such a long time without these questions being asked.

The others ask them, but it is not the same.

What comparison do you think there can be between 20,000 who are separated and 200,000,000 who belong, and who will die for one another? An immortal body.

We will stand by one another until death. Lamy.

We are driving back our enemies. M. Puys.

Kings, Pope. 3 Reg. 246.

Everything depends on probability.

The world naturally desires a religion, but a comfortable one.

Grant me this principle, and I will prove everything for you. The fact is that the Society and the Church are in the same boat.

Without these principles nothing can be proved.

We cannot live for long in a state of blatant irreligion, or naturally when practising great austerity. An easygoing religion is likely to last. We seek them out of licentiousness.

I should like to prove it to you by a strange assumption. I am going to say therefore . . . if God did not preserve us by a special providence for the good of the Church, I can still show you that speaking even in human terms we cannot perish.

I do not know whether they could do better with individuals who did not wish to rule by the sword.

6 . . . Uprightness and good faith in religion.—6. 452. Foster-kings.—4. Hated for their virtues.—Apol. Univers. 159. Decree of the Sorbonne.—The kings 241. 228.—Jesuits hanged, 112.—Religion and the Society.—*Jesuita omnis homo*[1]. —Schools, relations, friends, children to choose.

Constitutions.

[1] Every man a Jesuit.

253. Poverty, ambition.

257. Mainly princes, great noblemen who can help or hinder.

12. Useless, rejected. Good complexion. Wealth, nobility, etc.

What! You mean to tell me that you were afraid that one would fail through receiving them earlier?

27, 47. Give his capital to the Society for the glory of God. *Dec*[larations].

51, 52. Union of feelings. *Decl.* submit to the Society and in this way preserve uniformity. Now today uniformity lies in diversity because that is what the Society wants.

65. Rare, learned, pious people. But today opinion is changing.

23, 74. Beg.

19. Not to give to relatives, and rely on the advisers provided by the superior.

1. Not to practise examination of conscience. *Decl.*

2. Complete poverty. No masses, nothing for preaching the sermon, or by way of compensatory alms.

4. *Decl.* same authority as the *Const. Fin.*: read the *Cons.* each month.

149. The *Declarations* spoil everything.

154. Nor egg people on to give perpetual alms, nor demand them as of right, nor collecting boxes. *Decl.*: '*Non tanquam Eleemozina.*'

200. 4. Keep us informed of everything.

190. *Const.* does not want a troupe. *Decl.* troupe interpreted.

A universal and immortal body.—Affection for the community great and without scruple, dangerous. We should all be rich through religion if it were not for our Constitutions: therefore we are poor. And through the true religion and without it we are strong.

Cl . . . placent . . .—Our generals fear loss of reputation;—on account of external occupations, 208, 152, 150; on account of the Court, 209, 203, 216, 218;—because they did not follow the safest and most reliable opinion, St. Thomas, etc., 215, 228.—

Stipendium contra Consti, 218.—Women, 225, 228.—Princes and politics, 227, 168, 177.

Probability. Novelty, 279, 156.—Novelty, Truth.—In order to pass the time and amuse oneself rather than to help souls, 158.—Lax views, 160.—Mortal into venial sin. Contrition, 162. —Politics, 162.—Anticipators . . . or, 162.

The comforts of life are increasing with the Jesuits, 166.— Very evident and false which deceive them, 192 *ad.*—Complaints from the generals: not from St. Ignatius, not from Laynez, a few from Borgia and Aquaviva; innumerable from Mutius, etc. Père Lemoine: 10,000 *écus*, outside his province.

See how weak human foresight is: all the things that made our first generals fear the destruction of our order; it was by them that it grew, by the great nobility, by the contradictions of our Constitutions, by the multitude of religious, the variety and novelty of opinions, etc., 182, 157.

Politics, 181.

The first spirit of the order extinguished, 170, 171 *ad* 174, 183 *ad* 187.

Non e più quella. Vittelescus, 183.   (956)

780. If by postponing judgement we condemned, you would be right. Uniformity without variety is useless to others, variety without uniformity fatal for us. One harmful outside, the other inside.   (892)

781. We have turned variety into uniformity because we are all uniform owing to the fact that we have all become alike.   (—)

782. Letter on the forcible establishment of Jesuits everywhere.

Supernatural blindness.

This moral system which has at the head a crucified God.

Such are those who have taken a vow to obey *tanquam Christo.*

The decadence of the Jesuits.

Our religion which is wholly divine.

A casuist: Mirouër.

If you think him good, it is a good sign.

It is a strange thing that there is no way of giving them any idea of religion.

A crucified God.

By isolating the punishable case of the schism, they will be punished.

But what an upheaval! Children by embracing it love those who corrupt them. Enemies abhor them. We are witnesses.

For the great majority of casuists, so far from being a subject of accusation against the Church, it is on the contrary a subject of lamentation by the Church.

And in order that we may not be suspect like the Jews who are the custodians of the books, which are not suspect to the Gentiles, they bring us their Constitutions. (953)

783. *Montalte*[1]. Lax views are so popular that it is strange that theirs should cause scandal. It is because they have gone too far. And, what is more, there are plenty of people who see the truth and cannot reach it. But there are few who do not know that the purity of religion is an antidote to our corruption. Ridiculous to say that an eternal reward is offered in return for Escobartine morals. (915)

784. *Probability*. Each of us can give, none can take away. (913)

785. Unrepentant sinners, righteous men without charity, a God without power over the will of men, a predestination without mystery! (884 *bis*)

786. Can it be anything but the indulgence of the world which makes you think that things are probable? Will you convince us that it is the truth and that, if duelling were not fashionable, you would think it probable that it is permissible to fight a duel when the thing is considered in itself? (910)

787. *Diana*, 11. It is to what Diana does ...

11. 'It is lawful not to bestow livings, which do not involve care of souls, on the most deserving.' The Council of Trent appears to say the opposite; but this is how he proves it: 'for if that were so, all prelates would be damned because they all behave in that way.'

11. 'The king and the Pope are not compelled to choose the

---

[1] Pseudonym used by Pascal in writing the *Provinciales*.

worthiest.' If that were so, the Pope and the kings would bear a terrible responsibility.—21. And in another place: 'If this view were not true, penitents and confessors would have a great deal of trouble, and that is why I hold that they should adopt it in practice.'

22. And in another place where he lays down the conditions which are necessary to turn a sin into a mortal sin, he introduces so many qualifications that it is scarcely possible to commit a mortal sin; and after proving it, he exclaims: 'Oh, how light and gentle is the yoke of the Lord!'

11. And elsewhere: 'We are not obliged to give alms from what we can spare to relieve the ordinary necessities of the poor: if the contrary were true, we should be obliged to condemn the majority of the rich and their confessors.'

These arguments exasperate me, and I said to the Father: 'But who prevents us from saying that they are?'

'It is what he had foreseen in this passage,' he replied, 'where after saying: 22 "If it were true that the richest were damned," he adds: "To that, Arragonius replies that they are, too, and Baunez, who was a Jesuit, adds that their confessors are in the same position; but I reply, with Valentia, another Jesuit, and other writers, that there are several grounds on which the rich and their confessors can be excused." '

I was enchanted by this reasoning when he ended by saying: 'If this were true of restitution, what a lot of restitutions there would be!'

'Oh, Father,' I said, 'what a reason!'

'Oh,' the Father said to me, 'there's an accommodating man for you!'

'Oh, Father,' I replied, 'what a lot of people would be damned without your casuists! Oh, Father, how wide you make the path which leads to heaven! Oh, what a lot of people there are who find it! Here's one . . .' (928)

788. The servant does not know what the master is doing because the master only tells him what his job is and not the reason for it; and that is why he submits cringingly and often sins against the end. But Jesus Christ has told us the end.

And you destroy that end. (897)

789. Digressions. Small turns; it is fitting. Are you angry with [me] for standing clear? The Fathers and the . . .

I have noticed them since; because I had not known them . . . (938)

790. They take refuge in the crowd and call numbers to their aid. Uproar. (260)

791. We must hear both sides; that is what I am careful to do. When we only hear one side, we are always on that side; but the other makes us change our mind; instead of this, in the present instance the Jesuit confirms it.

Not what they do, but what they say.

It is only against me that they are raising a hue and cry. It is all right by me. I know to whom I am answerable.

J.C. was a stumbling block. Liable to condemnation, condemned.

Politics. We have found two obstacles in the way of alleviating the lot of mankind: one comes from the inner laws of the Gospel, the other from the external laws of the State and religion. We are masters of the former: this is what we have made of the latter: *Amplianda restrengenda. A majori ad minus.* Junior.

Probable. If such bad reasons as these are probable, everything must be.

They argue like people who prove that it is night at midday.

1st argument: *Dominus actum conjugalium.* Molina.

2nd argument: *Non potest compensari* (Less[ius]).

Do not use holy, but abominable axioms against them.

Bauny burner of barns.

Mascarenas. Council of Trent for priests in a state of mortal sin: *quam primum* . . . (926)

792. *Probable.* Let us see whether we are genuinely seeking God compared with the things of which we are fond: it is *probable* that this meat will not poison me; it is *probable* that I shall not lose my case by not lobbying . . .

Probable. If it were true that serious writers and arguments are sufficient, I say that they are neither serious nor reasonable. What! according to Molina a husband can take advantage of his wife. Is the reason that he gives reasonable? And is the restraint of Lessius any more so?

And you, are you really bold enough to play about with the king's decrees like that and say that it is not duelling to go into a field and wait for a man?

That the Church has certainly forbidden duelling, but not going for a walk?

and also usury, but not . . .

and simony, but not . . .

and vengeance, but not . . .

and sodomites, but not . . .

and the *quam primum*, but not . . .   (922)

793. *Pope.* We like security. We like the Pope to be infallible in matters of faith, and grave doctors on moral questions in order to feel reassured.   (880)

794. They assert that the Church says what she does not say, and that she does not say what she does say. (—)

795. *Generals.* They are not satisfied with introducing such behaviour into our temples: *templis inducere mores*; they not only expect people to put up with them in the Church, they want to drive out those who do not belong, as though they had become the strongest party . . .

Mohatra: it is not the sign of a theologian to be surprised by him.

Who would have told your generals that the time was so close when they would force such behaviour on the universal Church, and describe the refusal to admit such disorders as war: *et tanta mala pacem.*   (934)

796. Those unfortunate beings who have compelled us to speak of the essence of religion.   (883)

797. Sinners absolved without penance; righteous men sanctified without charity; all Christians without the grace of Jesus Christ, God without power over men's wills, a predestination without mystery, a redemption without certainty!
                                                              (884)

798. Miracles are no longer necessary because we have already had them. But when tradition is no longer heeded, when nothing is offered but the pope, when he has been imposed upon: and when the real source of truth, which is tradition, has been excluded; and when the pope, who is the custodian of tradition, is biased, truth is no longer free to show itself: then as men no longer speak of truth, truth itself must speak to men. That is what happened in the time of Arius. (Miracles under Diocletian and Arius.) (832)

799. [See the discourses in the Jansenist's second, fourth and fifth letters. They are highminded and serious.]

[I dislike equally the clown and the pompous man.] One would not want either as a friend.

We only judge by ear because we lack heart.

[After my eighth letter, I thought that I had written enough by way of reply.] (30)

800. What would have become of the Jesuits without probability, and of probability without the Jesuits?

Take away *probability* and it is impossible to go on pleasing people; bring in *probability* and you cannot go wrong. At other times, it was difficult to avoid sins and difficult to atone for them; nowadays there are all sorts of dodges for avoiding them and atonement is simple. (918)

801. They turn the exception into the rule.

The ancients gave absolution before penance? Do it as an exception. But you turn the exception into a rule without exception, so that you will no longer admit that there is an exception to the rule. (904)

802. *Rarum est enim ut satis se quisque vereatur.*[1]

Tot circa unum caput tumultuantes deos.[2]

Nihil turpius quam cognitioni assertionem praecurrere.[3]

---

[1] It is rare for a man to respect himself sufficiently (Quintilian, x, 7. Quoted after Montaigne, I, 39).

[2] So many gods busy about a single man (Seneca, *Suasoriae*, I, iv. Quoted after Montaigne, II, 13).

[3] Nothing is more shameful than to make assertion and decision precede perception and knowledge (Cicero, *Acad.*, I, 12. Quoted after Montaigne, III, 13).

Nec me pudet ut istos fateri nescire quod nesciam.[1]

Melius non incipient.[2]   (364)

803. What good has it done you to accuse me of making mock
of holy things? You will fare no better if you accuse me of being
an impostor.

I have not said all that I have to say, as you will soon see.

I am not a heretic; I have not subscribed to the five propositions. You claim that I have, but you produce no evidence. I
maintain that you said it, and I can prove it.

Ex senatus-consultis et plebiscitis . . .[3]

 Look up similar passages.

I am very glad that you are saying the same thing as myself.
Elidere Caramuel.

Are you threatening me?

I tell you that you are impostors; I have proved it, and you
have the impertinence not to hide the fact.—Brisacier. Menier.
D'Alby—and you authorise it, *elidere*.

When you thought that M. Puys was an enemy of the
Society, you alleged that he was unfit to be a parish priest;
ignorant, heretical, a man of bad faith and loose morals. Since
then, he has become a worthy priest, a man of good faith and
exemplary morality.

As you have only touched on that one point, it is tantamount
to approving all the rest. *Me causam fecit.*

Slander, *haec est magna caecitas cordis* (is a great blindness of
the heart); not to see the evil of it: *haec est major caecitas cordis* (is
a greater blindness of the heart); to defend instead of confessing
it as a sin: *tunc homines concludit profunditas iniquitatis*, etc. (This is
a sign of the profundity of man's iniquity.)—230, Prosper.

The great nobles are taking different sides in the civil war,
and so do you in the civil war of mankind.

---

[1] I am not ashamed like these people to admit that I do not know what I
do not know (Cicero *Tusc.*, I, xxv. Quoted after Montaigne, III, 11).

[2] They will find it easier not to begin than to stop (Seneca, *Ep.* LXXII.
Quoted after Montaigne, II, 10).

[3] It is in virtue of the senatus-consultus (that crimes are committed)
(Seneca, *Ep.*, xcv).

I want to say it to your face, so that what I say will have greater force.

I am certain of the approval of those who study the texts. But those who only read the titles, and they are the great majority, might take your word for it; members of religious orders must not be impostors—our own have already been disabused by the [pertinence of the] quotations. The others must be disabused by *elidere*.

It is not that I do not see how embarrassed you are; because if you wished to unsay what you have said, it would be done, but, etc.

. . . The saints enter into all sorts of subtleties in order to show that they are criminals and blame themselves for their finest actions. And these people invent all sorts of subtleties in order to excuse their worst actions.

A building which looks equally well from outside, but is constructed on shaky foundations, is the work of the wise pagans: and the devil deceives men by an apparently similar building which rests on an entirely different foundation.

Never has a man had such a good cause as mine; and never has anyone presented such an easy target as you.

Men of the world do not imagine that they are on the right path.

Do not argue that this is something that happens in the course of a dispute: if your works were printed in full and in French, everybody would be able to judge for himself.

I ask people to do me the justice of not taking their word for it any more.

The more they insist on my personal weakness, the more they acknowledge the justice of my cause.

You declare that I am a heretic. Is such a thing permissible? And if you are not afraid that men will do me justice, are you not afraid that God will?

You are aware of the power of truth, and you will yield to it . . .

It would be necessary to force people to believe you under pain of mortal sin. *Elidere*.

It is a sin to believe brazenly in evil speaking: *Non credeba(nt) temere calumniatori* (They did not brazenly believe the slanderer). St. Aug.: *Fecitque cadendo undique me cadere*, by the axiom of evil speaking.

There is something supernatural about such blindness. *Digna necessitas.*

Mentiris impudentissime (You will be impudent liars).

230. It is a grave sin to defend it.—*Elidere.*

340-23. The doom of the wicked.

Doctrina sua noscetur vir. (A man is known by his teaching.)

66. *Labor mendacii* (the work of lying).—80, alms.

False piety, a twofold sin.

Am I single-handed against thirty thousand? Not at all. You, stick to the Court; and you, to fraud; I, to truth: it is my whole strength; if I lose it, I am lost. I shall not lack accusers or persecutors. But I possess truth, and we shall see who will prevail.

I am not fit to defend religion, but you are not fit to defend error. And I hope that God in his mercy, not heeding the evil that is in me and heeding the good that is in you, will grant us the grace not to let truth succumb in my hands, and not to let a lie . . .   (921/362)

804. The world must be very blind if it believes you.   (937)

805. The man who is condemned by Escobar will be well and truly condemned!   (932)

806. End. Is one safe? Is this principle a sound one? Let us look at it. Self-witness—nil. St. Thomas.   (941)

807. You never accuse me of being wrong about Escobar because his work is there for people to read.   (939)

808. 'We ourselves have not received any general precepts. If you look at our Constitutions, you will hardly recognise us: they make out that we are beggars who are shut off from courts—and yet, etc. But it does not mean that the Constitutions have been infringed, for the glory of God is everywhere.'

'There are different ways of getting there. St. Ignatius chose some of them; and now we choose others. It was better in the beginning to preach poverty and withdrawal from the world;

it was better later on to follow a different course. For it would have been frightening to begin with the difficult things: it is contrary to human nature.'

'It does not affect the general rule, thàt we must observe the Institutions, because that would lead to abuses. You will not find many like us who know how to get on in the world without growing vain.'

'Two obstacles: the Gospel; laws of the State.' '*A majori ad minus*.' Junior.—*Unam sanctam*. The Jansenists will be punished for it.

God clearly protects us against rash judgements and scruples. *Falso crimine*. Subtlety for its own sake.—The whole of truth on one side; we extend it to both.

Father St. Jure.—Escobar.—*Tanto viro*.—Aquiviva, 14 December, 1621. Ta[nn]er, 9, 2, dub. 5; n. 86.—Clement and Paul V.—St. Teresa, 474.—Romance, rose.

When it comes to speaking of personal vices.—Fine letter of Aquiviva's, 18 June, 1611, against probable opinions. St. Augustine, 282.—And for St. Thomas in the places where he deals explicitly with the matter.—*Cl. Place* . . . 277.—And novelties.— And it is no excuse in the eyes of superiors not to have known, because they should have known, 279, 194, 192.—For morality, 283, 288.—Acquoquiez heard women's confessions, 360.—The Society is important to the Church, 236, in a good and a bad sense, 156.   (957)

809. *Heretics*. Ezechiel. All the heathen spoke evil of Israel, and the prophet too: and the Israelites were far from being in the position to say to him: 'You talk like the heathen' because his greatest strength lay in the fact that the heathen spoke like him.

(886)

810. The absurdly exaggerated idea that you have of the importance of your Society has made you introduce these horrible methods. It is perfectly clear that it is this that has led you to indulge in a campaign of slander, since you blame in me, as horrible, the least deceits which you excuse in yourselves, because you regard me as an individual and yourselves as the *Imago*.

Are you likely to encourage your children if you condemn them when they serve the Church?

It is a trick of the devil to use for other purposes the arms with which those people would fight heresy.

You are a bunch of evil politicians.

It seems clear that your praises are follies which have replaced fairy stories like the privilege of escaping damnation.   (927)

811. Untrustworthy people without faith, without honour, without truth, with deceitful hearts and tongues who resemble, as people complained of you in other times, the amphibious animal in the fable which belonged to an ambiguous species somewhere between fish and fowl.

P[ort]-Royal is quite as good as Voltigerode.

In so far as your device is just when looked at from this angle, it is unjust in precisely the same degree when looked at in the light of Christian piety.

It is important to kings and princes to be esteemed for their piety; and in order to achieve it they must be shriven by you.

(924)

812*.

Notes in an Unknown Hand	*Notes by Pascal*
Ep. 16. AQUIVIVAE.	
De formandis concionatoribus.	
— p. 373. *Longe falluntur qui ad . . . irrigaturae.*	Read the Fathers in order to make them fit in with his imagination instead of modelling his thought on that of the Fathers.
Ep. 1. Mutii VITELESCI.	
— p. 389. *Quamvis enim probe norim . . . et absolutum.*	
— 390. *Dolet ac queritur . . . esse modestiam.*	Modesty.
— p. 392. *Lex ne dimidiata . . . reprehendit.*	Mass. I do not know what he means.
— p. 408. *Ita feram illam . . . etiam irrumpat.*	Politics.

Notes in an Unknown Hand	*Notes by Pascal*
— p. 409. *Ad extremum pervelim . . . circumferatur.*	Owing to a misfortune, or rather a singular piece of good fortune for the Society, what one member does is attributed to all.
— p. 410. *Quaerimoniae . . . deprehendetis,* p. 412.	Strict obedience to the bishops. Let it not appear that we are setting ourselves up as a challenge to them, in the manner of St. Xavier.
— p. 412. *Ad haec si a litibus . . . aviditatis.*	Wills, lawsuits.
— p. 413. *Patris Borgiae . . . illam futuram.*	They add to, they even invent, untrue stories.
— p. 415. *In res domesticas . . . nunc dimittis,* etc.	
Ep. 2. Mutii VITELESCI	
— p. 432. *Quarto nonnulorum . . . quam ardentissime possum urgere.*	Probability: *tueri potius potest— probabilis est—autore non caret.*
— p. 433. *Quoniam vero de loquendi licentia . . . aut raro plectatur.*	Failure to punish slanderers.
Ep. 3. Mutii VITELESCI	
— p. 437. *Nec sane dubium . . . nihil jam detrimenti acceperit.*	Avoid the ruin of the Society.
— p. 440. *Ardentissime Deum exoremus . . . operari non est gravatus et tu fili,* etc. Ezech. 37.	
— p. 441. *Secundum caput . . . tanti facimus.*	Disobedience in order to make a name for themselves.
— p. 442. *Haec profecto una si deficiet . . . qui haec molitur,* etc.	Disobedience, seek the support of the great.

Notes in an Unknown Hand	*Notes by Pascal*
— p. 443. *Ex hoc namque vitio . . . importunum praebeas.*	They behave indecently which is contrary to the Constitutions of the Society, and say that it is owing to the importunity of the nobility; but it is they who are importunate so that we must either have them for our enemies if we refuse to do what they want, or bring about the downfall of the Society if we grant their wish.
— p. 443. *Spectabit tertium caput . . . mutatus est color optimus.*	Chastity.
— p. 445. *De paupertate . . . non adversentur veritati.*	Poverty. Laxity of opinions contrary to truth.
— p. 445. *Nobilis quidam Romae . . . collocabit.*	
— p. 446. *Faxit Deus . . . atque si praetermitterentur.*	Vines, etc. (958)

813. We never plunge so wholeheartedly and so gaily into evil doing as when we do it to salve our conscience.   (895)

814. These women, who are amazed when they are told that they are on the road to perdition; that their confessors are leading them in the direction of Geneva; that they are giving them the idea that Jesus Christ is not in the Eucharist or on the right hand of the Father, know that it is all false. They therefore offer themselves to God in this state: *Vide si via iniquitatis in me est.* What will happen next? God will make the place, which is said to be the temple of the devil, his own temple. They say that the children must be taken away from it: God heals them where they are. They say that it is hell's arsenal: God turns it into the sanctuary of his grace. In short, they are threatened with all the furies and all the vengeances of heaven; and God loads them with his favours. We should have to be out of our senses to infer from this that they are on the road to perdition.

(We no doubt have the same signs of it as St. Athanasius.)
(841)

815. By demonstrating truth we make people believe it; but by displaying the injustice of the masters we do not put it right. We quieten conscience by pointing out error; we do not safeguard our purse by revealing injustice. (893)

816. [We must be sober in our judgement of the divine ordinances, Father.

St. Paul on the island of Malta.] (853)

817. . . . And they are preparing to drive out of the Church those who refuse the undertaking. In t[ruth] . . .

Everyone asserts that they are. M. Arnauld and his friends protest that he condemns them as they stand and wherever they are to be found; that, if they are in Jansen, he condemns them there; that he still condemns them if they are not there; if the heretical sense of the propositions which the Pope has condemned is to be found in Jansen, let him condemn Jansen.

But you are not satisfied with these declarations: you want him to assert that the propositions are to be found, word for word, in Jansen. He has replied that he cannot make such a declaration because he does not know whether it is true, that he and countless other people have searched for them but have failed to find them there. They asked you and the others to quote the pages where they occur; no one has ever done so.

And despite the fact that he condemns everything that the Church condemns, you are trying to drive him out of the Church solely on the grounds that he refuses to admit that particular words or a particular meaning occur in a book in which he has never found them, and where no one is able to point them out to him. In truth, Father, it is such a frivolous pretext that the Church has probably never known such a strange, unjust, tyrannical proceeding.

The Church can of course compel. Clement VIII: *Si quis dixerit* . . . That to a heretic . . .

It is not necessary to be a theologian to see that their heresy amounts to nothing more than their opposition to you. I am conscious of it myself, and the proof lies in the fate of all those who have attacked you: the Jansenist priests at Rouen. The Caen Vow.

You think that your intentions are so honest that you make them the subject of a vow.

Two years ago their heresy was the Bull; last year it was an interior heresy; six months ago it was *totidem* ('so often'); today it is the meaning of Jansen.

Is it not perfectly clear that your one desire is to brand them as heretics? Blessed Sacrament, Preface, Villeloin.

It was on behalf of others that I attacked you.

It is ridiculous of you to make such a fuss about the propositions. It is nothing; it must be understood.

I will mention no names; but when people knew what you were up to, seventy rose in opposition—date the decree—so that the person whom you had not managed to convict of heresy out of his own mouth, etc.

Who can be angry with me for pointing out that everything—even the most horrible—is to be found in your own authors? It is common knowledge.

Is that all you can find to answer? And is this your only method of proving it?

He knows that the answer is either yes or no, or he is a doubter: either a sinner or a heretic—Jansen—Aurelius—Arnauld—*Provinciales*.

We need only consider the heathen. The same light which reveals supernatural truths shows that they are without error, instead of which the light that, etc.

After Pelagius. Therefore there is nothing strange about it. —Spurious right. Baronius.—I myself would sooner be an impostor than, etc.

A contingent of lost souls.

All the alms-boxes at St. Merry might be opened without your being any less innocent. And . . .

What is your reason for it? You say that I am a Jansenist, that Father R. upholds the five propositions, and that therefore I uphold them: three lies.

And I beg you not to come and tell me that it was not you who started it all. Spare me the answer.

The Pope has not condemned two things. He has only condemned the meaning of the propositions; are you going to claim that he has not condemned it? 'But the meaning of Jansen is there,' said the Pope. I can see very well that the Pope thought so because of your *totidem*. But he did not say so under pain of excommunication.

How could he have failed to believe it, and the French bishops as well? You said it *totidem*, and they did not know that you were capable of saying it, even though it was not true. Frauds! You had not seen my fifteenth letter.

How could Jansen's meaning be found in propositions which were not by him?

Either it is in Jansen, or it is not. If it is there, then he is condemned on that point; if not, why are you trying to have him condemned?

If only they would condemn one of the propositions of your Father Escobar, I should appear with Escobar in one hand and the condemnation in the other, and argue the case in due form.

(925)

818. Every time the Jesuits trick the Pope, they make the whole of Christendom guilty of perjury.

The Pope is very easy to trick because of the demands on his time and his trust in the Jesuits; and the Jesuits are very good at tricking people by means of slander. (882)

819. . . . Now probability is as necessary for the other precepts as for those of Lamy and the slanderer.

A fructibus eorum . . . —Judge the quality of their faith by their morals.

Probability is of little use without corrupt means, and the means are nothing without probability.

It is pleasant to be able to do well and to know how to do well: '*Scire et posse.*' Grace and probability provide the means because we can account to God by relying on their authors.

(942)

820. Will *Est et non est* be accepted in faith itself as well as in morality? If it is so inseparable from it in men's actions.

When St. Xavier performed miracles.—[St. Hilary.—Wretched creatures to force us to bring in miracles]. [*Vae qui conditis.*]

Unjust judges, do not draw up laws to suit the time; judge according to those which are already established, and by yourselves: *Vae qui conditis leges iniquas.*

Continual miracles, false ones.

In order to weaken your opponents, you disarm the whole Church.

If they say that our salvation is in the hands of God, they are 'heretics'.

If they say that they submit to the Pope, it is a piece of 'hypocrisy'.

If they are ready to subscribe to all her constitutions, it is not enough.

If they say that we must not kill for an apple, 'they are fighting against the moral code of Catholics'.

If miracles are performed among them, it is not a sign of sanctity, but means that they are tainted with heresy.

The reason why the Church has survived is that truth has not been challenged or, if it has, there has been the Pope, and if not, there has been the Church. (849)

821. There is such a vast gap between the merits which he imagines that he possesses and his stupidity, that no one would have thought him capable of such a huge miscalculation. (946)

822. After so many signs of piety, they are still persecuted, which is the surest guarantee of piety. (860)

823. The Day of Judgement.

So that, Father, is what you call the meaning of Jansen; it is what you have given the Popes and the bishops to understand!

If the Jesuits were corrupt, and if it were true that we were alone, it would be all the more reason for staying where we are.

Quod bellum firmavit, pax ficta non auferat.

Neque benedictione, neque maledictione movetur, sicut angelus Domini.

People attack the greatest of the Christian virtues, which is the love of truth.

If that is the meaning of the signature, perhaps I may be permitted to explain it so that there will be nothing equivocal about it: because there are people who think that to sign is a mark of assent.

If the registrar did not sign, the decree would be invalid; if the Bull were not signed it would be valid; it is therefore not . . .

'But you may be mistaken?' I swear that I believe that I may have made a mistake; but I do not swear that I believe that I have made a mistake.

We are not guilty for not believing and we shall be guilty if we swear without believing . . . fine questions; it . . .

I am sorry to have to say this: I am simply giving an account.

With Escobar, it gives them the upper hand; but they do not see it in that way: and show their annoyance at finding themselves between God and the Pope . . .   (945)

824. It is a good thing that they perpetrate injustices for fear that it may appear that the Molinists have acted with justice; and so they should not be spared.—They are capable of committing them.   (936)

825. Annat. He plays the part of the disciple without ignorance, and of the master without presumption.   (946 *bis*)

826. In Paul IV's bull, *Cum ex apostolatus officio*, published in 1558:

'We order, legislate, decree, define that all and each of those who find that they have been inveigled or have fallen into heresy or schism, whatever their quality or condition, whether laymen, ecclesiastics, priests, bishops, archbishops, patriarchs, primates, cardinals, counts, marquesses, dukes, kings and emperors, beyond the sentences and punishments mentioned above, should by that fact alone, without any ministry of right or fact, be deprived in all and for all, in perpetuity, of their orders, sees, benefices, offices, kingdoms, empires, and never be permitted to return to them.

'Let us leave [such people] to the discretion of the secular power to be punished, not granting any other grace to those who, by true repentance, renounce their errors, except that by the benevolence and clemency of the Holy See, they may be considered fit to be enclosed in a monastery there to do perpetual penance on bread and water; but that they should remain for ever deprived of all dignities, orders, prelacies, counties, duchies, kingdoms. And that those who conceal and defend them, will by that very act be judged excommunicate and infamous, deprived of all kingdoms, duchies, goods and possessions, which will belong by right and property to those who are the first to seize them.

'*Si hominem excommunicatum interfecerunt, non eos homicidas reputamus, quod adversus excomminicator zelo catholicae ardentes aliquem eorum trucidasse contigerit*'. 23, *qu*. 5. of Urban II.[1]   (951)

827. After being thoroughly harassed, they will send you back home.

Appeals are just as weak a means of consolation as abuses because when a great source of abuse has been removed . . . besides the fact that the majority will not have the means to come from the depths of Périgord or Anjou to plead before the Parliament of Paris . . . besides the fact that they will always have the decrees of the Council to forbid these appeals as abuses.

For though they cannot obtain what they have asked for, the fact that they have asked for it will quickly reveal their power, which is all the greater because it has prompted them to ask for something so unjust that it was evident that they would not obtain it.

That only helps us to arrive at a better understanding of their intention and the necessity of not authorising by registration the Bull which they wish to use as a basis for the new establishment. It is not a question of a simple Bull, but of a basis.

On leaving the palace . . .

[1] Those men shall not be accounted guilty of murder who in the zeal of their Catholic faith against those who have been excommunicated kill some of them.

121. The Pope forbids the king to marry his children without his consent, 1294.

Scire te volumus, 124, 1302.

The puerile ...   (950)

828. The Jansenists resemble the heretics by their zeal for moral reform; but you resemble them by what is bad in them.   (887)

829. Those who have written it in Latin speak French. Since the evil lay in putting it into French, it was essential to condemn them.

There is only one heresy which is explained differently in the schools and in the world.   (933)

830. 3. Unless they abandon probability, their good precepts are as far from being holy as their bad, because the authority behind them is human; and so, if they are more righteous they will be more reasonable, but not holier. They cling to the wild stalk on to which they have been grafted.

If what I say does not help to enlighten you, it will help to enlighten the people.

If they are silent, the stones will speak.

Silence is the greatest of persecutions: the saints have never been silent. It is true that you have to have a vocation, but it is not from the decrees of the Council that you will learn whether you have been called; it is from the necessity of speaking. Now, after Rome had spoken, when it was thought that she had condemned the truth, and that they had written it; and that the books which said the opposite were censured, it is necessary to shout all the louder because one has been censured unjustly and because they are trying to stifle one's voice by force, until a Pope arrives on the scene who will listen to both parties and consult antiquity in order to ensure that justice is done.

Therefore good popes will still find the Church in a state of uproar.

The Inquisition and the Society—the two scourges of truth.

Why do you not accuse them of Arianism? For they have said that Jesus Christ is God: perhaps they do not mean it in the natural sense, but in the same way that it is said, *Dii estis.*

372

If my letters are condemned in Rome, what I condemn in them will be condemned in heaven.

Ad tuum, Domine Jesu, tribunal appello.

You yourselves are liable to corruption.

When I found myself condemned, I was afraid that I had written badly, but the example of so much pious writing leads me to the opposite conclusion. It is not permissible to write well!

So corrupt is the Inquisition, or so ignorant!

'It is better to obey God than men.'

I fear nothing; I hope for nothing. The bishops are not like that. Port-Royal is afraid, and it is a bad policy to separate them because they will no longer be afraid and will make themselves feared.

I am not afraid of your censures: they are mere words unless they are in conformity with tradition.

Do you censure everything? What! Even my respect? No. Then tell me what, or you will achieve nothing unless you point out what is evil, and explain why it is evil. And that is what they will have great difficulty in doing.

Probability. They have given an amusing explanation of certainty; for after demonstrating that all their paths are certain, they no longer describe as certain the one that leads to heaven, without any danger of not reaching it, but the one that gets us to heaven without any danger of diverging from that path. (920)

831. *Pro.* Those who love the Church bewail the fact that morals are becoming corrupt; but at least the laws remain. But morals corrupt the law: the model is ruined.   (894)

832. The casuists leave the decision to a corrupt reason and the choice of solution to a corrupt will, with the result that everything that is corrupt in the nature of man will play its part in his conduct.   (907)

833. What ruins comparisons between what happened in the Church in earlier times and what happens today is that we usually regard St. Athanasius, St.Teresa and the rest as being crowned with glory and years, judged before us as though they were gods. At present when time has thrown light on such

matters, it does appear like that. But at the time when they persecuted him, the great saint was simply a man named Athanasius; and St. Teresa a woman. 'Elias was a man like ourselves and subject to the same passions as ourselves,' said St. [James] in order to disabuse Christians of the false idea which makes us reject the example of the saints as being completely beyond our reach. 'They were saints,' we say; 'they were not like us.' What happened then at the time? St. Athanasius was a man named Athanasius who was accused of several crimes, condemned by this or that council for such and such a crime; all the bishops assented and finally the Pope himself. What did people say to those who resisted? That they were disturbers of the peace, that they were schismatics, etc.

Zeal, light. Four kinds of person: those who possess zeal without knowledge, knowledge without zeal, neither knowledge nor zeal, and zeal and knowledge. The first three condemned him; the last absolved him, were excommunicated by the Church, and nevertheless saved the Church. (868)

834. That they treated them as humanely as possible in order to preserve a middle course between love and truth, and the duty of charity.

That piety does not consist in never rising up against one's brothers: it would be very easy, etc. It is a form of false piety to keep the peace at the expense of truth; it is also a form of false zeal to preserve truth by offending against charity. Therefore they made no complaint.

Their precepts have their time and place.

Their vanity tends to arise from their errors.

They resemble the Jews by their faults and the martyrs by their torments.

Yet they do not repudiate any of them ... They only had to take an extract and repudiate it.—*Sanctificat proelium*—M. Bourseys. At any rate, they cannot deny that he would be opposed to condemnation. (930)

835. Just as the only object of peace in States is to safeguard the possessions of their peoples, so the only object of peace in the Church is to safeguard truth which is her good, and the treasure

where her heart is. And just as it would be contrary to the aims of peace to allow an enemy to penetrate into a State in order to plunder it without resisting him for fear of causing a disturbance (for since peace is only just and useful for the protection of possessions, so it becomes unjust and pernicious when it permits their loss, and war which can defend them becomes just and necessary); so, in the Church, when the enemies of the Faith offend against truth by trying to tear it out of the hearts of the faithful in order to set up error in its place, would it be a service to the Church or a betrayal of her to remain at peace in such circumstances? And is it not evident that, as it is a crime to disturb the peace where truth reigns, it is also a crime to remain at peace when truth is being attacked? There is therefore a time when peace is just and another when it is unjust. It is written that 'there is a time for peace and a time for war'; it is the interests of truth which distinguish the two. But there is not a time for truth and a time for error; on the contrary, it is written that 'the truth of God remains for ever'; and that is why Jesus Christ, who said that he had come to bring peace also said that he had come to bring the sword; but he did not say that he had come to bring truth and falsehood. Truth is therefore the first rule and the final end of things. (949)

836. *On confession and absolution without signs of repentance.* God looks only at the inner man: the Church can only judge by externals. God gives absolution as soon as he sees repentance in our heart; the Church when it is apparent from our actions. God will make a church pure within, which by its interior and purely spiritual holiness confounds the interior impiety of the proud and the Pharisees; and the Church will create an assembly of men whose morality is outwardly so pure that it confounds the morality of the heathen. If there are hypocrites who are not so well disguised that she does not fail to perceive their poison, she suffers them: for though they are not yet accepted by God, whom they cannot deceive, they are accepted by men whom they do deceive. And so she is not dishonoured by their behaviour which appears saintly.

But you want the Church to judge neither by the interior,

because it belongs to God, nor by the exterior because God only pays attention to the interior; and so, by depriving her of any choice in the matter, you keep in the Church the most licentious of men and those who do her such dishonour that the synagogues of the Jews and [the] sects of the philosophers would have rejected them as unworthy and detested them as impious.

(905)

837. The Jesuits. The Jesuits wanted to join God to the world and have only earned the contempt of God and the world. For in the eyes of conscience this is obvious; and in the eyes of the world, they are no good at plotting. They are powerful, as I have often observed, but only in comparison with the other religious orders. They will have sufficient authority to get a chapel built and obtain a place at a jubilee, but not to be able to capture episcopal sees, or hand out livings. On their own admission, their position as monks living in the world is a silly one (P. Brisacier, *Bénédictins*). Yet . . . you yield to people who are stronger than yourselves, and you use all your petty authority to oppress those who are less worldly wise than yourselves.

(935)

838. . . . So that if it is true, on the one hand, that a handful of lay monks and a few corrupt casuists, who are not members of the hierarchy, have been involved in this sort of trickery, it is a definite fact, on the other, that the true pastors of the Church, who are the veritable custodians of the divine word, have preserved it immutably against those who have set out to ruin it.

The faithful therefore have no excuse for following those examples of doctrinal laxity, which only reach them through the unfamiliar hands of the casuists, instead of the sound doctrine which comes to them through the paternal hands of their own pastors.

And unbelievers and heretics have no grounds for claiming that these abuses are a sign of the weakening of the providence of God in his Church, because the Church, properly speaking, is in the body of the hierarchy, and so far from our being entitled to assume from the present state of affairs that God

376

has abandoned it to corruption, it has never been more apparent than it is today that God is openly protecting it against corruption.

For if a few of these men, who through an extraordinary vocation professed to turn their backs on the world and don the habit of a religious to live in a more perfect state than the common run of Christians, have indulged in extravagances which arouse a feeling of horror in the ordinary Christian and become for us what the false prophets were for the Jews, it is a private and personal misfortune which is certainly to be deplored, but from which we can draw no general conclusion about God's solicitude for his Church; because all these things were clearly foretold, and because it was announced long ago that temptations of this nature would occur among people of this kind, that, when we are properly instructed, we see in it a sign of God's guidance rather than of his forsaking us.   (889)

839. We must make it clear to heretics, who rely on the teaching of the Jesuits, that it is not the teaching of the Church . . . the doctrine of the Church; and that our divisions do not affect our unity.   (891)

840. It is a matter of indifference to the heart of man whether he believes that there are three or four persons in the Trinity; but not, etc. Whence it comes that they grow hot under the collar when arguing in favour of one and not the other.

It is a good thing to do one; but we must not neglect the other. The same God who says to us, etc.

And thus anyone who believes one and not the other, does not believe it because God has said it, but because his covetousness does not deny it and he is very glad to concur, and therefore to have the testimony of his conscience without any trouble, which tells him . . . But it is a false testimony.   (940)

841. As the two main interests of the Church are safeguarding the faith of her people and the conversion of heretics, we are overwhelmed with grief at the sight of the factions which today are being formed for the express purpose of introducing the errors most calculated to prevent heretics from ever entering our communion, and to infect with a deadly corruption those devout and Catholic people who have remained with us. The campaign which today is being waged openly against the truths of religion, particularly those which are the most important for salvation, not only fills us with disgust, but also with fear and trembling because, apart from the feeling that every Christian ought to have about the spread of such disorders, we have the additional obligation to put a stop to them and to use the authority that God has given us to ensure that the peoples whom he has entrusted to us, etc.   (952)

842. B. You are ignorant of the prophecies if you did not know that all these things were bound to happen: princes, prophets, pope, and even priests; and yet the Church must survive.

By the grace of God we have not yet reached this point. Woe to these priests! But we hope that God will have mercy on us and that we shall not come to such a pass ourselves.

I. St. Peter, chap. II: false prophets of the past, the types of those to come.   (888)

843. But is it *probable* that *probability* will offer reassurance?

Difference between peace of mind and moral certainty. Nothing gives so much assurance as truth; nothing is so conducive to peace as the genuine search for truth.   (908)

844. All their casuists put together cannot bring reassurance to a conscience which has fallen into error, and that is why it is important to choose good guides.

Thus, they will be doubly guilty: for having followed paths which they should not have followed, and for listening to doctors to whom they should not have listened.   (909)

845. If St. Augustine reappeared today and had as little authority as his defenders, he would achieve nothing. God guided his Church well by sending him earlier, and investing him with the proper degree of authority.   (869)

846. We must not judge the Pope's position by a few words from the Fathers (as the Greeks said at one of the councils,— important rules), but by the actions of the Church and the Fathers, and by the canons.

Duo aut tres in unum. Unity and plurality: error to exclude one of the two, as those papists do who exclude plurality, or the Huguenots who exclude unity.   (874)

847. The Pope occupies the first place. What other man is known to everybody? What other is recognised by all as having power to speak for the whole body because he holds the main branch which spreads everywhere?

How easy it would have been for it to degenerate into tyranny! That is why Jesus Christ gave them the precept: *Vos autem non sic.*   (872).

848. *Church, Pope, Unity, Plurality.* When we consider the Church as a unity the Pope, who is its head, is everything. When we consider it as plurality, the Pope is only a part. The Fathers sometimes regarded it from one point of view, sometimes from the other; and so they spoke of the Pope with different voices. (St. Cyprian: *Sacerdos Dei.*) But by establishing one of these two truths, they did not rule out the other. Plurality, which is not reduced to unity, is a form of confusion; unity which is not dependent on plurality is tyranny.

There is hardly a country left except France where it is permissible to say that the Council is above the Pope.   (871)

849. It is idle for the Church to use words like anathemas, heresies, etc.: people use them against her.   (896)

850. The Pope hates and fears scholars who have not taken a vow of obedience to him.   (873)

851. *Popes.* Kings dispose of their empires; but the Popes cannot dispose of theirs.   (877)

852. *P. P. Popes.* God does not perform miracles in the ordinary conduct of his Church. It would be a strange one if infallibility belonged to one man; but it appears so natural for it to reside in the multitude because the hand of God is hidden behind natural events, as in all his other works.   (876)

853. Bind and unloose. God did not wish to give absolution without the Church. Since she plays a part in the offence, he wishes her to play a part in its forgiveness. He associates her with this power as kings do their parliaments; but if she gives absolution or binds without God, she is no longer the Church: so it is with parliament; for though the king may have pardoned a man, it must be ratified; yet if parliament ratifies without the king, or if it refuses to ratify at the king's command, it is no longer the king's parliament, but a body in revolt. (870)

854. Would the Pope be dishonoured if he derived his light from God and tradition? And should we not dishonour him if we separated him from this holy union, etc. (875)

855. Tertullian: *nunquam Ecclesia reformabitur.* (890)

856. The Church teaches and God inspires, both of them infallibly.

The action of the Church only serves to prepare us for grace or damnation. What she does is sufficient to condemn, not to inspire. (881)

857. Fine state of the Church when she is no longer sustained by anything except God. (861)

858. Venice. What advantage will you derive from it, except that princes need it, and their peoples have a horror of it? If they had asked you, and if, in order to secure it, they had begged for assistance from Christian princes, you could have made the search effective. But that for a period of fifty years all the princes applied themselves to it without results, and that it required such a pressing need to obtain it. . . . (954)

859. They cannot have perpetuity and they seek universality; and on that account they reduce the whole Church to a state of corruption, so that they may be taken for saints. (898)

860. *Pope.* There is a contradiction; for on the one hand they say that one must follow tradition and dare not repudiate it; and on the other, they will say whatever suits them. People will always believe the former because not to believe it would be against their own interests. (944)

861. *Probability.* The ardour of the saints in seeking truth was a waste of time if the probable is certain. The fear of the saints who always followed the most reliable guide (St. Teresa having always followed the advice of her confessor). (917)

862. *Casuists.* A substantial almsgiving, a reasonable penance.

Although we cannot point out the righteous man, we can see clearly who is not righteous. It is amusing of the casuists to think that they can interpret it in the way they do.

People who grow used to speaking badly and thinking badly.

The fact that there are so many of them, far from being a sign of perfection, is a sign of the opposite.

The humility of one man is responsible for the pride of many. (931)

863. Truth has become so obscured in these days, and falsehood so firmly established, that unless we loved truth, we should be unable to recognise it. (864)

864. Two kinds of people equate such things as feast days and working days, Christians and priests, the different sins, etc. This leads some of them to the conclusion that what is wrong for priests is also wrong for other Christians; others to the conclusion that what is not wrong for Christians is permissible for priests. (866)

865. All the religions and sects of the world have had natural reason for their guide. Christians alone have been compelled to take their rules from outside themselves and to find out about those which Jesus Christ left to the ancients to be handed on to the faithful. This compulsion wearies the good Fathers. Like other people they want freedom to follow their own imagination. In vain we cry out to them, as the prophets in earlier times said to the Jews: 'Go to the heart of the Church; find out about the laws that the ancients left behind them, and follow these paths.' They replied like the Jews: 'We will not walk in them; but we will follow the thoughts of our hearts'; and they said: 'We will be like the other nations.' (903)

866. *Perpetuity.* Is your character founded on Escobar?

Perhaps you have reasons for not condemning them: it is enough for you to understand that I am addressing you. (—)

867. *Perpetuity.* Molina: novelty. (844 *bis*)

868. *Probability.* They have some true principles; but they abuse them. Now, the abuse of truths ought to be as severely punished as the introduction of falsehood.

As though there were two hells, one for sins against charity, the other for sins against justice! (916)

869. They are the effects of the sins of the peoples and the Jesuits: the great desire for flattery; the Jesuits wished to be popular with the great. They all deserved to be abandoned to the spirit of falsehood, some in order to deceive, others in order to be deceived. They were greedy, ambitious, sensual: *Coacervabunt sibi magistros.* Worthy disciples of such masters, *digni sunt,* they have sought flatterers and have found them. (919)

870. Sudden death is the one thing of which they are afraid, and that is why confessors are always to be found at the homes of the great. (216)

5. NOTES FOR 'AN ACCOUNT OF THE MIRACLE PERFORMED ON MLLE PÉRIER'

871. The points that I want to put to M. l'abbé de Saint-Cyran are the following. But, as I have not kept a copy of them, I shall have to ask him to be good enough to return the manuscript with his replies.[1]

1. Whether, for an effect to be miraculous, it is necessary that it should be beyond the power of men, devils, angels and the whole of created nature.

Theologians maintain that miracles are supernatural either in substance, quoad substantiam, *like the penetration of two bodies, or the presence of the same body in two places and at the same time; or that they are supernatural in the manner in which they are produced* quoad modum: *as, for example, when they are produced by means which do not possess any natural properties capable of producing them as, for example, when J. C. healed the eyes of the blind man with mud and the mother-in-law of Peter by bending over her, or the woman suffering from a flux by touching the hem of his garment. . . . And the majority of the miracles which He does in the Gospels are of the second kind. Such, too, is the curing of a fever or other disease which is done instantaneously,*

---

[1] Saint-Cyran's replies are given in italics. *Tr.*

or more perfectly than nature could do it, by touching a relic or by invoking the name of God, so that the view of the man who puts forward these difficulties is correct and in conformity with the views of all theologians, even those of the present day.

2. Whether it is not sufficient that it should be beyond the natural properties of the means employed; my idea being that every effect is miraculous (when it) exceeds the natural properties of the means used. Thus, I call miraculous the healing of a sick person by touching a holy relic, the curing of a madman by invoking the name of Jesus, etc., because these effects exceed the natural power of the words with which we invoke God and the natural properties of a relic [which] cannot heal sick people and drive away devils. But I do not call it miraculous to drive out devils by the arts of the devil; because when one employs the arts of the devil in order to drive out the devil, the effect does not exceed the natural properties of the means used; and so it appeared to me that the true definition of miracles is the one that I have just given.

What the devil is capable of doing is no more miraculous than what can be done by an animal, though a man could not do it by himself.

3. Whether St. Thomas is not opposed to this definition, and whether it is not his view that an effect, to be miraculous, must exceed the powers of the whole of created nature.

St. Thomas holds the same views as other theologians, though he divides the miracles of the second kind into two classes: miracles quoad subjectum, *and miracles* quoad ordinem naturae. *He says that the first are those which nature could produce absolutely, but not in such a subject, as she can produce life, but not in a dead body; and that the second are those which she can produce in a subject, but not by such means and with such promptness, as, for example, healing in a moment and simply by touch a fever or a disease, which are not in themselves incurable.*

4. Whether known, declared and recognised heretics can perform true miracles to confirm error.

True miracles can never be performed by anybody, whether Catholic or heretic, saint or evil-doer, in such a way as to confirm an error because it would mean that God approved and set his seal on an error as a false witness, or rather as false judge; that is a definite fact.

5. Whether known and declared heretics can perform miracles like the curing of illnesses which are not mortal; for example, whether they can cure a fever to confirm an erroneous proposition: according to Father Lingendes' teaching they can.

[*No reply to this question.*]

6. Whether known and declared heretics can perform miracles which are beyond the powers of created nature by invoking the name of God and by a holy relic.

They can in order to confirm a truth, and history provides us with examples of it.

7. Whether undeclared heretics, who have not left the Church, but who have nevertheless fallen into error and who have not declared themselves against the Church so that it will be easier for them to seduce the faithful and strengthen their party, can by invoking the name of Jesus or by a holy relic perform miracles which are beyond the powers of nature, or even whether they can perform those which are merely beyond the powers of man such as curing on the spot illnesses which are not incurable.

Undeclared heretics have no greater power of working miracles than declared heretics because nothing is hidden from God, who is the sole author and worker of miracles, whatever their kind, provided that they are true miracles.

8. Whether miracles produced by invoking the name of God or by the introduction of divine things, are not the signs of the true Church, and whether all Catholics have not maintained the affirmative against heretics.

All Catholics agree and first and foremost Jesuit writers. We need only to read Bellarmine. Even when heretics have performed miracles, which has happened in earlier times though only on rare occasions, these miracles were signs of the Church because they were only performed in order to confirm the truth that the Church teaches, and not the error of the heretics.

9. Whether heretics have ever performed miracles, and if so of what kind.

There are very few which are well attested; but those of which people speak are miraculous only quoad modum, *that is to say, natural effects produced miraculously and in a manner which is outside the natural order.*

10. Whether the man in the Gospels who drove out devils in
the name of Jesus Christ and of whom Jesus Christ said 'he who
is not against us is for us', was the friend or enemy of Jesus
Christ, and what interpreters of the Gospels have to say about
him. I am asking this because Father Lingendes taught that the
man was opposed to Jesus Christ.

*There is sufficient evidence in the Gospels to show that he was not
opposed to Jesus Christ; the Fathers agree on this, and almost all the
Jesuit writers.*

11. Whether Antichrist will work miracles in the name of Jesus
Christ or in his own name.

*As he will not come in the name of Jesus Christ but, according to the
Gospels, in his own name, so he will not perform miracles in the name of
Jesus Christ, but in his own name and in opposition to Jesus Christ in
order to destroy the faith and his Church; for this reason they will not be
true miracles.*

12. Whether the oracles were miraculous.

*The miracles of the heathen and of idols were no more miraculous
than the manifestations of devils and magicians.* (App. xiii)

872. The second miracle may pre-suppose the first; the first cannot pre-suppose the second. (810)

873. *Beginning.* Miracles set the seal on doctrine, and doctrine
sets the seal on miracles.

There are true and false miracles. We need a sign to distinguish between them; otherwise they would be useless. Now,
they are not useless: on the contrary, they are one of the foundations of faith. But the rule that he gives us must be such that it
does not destroy the proof provided by true miracles, which is
the principal aim of miracles.

Moses has given two: that the prophecy is not fulfilled,
Deut., xviii, and that they do not lead to idolatry, Deut., xiii;
and Jesus Christ one.

If doctrine determines miracles, miracles are useless for doctrine. If miracles determine . . .

Objection to the rule. The times have changed. One rule in
Moses' time, another in our own. (803)

874. *Reasons why people do not believe.*

Joh., XII, 37. *Cum autem tanta signa fecisset, non credebant in eum, ut sermo Isaiae impleretur. Excaecavit,* etc.

Haec dixit Isaias, quando vidit glorium ejus et locutus est de eo.

'*Judaei signa petunt et Greci sapientiam quaerunt, nos autem Jesus crucifixum.*' *Sed plenum signis, sed plenum sapientia; vos autem Christum non cruxifixum et religionem sine miraculis et sine sapientia.*[1]

The reason why people do not believe true miracles is their lack of charity. Joh.: *Sed non creditis, quia non estis ex ovibus.*[2]

The reason why they believe false miracles is lack of charity. I. Thess. II.

Foundation stone of religion. It is miracles. What then? Does God speak against miracles, against the foundation stone of the faith that we have in him? If there is a God, it is necessary that God's faith should be on earth. Now the miracles of Jesus Christ were not foretold by Antichrist, but the miracles of Antichrist were foretold by Jesus Christ; and so, if Jesus Christ was not the Messiah, he would have led us into error; but Antichrist cannot very well lead us into error. When Jesus Christ foretold the miracles of Antichrist, did he think that he was destroying faith in his own miracles?

Moses foretold Jesus Christ and ordered people to follow him; Jesus Christ foretold Antichrist and forbade people to follow him.

It was impossible, in the time of Moses, for people to have reservations about their belief in Antichrist because he was unknown to them; but it is very easy in the time of Antichrist to believe in Jesus Christ who is already known to us.

There is no reason for believing in Antichrist which is not a reason for believing in Jesus Christ; but there are reasons for

[1] Such great miracles he did in their presence, and still they did not believe in him; this was in fulfilment of the words spoken by the prophet Isaias . . . He has blinded their eyes, etc.

Isaias said this, as one who had seen his glory; it was of him that he spoke.

'Here are the Jews asking for signs and wonders, here are the Greeks intent on their philosophy; but what we preach is Christ crucified' (I Cor. 22-23). But full of signs, but full of wisdom; and you preach a Christ who was not crucified and a religion without miracles or a philosophy (Pascal).

[2] And still you will not believe me; that is because you are no sheep of mine.

believing in Jesus Christ which are not reasons for believing in
the other.   (826)
875. I assume that people believe in miracles. You corrupt religion either in favour of your friends, or in opposition to your
enemies. You deal with it according to your own pleasure.

(855)
876. If there were no false miracles, there would be certainty.

If there were no test for distinguishing between true and
false, miracles would be useless, and there would be no grounds
for belief.

Now there is, humanly speaking, no human certainty, except reason.   (823)
877. Judges, XII, 23: 'If the Lord meant us harm . . . he would
not have shewn us this marvellous sight, nor told us what is to
befall.'

Ezechias. Sennacherib.

Jeremias. Hanarias, a false prophet, dies during the seventh
month.

II Mach., III: The temple on the point of being sacked,
miraculously preserved.—II Mach., XV.

III Kings, XVII: The widow to Elias who had raised her
child from the dead: 'This proves to me that thou art God's servant indeed, and his promise on thy lips is true.'

III Kings, XVIII: Elias with the prophets of Baal.

Never in a dispute about the true God, about the truth of
religion, has a miracle been performed in support of error and
not of truth.   (827)
878. This is not the home of truth; truth wanders unrecognised
among men. God has hidden it behind a veil which prevents it
from being recognised by those who do not hear its voice. The
way is open to blasphemy, even against those truths which at
any rate are perfectly plain. If the truths of the Gospel are proclaimed, so too are things which are contrary to them, and the
questions at issue are obscured, with the result that people cannot distinguish between them. And they ask: 'What have you
got that we should believe you rather than the others? What
proof can you give? You have only words, and so have we. If

you had miracles, well and good!' It is true that teaching must
be supported by miracles which are misused so that people can
blaspheme against doctrine. And if miracles occur, people
say that without doctrine miracles are not enough; and
that is another truth which is used for blaspheming against
miracles.

Jesus Christ healed the man who was born blind, and performed a large number of miracles on the sabbath, which
blinded the eyes of the Pharisees who said that the miracles
must be judged by his teaching.

'We know for certain that God spoke to Moses; we know
nothing of this man, or whence he comes.' What is wonderful is
that you do not know where he comes from; and yet he performs such miracles.

Jesus Christ did not speak against God or against Moses.

Antichrist and the false prophets, who were foretold in both
the Old and the New Testaments, will speak openly against
God and against Jesus Christ. Who is not against . . . God
would not permit anyone who was a secret enemy to work
miracles in public.

Never in a public debate, in which both parties claim to be
on the side of God, Jesus Christ and the Church, are miracles
on the side of false Christians, or is the other side without
miracles?

'He must be possessed.' John, x, 21. And the others said:
'Has a devil power to open blind men's eyes?'

The proofs which Jesus Christ and the Apostles drew from
Scripture are not conclusive: for they simply tell us that Moses
said that a prophet would come, but this does not prove that
he was the prophet, and that is the crux of the matter. These
passages therefore only serve to show that one is not against
Scripture and that there is no conflict, but not that there is
agreement. Now, that is sufficient—the exclusion of conflict,
with miracles.

God and men are bound by mutual obligations. We must be
forgiven the word. *Quod debui?* 'Make a trial of me,' said God in
Isaias.

God must fulfil his promises, etc.

Men owe it to God to accept the religion that he gave them. God owes it to men not to lead them into error. Now, they would be led into error if the miracle-workers preached a doctrine which did not appear obviously false by the light of common sense, and if one great miracle-worker had not already warned them against believing in them.

Thus if there were division in the Church and if the Arians, for example, who claimed like Catholics to take their stand on Scripture, had performed miracles and the Catholics had not, people would have been led into error.

For just as a man who proclaims the secrets of God to us is not worthy of credence on his private authority, and on this account the unbelievers doubt them, so if a man who in order to prove that he is in contact with God, raises the dead, foretells the future, moves the seas, cures the sick, there is none among the unbelievers who does not yield to him, and the unbelief of Pharaoh and the Pharisees is the result of a supernatural hardening of the heart.

There is therefore no difficulty when we find miracles and sound doctrine in the same camp. But when we find miracles and suspect doctrine in the same camp, we must make up our minds which is the clearer. Jesus Christ was suspect.

Bar-Jesus blinded. The power of God overwhelms that of his enemies.

The Jewish exorcists defeated by the devils saying: 'I know Jesus and Paul, but who are you?'

Miracles are for the sake of the doctrine, and not the doctrine for the sake of the miracles.

If the miracles are true, will all doctrine be accepted? No. That will never happen. *Si angelus . . .*

Rule: We must judge the doctrine by the miracles; we must judge the miracles by the doctrine. That is true and not a contradiction.

For we must distinguish between the times.

How pleased you are to know the general rules because you think that this will enable you to sow the seeds of disquiet and ruin everything! We shall prevent you, Father: truth is one and indivisible.

God's duty to us makes it impossible that a man who conceals his subversive doctrines and declares himself in agreement with the teaching of the Church, should perform miracles which would have the effect of secretly instilling a false and insidious teaching: such things cannot happen.

And still less that God, who knows the hearts of men, should work miracles in support of such a man. (843)

879. Jesus Christ says that the Scriptures bear witness to him, but he does not show in what manner.

Even the prophecies could not prove the claims of Jesus Christ during his lifetime; and so, one would not have been guilty for not believing in him before his death, if the miracles had not been sufficient without the teaching. Now those who did not believe in him, while he was still alive, were sinners, as he himself says, and had no excuse. Therefore, it was necessary for them to be given a demonstration which they refused to accept. Now they did not have the Scriptures, but only the miracles; therefore they were sufficient when the teaching did not conflict with them, and they should have believed in them.

John, VII, 40. *Controversy among the Jews, as among Christians today.* Some believed in Jesus Christ; others did not believe because of the prophecies which said that he would be born at Bethlehem. They should have taken care to find out whether he was born there or not. For his miracles were convincing; they should have looked into the supposed contradictions between his teaching and Scripture; and the obscurity was not an excuse, but blinded them. Thus, those who refuse to believe in miracles today on account of some supposed and fanciful contradiction, cannot be excused.

The Pharisees said to people who believed in him on the strength of the miracles: 'This people is accursed who do not know the law.' But was there a prince or a Pharisee who believed in him? Nicodemus answered: 'Does our law judge a man before hearing him [and still more, such a man who works such miracles].' (829)

880. There is a great difference between not being for Jesus
Christ and saying so, and not being for Jesus Christ and pretending to be. Some can work miracles and not others; because
it is evident that some are against the truth and not others; and
so the miracles are plainer.   (836)

881. It is so obvious that we must love only one God that it
does not take miracles to prove it.   (837)

882. There is a great difference between tempting people and
leading them into error. God tempts, but he does not lead us
into error. To tempt is to provide occasions when, without being under any compulsion, if we do not love God, we shall perform a certain action. To lead into error is to place a man
under the necessity of accepting and following something false.
                                                                (821)

883. Jesus Christ proved that he was the Messiah not by verify-
ing his teaching against Scripture and the prophecies, but always by his miracles.

He proved that he could forgive sins by performing a
miracle.

Rejoice not in your miracles, said Jesus Christ, but rejoice
because your names are written in heaven.

If they do not believe Moses, they will not believe one who
has risen from the dead.

Nicodemus recognised from his miracles that his teaching
was from God: *Scimus quia venisti a Deo magister; nemo enim potest
haec signa facere quae tu facis nisi Deus fuerit cum illo.*[1]

He did not judge the miracles by the teaching, but the
teaching by the miracles.

The Jews had a doctrine of God, as we have one of Jesus
Christ, which was confirmed by miracles; with a prohibition
against believing all the miracle-workers and, what is more,
an order to refer to the high priests and submit to their view.

And so they had precisely the same reasons for not believing
in their prophets as we have for refusing to believe in miracle-
workers.

---

[1] We know that thou hast come from God to teach us; no one, unless
God were with him, could do the miracles which thou doest (John III, 2).

And yet they were greatly to blame for refusing to believe the prophets on the strength of their miracles, and Jesus Christ; and would not have been to blame if they had not seen the miracles: *Nisi fecissem . . . peccatum non haberent.*[1] Therefore all belief is based on miracles.

Prophecy is not described as miraculous: just as St. John speaks of the first miracle at Cana, then of what Jesus Christ said to the woman of Samaria which revealed her hidden life, and then healed the son of a ruler, and St. John called it 'the second sign'.   (808)

884. The miracles and truth are necessary because it is essential to convince the whole man, body and soul.   (806)

885. *Si tu est Christus, dic nobis.*

Opera quae ego facio in nomine patris mei, haec testimonium per-hibent de me. Sed vos non creditis quia non estis ex ovibus meis. Oves mei vocem meam audiunt.

Joh., VI, 30: *Quod ergo tu facis signum ut videamus et credamus tibi?—Non dicunt: Quam doctrinam praedicas?*

Nemo potest facere signa quae tu facis nisi Deus fuerit cum eo.

II Mach., XIV, 15: *Deus qui signis evidentibus suam portionem protegit.*

Volumus signum videre de caelo, tentantes eum. Luke, XI, 16.

Generatio prava signum quaerit; et non dabitur.

Et ingemiscens ait: Quid generatio ista signum quaerit. Mark, VIII, 12. It demanded a sign with bad intentions.

Et non poterat facere. And nevertheless he promised them the sign of Jonas, the great and incomparable sign of his resurrection. *Nisi videritis signa, non creditis.* He does not blame them for not believing without miracles, but for not believing without actually seeing them for themselves.

The Antichrist *in signis mendacibus,* said St. Paul.

Secundum operationem Satanae, in seductione iis qui pereunt eo quod charitatem veritatis non receperunt ut salvi fierent, ideo mittet illis Deus optationes erroris ut credant mendacio.

As in a passage of Moses: *tentat enim vos Deus, utrum diligatis eum.*

---

[1] If I had not done . . . they would not have been in fault (John xv, 24).

Ecce prae dixi vobis: vos ergo videte.[1]   (842)

886. In the Old Testament when someone turns you away from
God. In the New when someone turns you away from Jesus
Christ.

Those are the cases for rejecting belief in particular miracles.
There should be no others.

Does it follow from this that they would have the right to
reject all the prophets who came to them? No. They would
have committed a sin by not rejecting those who denied God,
and would have committed a sin by rejecting those who did not
deny God.

First of all, therefore, when we see a miracle we must either
admit it, or there must be some special ground for rejecting it.
We must see whether it is a denial of God, or Jesus Christ, or
the Church.   (835)

887. 'Let my actions convince you where I cannot.' He refers
to his miracles as though they were more powerful.

---

[1] If thou art the Christ, tell us (Luke XXII, 66).

All that I do in my Father's name bears me testimony, and still you will
not believe me; that is because you are no sheep of mine. My sheep listen
to my voice (John X, 26-27).

Why then, what miracle canst thou do? We must see it before we trust
thee; what canst thou effect? (John VI, 30). They do not say: What is your
teaching (Pascal).

No one, unless God were with him, could do the miracles which thou
doest (John III, 2).

Was he not wont to protect them with signal marks of his favour (II
Mach., XIV, 15).

While others, to put him to the test, would have him shew a sign out of
heaven.

The generation that asks for a sign is a wicked and unfaithful generation
(Matt. XII, 39).

And he sighed deeply in his spirit, and said, Why does this generation
ask for a sign? (Mark VIII, 12).

Nor could he do any wonderful works there (Mark VI, 5).

If you do not see miracles you do not believe.

He will come, when he comes, with all Satan's influence to aid him;
there will be no lack of power, of counterfeit signs and wonders; and his
wickedness will deceive the souls that are doomed, to punish them for refusing that fellowship in the truth which would have saved them (II Thess.,
II, 9).

God is putting thee to the proof, to see whether he has the love of thy
whole soul or not (Deut. XIII, 2).

Mark well, I have given you warning of it (Matt. XXIV, 26).

The Jews, as well as Christians, had been told that they must not always believe the prophets; but nevertheless the Scribes and Pharisees laid great emphasis on his miracles and tried to show that they were false, or were the work of the devil: because once they had admitted that they were from God they would have been compelled to believe.

Today, there is no need to draw this distinction. It is, however, very easy to do: those who do not deny either God or Jesus Christ, do not perform miracles which are not certain. *Nemo facit virtutem in nomine meo, et cito possit de me male loqui.*[1]

But we do not need to draw this distinction. Here is a sacred relic. Here is a thorn from the crown of the Saviour of the world over whom the prince of this world has no power, which performs miracles by the very power of the blood that he shed for us. Here is God himself choosing this house to give a demonstration of his power.

It is not men who work miracles through some unknown and dubious virtue of their own which makes us draw a difficult distinction. It is God himself; it is the instrument of the Passion of his only Son who, being in several places, chose this one, and made men come from every direction to receive these miraculous comforts in their ailments. (839)

888. Joh., VI, 26. *Non quia vidistis signa sed quia saturati estis.*[2]

Those who follow Jesus Christ because of his miracles honour his power in all the miracles that he wrought; but those who, professing to follow him on the strength of his miracles, only follow him in reality because he consoles them and loads them with the rewards of the world, try to discredit his miracles when they are an obstacle to their comfort.

Joh., IX: *Non est hic homo a Deo, qui sabbatum non custodit: Alii: Quomodo potest homo peccator haec signa facere?*[3]

Which is the clearer?

---

[1] No one who does a miracle in my name will lightly speak evil of me (Mark IX, 13).

[2] It is not because of the miracles you have seen; it is because you were fed with the loaves and had your fill.

[3] This man can be no messenger of God; he does not observe the sabbath. Others asked, How can a man do miracles like this, and be a sinner?

This house is God's; because wonderful miracles are performed there. The others: this house is not God's because the inhabitants do not believe that the five propositions are in Jansen.

Which is the clearer?

Tu quid dicis? Dico quia propheta est. Nisi esset hic a Deo, non poterat facere quidquam.[1]   (834)

889. *Dispute.* Abel, Cain; Moses, magicians; Elias, false prophets; Jeremias, Hananias; Michea, false prophets; Jesus Christ, Pharisees; St. Paul, Bar-Jesus; Apostles, exorcists; Christians and infidels; Catholics and heretics; Elias, Enoch; Antichrist.

Truth always prevails in miracles. The two crosses.   (828)

890. Jer., XXIII, 32, the miracles of the false prophets. In Hebrew and Vatable, there are tricks.

Miracle does not always mean a miracle. I Kings 15, *miracle* means fear and so it is in Hebrew and Job obviously, XXXIII, 7. And again Is., XXI, 4; Jer., XLIV, 12.

Portentum means *simulacrum*, Jer., L, 38; and this is so in Hebrew and in Vatable.

Is., VIII, 18: Jesus Christ says that he and his will be in *miracles*.   (819)

891. The Church has three sorts of enemy: the Jews who have never been part of her body; the heretics who have left her; and the bad Christians who rend her from within.

These three different kinds of enemy usually attack her in different ways. But in the case of miracles they all attack in the same fashion. As they are all without miracles, they all have the same interest in discrediting them, and have all made use of this pretext: that one must never judge doctrine by miracles, but miracles by doctrine. There were two parties among those who listened to Jesus Christ: some who accepted his teaching because of his miracles; others who said ... There were two parties in the time of Calvin ... Today there are the Jesuits, etc. (840)

---

[1] What account dost thou give of him? Why, he said, he must be a prophet. No, if this man did not come from God, he would have no powers at all (John IX, 17, 33).

892. Unjust persecutors of those whom God clearly protects:

If they complain about your excesses, 'they speak like heretics';

If they say that the grace of Jesus Christ draws distinctions, 'it is a sign of their heresy'.

It is said: 'Believe in the Church', but it is not said: 'Believe in the miracles', because the second is natural and not the first. One needed precepts, not the other.

Ezechiel. It is said: Listen to the people of God who talk like that.—Ezechias.

The synagogue was a symbol, and therefore did not pass away, yet it was nothing but a symbol and therefore decayed. It was a symbol which contained truth, and therefore went on existing until there was no longer any truth in it.

Reverend Fathers, it was all a matter of symbols. The other religions disappeared; ours did not.

Miracles are more important than you think: they contributed to the foundation of the Church, and will contribute to her continued life until the coming of Antichrist, until the end.

The two Witnesses.

In the Old Testament and the New, miracles have a symbolical meaning. Salvation is a thing of no value except to show that we must submit to created things: a symbol of the sacrament. (852)

893. Men have always spoken of the true God, or the true God has spoken to men. (807)

894. Montaigne opposed to miracles.

Montaigne in favour of miracles. (814)

895. God either reduced the false miracles to nothing, or he foretold them; and, in one way or another, he raised himself above what is supernatural for us, and raised us ourselves to the same level. (824)

896. Heretics have always fought against the three signs which they do not possess. (845)

897. *Miracles.* How I hate those who profess to doubt miracles! Montaigne speaks of them appropriately in two places. In one

of them, we see how circumspect he is; in the other, that he nevertheless believes in them and makes fun of those who do not.

However it may be, the Church is without proofs if the unbelievers are right. (813)

898. If the devil supported doctrines which destroyed him, he would be divided, as Jesus Christ said. If God supported a doctrine which destroys the Church, he would be divided: *Omne regnum divisum.*

Jesus Christ worked against the devil and destroyed his hold on men's hearts, of which exorcism is the outward sign, in order to establish the Kingdom of God. And so he adds: *In digno Dei ... regnum Dei ad vos.*[1] (820)

899. 'When a strong man, fully armed, mounts guard over his own palace, his goods are left in peace' (Luke, XI, 21).

(300)

900. *First objection*: 'Angel of heaven. We must not judge truth by miracles, but miracles by truth. Therefore miracles are useless.'

Now, they help; we must not be against truth, therefore what Father Lingendes has said, that 'God will not permit a miracle to lead people into error' . . .

When there is dissension within the same Church, a miracle will decide the issue.

Second objection. 'But Antichrist will work wonders.'

Pharaoh's magicians did not promote error. Thus we cannot say to Jesus Christ on the strength of Antichrist: 'You have led me into error.' For Antichrist will work miracles against the Church with the result that they will not be liable to breed error.

Either God will not permit false miracles, or he will perform greater ones.

[Jesus Christ exists since the beginning of the world: that is more powerful than all the miracles of Antichrist.]

If, in the same Church, a miracle were performed in sup-

---

[1] If I, through God's power . . . then it must be that the kingdom of God has suddenly appeared among you (Luke XI, 20).

port of error, we should be led into error. The schism is obvious, the miracle is obvious. But schism is a more obvious sign of error than a miracle is of truth: therefore a miracle cannot lead people into error.

Ubi est Deus tuus? Miracles reveal him, and are a flash of lightning. (846)

901. The five propositions were equivocal; they are no longer so. (831)

902. That the five propositions were condemned is not a miracle because truth was not in danger. But the Sorbonne . . . but the Bull . . .

It is impossible that those who love God with all their heart should fail to recognise the Church, so evident is it.—It is impossible for those who do not love God to be convinced by the Church.

Miracles have such power that it was necessary for God to warn people not to think about them in opposition to him, so clear is it that there is a God; without the warning they might have been a source of unrest.

And thus, so far from these passages, Deut., xiii, militating against the authority of miracles, nothing reveals their strength more clearly. It is the same with Antichrist: 'so that if it were possible, even the elect would be deceived.' (850)

903. The three characteristics of religion: perpetuity, the good life, miracles. They destroy perpetuity by probability; the good life by their moral system; miracles, by undermining either their validity or their importance.

If we believed them, the Church has nothing to do with perpetuity, holiness or miracles. Heretics deny them, or deny their importance; so do the Jesuits. But we should have to be lacking in sincerity to deny them, or to have lost our wits to deny their importance.

No one has ever let himself be martyred on account of miracles which people claim to have seen; the foolishness of men may drive them to suffer martyrdom for those which the Turks believe on the authority of tradition, but not for those which people have seen. (844)

904. *Miracle.* It is an effect which goes beyond the natural power of the means employed to produce it; a non-miracle is an effect which does not go beyond the natural power of the means employed. Thus those who bring about cures by invoking the devil do not perform a miracle; because it does not go beyond the natural power of the devil. But . . .   (804)

905. *Blindness of Scripture.* 'Scripture,' said the Jews, 'maintains that we shall not know whence Christ will come (Job, VII, 27, and XII, 34). Scripture says that Christ will abide for ever, and he declares that he will die.'

Thus, says St. John, they did not believe though he had performed so many miracles in order that the word of Isaiah should be fulfilled: 'He has blinded their eyes, etc.'   (573)

906. Abraham, Gideon: [signs] above revelation. The Jews were blind in judging miracles by Scripture. God has never abandoned his true worshippers.

I prefer to follow Jesus Christ rather than anyone else because he has miracles, prophecies, teaching, perpetuity, etc.

Donatists: no miracles, which compels us to say that it is the devil.

The more we particularise, God, Jesus Christ, the Church.
     (822)

907. Miracles enable us to discriminate between things which are doubtful: between the Jewish people and the heathen; Jew and Christian; Catholic and heretic; slandered and slanderers; between the two crosses.

But miracles would be useless to heretics; because the Church, with the authority of the miracles that created belief, tells us that they do not possess the true faith. There is no doubt that they do not possess it because the first miracles of the Church rule out belief in theirs. There is therefore miracle against miracle, and the first and greatest support the Church.
     (841)

908. The story of the man born blind.

What does St. Paul say? Does he recite the prophecies at every moment? Not at all; he speaks of his miracle. What does Jesus Christ say? Does he recite the prophecies? No; his death had not yet fulfilled them; but he says: *si non fecissem*. Believe the works.

Two supernatural foundations of our religion which is wholly supernatural: one visible, the other invisible. Miracles with grace; miracles without grace.

The synagogue, which has been treated lovingly as a symbol of the Church, and with hatred because it was only a symbol of it, was restored when on the point of collapse at a time when it stood well with God; it is therefore a symbol.

Miracles are proof of the power that God has over men's hearts through the power that he wields over their bodies.

The Church has never recognised a miracle which took place among heretics.

Miracles, the mainstay of religion: they were the mark of the Jews, Christians, the saints, the innocents, the true believers.

A miracle among schismatics is not so much to be feared; for the schism, which is more evident than a miracle, is a visible sign of their error. But when there is no schism and the error is being debated, a miracle makes a distinction possible.

Si non fecissem quae alius non fecit.[1] Wretched people who have forced us to speak of miracles.

Abraham, Gideon: faith confirmed by miracles.

Judith. The voice of God is finally heard in the last persecutions.

If the cooling of charity leaves the Church almost without true worshippers, miracles will produce them. They are the ultimate effects of grace.

Supposing a miracle took place among the Jesuits!

When a miracle disappoints the expectations of those among whom it occurs and there is a lack of proportion between the state of their faith and the instrument of the miracle, it ought to bring about a change in them. But it is otherwise with you. There would be just as much reason for saying that if the Eucharist brought a dead man back to life, we should have to turn Calvinist rather than remain Catholic. But when it fulfils

[1] If I had not done what no one else ever did in their midst (John xv, 24).

expectations, and those who hoped that God would bestow his blessing on their remedies find themselves healed without any remedies . . .

Unbelievers. There has never been a sign from the devil without a more powerful sign from God, or at any rate without its being foretold that such a thing would happen. (851)

6. NOTES FOR A PREFACE TO A TREATISE ON GEOMETRY OR LOGIC

909. Various kinds of right understanding; some display it in one field and not in others where they talk nonsense.

Some draw sound conclusions from few principles, and that shows rightness of judgement.

Others draw sound conclusions from things involving many principles.

For example, some have a very good understanding of the properties of water which involves few principles; but the conclusions are so complex that only extreme clarity of mind can follow them.

This would probably not turn such people into great mathematicians because mathematics includes a great many principles, and because intelligence can be of such a kind that it is well able to understand a few principles completely, but cannot grasp subjects involving a great many principles at all.

There are therefore two kinds of intelligence: one can penetrate quickly and deeply into the implications of principles, and that is the exact mind; the other understands a great number of principles without confusing them, and that is the mathematical mind. One shows strength and directness of mind; the other breadth of mind. Now we can have one without the other because the mind can be powerful and narrow; it can also be broad and flabby. (2)

910*. Difference between the mathematical and the intuitive mind. In one, the principles are obvious, but remote from common use;

with the result that we are faced with the difficulty of turning our head in an unaccustomed direction; but when we do so, we see the principles clearly; and we should have to have a thoroughly illogical mind to argue wrongly from principles which are so transparent that it is practically impossible to overlook them.

But with the intuitive mind the principles are in common use and plain for everyone to see. There is no need to turn our head, or to over-tax ourselves; it is simply a matter of possessing good eyesight, but it must be really good: because the principles are so intricate and so numerous that it is practically impossible not to miss some of them. Now the omission of a principle leads to error; therefore it is necessary to be very clear-sighted to perceive all the principles, and after that to possess an exact mind in order not to argue falsely from known principles.

All mathematicians would therefore be intuitive if they had clear sight because they do not argue falsely from known principles; and people with intuitive minds would be mathematicians if they could bend their minds to the unaccustomed principles of mathematics.

The reason why some intuitive minds are not mathematicians is that they are incapable of applying themselves to the principles of mathematics; but the reason why mathematicians are not intuitive is that they do not see what is in front of them, and that being used to the clear, unadorned principles of mathematics and to arguing when they have had a good look at their principles and obtained a firm grasp of them, they became lost among the subtleties when principles cannot be grasped in that way. We can scarcely see them; we feel rather than see them; we have the greatest difficulty in making people feel them who are incapable of feeling them on their own account: these matters are so subtle and so involved that we need a very clear and very delicate sense of perception to feel them and to judge them rightly and fairly in accordance with this feeling, usually without being able to give an orderly demonstration of them as in mathematics because we do not perceive the principles governing them, and because the task imposed on us would be endless. What is necessary is to take the matter in at a glance, and not by a process of rational argument, at least up to a certain point. Thus it is rare for mathematicians to be intuitive thinkers because mathematicians want to treat intuitive matters mathematically and make themselves ridiculous by attempting to begin with definitions and then going on to principles, which is not the way to tackle an argument of this kind. It is not that the mind does not do it; but it does it silently, naturally and without artifice, for expression eludes everyone, and feeling only belongs to the few.

And conversely, intuitive minds being accustomed to judging things at a glance, are so astonished when they come across propositions which are incomprehensible to them and can only be grasped by means of definitions and principles which are so tenuous that they are not used to examining them in detail—that they find them repellent and give up in disgust.

But inaccurate minds are neither intuitive nor mathematical.

It follows that mathematicians who are merely mathematicians possess right judgement, but only as long as you explain everything to them in terms of definition and principle; otherwise they are hopelessly inaccurate because they only function accurately when operating in accordance with well-tried principles.

And those who are intuitive and nothing but intuitive do not possess the patience to go back to first principles in speculative or imaginative matters, which they have never encountered in life and with which they are completely unfamiliar. (1)

911. *Mathematics, intuition.* True eloquence makes light of eloquence; true morality makes light of morality; in other words, moral judgement makes light of intellectual judgement—which has no rules.

For feeling belongs to judgement as knowledge does to mind. Intuition is a faculty of judgement, as mathematics is of mind.

To make merry over philosophy is to be truly a philosopher.

(4)

912. The examples that we choose to prove other things—if we wanted to prove the examples, we should take other things to

furnish the examples; for since we always believe that the difficulty lies in what we want to prove, we find the illustrations clearer and helpful in proving it.

Thus, when we want to demonstrate some general proposition, we must cite the rule governing a particular case; but if we want to demonstrate a particular instance, we must begin with the [general] rule. For we always find that the thing we want to prove is obscure, and that the thing we use as a proof is clear; because when we put forward something to be proved, we begin with the assumption that it is obscure and, conversely, that the argument used to prove it is clear, and in that way come to understand it easily. (40)

913. All sound principles are at work in the world; all that we need to do is to apply them. For example, no one doubts that he must risk his life for the common good; but not for religion.

There is bound to be inequality among them—true enough; yet once this is granted, the door is open not only to great oppression, but to sheer unadulterated tyranny.

We need a little mental relaxation; but it opens the door to great abuses.—Limits must be imposed on them.

There are no limits in things: the law tries to introduce some, but the mind cannot tolerate it. (380)

914. Feeling. Memory and joy are feelings; and even mathematical propositions become a matter of feeling because reason makes feelings natural, and natural feelings are obliterated by reason. (95)

915. Those who are accustomed to judging by their feelings understand nothing about reasoning because they want to grasp things intuitively, and are not accustomed to seeking principles. People of the opposite disposition, who are accustomed to arguing from principles, understand nothing about matters of feeling because they seek principles and are incapable of grasping things intuitively. (3)

916. There are plenty of warped minds. (568)

7. NOTES FOR THE *TROIS DISCOURS SUR LA CONDITION DES GRANDS*

917. God
has created everything for himself;
has given the power of pain and pleasure for himself.
You can apply it to God or to yourself.
If to God, the Gospel is the rule.
If to yourself, you will be taking the place of God.

As God is surrounded by people filled with charity, who ask
him for the gifts of charity which are in his power, so . . .

Know yourself therefore and know that you are only a king
of concupiscence, and follow the paths of concupiscence. (314)

918. *King and tyrant.* I, too, shall have my hindsight.

I shall be careful every time I go on a journey.

Greatness of establishment, respect for establishment.

The pleasure of the great lies in being able to make people
happy.

The essence of wealth is to be given away liberally.

The essence of everything must be sought. The essence of
power is to give protection.

When power attacks the smirk, when a private soldier seizes
a judge's hat and sends it flying out of the window . . .   (310)

919. A true friend is such an asset even for the greatest in the
land because he can speak well of them and support them behind their backs, that they do their utmost to have friends. But
let them choose wisely; if they put themselves out for fools, they
will be wasting their time, however well the fools may speak of
them; if they are weak, the fools will not speak well of them because they have no authority; they will slander them in order
to resemble the company they keep.   (155)

8. MISCELLANEOUS NOTES

920. Children are astonished to find that their companions are respected. (321)

921. The body is nourished by degrees. Plenty of food and little substance. (356)

922. *Spongia solis* (Streaks of sunlight). When we always see the same effect produced, we conclude that it is due to some natural necessity, such as the fact that there will be daylight tomorrow, etc. But nature often gives us the lie, and does not conform to its own rules. (91)

923. Do you want people to think well of you? Don't say a word about it. (44)

924. He no longer loves the person whom he loved ten years ago. I can well believe it: she is no longer the same person; neither is he. He was young then and so was she; she is quite different now. He might still be fond of her if she were the same person that she used to be. (123)

925. Rivers are roads which move, and take us where we want to go. (17)

926. If we do not happen to know the truth about a thing, it is just as well that there should be a common error which determines public opinion as, for example, the moon to which we attribute the changes of the seasons, the progress of illnesses, etc.; because the principal malady of man is his restless curiosity about things which he cannot know; and it is not so bad for him to be in a state of error as in a state of useless curiosity. (18)

927. The literary style of Epictetus, Montaigne and Solomon of Tultia is the commonest, the one which insinuates itself most effectively into our minds, which remains longest in our memory and which is most frequently quoted because it consists entirely of commonplace thoughts about everyday events; for example, when we speak of the common error that the moon is the cause of everything, we never fail to quote Solomon of

Tultia as saying that, when we do not know the truth about anything, it is just as well that there should be a common error, etc., which is what the other party thinks.   (18 *bis*)

On Reading

928. It is, to use a curious expression, wholly the body of Jesus Christ, but we cannot say that it is the whole body of Jesus Christ.[1]

The indestructible union of two things does not enable us to say that one becomes the other.

Thus the soul is united to the body.

Fire to the wood without change.

But a change is necessary to turn the form of one into the form of the other.

Thus the union of the Word with humanity.

Because my body without my soul would not be the body of a man, my soul united to any sort of matter will form my body.

It does not distinguish the necessary condition from the sufficient: union is necessary, but not sufficient.

The left arm is not the right.

Impenetrability is a property of matter.

Numerical identity in relation to the same time requires identity of matter.

Thus if God united my soul to a body in China, the same body *idem numero* would be in China.

The same river which is flowing over there is *idem numero* that flowing at the same time in China.   (512)

929. It is a heresy always to explain *omnes* by 'all', and a heresy not to explain that it sometimes means 'all'. *Bibite ex hoc omnes*[2]: the Huguenots are heretical in explaining it by 'all'. *In quo omnes peccaverunt*[3]; the Huguenots are heretical in excepting the children of the faithful. We must therefore follow the Fathers and

---

[1] Pascal is here referring to the Eucharist. *Tr.*
[2] Drink, all of you, of this (Matt. xxvi, 27).
[3] It was through one man that guilt came into the world (Rom. v, 12).

tradition in order to know when, because there is danger of heresy on both sides.   (775)

930. 'Pray lest you enter into temptation.' It is dangerous to be tempted; and those who are, are tempted because they do not pray.

Et tu conversus confirma fratres tuos.[1] But beforehand, *conversus Jesus respexit Petrum.*[2]

St. Peter asked permission to strike Malchus and struck without waiting for an answer, and Jesus Christ replied afterwards.

The word *Galilee*, which the crowd of Jews murmured as though by chance, when accusing Jesus Christ before Pilate, gave Pilate an excuse for sending Jesus Christ to Herod; which was the fulfilment of the prophecy that he would be judged by both Jews and Gentiles. What appeared to be a matter of chance was the cause of the fulfilment of the prophecy.   (744)

931. There is one recipe for the agreeable and the beautiful which is based on a certain correspondence between our nature, whether it is weak or strong, and the thing that gives pleasure.

Everything that conforms to this standard gives us pleasure, whether it happens to be a house, a song, a speech, verse, prose, a woman, birds, rivers, trees, rooms, clothes, etc. Anything that does not conform to it is displeasing to people of good taste.

And, just as there is a perfect correspondence between a song and a house when they are based on a good model because they resemble in their different ways the unique model, so there is a perfect correspondence between things based on a bad model. It is not that the bad model is unique because their number is infinite; but every bad sonnet, for example, whatever the false model on which it is based, exactly resembles a woman dressed according to the same pattern.

Nothing shows more clearly how ridiculous a bogus sonnet is than to consider its nature and the model, then to imagine a woman or a house constructed according to that particular model.   (32)

---

[1] It is for thee to be the support of thy brethren (Luke XXII, 32).
[2] And the Lord turned, and looked at Peter (Luke XXII, 61).

932. Poetic beauty. Just as we speak of poetic beauty, so we should speak of mathematical beauty, and medicinal beauty; but we do not do so: and the reason is that we know perfectly well what the object of mathematics is, and that it consists of proofs; what the aim of medicine is, and that it lies in healing; but we do not know the nature of the charm which is the object of poetry. We cannot discover the natural model which must be copied; and in default of such knowledge people have invented certain odd terms: 'golden age', 'marvel of our time', 'fatal', etc., and this jargon is called poetic beauty.

But anyone who imagines a woman fashioned in this way, which consists of using big words to say little things, will picture a pretty girl tricked out with mirrors and chains. This will make him laugh because he has a much better idea of the source of a woman's charm than he has of that of verse. But those who did not understand the matter would admire her in such a rig-out; and there are many villages where she would be taken for the queen; that is why we call sonnets using that model 'village queens'. (33)

933. Anyone who wants can become a priest, as under Jeroboam.

It is a horrible thing to suggest that the discipline of the Church today is so good that it would be a crime to wish to change it. At other times, it was unquestionably good, and we find that it could be changed without anyone pretending that it was a sin to do so; and now, such as it is, we are told that we ought not to want to see it changed!

It was permissible to change the practice of not ordaining men priests except with such circumspection that there were hardly any men who were fit to be priests; and it is apparently not permissible to complain about a practice which produces so many bad ones. (885)

934. We enjoy seeing the error, the passion of Cleobuline because she is unaware of it herself. Only her ignorance prevents it from being disgusting. (13)

935. *Montaigne.* What is good in Montaigne can only be acquired with difficulty. What is bad in him—I mean apart from

morals—could have been put right in a moment if someone had warned him that he told too many stories, and that he talked too much about himself. (65)

936. *Montaigne.* Montaigne has great faults. The use of licentious words; which is worthless in spite of what Mademoiselle de Gournay said. Credulous, *people without eyes.* Ignorance, *quadrature of the circle. Greater world.* His views on voluntary homicide, on death. He encourages an indifference towards salvation, *without fear and without repentance.* Since his book was not written in order to bring people to religion, he was under no obligation to do it: but we are always under an obligation not to turn people away from religion. We may find excuses for his sentiments which on certain occasions were decidedly free and salacious (730, 331), but there is no excuse for his thoroughly pagan views on death; for we must abandon religion entirely if we do not at least intend to die a Christian death; now all through his book he thinks only of dying in a soft and cowardly manner.

(63)

937. We are astonished to hear people say that warmth is only the movement of a few globules, and light the *conatus recedendi* that we feel. What! Pleasure nothing more than the ballet dance of our spirits? We had formed a very different idea of it! And such feelings seem to us to be as far removed from others that we declare to be the same as those with which we compare them! The awareness of fire, the heat that affects us in a manner which is entirely different from touch, the reception of sound and light—it all appears mysterious to us and yet it is as crude as a blow with a hammer. It is true that the smallness of the spirits which enter our pores affects other nerves, but there are always some nerves which are affected. (368)

938. Denys possessed charity: he was in the right place. (568)

939. *Epigrams of Martial.* Men enjoy playing dirty tricks; not on the infirm or the unfortunate, but on the proud. We deceive ourselves in a different way.

For concupiscence is the source of all our impulses, and our humanity, etc.

We must seek to please those who are human and tender.

The one about the two one-eyed men is valueless because it brings them no comfort, but boosts the reputation of the author. Everything which is merely for the benefit of the author is worthless. *Ambitiosa recidet ornamenta.*[1]   (41)

940. A sneeze absorbs all the faculties of our being in precisely the same way as labour[2]; but it does not furnish the same arguments against the greatness of man because it happens against his will. And though he causes it himself, it is nevertheless against his will; it is not done for the sake of the thing itself, but for a different end: and so it is not a sign of the weakness of man and of his servitude when subjected to such an action.

It is no shame to man to succumb to pain, and it is a source of shame to him to succumb to pleasure. This is not due to the fact that pain comes to us from somewhere else, and that we ourselves pursue pleasure; for we may seek pain and succumb to it deliberately without being guilty of that kind of baseness. Why then is it a glorious thing for reason to succumb to pain, and a disgrace to succumb to pleasure? It is because it is not pain that tempts and attracts us; it is we ourselves who choose it and seek to place ourselves in its power, so that we are masters of the situation, and for that reason it is man who succumbs to himself; but with pleasure, it is man who succumbs to pleasure. Now it is only mastery and control which lead to glory, and servitude which brings shame.   (160)

Apparent contradictions

941. C. C. *Homo existens te Deum facis.*
Scriptum est: 'Dii estis' et non potest solvi Scriptura.
C.C. *'Haec infirmitas non est ad vitam et est ad mortem.*
'Lazarus dormit,' et deinde dixit: Lazarus mortuus est.[3]   (754)

---

[1] He cuts out superfluous ornaments (Horace, *Ars poetica*, 447).
[2] *Besogne* in this context means physical love. *Tr.*
[3] It is because thou, who art a man, dost pretend to be God. ——Is it not written in your law, I have said, You are gods? . . . and we know that the words of Scripture have binding force (John x, 33-35). The end of this sickness is not death; it is meant for God's honour. Lazarus is at rest now. So now Jesus told them openly, Lazarus is dead (John xi, 4, 11, 14).

942. How many stars have been discovered by telescopes which were previously non-existent for our philosophers! We relied frankly on Holy Scripture for the number of stars, saying: 'We know that there are only a thousand and twenty-two of them.'

There is grass on the earth; we see it.—From the moon we should not see it.—And on the grass hairs; and in the hairs little animals; but after that, nothing more.—O presumptuous man! —Mixtures are formed of elements; and the elements not.— O presumptuous man! here is a delicate joint.—We must admit that there are some things which we do not see.—We must therefore speak like the others, but not think like them.

(266)

943. When we try to push virtues to extremes in either direction, vices appear which insinuate themselves imperceptibly into them, by invisible ways in the direction of the small infinite; and a swarm of vices from the direction of the great infinite, with the result that we are lost among the vices and no longer see the virtues.

We even attack perfection itself. (357)

944. Words arranged in a different order have a different meaning, and meanings in a different order create different effects.

(23)

945. *Ne timeas pusillus grex. Timore et tremore.—Quid ergo? Ne timeas, [modo] timeas*: Do not be afraid provided [that] you are afraid; but if you are not afraid, be afraid.

Qui me recipit, non me recipit, sed eum qui me misit.

Nemo scit, neque Filius.

Nubes lucida obumbravit.[1]

St. John was to turn the hearts of the fathers towards the children, and Jesus Christ to create division between the two. Without contradiction. (776)

946. I believe that Joshua was the first of the men of God to

---

[1] Do not be afraid, you, my little flock (Luke xii, 32). You must work to earn your salvation, in anxious fear (Philip ii, 12). Whoever welcomes me, welcomes, not me, but him that sent me (Mark ix, 36). No one knows, not even the Son (Mark xiii, 32). A shining cloud overshadowed him (Matt. xvii, 5).

have this name, as Jesus Christ was the last of the people of God. (627)

947. If there has ever been a time when we should make profession of two conflicting truths, it is when we are reproached for omitting one of them. Therefore the Jesuits and the Jansenists are wrong to conceal them; but the Jansenists more so because the Jesuits have been more successful in making profession of both. (865)

948. M. de Condren: 'There is no comparison,' he says, 'between the union of saints and that of the Blessed Trinity.'

Jesus Christ says the opposite. (943)

949. The dignity of man lay, in his innocence, in making use of and lording it over creatures, but today it lies in separating himself from them and subjecting himself to them. (486)

950. *Meanings.* A single meaning changes according to the words that we use to express it. Meanings acquire their dignity from the words instead of bestowing it on them. We must look for examples . . . (50)

951. Effects, *in communi* and *in particulari*. The semi-Pelagians are wrong in saying *in communi*, what is only true *in particulari*; and the Calvinists, in saying *in particulari* what is true *in communi* (so it seems to me). (777)

Rhetoric . . .

952. [Chance provides us with thoughts, and chance obliterates them; no art is necessary for acquiring or preserving them.

A thought escapes me; I wanted to write it down; instead I write that it has escaped me.] (370)

953.   Nature differentiates   artifice imitates
          and imitates,   and differentiates.

(120)

954. *Nature imitates itself.* Nature imitates itself: a seed, which falls on good ground, grows; a principle, which falls into a good mind, grows;

Numbers imitate space though by their nature they are so different.

Everything is made and guided by the same master: the root, the branches, the fruit; principles, consequences.   (119)

955. Eloquence is a portrait of thought; and so those, who after drawing a portrait add something more, produce a picture instead of a portrait.   (26)

956. Eloquence moves us by gentleness and not by authority: as a tyrant, not as a king.   (15)

957. When some feeling or effect is described in a natural style, we feel within ourselves the truth of what we hear without previously knowing that it was there. We are therefore well disposed towards the person who made us feel it, because he has not made a display of his own riches but of ours; and so the benefit that he has conferred on us makes him sympathetic; apart from the fact that our similarity of outlook necessarily arouses our sympathy.   (14)

958. *Eloquence.* We need the agreeable and the real; but the agreeable must itself be drawn from the real.   (25)

959. In every discussion and speech we must be able to say to those who take offence at what we say: 'What are you complaining about?'   (188)

960. There are many people who go and hear a sermon in the same way that they go to vespers.   (8)

961. Perpetual eloquence is wearisome.

Princes and kings sometimes play. They are not always on their thrones; it bores them: greatness needs to be laid aside in order to be felt. Continuity is displeasing in everything; cold is welcome because it enables us to warm ourselves.

Nature operates by progression, *itus et reditus.*
AA. It passes by and returns, then goes further, then half the distance, then further than ever, etc.

The ebb and flow of the sea occurs like that, the sun seems to move like that.   AA   AAA   AAA.   (355)

962. If we know a person's main interest in life, we can be sure of making ourselves agreeable to him; and nevertheless the idea

that each of us has formed of what is good reflects whims which operate against our own interest; it is a peculiarity which throws us off balance. (106)

963. There are people who speak well and do not write well. It is because the place and the audience warm them up, and enable them to find more to say than would otherwise be possible. (47)

964. Scaramouche, who only thinks of one thing.

The doctor who goes on talking for a quarter of an hour after he has said everything, so filled is he with a desire to talk. (12)

965. The man who says smart things—bad character. (46)

966. All the sham beauties that we criticise in Cicero have their admirers in plenty. (31)

967. If lightning struck low-lying places, etc., poets and people who are only capable of arguing about things of this kind would have no proofs. (39)

968. Mask nature and disguise it. Do not talk about kings, popes, bishops; say *august monarch*, etc.; not Paris, but *capital of the kingdom*. There are times when we must call Paris, Paris, and others when we must speak of the capital of the kingdom. (49)

969. *Miscell.* When we find words repeated in a speech, try to alter them, and find that they are so apposite that we should spoil the speech, we must leave them in; they are the hall-mark; it is the work of envy which is blind, and does not know that repetition is not wrong in its proper place; for there is no general rule. (48)

970. I dislike apologies like these: 'I have put you to a lot of trouble; I am sorry to bother you; I am afraid that it's too long.' You either enlist people's sympathies or you irritate them. (57)

971. *Miscell. Language.* Those who indulge in antitheses by forcing the meaning of words are like people who put in false windows for the purpose of symmetry:

Their rule is not to speak precisely, but to execute precise figures. (27)

972. *Miscell.* Manner of speaking: 'I had wished to apply myself to it.' (54)

973. Carriage which has fallen *on its side* or *overturned*, according to the meaning.[1]

Spill or *pour* according to the sense. (Speech by M. le M[aître] on the Franciscan by force.) (53)

974. Symmetry. In anything one takes in at a glance; based on something that there is no reason for doing differently:

and also based on the face of man,

whence it comes that we only desire symmetry in breadth, and not in height or depth. (28)

975. You can divine sympathy for you in your grief. M. le Cardinal did not wish anyone to see through him.

'My mind is filled with anxiety.' 'I am filled with anxiety' is better. (56)

976. 'Extinguish the torch of sedition': too flowery.

'The restlessness of his genius': two daring words too many. (59)

977. A king likes to hear himself addressed as 'prince' because it reduces his rank. (42)

978. You have been ungracious and say: 'Please forgive me.' Without the apology, I should not have noticed the offence. 'Saving your reverence . . .' Nothing is wrong but their apology. (58)

979. Nobody says 'courtiers' except those who are not courtiers; 'pedants' except a pedant; 'provincials' except a provincial, and I will wager that it was the printer who put it into the title of the *Lettres au Provincial*. (52)

980. The *aperative* power of a key; *drawing* power of a hook. (55)

981. The more wit we have, the greater the number of people whom we are inclined to think original. Ordinary people do not notice any difference between men. (7)

982. Compared with other people, those who judge a work of

---

[1] In French: *carrosse versé* or *renversé. Répandre* (spill or spread): *verser* (overflow or pour). *Tr.*

art without rules are in the same position as people who have no watches compared with those who have. One says: 'Two hours ago'; the other: 'Only three-quarters of an hour.' I look at my watch; I say to one: 'You're bored,' and to the other: 'You hardly notice time.' For it was an hour and a half ago. I laugh at those who tell me that time hangs heavily on my hands, and that I count it according to whim; they do not know that I was going by my watch. (5)

983. The variety is so great that every tone of voice, every style of walking, coughing, blowing one's nose, sneezing . . . We distinguish grapes from other fruits and among grapes, muscatels, then Condrieu, then Desargues, and then this cutting. Is that all? Has it ever produced two bunches alike? And has a bunch two grapes which are alike? etc.

I have never judged the same thing in precisely the same way. I cannot judge my work while I am doing it; I must do as painters do and step back to get a proper view; but not too far back. How far then? Your guess is as good as mine. (114)

984. No one is accepted in society as a connoisseur of verse unless he has hoisted the sign of poet or mathematician, etc. But people with universal minds do not need a sign, and scarcely notice any difference between the trade of the poet and that of the embroiderer.

People with universal minds are not described as poets or mathematicians, etc., but they are all those things, and are good judges of them as well. No one would guess it from meeting them. They will talk about the subject that was being discussed when they came in. We are not more aware of one quality in them than another unless they have occasion to make use of it; then we remember because it is equally in keeping with their character that we do not say of them that they speak well when no one is discussing language, and that we do say of them that they speak well when it is being discussed.

We are therefore bestowing false praise on a man if we say of him, when he comes in, that he is a very gifted poet; and it is a bad sign if we do not appeal to such a man when we need an opinion on a piece of verse. (34)

985. Man has many needs: he only cares for those who can satisfy them all. 'He's a good mathematician,' people say.— But I do not care a fig for mathematics; he might take me for a proposition.—'He's a good soldier.'—He might take me for a beleaguered fortress. I therefore need a man of the world who will be able to fit in with all my needs generally. (36)

986. His rule is universality.

Poet and not truly a man of the world.[1]

Beauties of omission, judgement. (30)

987. *Man of the World*. We must be in a position to [say] not: he is a mathematician, or a preacher, or eloquent, but that he is a man of the world. This universal quality is the only one that appeals to me. It is a bad sign if, on seeing a man, we remember his book; I should prefer not to be aware of any quality until we actually meet it, and the moment comes to make use of it (*Ne quid nimis*), for fear that one quality might be preponderant and give a man a label; we do not want to feel that he is a good talker except when it is the right moment for good talk; but let us be sure to recognise it then. (35)

988. Poet, and not truly a man of the world. (38)

989. Languages become ciphers, not when letters are changed into letters but words into words, so that an unknown language can be deciphered. (45)

990. *Language*. We must not turn our mind to other subjects except to rest it, and only then when it is the proper time for rest; rest it when it is necessary and not otherwise; for anyone who rests at the wrong time is tiring; and anyone who tires at the wrong time is restful because we drop everything on the spot; so bent is the evil of concupiscence on making us do the exact opposite of what anyone wants without giving us the least pleasure, which is the money for which we are ready to give everything that anyone asks. (24)

991. In the same way that we spoil our minds, we also ruin our feelings.

---

[1] In French: *honnête homme*. *Tr.*

Mind and feeling are formed by conversation. We spoil our minds and feelings by conversation. Thus good or bad conversation improves or ruins our minds and feelings. It is therefore very important to be able to choose the people we converse with in order to improve and not to spoil them; and we can only choose provided that we have already trained our minds and feelings and not spoilt them. This creates a circle from which those who emerge are very fortunate. (6)

Bibliography

Concordance

Index

SELECT BIBLIOGRAPHY

In the absence of a contrary indication books in English are published in London and books in French in Paris.

ADAM, A. *Histoire de la littérature française au dix-septième siècle*, T. II. L'Époque de Pascal, Domat, 1951, 420 pp.
> (Pascal, pp. 185-301.)

BÉGUIN, A., *Pascal par lui-même* (Écrivains de Toujours, No. 6), Éditions du Seuil, 1952, 192 pp.

BOUTROUX, E., *Pascal* (Les Grands Écrivains Français), Hachette, 1900, 205 pp.

BREMOND, H., *Histoire littéraire du sentiment religieux en France*, IV. La Conquête Mystique, (2) L'École de Port-Royal, Bloud et Gay, 1920, 604 pp.
> (La Prière de Pascal, pp. 318-417.)

CHEVALIER, J., *Pascal*, Plon, 1922, new ed., 1949. Eng. tr., Sheed & Ward, 1930, 336 pp.

CRISTIANI, L., *L'Hérésie de Port-Royal* (Bibliothèque Ecclesia, No. 11), Fayard, 1955, 187 pp.
> (Useful short introduction to the Jansenist controversy.)

ELIOT, T. S., *Essays Ancient and Modern*, Faber & Faber, 1936, 190 pp.
> ('The *Pensées* of Pascal', pp. 137-159.)

GUITTON, J., *Pascal et Leibnitz*, Étude sur deux Types de Penseurs (Philosophie de l'Esprit), Aubier, 1951, 181 pp.

GUARDINI, R., *Christliches Bewusstsein*, Versuche über Pascal, 3rd ed., Kösel, Munich, 1956, 317 pp. French tr. 1951.

HUXLEY, A., *Do What You Will*, Chatto & Windus, 1929, 310 pp.
> (Pascal, pp. 227-310.)

KNOX, R.A., *Enthusiasm*, Clarendon Press, Oxford, 1950, 622 pp.
> (Jansenism, pp. 176-230.)

LAFUMA, L., *Histoire des Pensées de Pascal* (1656-1952), Éditions du Luxembourg, 1954, 148 pp.
> (Good survey of all the important editions of the *Pensées*.)
Recherches pascaliennes, Delmas, 1949.

MAURIAC, F., *Blaise Pascal et sa soeur Jacqueline* (Le Passé Vivant), Hachette, 1931, 254 pp.

MESNARD, J., *Pascal l'homme et l'oeuvre* (Connaissance des Lettres, No. 30), Boivin, 1951, 192 pp. Eng. tr., *Pascal His Life and Works*, Harvill Press, 1952, 211 pp.
> (Best short up-to-date introduction.)

Select Bibliography

MORTIMER, E., *Blaise Pascal: The Life and Work of a Realist*, Methuen, 1959, 240 pp.
>
> (Good introduction.)

SAINTE-BEUVE, C. A., *Port-Royal*, 7 vols., 1840-1859; 3 vols. (Bibliothèque de la Pléiade), Gallimard, 1954.
>
> (Still one of the indispensable works.)

STROWSKI, F., *Pascal et son temps*, 3 vols., Plon, 1907-8, T. I, 286 pp., T. II, 407 pp., T. III, 430 pp.
>
> (Admirable study of the age.)

VALÉRY, P., 'Variation sur une "Pensée"' in *Variété* I, 1923, pp. 140-153.

Various writers, *Blaise Pascal L'Homme et l'oeuvre* (Cahiers de Royaumont: Philosophie No. 1), Éditions de Minuit, 1956, 478 pp.

CONCORDANCE

Showing the order adopted by Louis Lafuma (2nd Edition, Delmas, 1952), Léon Brunschvicg (Hachette), and Jacques Chevalier (Bibliothèque de la Pléiade, 1954).

Lafuma	Brunschvicg	Chevalier	Lafuma	Brunschvicg	Chevalier
1	105	161	35	187	1
2	274	474	36	241	458
3	29	36	37	442	428
4	22	65	38	290	486
5	9	93	39	421	333
6	10	43	40	74	188
7	252	470	41	494	436
8	19	63	42	449	418
9	276	473	43	562	74
10	197	339	44	373	71
11	194	335	45	21	69
12	195	334	46	120	27
13	229	414	47	61	70
14	560	640 & (a)	48	62	76
15	194 *ter*	335/336	49	242	366
16	560 *bis*	640 & (a)	50	133	115
17	556	602	51	338	313
18	419	332	52	410	268 (a)
19	243	6	53	161	178
20	198	340	54	113	173
21	196	338	55	955	IV
22	193	361 (a)	56	318	302 (a)
23	191	13	57	292	233 (b)
24	596	404	58	381	85
25	227	353	59	367	96
26	244	362	60	67	196
27	184	365	61	127	199
28	257	364	62	308	293
29	60	73	63	330	297
30	248	471	64	354	318
31	602	405	65	436	197 & (a)
32	291	232	66	156	155
33	167	215	67	320	296
34	246	441	68	149	152

Concordance

Lafuma	Brunschvicg	Chevalier	Lafuma	Brunschvicg	Chevalier
69	317 bis	303 (a)	114	326	288
70	374	185	115	879	811
71	376	186	116	205	88
72	117	126	117	174 bis	169 & (a)
73	164	211	118	165 bis	212
74	158	154	119	405	143
75	71	84 (b)	120	66	81
76	141	177	121	110	170
77	134	116	122	454	137
78	69	84 (a)	123	389	367
79	207	90	124	73	189
80	136	175	125	437	270
81	82	104, 92	126	174	169 & (a)
82	83	92	127	414	184
83	163	180 (a)	128	171	217
84	172	168	129	399	256
85	366	95	130	441	421
86	132	179	131	406	144
87	305	291	132	439	422
88	293-154	233/233 (a)	133	90, 87	105, 106, 117
89	388	381	134	408	279
90	162	180	135	85	109
91	404	276	136	102	140
92	76	193	137	407	141
93	153	150	138	84	108
94	150	153	139	173	190
95	333	301	140	186	9 (a)
96	401	277	141	455	136
97	436 bis	197 & (a)	142	214	142
98	390	385	143	109 bis	{166 {167
99	100	130			
100	275	475	144	109	100
101	42	132 (a)	145	448	417
102	112	171	146	372	100
103	111	172	147	124	114
104	181	164	148	175	220
105	379	326	149	108	174
106	332	244	150	456	138
107	296	234	151	258	363
108	294	230	152	212	350
109	309	237	153	88	111
110	177	224	154	101	131
111	151	149	155	351	321
112	295	231	156	165	212
113	155	157	157	152	146

Concordance

Lafuma	Brunschvicg	Chevalier		Lafuma	Brunschvicg	Chevalier
158	126	160		203	176	221
159	128	200		204	306	290
160	131	201		205	393	286
161	417	315		206	122	112
162	94	121		207	304	289
163	129	198		208	320	296
164	457	139		209	342	260
165	94 bis	121		210	403	283
166	359	325		211	343	261
167	323	306		212	339 bis	355
168	118	129		213	392	383
169	147	145		214	282	479
170	317	303		215	339	258
171	299	238		216	344	272
172	271	464		217	348	265
173	327	308		218	397	255
174	79	192		219	349	356
175	878	821		220	398	269
176	297	235		221	409	268
177	307	292		222	402	284
178	302	241		223	400	278
179	315	299		224	277	477
180	337	312		225	278	481
181	336	311		226	146	210
182	335	310		227	411	274
183	328	309		228	369	97
184	313	295		229	353	323
185	316	298		230	341	259
186	329	300		231	340	262
187	334	247		232	365	263
188	80	101		233	346	257
189	536	102		234	423	331
190	467	691		235	148	151
191	324	307		236	418	328
192	298	285		237	416	314
193	322	305		238	157	156
194	89	449		239	125	159
195	325	287		240	92	119
196	331	294		241	93	120
197	303	242		242	415	254
198	312	236		243	396	271
199	452	133		244	116	125
200	311	243		245	420	330
201	301	240		246	434	438
202	96	123		247	438	415

Concordance

Lafuma	Brunschvicg	Chevalier		Lafuma	Brunschvicg	Chevalier
248	424	437		293	394	389
249	413	3ı7		294	391	387
250	588 bis	828		295	432	384
251	70	84 (c)		296	51	386
252	443	427		297	78	195
253	412	316		298	385	228
254	97	127		299	361	375
255	377	187		300	425	370
256	81	103		301	426	368
257	358	329		302	544	721
258	180	223		303	74 bis	188
259	215	219		304	363	371
260	532	683		305	462	378
261	386	380		306	422	693
262	580	416		307	182	165
263	490	450		308	488	429
264	145	209		309	430	483
265	170	216		310	288	839
266	169	214		311	478	701
267	168	213		312	427	275
268	469	443		313	477/606	703
269	139	205		314	199	341
270	142	206		315	557	603
271	166	218		316	558	604
272	143	207		317	586	599
273	130	202		318	769	652
274	137	204		319	559	606, 446
275	140	176		320	574	579
276	135	203		321	575	580
277	138	205 (a)		322	202	572 (b)
278	466	692		323	445	448
279	509	377		324	857	786
280	463	379		325	230	447
281	464	390		326	226	361
282	360	376		327	211	351
283	461	373		328	213	349
284	350	374		329	238	455
285	525	392		330	237	454
286	465	391		331	281	478
287	395	273		332	190	12
288	220	348		333	225	360
289	378	327		334	236	453
290	375	252		335	204	344 (& a)
291	387	382		336	257	364
292	219	347		337	221	354

Concordance

Lafuma	Brunschvicg	Chevalier	Lafuma	Brunschvicg	Chevalier
338	189	11	383	527	75
339	200	342	384	98	124
340	218	346	385	208	89
341	210	227	386	37	42
342	183	226	387	86	110
343	233	451	388	163 bis	180 (a)
344	231	444	389	693	393
345	203	343	390	72	84
346	234	452	391	347	264
347	121	128	392	206	91
348	232	445	393	517	657
349	239	456	394	431	388
350	240	457	395	660	557
351	262	282	396	245	482
352	269	463	397	595	399
353	224	359	398	592	396
354	812	625	399	489	431
355	268	461	400	235	452 (a)
356	696	524 (c)	401	597	401
357	185	9	402	435	439
358	273	4	403	599	402
359	270	462	404	451	134
360	563	2	405	453	135
361	261	248	406	528	678
362	384	250	407	551	733
363	747 bis	779 (a)	408	491	432
364	256	781	409	433	426
365	838	620	410	493	435
366	255	780	411	650	552
367	272	465	412	598	400
368	253	3	413	251	834
369	811	624	414	468	700
370	265	459	415	628	412
371	947	XLII	416	594	398
372	254	280	417	479	433
373	267	466	418	492	434
374	260	249	419	589	824
375	99	472	420	259	485
376	279	480	421	593	397
377	345	266	422	487	430
378	561	814	423	774	642
379	604	726	424	747	516
380	547	730	425	590	395
381	543	5	426	780	646
382	549	728	427	450	419

Concordance

Lafuma	Brunschvicg	Chevalier	Lafuma	Brunschvicg	Chevalier
428	798	742	473	815	626
429	615	830	474	263	440
430	570	571	475	833	LV
431	816	281	476	830	621
432	789	638	477	817	825
433	523	675	478	818	825 (a)
434	223	358	479	647	549
435	751	591	480	657	562 (b)
436	444	833	481	674	572 (a)
437	430 bis	483	482	653	562 (d)
438	511	605	483	681	568 (a)
439	566	573	484	667	519 (a)
440	796	633	485	900	550 (b)
441	581	596	486	648	550
442	771	658	487	697	567
443	578	582	488	649	551
444	795	637	489	758	589
445	645	561	490	662	577
446	510	484	491	684	558
447	705	524	492	728	535 (c)
448	765	601	493	685	559
449	585	598	494	678	566
450	601	413	495	757	590
451	228	352	496	762	521
452	565	588	497	686	559 (a)
453	559 bis	446, 606	498	746	494
454	201	420	499	677	565
455	863	789	500	719	535 (b)
456	428	7	501	680	568
457	577	510	502	683	569
458	622	410	503	692	570
459	289	487	504	670	583
460	567	791	505	545	689
461	576	581	506	687	555
462	862	788	507	745	515
463	583	792	508	642	541
464	568	587	509	643	560
465	899	820	510	691	558 (a)
466	737	600	511	794	632
467	741	538	512	644	542
468	217	345	513	572	589 (a)
469	588	828	514	676	564
470	805	745	515	688	554
471	222	357	516	682	568 (b)
472	285	836	517	659	556

Lafuma	Brunschvicg	Chevalier	Lafuma	Brunschvicg	Chevalier
518	571	574	563	612	500
519	675	563	564	632	411 (a)
520	646	773	565	633	411 (b)
521	651	553	566	634	411
522	669	583 (a)	567	626	491
523	656	549 (b)	568	587	827
524	766	619	569	624	489
525	664	576	570	204 bis	344 (& a)
526	663	575	571	703	502
527	666	722	572	629	511 (a)
528	519	670	573	625	490
529	782	649	574	702	501
530	673	572, 586	575	283	72
531	671	584	576	742	540
532	665	608	577	786	631
533	661	724	578	772	650
534	658	562 (e)	579	809	627 (a)
535	654	562 (& a), 740	580	799	743
536	635	512 (a)	581	743	539
537	446	421 (a)	582	638	509
538	690	493	583	763	635
539	614	777	584	764	634
540	613	776	585	793	829
541	616	774	586	797	744
542	655	549 (a)	587	801	739
543	605	727	588	640	505
544	867	816	589	607	524 (e)
545	609	497	590	569	785
546	607	495	591	639	508
547	689	492	592	752	592
548	608	496	593	800	741
549	630	512	594	701	503, 544
550	617	775	595	755	644
551	621	409	596	699	525
552	620	408	597	178	225 (a)
553	631	511	598	600	403
554	610	498	599	802	738
555	619	407	600	740	488
556	618	406	601	546	690
557	630	512	602	548	729
558	591	394	603	714	535 (d)
559	750	518	604	641	506
560	766	619	605	792	636
561	859	783	606	700	545
562	858	778	607	784	607

Concordance

Lafuma	Brunschvicg	Chevalier	Lafuma	Brunschvicg	Chevalier
608	768	610	653	778	644 (b)
609	440	423	654	704	504
610	788	826	655	760	519
611	787	630	656	736	618
612	179	225	657	731	612 (a)
613	759	513	658	568	587
614	773	642 (a)	659	712	530
615	730	614	660	698	523
616	733	616	661	726	532, 533, 535 (a)
617	694	522	662	722	534
618	770	611	663	761	520
619	732	617	664	713	531
620	734	543	665	652	562 (c)
621	725	532 (a)	666	623	529 (a)
622	748	517	667	537	684
623	710	528	668	526	677
624	708	546	669	529	679
625	716	535 (f)	670	524	676
626	706	526	671	767	641
627	709	547	672	539	686
628	753	593	673	541	688
629	724	535	674	538	685
630	738	536	675	481	714
631	720	535 (j)	676	482	709
632	723	548	677	209	158
633	637	507	678	472	702
634	695	524 (d)	679	914	XIX
635	756	595	680	249	467
636	727 bis	612	681	496	717
637	729	615	682	747 ter	779
638	735	613	683	672	585
639	718	535 (h)	684	474	705
640	707	527	685	611	499
641	749	514	686	480	708
642	783	651	687	473	704
643	717	535 (g)	688	483	710
644	713 bis	531	689	476	707
645	739	537, 609	690	475	706
646	711	529	691	503	673
647	727	612	692	484	713
648			693	535	682
649	714	535 (d)	694	500	715
650			695	579	787
651	721	535 (i)	696	458	696
652	715	535 (e)	697	515	666

Concordance

Lafuma	Brunschvicg	Chevalier	Lafuma	Brunschvicg	Chevalier
698	779	83	743	856	L
699	485	712	744	498	723
700	534	681	745	668	648
701	502	672	746	790	636 (a)
702	495	716	747	540	687
703	159	148	748	550	732
704	911	XXXII	749	505	656
705	906	720	750	499	719
706	383	87	751	555	737
707	382	86	752	552	735
708	507	653	753	107	163
709	923	468	754	371	99
710	912	20	755	471	832
711	352	322	756	144	80
712	501	718	757	530	680
713	11	208	758	64	79
714	103	182	759	506	655
715	497	725	760	192	337
716	68	82	761	75	191
717	447	425	762	520	669
718	673	572, 586	763	513	659
719	533	694	764	531	662
720	459	697	765	521	674
721	460	698	766	516	668
722	250	469	767	522	667
723	104	183	768	901	550 (a)
724	518	663	769	508	654
725	264	253	770		
726	542	195	771	781	645
727	280	476	772		
728	470	699	773	636	524 (a)
729	825	762	774	514	661, 664
730	284	835	775	925	I
731	286	837	776	948	XLV
732	287	838, 840	777	902 bis	251
733	848	769	778	902	251
734	584	647	779	956	X
735	847	770	780	892	XI, LXVII
736	564	831	781	—	LXVIII
737	—	pp. 553-4	782	953	XIV
738	582	597	783	915	XX
739	553	736	784	913	XXIV
740	504	671	785	884 bis	802 (a)
741	785	731	786	910	XXXI
742	554	734	787	928	II

Concordance

Lafuma	Brunschvicg	Chevalier	Lafuma	Brunschvicg	Chevalier
788	897	797	833	868	803
789	938	XLVIII	834	930	XV
790	260	249	835	949	822
791	926	IX	836	905	819
792	922	XXX	837	935	XXXV
793	880	806	838	889	802
794	—	LXIX	839	891	XLIX
795	934	XVI	840	940	XIII
796	883	XLVII	841	952	XLVI
797	884	802 (a)	842	888	802 (c) (d)
798	832	LIII	843	908	XXVI
799	30	32	844	909	717
800	918	XXXIV	845	869	804
801	904	XXII	846	874	808
802	364	372	847	872	810
803	921/362	III—371	848	871	809
804	937	XXXVII	849	896	799
805	932	XXXIX	850	873	LXIV
806	941	XXVIII	851	877	812
807	939	XLI	852	876	807
808	957	VIII	853	870	818
809	886	800	854	875	813
810	927	V	855	890	816 (a)
811	924	VI	856	881	817
812	958	XII	857	861	784
813	895	794	858	954	XLIV
814	841	766, LIV	859	898	798
815	893	795	860	944	XXIII
816	853	LX (a)	861	917	XXVII
817	925	I	862	931	XXI
818	882	LXV	863	864	793
819	942	XLI	864	866	19
820	849	805, LX	865	903	815
821	946	XLIII	866	?	LXX
822	860	782	867	844 bis	LVI II, LXXI
823	945	823	868	916	XXV
824	936	XXXVI	869	919	XXXIII
825	946 bis	XLIII	870	216	222
826	951	XVII (a)	871	App. XIII	L—LXIII
827	950	XVIII	872	810	627 (b)
828	887	802 (b)	873	803	750
829	933	XXXVIII	874	826	760
830	920	XXIX, LXVI	875	855	LXII
831	894	796	876	823	759
832	907	XVIII	877	827	756, 756 (a)

Concordance

Lafuma	Brunschvicg	Chevalier	Lafuma	Brunschvicg	Chevalier
878	843	754	921	356	320
879	829	623	922	91	118
880	836	751	923	44	15
881	837	629	924	123	113
882	821	758	925	17	45
883	808	627	926	18	147
884	806	746	927	18 *bis*	44 (a)
885	842	627 (a)	928	512	639
886	835	752	929	775	643
887	839	753	930	744	181, 665
888	834	LVI	931	32	37
889	828	766 (a)	932	33	38
890	819	755 (a)	933	885	801
891	840	LVII	934	13	208 (a)
892	852	765, 772, 800 (a)	935	65	78
		LXI	936	63	77
893	807	748	937	368	94
894	814	497 (a)	938	568	587
895	824	761	939	41	34, 132
896	845	LIX	940	160	267
897	813	749	941	754	594
898	820	757	942	266	460
899	300	239	943	357	324
900	846	768	944	23	66
901	831	LII	945	776	644 (a)
902	850	764, LI	946	627	524 (b)
903	844	LVIII, LXXI	947	865	790
904	804	755	948	943	711
905	573	578	949	486	424
906	822	763	950	50	51
907	841	766, LIV	951	777	660
908	851	747, 767, 771,	952	370	98
		LXIII	953	120	27
909	2	22	954	119	31
910	1	21	955	26	48
911	4	24	956	15	244 (a)
912	40	67	957	14	44
913	380	229	958	25	47
914	95	122	959	188	10
915	3	23	960	8	18
916	568	587	961	355	319
917	314	246	962	106	162
918	310	245	963	47	62
919	155	157	964	12	208 (b)
920	321	304	965	46	14

Concordance

Lafuma	Brunschvicg	Chevalier		Lafuma	Brunschvicg	Chevalier
966	31	33		979	52	54
967	39	35		980	55	56
968	49	52		981	7	17
969	48	61		982	5	25
970	57	58		983	114	28
971	27	49		984	34	39
972	54	55		985	36	41
973	53	53		986	30	32
974	28	50		987	35	40
975	56	57		988	38	32
976	59	60		989	45	30
977	42	132 (a)		990	24	46
978	58	59		991	6	26

INDEX TO THE PENSEÉS

References are to the numbers of the Lafuma edition,
not to page numbers

Abraham, took nothing for himself, 701; and Gideon, 906

absolution, it is not absolution alone . . . 709; without repentance, 836; God did not wish to give absolution without the Church, 853

Adam, glorious state of, 14; and Jesus Christ, 309; *forma futuri*, 523

Alexander, example of A's chastity, 714

amusements *see* distraction

angel, who tries to play the angel . . . 257; man equal to the angels, 236; neither angel nor beast, 275

animals, do not admire one another, 96

Antichrist, whether he will come in own name or that of Jesus Christ, 871; miracles of, cannot lead to error, 874; foretold, 878; Church will endure until coming of, 892; signs of, 900

Apostles, hypothesis that they were rogues, 513, 587; deceived or deceivers, 599

Aquinas, St. Thomas, and order, 47; on vanity, 51; on miracles, 871

Arcesilaus, reverted to dogmatism, 290

Archimedes, his inventions, 585

Aristotle, like other men, 196

Athanasius, St., a man like ourselves, 833

atheism, sign of a powerful mind, 333

atheists, pity them, 332; what right have they to say . . . 471

Augustine, St., if he returned today, 845; saw that we work for the uncertain, 346; on submission of reason, 359

Augustus, and Herod's son, 612

authority, the rule of your faith, 374

beast, man on the level of the beasts, 236; who tries to play the angel . . . 257; neither angel nor beast, 275

beauty, model of, 931; poetic, 932

belief, importance of, 374; three methods of, 396; those who believe without reading . . . 731; do not be surprised to find . . . 730

Index

Copernicus, opinion of, 346

Corneille, "un je ne sais quoi," 90; inhuman character of, 719

correct, when we wish to correct someone . . . 5

Cromwell, was about to lay waste all Christendom . . . 203

Daniel, the seventy weeks of, 632; prophecies, 662

death, preferred to peace, 66

deference, meaning of, 69, 170

deism, almost as far removed from true religion as atheism, 17

Des Barreaux, brute-beasts, 249

Descartes, write against those who probe too deeply into the sciences, 92; we must say in general . . . 174; useless and unreliable, 297

despair, what drives us to, 383

dispute, the truth prevails, 889

disorder, those who live in a state of, 706

distraction, based on wretchedness, 33, 118; greatest of our miseries, 128; if men were happy . . . 267; king's distractions, 270; all his special occupations . . . 274; this man, overwhelmed by grief, 275

dogmatism, and scepticism, 287

doubt, a great misfortune, 11, 15; when we should, 355

dream, life a, 261

Eat, not bored when eating, 725

ebb, it is a horrible thing . . . 152

eclipses, said to foreshadow misfortune, 139

eloquence, a picture of thought, 955; true eloquence makes light of, 911; continual eloquence wearies, 961; we need the agreeable, 958

Epaminondas, 229

Epictetus, 188, 190, 278

error, Church's struggle against conflicting errors, 462; miracles and error, 871

Esdras, against the story of, 564-5; if the story is credible, 566

Eternal Being, existed always, 453

Eucharist, absurdity of not believing in, 353; and symbols, 535; whole body of Jesus Christ, 928

evil, is easy, 134

exterior, must be joined to interior, 722

Faces, similar, 50

faith, different from proof, 30; nature of, 225; impossible to know truth without, 300; above the senses, 370; gift of God, 376; and miracles, 474; not in our power, 766

Index

441

opinion, sound opinions of the people, 180, 182, 184, 185; uses power, 197; queen of the world, 200; happiness lies in the good opinion of men, 223; of half a dozen people, 235

order, order of my material new, 4; I will set down my thoughts without any order, 44; why divide my moral system . . . 46

orders, the three, 585

organ, and man, 103

Painting, a form of vanity, 77

parakeet, beak of, 211

passions, great and small have the same, 258

patriarchs, long lives of, 567

penance, alone of all the mysteries . . . 533

people, universal, 984

perpetuity, of religion, 540; of the Messiah, 541, 550

Perseus, 52

persons, three sorts of, 336

persuading, two ways of, 378

Peter, St., did not stand on ceremony, 683

philosophers, have desired to be loved and admired, 280; did not prescribe feelings, 285; falsity of, 288; confuse the ideas of things, 390; have consecrated the vices . . . 691

philosophy, not worth an hour's labour, 174; to make light of . . . 911

piety, is painful, 744

Plato, like other men, 196

please, by knowing a man's dominant passion, 962

pleasure, what is the sign of, 212; shameful to succumb to, 940

Pope, is first, 847; and Church, 848; hates and fears scholars, 850; and kings, 851; would be dishonoured, 854

Port-Royal, children of, 111; as good as Voltigerod, 811

poverty, "I love . . .", 748

prayer, why God established, 763

precipice, rush towards, 342

present, never our goal, 84

pride, hides and reveals misery, 119; outweighs and banishes all miseries, 131; curiosity only vanity, 157; what constitutes, 383; persuades the presumptuous, 668

priests, become a priest, 932

principles, true, 293; and instinct, 331

probability, 784, 791, 794, 797, 800, 830, 843, 861, 868, 869

progress, everything tends towards perfection, 153